Frommer's®

Denver, Boulder & Colorado Springs

10th Edition

by Eric Peterson

Here's what the critics say about Frommer's:

"Amazingly easy to use. Very portable, very complete."
—**BOOKLIST**

"Detailed, accurate, and easy-to-read
information for all price ranges."
—**GLAMOUR MAGAZINE**

"Hotel information is close to encyclopedic."
—**DES MOINES SUNDAY REGISTER**

"Frommer's Guides have a way of giving
you a real feel for a place."
—**KNIGHT RIDDER NEWSPAPERS**

WILEY

Wiley Publishing, Inc.

Published by:

WILEY PUBLISHING, INC.

111 River St.
Hoboken, NJ 07030-5774

Copyright © 2009 Wiley Publishing, Inc., Hoboken, New Jersey. All rights reserved. No part of this publication may be reproduced, stored in a retrieval system or transmitted in any form or by any means, electronic, mechanical, photocopying, recording, scanning or otherwise, except as permitted under Sections 107 or 108 of the 1976 United States Copyright Act, without either the prior written permission of the Publisher, or authorization through payment of the appropriate per-copy fee to the Copyright Clearance Center, 222 Rosewood Drive, Danvers, MA 01923, 978/750-8400, fax 978/646-8600. Requests to the Publisher for permission should be addressed to the Permissions Department, John Wiley & Sons, Inc., 111 River Street, Hoboken, NJ 07030, 201/748-6011, fax 201/748-6008, or online at http://www.wiley.com/go/permissions."

Wiley and the Wiley Publishing logo are trademarks or registered trademarks of John Wiley & Sons, Inc. and/or its affiliates. Frommer's is a trademark or registered trademark of Arthur Frommer. Used under license. All other trademarks are the property of their respective owners. Wiley Publishing, Inc. is not associated with any product or vendor mentioned in this book.

ISBN 978-0-470-38228-8
Editor: Matthew Brown
Production Editor: M. Faunette Johnston
Cartographer: Andrew Dolan
Photo Editor: Richard Fox
Production by Wiley Indianapolis Composition Services

Front cover photo: The Colorado Balloon Classic in Memorial Park, Colorado Springs

For information on our other products and services or to obtain technical support, please contact our Customer Care Department within the U.S. at 800/762-2974, outside the U.S. at 317/572-3993 or fax 317/572-4002.

Wiley also publishes its books in a variety of electronic formats. Some content that appears in print may not be available in electronic formats.

Manufactured in the United States of America

5 4 3 2 1

CONTENTS

4 SUGGESTED ITINERARIES IN DENVER, BOULDER & COLORADO SPRINGS   45

5 SETTLING INTO DENVER   49

6 WHAT TO SEE & DO IN DENVER   79

7 BOULDER   122

**APPENDIX: FAST FACTS, TOLL-FREE
NUMBERS & WEBSITES** 224

INDEXES 236

LIST OF MAPS

ABOUT THE AUTHOR

A Denver-based writer, **Eric Peterson** has contributed to numerous Frommer's guides covering the American West and has authored *Frommer's Montana & Wyoming, Frommer's Yellowstone & Grand Teton National Parks,* and *Ramble California* (www.fulcrum-books.com). He also writes about travel and other topics for such publications as *ColoradoBiz, United Hemispheres, Delta Sky,* and the *New York Daily News.*

ACKNOWLEDGMENTS

The author wishes to thank for their help Rich Grant, Angela Berardino, and Carrina Junge with the Denver Metro Convention and Visitors Bureau; Kim Farin with the Boulder Convention and Visitors Bureau; Lisa Amend with the Colorado Springs Convention and Visitors Bureau; and Suzy Blackhurst with the Estes Park Convention and Visitors Bureau.

AN INVITATION TO THE READER

In researching this book, we discovered many wonderful places—hotels, restaurants, shops, and more. We're sure you'll find others. Please tell us about them, so we can share the information with your fellow travelers in upcoming editions. If you were disappointed with a recommendation, we'd love to know that, too. Please write to:

Frommer's Denver, Boulder & Colorado Springs, 10th Edition
Wiley Publishing, Inc. • 111 River St. • Hoboken, NJ 07030-5774

AN ADDITIONAL NOTE

Please be advised that travel information is subject to change at any time—and this is especially true of prices. We therefore suggest that you write or call ahead for confirmation when making your travel plans. The authors, editors, and publisher cannot be held responsible for the experiences of readers while traveling. Your safety is important to us, however, so we encourage you to stay alert and be aware of your surroundings. Keep a close eye on cameras, purses, and wallets, all favorite targets of thieves and pickpockets.

Other Great Guides for Your Trip:

Frommer's Colorado
Frommer's National Parks of the American West
Frommer's Arizona
Frommer's New Mexico
Frommer's Utah

FROMMER'S STAR RATINGS, ICONS & ABBREVIATIONS

Every hotel, restaurant, and attraction listing in this guide has been ranked for quality, value, service, amenities, and special features using a **star-rating system.** In country, state, and regional guides, we also rate towns and regions to help you narrow down your choices and budget your time accordingly. Hotels and restaurants are rated on a scale of zero (recommended) to three stars (exceptional). Attractions, shopping, nightlife, towns, and regions are rated according to the following scale: zero stars (recommended), one star (highly recommended), two stars (very highly recommended), and three stars (must-see).

In addition to the star-rating system, we also use **seven feature icons** that point you to the great deals, in-the-know advice, and unique experiences that separate travelers from tourists. Throughout the book, look for:

Finds	Special finds—those places only insiders know about
Fun Facts	Fun facts—details that make travelers more informed and their trips more fun
Kids	Best bets for kids, and advice for the whole family
Moments	Special moments—those experiences that memories are made of
Overrated	Places or experiences not worth your time or money
Tips	Insider tips—great ways to save time and money
Value	Great values—where to get the best deals

The following **abbreviations** are used for credit cards:

AE	American Express	DISC	Discover	V	Visa
DC	Diners Club	MC	MasterCard		

FROMMERS.COM

Now that you have this guidebook to help you plan a great trip, visit our website at **www.frommers.com** for additional travel information on more than 4,000 destinations. We update features regularly to give you instant access to the most current trip-planning information available. At Frommers.com, you'll find scoops on the best airfares, lodging rates, and car rental bargains. You can even book your travel online through our reliable travel booking partners. Other popular features include:

- Online updates of our most popular guidebooks
- Vacation sweepstakes and contest giveaways
- Newsletters highlighting the hottest travel trends
- Podcasts, interactive maps, and up-to-the-minute events listings
- Opinionated blog entries by Arthur Frommer himself
- Online travel message boards with featured travel discussions

What's New in Denver, Boulder & Colorado Springs

Colorado's Front Range cities of Denver, Boulder, and Colorado Springs offer a rich combination of old and new. They lure travelers with both their city attractions, such as museums, galleries, and historic sites; as well as their outdoor recreational opportunities and proximity to some of America's most beautiful mountains. Here you can sleep in a grand historic hotel, awake to a gourmet breakfast, hike or ride to the top of a spectacular mountain (or, in winter, ski down one), and be back in town in time for the ballet.

Growth, which Coloradans see as both a blessing and a curse, is the main agent of change in the area. And more could be coming after the Democratic National Convention thrust the city onto the national stage in August 2008. Following are some of the changes, including some exciting new things to watch for in Denver, Boulder, and Colorado Springs.

SETTLING INTO DENVER Southwest Airlines has continually expanded at Denver International Airport since its first flights touched down there in 2006. The light-rail has grown significantly in recent years. Four new lines have been created: The **E Line** runs along I-25 from Broadway to Lincoln Avenue in the south suburbs; the **F Line** connects 18th and California streets downtown with Lincoln Avenue; the **G Line** runs from Nine Mile in Aurora at I-225 and Parker Road to Lincoln; and the **H Line** connects Nine Mile and 18th and California.

Downtown Denver has a pair of new lodging options: the swank **Ritz-Carlton, Denver,** 1881 Curtis St. (© 303/312-3800); and **The Curtis,** 1405 Curtis St. (© 800/525-6651 or 303/572-3300), a fun and pop-culture-loving hotel. Denver also boasts some excellent new restaurants, including **Duo,** 2413 W. 32nd Ave. (© 303/820-2282), serving terrific interpretations of American standards in a warm space in the Highlands neighborhood; and **Encore,** 2250 E. Colfax Ave., (© 303/399-5353), a slick new Mediterranean eatery at the renovated theater complex now anchored by the Tattered Cover Book Store. See chapter 5 for details.

WHAT TO SEE & DO IN DENVER The **Museum of Contemporary Art Denver,** 1485 Delgany St. (© 303/298-7554), opened its terrific new building in 2007, a stark, avant-garde structure that puts the artists on center stage. Six Flags sold **Elitch Gardens Theme Park,** Speer Blvd. at I-25 (© 303/595-4386), but little has changed except for the banishment of Looney Tunes characters and Batman. New in 2009, the **Denver Museum of**

Nature & Science, in City Park, 2001 Colorado Blvd. (© 303/322-7009), will open "Expedition Health" a state-of-the-art exhibit giving visitors an eye-opening look at the workings of their own bodies.

The **Colorado Rapids** (© 303/405-1100; www.coloradorapids.com) of Major League Soccer now play home games at the new Dick's Sporting Goods Park in Commerce City. Flying Dog bolted to Maryland, but **Great Divide Brewing Co.** opened an excellent new tap room at its downtown brewery, 2201 Arapahoe St. (© 303/296-9460, ext. 26). See chapter 6 for details.

BOULDER In 2007, the stalwart Pearl Street burger joint **Tom's Tavern** shut its doors after 49 years, following the death of owner Tom Eldridge. Also closing since the last edition of this book: **Trilogy Wine Bar** and **Rhumba.** As for openings, **Black Cat,** 1964 13th St. (© 303/444-5500), sources a good deal of its ingredients from owner-chef Eric Skokan's half-acre garden. The new outdoor shopping center, **Twenty Ninth Street,** centered on the former site of the long-languishing Crossroads Mall at the intersection of Canyon Boulevard and 29th Street (© 303/440-0722), is now open for business. See chapter 7.

COLORADO SPRINGS In 2007, long-time Manitou Springs favorite **Adam's Mountain Cafe,** 934 Manitou Ave. (© 719/685-1430), relocated from its Cañon Avenue address to the ground floor of the restored Spa Building. Thankfully, the tasty, healthy food and country-meets-French–Victorian vibe remain. The Hawaiian taco joint **La'au's,** 830 N. Tejon St. (© 719/578-5228), is a new favorite for Colorado College students—and for travelers pinching their pennies.

At **Garden of the Gods,** 1805 N. 30th St. (© 719/634-6666), the excellent multimedia theater presentation, *How Did Those Red Rocks Get There?* was newly remade by local filmmaker John Bourbonais for 2008. A major expansion at the **Colorado Springs Fine Art Center,** 30 W. Dale St. (© 719/634-5581), doubled the gallery space and won raves from critics. New in 2008 at the **Cheyenne Mountain Zoo,** 4250 Cheyenne Mountain Zoo Rd. (© 719/633-9925), the $8.2-million "Rocky Mountain Wild" lets visitors get up close and personal with mountain lions, grizzly bears, moose, and other local denizens. See chapter 8.

The Best of Denver, Boulder & Colorado Springs

The old and the new, the rustic and the sophisticated, the urban and the rural—you'll find all these elements practically side by side in and immediately adjacent to the cities of Denver, Boulder, and Colorado Springs.

Founded in the mid–19th century by both East Coast gold-seekers and European and Asian immigrants in search of a better life, these cities on the Front Range of the majestic Rocky Mountains weren't as wild as Colorado's mountain towns (such as Telluride and Creede), but they did have their day. According to historian Thomas Noel, in 1890 Denver had more saloons per capita than Kansas City, St. Louis, New Orleans, or Philadelphia. But these Colorado cities soon became home to a more sophisticated westerner—the mine owner instead of the prospector, the business owner rather than the gambler.

Today, these thoroughly modern cities have virtually all the amenities you'd expect to find in New York or Los Angeles: opera, theater, contemporary dance, art, excellent restaurants, and sophisticated hotels and convention centers. You'll also find historic Victorian mansions, working steam trains, and old gold mines. You can go horseback riding, hiking, skiing, or shopping; do the Texas two-step to a live country band; or spend hours browsing through a huge four-story bookstore, a gigantic model-train shop, or the world's largest hardware store. You might also join the locals at what many of them enjoy most: being outdoors under the warm Colorado sun—so don't forget your hiking boots, mountain bike, skis, sunscreen, and sunglasses.

Although Denver is certainly a city, bustling and growing, it's still comfortable and fairly easy to explore. Boulder and Colorado Springs call themselves cities, but I like to think of them more as big Western towns, where the buildings aren't very tall and there's lots of open space. In all three places, the residents are friendly, relaxed, and casual.

In this book, I thoroughly explore Denver, Boulder, and Colorado Springs. But I also look at some of the nearby attractions where the locals spend their weekends, including the state's most-visited natural wonder, Rocky Mountain National Park.

1 FROMMER'S FAVORITE DENVER, BOULDER & COLORADO SPRINGS EXPERIENCES

- **Hitting Lower Downtown and Larimer Square (Denver):** Once neglected and even a bit dangerous, Lower Downtown (LoDo) and Larimer Square are now well-preserved historic gems, heavy with redbricks and activity of all kinds. LoDo is where you'll find Coors Field (home of baseball's Colorado Rockies), plus galleries, nightspots, restaurants, and Mayor John Hickenlooper's long-standing microbrewery, the Wynkoop Brewing Company, right across from Union Station. Larimer Square is abuzz with commercial activity and has more good restaurants than any other block in Denver. See p. 84.

- **Visiting the Denver Art Museum (Denver):** With a striking new expansion doubling its size, the Denver Art Museum now has one of the country's top collections of Western art, ranging from 19th century to contemporary, as well as an excellent American Indian collection. The expansion features a jagged, avant-garde design by renowned architect Daniel Libeskind. See p. 79.

- **Shopping for Duds at Rockmount Ranch Wear (Denver):** The inventors of the Western snap shirt have gone into the retail business after sticking strictly to manufacturing and wholesale since 1946. Their downtown store is a three-generation family operation, and browsing the racks is something of an education on the history of Western wear. Rock stars regularly stop by while in Denver; Bob Dylan wears Rockmount's dusters onstage. See p. 104.

- **People-Watching on Pearl Street Mall (Boulder):** This 4-block-long tree-lined pedestrian mall marks Boulder's downtown core and its center for dining, shopping, strolling, and loafing in the sun. It's also the best spot in Colorado for observing your fellow humans. Here you'll see students, local businesspeople, and tourists as they watch the musicians, mimes, jugglers, and other street entertainers who hold court on the landscaped mall day and night, year-round. See p. 139.

- **Touring Celestial Seasonings (Boulder):** The nation's leading producer of herbal teas offers a tour that excites the senses as it takes you behind the scenes into the world of tea. The company, which began in a Boulder garage in the 1970s, now produces more than 50

varieties of tea from more than 75 different herbs and spices, imported from 35 countries. Guided tours move from a consumer taste test in the lobby to marketing displays, and finally into the production plant, where the overpowering "Mint Room" is a highlight. See p. 142.

- **Watching the Colorado Shakespeare Festival (Boulder):** Among the top Shakespearean festivals in the United States, this 2-month event offers more than a dozen performances of each of four of the Bard's plays each summer. Actors, directors, designers, and everyone associated with the productions are fully schooled Shakespearean professionals. During the festival, company members conduct 1-hour backstage tours before each show. See p. 154.

- **Hiking the Mills Lake Trail (Rocky Mountain National Park):** Although it's packed at first, this moderately rated trail usually becomes much less crowded after you've logged a few miles. At trail's end (elevation 10,000 ft.), towering peaks surround a gorgeous mountain lake. The lake is an excellent spot for photographing dramatic Longs Peak, especially in late afternoon or early evening, and it's the perfect place for a picnic. See chapter 7.

- **Taking in Garden of the Gods (Colorado Springs):** There's nothing like sunrise at Garden of the Gods, with its fantastic and sometimes fanciful red-sandstone formations sculpted by wind and water over hundreds of thousands of years. Although you can see a great deal from the marked view points, it's worth spending some time and energy to get away from the crowds on one of the park's many trails, to listen to the wind, and to imagine the gods cavorting among the formations. See p. 191.

- **Riding Pikes Peak Cog Railway (Colorado Springs):** Perhaps no view in Colorado equals the 360-degree

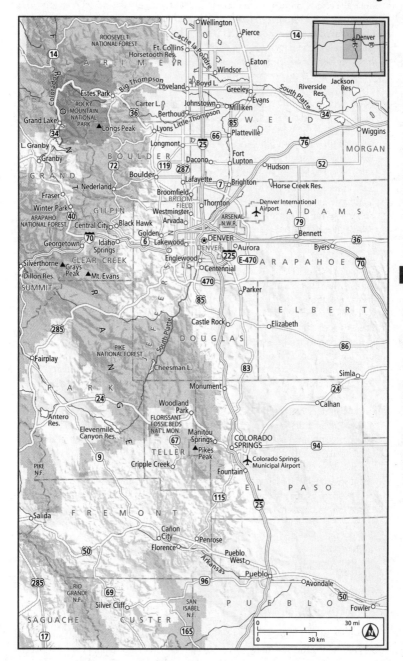

panorama from the summit of Pikes Peak. For those who enjoy rail travel, spectacular scenery, and the thrill of mountain climbing without all the work, this is the trip to take. The 9-mile route, with grades of up to 25%, takes 75 minutes to reach the top of 14,110-foot Pikes Peak. The journey is exciting from the start, but passengers really begin to ooh and aah when the track leaves the forest, creeping above timberline at about 11,500 feet. See p. 191.

2 BEST HOTEL BETS

- **Best Historic Hotels:** From its spacious, well-appointed lobby to the richly polished wood of its elegant Victorian and almost whimsical Art Deco rooms, the **Brown Palace Hotel,** 321 17th St., Denver (© **800/321-2599** or 303/297-3111), has an air of sophistication, refinement, and class. The Brown has operated continuously since August 1892. See p. 59.

  A handsome downtown establishment, the **Hotel Boulderado,** 2115 13th St., Boulder (© **800/433-4344** or 303/442-4344), has been skillfully renovated and restored. It retains its original Otis elevator, lovely leaded-glass ceiling, and spectacular cherrywood staircase, which caused quite a stir when the hotel opened in 1909. See p. 130.

  Designed by New York City architects in the Italian Renaissance style, **The Broadmoor,** Lake Circle, at Lake Avenue, Colorado Springs (© **800/634-7711** or 719/634-7711), opened in 1918. Colorado's most elegant and best-preserved hotel of the era, it's filled with objets d'art from around the world, including Oriental art from the Ming and Tsin dynasties and a huge carved wooden bar from an 1800s British pub. See p. 177.

- **Best for Business Travelers:** Rooms at **Hyatt Regency Denver,** 650 15th St., Denver (© **800/233-1234** or 303/436-1234), are the biggest in downtown Denver and feature ergonomic workstations; the location, next to the Colorado Convention Center, is convenient to the light rail. See p. 62.

- **Best for a Romantic Getaway:** Ideal for overnighting theatergoers—it's across the street from the Denver Center for the Performing Arts—the **Hotel Teatro,** 1100 14th St., Denver (© **303/228-1100**), is furnished with plenty of goods from the costume and props departments, and the luxurious feel helps make it the most romantic of all of the downtown properties. See p. 62.

  The Two Sisters Inn, 10 Otoe Place, Manitou Springs, outside Colorado Springs (© **800/2SISINN** or 719/685-9684), offers a cozy honeymoon cottage complete with fresh flowers, a big feather bed, a gas log fireplace, and lots of privacy. What more could you ask for? See p. 182.

- **Best Hotel Lobbies for Pretending You're Rich:** The lobby of the **Brown Palace Hotel** (Denver; see address and telephone above) features walls of Mexican onyx and a floor of white marble. The elaborate cast-iron grillwork surrounding the six tiers of balconies draws your eye to the stained-glass ceiling. Luncheon and afternoon tea are served in the lobby nearly every day.

  When it opened in 1918, the first guests at **The Broadmoor** (Colorado Springs; see address and telephone above) were millionaire John D. Rockefeller, Jr., and his party. When surrounded by priceless 17th-century art, it's easy to imagine yourself mingling with the wealthy, reading the financial news, and sipping a cognac by the hotel's elegant marble staircase.

- **Best Moderately Priced Hotels:** The colorful **Boulder Outlook,** 800 28th St. (© **800/542-0304** or 303/443-3322), is fun, fresh, and definitively Boulder, with such unique perks as two bouldering rocks (one is 11 ft. high, the other 4 ft.) and a fenced, 4,000-square-foot dog run. Best of all, the rates are typically cheaper than those of its chain counterparts. See p. 131.

  Also in Boulder, the **Colorado Chautauqua,** 900 Baseline Rd. (© **303/442-3282**), isn't exactly a hotel, but its lodge rooms and cottages are midpriced, and it's a National Historic Landmark to boot. See p. 132.

- **Best Inexpensive Lodging:** An apartment-turned-hostel near City Park, the **Innkeeper of the Rockies,** 1717 Race St., Denver (© **303/861-7777**), offers inexpensive bunks and private rooms a mile east of downtown. See p. 67.

  The Foot of the Mountain Motel, 200 Arapahoe Ave., at the mouth of Boulder Canyon, Boulder (© **866/773-5489** or 303/442-5688), is a nicely preserved relic with cozy rooms and easy access to the outdoors. See p. 132.

  Spread across numerous buildings near the University of Colorado campus, Boulder International Hostel, 1107 12th St. (© 888/442-0522 or 303/442-0522), is well kept, reputable, and perfect for those traveling on a budget. See p. 132.

- **Best Service:** Dedicated to providing guests with the best possible service, the **Brown Palace Hotel** (Denver; see address and telephone above) succeeds extremely well, and without pretension. Among other things, it offers 24-hour room service, concierge, and in-room massage.

  Taking good care of its guests is a point of pride for **The Broadmoor** (Colorado Springs; see address and telephone above): It offers 24-hour room service, a concierge, in-room massage, valet laundry, a shuttle bus between buildings, and a multitude of recreational activities, as well as almost anything else you might ask for.

- **Best Bed-and-Breakfast:** A great location, striking art, and modern convenience make **The Bradley,** 2020 16th St., Boulder (© **800/858-5811** or 303/545-5200), one of my very favorite B&Bs on the Front Range. See p. 130.

  At **Old Town GuestHouse,** 115 S. 26th St., Colorado Springs (© **888/375-4210** or 719/632-9194), each room is delightfully decorated around a theme, ranging from Saharan to Victorian. This B&B also has just enough in the way of modern convenience. See p. 181.

- **Best Views:** The gorgeous **St Julien,** 900 Walnut St., Boulder (© **877/303-0900** or 720/406-9696), is the nearest hotel to Boulder's even more gorgeous foothills. Rooms don't come cheap, but the views rival those from the windows of Colorado's ritziest mountain resorts. See p. 127.

  The **JW Marriott,** 150 Clayton Lane, Denver (© **800/327-0064** or 303/316-2700), the standout hotel in the tony Cherry Creek shopping district, looks out over the Denver Country Club and the creek itself. See p. 66.

- **Best for Families:** Two swimming pools, water slides, and a fabulous summer kids' program at **The Broadmoor** (Colorado Springs; see address and telephone above) will help keep youngsters busy while parents enjoy the golf courses, spa, and seemingly countless other facilities.

  At the **Hotel Monaco,** 1717 Champa St., Denver (© **800/397-5380** or 303/296-1717), kids get a kick out of the colorful decor, the complimentary goldfish, and the "Director of Pet Relations," a Jack Russell terrier named Lily Sopris. See p. 62.

3 BEST DINING BETS

- **Best Spots for a Romantic Dinner:** **Rioja,** 1431 Larimer Sq., Denver (℃ **303/820-2282**), is a quiet, slick, and dimly lit vehicle for chef-owner Jennifer Jasinski's inspired dishes. See p. 72.

  Frasca, 2328 Pearl St., Boulder (℃ **303/442-6966**), has impeccable service and peerless cuisine, drawn exclusively from the culinary traditions of Friuli-Venezia Giulia, a subalpine region in northeastern Italy. See p. 132.

  The Broadmoor's snazzy **Summit** (Colorado Springs; see address and telephone number above for The Broadmoor) is at once slick and romantic, with contemporary metalwork and a glassed-in, rotating turret behind the bar. The visual spectacle is aesthetically matched by the fare, which is innovative and adventurous. See p. 185.

- **Best Spots for a Celebration:** Owned by retired Denver Broncos quarterback John Elway, **Elway's,** 2500 E. 1st Ave., Denver (℃ **303/399-5353**), is a model of "New West" design, with a menu that melds swank and comfortable. The crowd is lively, and you might bump into Elway himself. See p. 75.

  Colorado Springs locals splurge on a night out at the **Cliff House Dining Room,** Cliff House Inn, 306 Cañon Ave., Manitou Springs (℃ **719/785-2415**). It offers an elegant Victorian atmosphere, superlative service, and innovative variations on old favorites, such as smoked bacon–scented petite prime-rib roast, with vegetables and potato purée. See p. 184.

- **Best Decor:** Occupying the same premises as when it opened in 1893, the **Buckhorn Exchange,** 1000 Osage St., Denver (℃ **303/534-9505**), still has a magnificent 19th-century hand-carved oak bar in the upstairs Victorian parlor and saloon. The downstairs features an amazing collection of taxidermy, a menagerie that includes everything from leopard to buffalo. See p. 68.

  In a converted Victorian, the Tibetan/Nepalese **Sherpa's,** 825 Walnut St., Boulder (℃ **303/440-7151**), has no shortage of Himalayan relics, photos, and art to look at, especially in the cozy bar that doubles as a library. See p. 137.

- **Best Values:** The all-you-can-eat buffet at **Govinda's Spiritual Food,** 1400 N. Cherry St., Denver (℃ **303/333-5461**), has one of the city's best salad bars, plus great soups, fresh-baked bread, and an array of meatless main dishes.

  You'll get fine food at reasonable prices in a casual atmosphere at the **Corner Bar** in the Hotel Boulderado, 2115 13th St., Boulder (℃ **303/442-4560**). See p. 137.

  It's amazing to find a restaurant that prepares so many different dishes well—candy, ice cream, Southwestern, Greek, basic American—and for such low prices. Perhaps that's why Colorado Springs residents have been coming to **Michelle's,** 122 N. Tejon St. (℃ **719/633-5089**), since it opened in 1952.

- **Best for Kids:** More a theme park than a restaurant, **Casa Bonita,** in the JCRS Shopping Center, 6715 W. Colfax Ave., Lakewood, west of Denver (℃ **303/232-5115**), has practically nonstop action, with divers plummeting into a pool beside a 30-foot waterfall, puppet shows, a video arcade, and a fun house. Yes, there's food, too: tacos and other standard Mexican fare, country-fried steak, and fried chicken, served cafeteria-style. See p. 78.

  There's something about trains that brings out the kid in all of us. **Giuseppe's**

Old Depot Restaurant, 10 S. Sierra Madre St., Colorado Springs (© 719/635-3111), has one parked outside the door and plenty more rolling by just outside the large windows. See p. 187.

- **Best Burgers & Beer:** Smack-dab on the pedestrian-only 16th Street Mall, **Paramount Cafe,** 519 16th St., Denver (© 303/893-2000), offers juicy burgers matched only by the people-watching patio. See p. 75.

- **Best People-Watching:** With outdoor seating just 2 blocks from home plate of Coors Field in downtown Denver, **Wynkoop Brewing Company,** 1634 18th St. (© 303/297-2700), is the place to sit and watch the world stroll by. See p. 74.

  Sitting inside or outside, you'll get a great view of the Pearl Street Mall at **14th Street Bar & Grill,** 1400 Pearl St., Boulder (© 303/444-5854). You'll see all kinds of people passing by—students and families, old and young, and even street entertainers, from musicians to mimes. See p. 135.

- **Best View:** Perched on the side of a mountain above Boulder, with a wall of windows framing the city below and plains beyond, **Flagstaff House Restaurant,** 1138 Flagstaff Rd. (© 303/442-4640), offers extraordinary views, especially as the sun sets or the city gradually disappears in a swirling snowstorm. See p. 133.

  Large picture windows at **Charles Court,** in The Broadmoor, Lake Circle, Colorado Springs (© 719/634-7711), give diners a splendid vista out over The Broadmoor's lake. See p. 184.

- **Best Wine List:** With more than 2,000 well-chosen selections, **Flagstaff House Restaurant** (Boulder; see address and telephone above) wins this category without question. See p. 133.

  The rotating wine turret holds about 400 of the 1,400 bottles on hand at the **Summit** (Colorado Springs; see address

and telephone above for The Broadmoor). See p. 185.

  The Palace Arms, at the Brown Palace Hotel (Denver; see address and telephone above), has one of the city's most widely respected and award-winning wine lists. See p. 69.

- **Best Desserts:** Homemade desserts at **The Kitchen,** 1039 Pearl St., Boulder (© 303/544-5973), include housemade ice cream, sticky toffee pudding, and other delectable treats.

  With all the fine restaurants that seem to specialize in desserts, the **Craftwood Inn,** 404 El Paso Blvd., Colorado Springs (© 719/685-9000), stands out, particularly for the way it combines raspberries and chocolate. See p. 184.

  While its taste in wine is also terrific, the desserts at Table 6, 609 Corona St., Denver (© 303/831-8800), are equally praiseworthy, especially the Nutella beignets and margarita nachos. See p. 77.

- **Best Fast Food:** At **Illegal Pete's,** 1447 Pearl St., Boulder (© 303/440-3955), you'll get a choice of unique burritos that are both mouthwatering and massive, as well as salads, chile, fish, chicken, and vegetarian tacos. See p. 137.

- **Best Natural Foods:** The Mile High City's vegetarians flock to **Water-Course,** 837 E. 17th Ave., Denver (© 303/832-7313), for such specialties as meatless tamales and banana-bread French toast. See p. 78.

  At the terrific new **Black Cat,** 1964 13th St., Boulder (© 303/444-5500), owner-chef Erik Skokan uses ingredients from his own half-acre farm in Boulder. See p. 133.

  Fresh and healthy are the key words at **Adam's Mountain Cafe,** 110 Cañon Ave., Manitou Springs, outside Colorado Springs (© 719/685-1430), which serves interesting dishes with a decidedly Mediterranean flair. See p. 189.

- **Best Sushi:** Ask any Denver resident: The **Sushi Den,** 1487 S. Pearl St.

(☎ **303/777-0826**), is the place to go for sushi. Located in south Denver in the charming Old South Pearl Street retail district, the Sushi Den is one of two locations worldwide—the other is in Fukuoka, Japan. See p. 77.

- **Best Italian Cuisine:** Traditional and innovative Italian flavors blissfully meet at **Panzano,** in Hotel Monaco, 909 17th St., Denver (☎ **303/296-3525**). Try the restaurant's specialty, *buridda,* a Genovese seafood stew with mussels, calamari, and shrimp in a savory lobster broth. See p. 72.
- **Best Seafood: McCormick's Fish House & Bar,** in the Oxford Hotel, 1659 Wazee St., Denver (☎ **303/825-1107**), flies in fresh seafood daily. Choices often include salmon from Alaska, mussels from Maine and Florida, and yellowfin tuna from Hawaii. See p. 73.
- **Best Vietnamese Cuisine:** The original Vietnamese restaurant in Denver, **T-Wa Inn,** 555 S. Federal Blvd., Denver (☎ **303/922-2378**), is the place to come for genuine Vietnamese cooking. The perfectly cooked and spiced entrees include several vegetarian plates, incredible shrimp and pork loin, and a number of spicy Thai dishes to boot. See p. 78.
- **Best American Cuisine:** The specifics change daily at **Flagstaff House Restaurant** (Boulder; see address and telephone above), but Rocky Mountain game highlights many of the dishes, each individually and creatively prepared with the freshest ingredients.

It certainly isn't cheap, but the creative and exquisitely prepared American cuisine served at Charles Court (Colorado Springs; see address and telephone above) is tough to beat.

- **Best Continental Cuisine:** Bone-in filet mignon with an imaginative wild mushroom and blue-cheese bread pudding at **Walter's Bistro,** 136 E. Cheyenne Mountain Ave., Colorado Springs (☎ **719/630-0201**), is just one highlight of this chic eatery at the foot of Cheyenne Mountain. See p. 185.
- **Best Mexican Cuisine: Amanda's Fonda,** 3625 W. Colorado Ave., Colorado Springs (☎ **719/227-1975**), is the handiwork of a family that has owned Mexican restaurants for five generations. Clearly they've honed the art of making remarkable chile in that time: Both the chile Colorado and the green chile are excellent. See p. 189.

Everything at **Jack-N-Grill,** 2524 N. Federal Blvd., Denver (☎ **303/964-9544**), has chile in it, roasted by the Martinez family on-site. Both the green and red chile are top-notch, as are the Mexican dishes and the fresh homemade salsa. See p. 78.

- **Best Regional Cuisine:** For carefully prepared Colorado game and other Western cuisine (such as venison, pheasant, and trout), visit the **Craftwood Inn** (Colorado Springs; see address and telephone above).

Denver, Boulder & Colorado Springs in Depth

Colorado's Front Range—with Denver, Boulder, and Colorado Springs being its core municipal components—contains a good two-thirds of the Centennial State's population. The people of this booming area occupy a precarious space between modern industrialized American life and the imposing high-elevation wildlands of the Rocky Mountains to the west. Each city has its own distinct dominant culture, from Denver's professionals and unshaven youths, to the college and hippie crowds in Boulder, to the more conservative and technical communities in Colorado Springs, but they all share the commonality of an enviable position on the cusp of the great outdoors.

1 DENVER, BOULDER & COLORADO SPRINGS TODAY

Colorado's major cities retain much of the casual atmosphere that has made them popular through the years, with both tourists and transplants. Many people moved here to flee the pollution, crime, and crowding of the East and West coasts, and some native and long-term Coloradans have begun to complain that these newcomers are bringing with them the very problems they sought to escape.

There is also a growing effort in Colorado to limit, or at least control, tourism. For instance, in 1995, just as the ski season was winding down, town officials in the skier's mecca of Vail reached an agreement with resort management to limit the number of skiers on the mountain and alleviate other aspects of overcrowding in the village. The word now from Vail and other high-profile Colorado tourist destinations is that visitors will be given incentives, such as discounts, to visit at off-peak times. In 2008, the idea of a toll in the mountains on I-70 surfaced at the Colorado State Capitol.

Several years ago, Colorado voters approved a measure that effectively eliminated state funding for tourism promotion. That resulted in the creation of the Colorado Tourism Authority, funded by the tourism industry, but debate continues over whether state government should take a more active role. Those in the tourism industry who run small businesses or are located away from the major attractions say they have been hurt by the lack of state promotion, whereas others insist that government assistance for one specific industry is inappropriate and argue that the tourism industry is doing very well on its own—too well, in some areas.

One problem is the increasingly popular Rocky Mountain National Park, which is not only attracting increasing numbers of out-of-state visitors but also becoming a popular day trip for residents of the fast-growing Front Range cities of Denver, Boulder, Colorado Springs, and Fort Collins. During the summer, park roads are packed and parking lots full to overflowing; in autumn, during the elk-rutting season, hundreds of people make their way to the Moraine Park and Horseshoe Park areas each evening. National Park officials say that motor vehicle noise is starting to have a negative effect on the experience, and disappointed visitors are asking where they can go to find serenity. A limited shuttle system has been put into effect in one of the busier areas, and park officials have begun studying ways to expand public transportation in the park, possibly by creating off-premises parking areas where day visitors could leave their vehicles and hop a shuttle.

2 LOOKING BACK AT DENVER, BOULDER & COLORADO SPRINGS

To explore Colorado today is to step into its past, from its dinosaur graveyards and impressive stone and clay cities of the Ancestral Puebloan people (also called the Anasazi) to reminders of the Wild West of Bat Masterson and Doc Holliday. The history of Colorado is a testimony to the human ability to adapt and flourish in a difficult environment. This land of high mountains and limited water continues to challenge its inhabitants today.

The earliest people in Colorado are believed to have been nomadic hunters who arrived some 12,000 to 20,000 years ago by way of the Bering Strait, following the tracks of the woolly mammoth and bison. Then, about 2,000 years ago, the people we call the Ancestral Puebloans arrived, living in shallow caves in the Four Corners area, where the borders of Colorado, Utah, Arizona, and New Mexico meet.

These hunters gradually learned farming and basket making, and then pottery making and the construction of pit houses—basically large underground pots. Eventually they built complex villages, examples of which can be seen at Mesa Verde National Park. For some unknown reason, possibly drought, they deserted the area around the end of the 13th century, probably moving south into present-day New Mexico and Arizona.

Although the Ancestral Puebloans were gone by the time the Spanish conquistadors arrived in the mid–16th century, in their place were two major nomadic cultures: the mountain dwellers of the west, primarily Ute; and the plains tribes of the east, principally Arapaho, Cheyenne, and Comanche.

Spanish colonists, having established settlements at Santa Fe, Taos, and other upper Rio Grande locations in the 16th

DATELINE

- **12,000** B.C. First inhabitants include Folsom Man.
- **3,000** B.C. Prehistoric farming communities appear.
- A.D. **1000** Ancestral Puebloan cliff-dweller culture peaks in Four Corners region.
- **Late 1500s** Spanish explore upper Rio Grande Valley; colonize Santa Fe and Taos,

New Mexico; and make forays into what is now southern Colorado.
- **1803** The Louisiana Purchase includes most of modern Colorado.
- **1805** The Lewis and Clark expedition sights the Rocky Mountains.
- **1806–07** Capt. Zebulon Pike leads first U.S. expedition into the Colorado Rockies.

- **1822** William Becknell establishes the Santa Fe Trail.
- **1842–44** Lt. John C. Frémont and Kit Carson explore Colorado and American West.
- **1848** Treaty of Guadalupe Hidalgo ends Mexican War, adds American Southwest to the United States.
- **1858** Gold discovered in modern Denver.

and 17th centuries, didn't immediately find southern Colorado attractive for colonization. Not only was there a lack of financial and military support from the Spanish crown, but the freedom-loving, sometimes fierce Comanche and Ute also made it clear that they would rather be left alone.

Nevertheless, Spain held title to southern and western Colorado in 1803, when U.S. President Thomas Jefferson paid $15 million for the vast Louisiana Territory, which included the lion's share of modern Colorado. Two years later the Lewis and Clark expedition passed by, but the first official exploration by the U.S. government occurred when Jefferson sent Capt. Zebulon Pike to the territory. Pikes Peak, Colorado's landmark mountain and a top tourist attraction near Colorado Springs, bears the explorer's name.

As the West began to open up in the 1820s, the Santa Fe Trail was established, cutting through Colorado's southeast corner. Much of eastern Colorado, including what would become Denver, Boulder, and Colorado Springs, was then part of the Kansas Territory. It was populated almost exclusively by plains tribes until 1858, when gold-seekers discovered flakes of the precious metal near the junction of Cherry Creek and the South Platte, and the city of Denver was established, named for Kansas governor James Denver.

The Cherry Creek strike was literally a flash in the gold-seeker's pan, but two strikes in the mountains just west of Denver in early 1859 were more significant: one at Clear Creek, near what would become Idaho Springs, and another in a quartz vein at Gregory Gulch, which led to the founding of Central City. The race to Colorado's gold fields had begun.

Abraham Lincoln was elected president of the United States in November 1860, and Congress created the Colorado Territory 3 months later. The new territory absorbed neighboring sections from Utah, Nebraska, and New Mexico to form the boundaries of the state today. Lincoln's Homestead Act of 1862 brought much of the public domain into private ownership and led to the plotting of Front Range townships, starting with Denver.

Controlling the American Indian peoples was a priority of the territorial government. A treaty negotiated in 1851 had guaranteed the entire Pikes Peak region to the nomadic plains tribes, but that had been negated by the arrival of settlers in the late 1850s. The Fort Wise Treaty of 1861 exchanged the Pikes Peak territory for 5 million fertile acres of Arkansas Valley land, north of modern La Junta. But when the Arapaho and Cheyenne continued to roam their old hunting grounds, conflict became inevitable. Frequent rumors and rare instances of hostility

- **1859** General William Larimer founds Denver. Major gold strikes in nearby Rockies.
- **1861** Colorado Territory proclaimed.
- **1862** Colorado cavalry wins major Civil War battle at Glorietta Pass, New Mexico. Homestead Act is passed.
- **1863–68** Ute tribe obtains treaties guaranteeing 16 million acres of western Colorado land.
- **1864** Hundreds of Cheyenne killed in Sand Creek Massacre. University of Denver becomes Colorado's first institution of higher education.
- **1870** Kansas City–Denver rail line completed. Agricultural commune of Greeley established by Nathan Meeker. Colorado State University opens in Fort Collins.
- **1871** General William Palmer founds Colorado Springs.
- **1876** Colorado becomes 38th state.
- **1877** University of Colorado opens in Boulder.
- **1878** Little Pittsburg silver strike launches Leadville mining boom, Colorado's greatest.

continues

against settlers led the Colorado cavalry to attack a peaceful settlement of Indians—who were flying Old Glory and a white flag—on November 29, 1864. More than 150 Cheyenne and Arapaho, two-thirds of them women and children, were killed in what has become known as the Sand Creek Massacre.

Vowing revenge, the Cheyenne and Arapaho launched a campaign to drive whites from their ancient hunting grounds. Their biggest triumph was the destruction of the northeast Colorado town of Julesburg in 1865, but the cavalry, bolstered by returning Civil War veterans, managed to force the two tribes onto reservations in Indian Territory in what is now Oklahoma—a barren area that whites thought they would never want.

Also in 1865, a smelter was built in Black Hawk, just west of Denver, setting the stage for the large-scale spread of mining throughout Colorado. When the first transcontinental railroad was completed in 1869, the Union Pacific went through Cheyenne, Wyoming, 100 miles north of Denver; 4 years later the Kansas City–Denver Railroad linked the line to Denver.

Colorado politicians had begun pressing for statehood during the Civil War, but it wasn't until August 1, 1876, that Colorado became the 38th state. Because it gained statehood less than a month after the 100th birthday of the United States,

Colorado became known as the Centennial State.

The state's new constitution gave the vote to blacks but not to women, despite the strong efforts of the Colorado Women's Suffrage Association. In 1893, women finally succeeded in winning the vote, 3 years after Wyoming became the first state to offer universal suffrage.

At the time of statehood, most of Colorado's vast western region was still occupied by some 3,500 mountain and plateau dwellers of a half-dozen Ute tribes. Unlike the plains tribes, their early relations with white explorers and settlers had been peaceful. Chief Ouray, leader of the Uncompahgre Utes, had negotiated treaties in 1863 and 1868 that guaranteed them 16 million acres—most of western Colorado. In 1873, Ouray agreed to sell the United States one-fourth of that acreage in the mineral-rich San Juan Mountains in exchange for hunting rights and $25,000 in annuities.

But a mining boom that began in 1878 led to a flurry of intrusions into Ute territory and stirred up a "Utes Must Go!" sentiment. Two years later the Utes were forced onto small reserves in southwestern Colorado and Utah, and their lands opened to white settlement in 1882.

Colorado's real mining boom began on April 28, 1878, when August Rische and George Hook hit a vein of silver carbonate

---

- **1879** Milk Creek Massacre by Ute warriors leads to tribe's removal to reservations.
- **1890** Sherman Silver Purchase Act boosts price of silver. Gold discovered at Cripple Creek, leading to state's biggest gold rush.
- **1893** Women win right to vote. Silver industry collapses following repeal of Sherman Silver Purchase Act.

- **1901–07** President Theodore Roosevelt sets aside 16 million acres of national forest land in Colorado.
- **1906** U.S. Mint built in Denver.
- **1913** Wolf Creek Pass highway is first to cross Continental Divide in Colorado.
- **1915** Rocky Mountain National Park established.
- **1934** Direct Denver–San Francisco rail travel begins.

Taylor Grazing Act ends homesteading.
- **1941–45** World War II establishes Colorado as military center.
- **1947** Aspen's first chairlift begins operation.
- **1948–58** Uranium "rush" sweeps western slope.
- **1955** Environmentalists prevent construction of Echo Park Dam in Dinosaur National Monument.

27 feet deep on Fryer Hill in Leadville. Perhaps the strike wouldn't have caused such excitement if Rische and Hook, 8 days earlier, hadn't traded one-third interest in whatever they found for a basket of groceries from storekeeper Horace Tabor, the mayor of Leadville and a sharp businessman. Tabor was well acquainted with the Colorado "law of apex," which said that if an ore-bearing vein surfaced on a man's claim, he could follow it wherever it led, even out of his claim and through the claims of others.

Tabor, a legend in Colorado, typifies the rags-to-riches success story of a common working-class man. A native of Vermont, he mortgaged his Kansas homestead in 1859 and moved west to the mountains, where he was a postmaster and storekeeper in several towns before moving to Leadville. He was 46 when the silver strike was made. By age 50, he was the state's richest man and its Republican lieutenant governor. His love affair with and marriage to Elizabeth "Baby Doe" McCourt, a young divorcée for whom he left his wife, Augusta, was a national scandal that became the subject of numerous books and even an opera.

Although the silver market collapsed in 1893, gold was there to take its place. In the fall of 1890, a cowboy named Bob Womack found gold in Cripple Creek, on the southwestern slope of Pikes Peak, west of Colorado Springs. He sold his claim to Winfield Scott Stratton, a carpenter and amateur geologist, and Stratton's mine earned a tidy profit of $6 million by 1899, when he sold it to an English company for another $11 million. Cripple Creek turned out to be the richest gold field ever discovered, ultimately producing $500 million in gold.

Unlike the flamboyant Tabor, Stratton was an introvert and a neurotic. His fortune was twice the size of Tabor's, and it grew daily as the deflation of silver's value boosted that of gold. But he invested most of it back in Cripple Creek, searching for a fabulous mother lode that he never found. By the early 1900s, the price of gold, like silver, began to be driven down by overproduction.

Another turning point for Colorado occurred just after the beginning of the 20th century. Theodore Roosevelt had visited the state in September 1900 as the Republican vice-presidential nominee. Soon after he became president in September 1901 (following the assassination of President McKinley), he began to declare large chunks of the Rockies forest reserves. By 1907, when an act of Congress forbade the president from creating any new reserves by proclamation, nearly one-fourth of Colorado—16 million acres in 18 forests—was national forest. Also during Roosevelt's term was the establishment

- **1967** Colorado legalizes medically necessary abortions.
- **1988** Sen. Gary Hart, a front-runner for the Democratic presidential nomination, withdraws from race after a scandal.
- **1992** Colorado voters approve a controversial state constitutional amendment barring any measures to protect homosexuals from discrimination.
- **1993** Denver becomes 15th U.S. city with three major professional sports teams by adding the Rockies, a new Major League Baseball franchise.
- **1995** The $4.2-billion state-of-the-art Denver International Airport opens, as does the $2.2-million Coors Field, home of Major League Baseball's Rockies. Denver gets its fourth major professional sports team, the Avalanche of the National Hockey League.
- **1996** The U.S. Supreme Court strikes down Colorado's 1992 constitutional amendment, stating that it could prevent homosexuals from enjoying basic constitutional rights granted to all Americans.

continues

in 1906 of Mesa Verde National Park, in the state's southwest corner.

Tourism grew hand in hand with the setting aside of public lands. Easterners had been visiting Colorado since the 1870s, when Gen. William J. Palmer founded a Colorado Springs resort and made the mountains accessible on his Denver & Rio Grande Railroad.

Estes Park, northwest of Boulder, was among the first resort towns to emerge in the 20th century, spurred by a visit in 1903 by Freelan Stanley. With his brother Francis, Freelan had invented the Stanley Steamer, a steam-powered automobile, in Boston in 1899. Freelan Stanley shipped one of his cars to Denver and drove the 40 miles to Estes Park in less than 2 hours, a remarkable speed for the day. Finding the climate conducive to his recovery from tuberculosis, he returned in 1907 with a dozen Stanley Steamers and established a shuttle service from Denver to Estes Park. Two years later he built the luxurious Stanley Hotel, still a hilltop landmark today.

Stanley befriended Enos Mills, a young innkeeper whose property was more a workshop for students of wildlife than a business. A devotee of conservationist John Muir, Mills believed tourists should spend their Colorado vacations in the natural environment, camping and hiking. As Mills gained national stature as a nature writer, photographer, and lecturer, he

urged that the national forest land around Longs Peak, outside Estes Park, be designated a national park. In January 1915, President Woodrow Wilson created the 400-square-mile Rocky Mountain National Park. Today it is one of America's leading tourist attractions, with more than 3 million visitors each year.

The 1920s saw the growth of highways and the completion of the Moffat Tunnel, a 6¼-mile passageway beneath the Continental Divide that in 1934 led to the long-sought direct Denver–San Francisco rail connection. Of more tragic note was the worst flood in Colorado history. The city of Pueblo, south of Colorado Springs, was devastated when the Arkansas River overflowed its banks on June 1, 1921; 100 people were killed, and the damage exceeded $16 million. The Great Depression of the 1930s was a difficult time for many Coloradans, but it had positive consequences: The federal government raised the price of gold from $20 to $35 an ounce, reviving Cripple Creek and other stagnant mining towns.

World War II and the subsequent Cold War were responsible for many of the defense installations that are now an integral part of the Colorado economy, particularly in the Colorado Springs area. The war also indirectly caused the other single greatest boon to Colorado's late-20th-century economy: the ski industry.

■ **1996** The Avalanche win the Stanley Cup, giving Colorado its first championship in any major league.

■ **1997** Weather wreaks havoc across the state. First, a summer rainstorm turns a small creek that runs through Fort Collins into a roaring river. Then, in late October, a 24-hour blizzard, the worst October storm in Denver since 1923, virtually shuts

down Interstate 25 from Wyoming to New Mexico and strands thousands at Denver International Airport.

■ **1997** Gary Lee Davis, convicted of the 1986 abduction and murder of a Colorado farm wife, is executed by lethal injection, the state's first execution in 30 years.

■ **1998** The Denver Broncos win the Super Bowl, defeating the Green Bay Packers.

The stunning victory saves the Broncos the indignity of becoming the first team to lose five Super Bowls.

■ **1999** The Broncos win the Super Bowl again, this time defeating the Atlanta Falcons.

■ **1999** The worst school shooting in United States history takes place in suburban Denver inside Columbine High School, leaving 15 dead.

Soldiers in the 10th Mountain Division, on leave from Camp Hale before heading off to fight in Europe, often crossed Independence Pass to relax in the lower altitude and milder climate of the 19th-century silver-mining village of Aspen. They tested their skiing skills, which they would need in the Italian Alps, against the slopes of Ajax Mountain.

In 1945, Walter and Elizabeth Paepcke—he the founder of the Container Corporation of America, she an ardent conservationist—moved to Aspen and established the Aspen Company as a property investment firm. Skiing was already popular in New England and the Midwest, but had few devotees in the Rockies. Paepcke bought a 3-mile chairlift, the longest and fastest in the world at the time, and had it ready for operation by January 1947. Soon, Easterners and Europeans were flocking to Aspen—and the rest is ski history.

The war also resulted in the overnight creation of what became at the time Colorado's 10th largest city, Amache, located in the southeastern part of the state. Immediately after the bombing of Pearl Harbor, the U.S. government began rounding up Americans of Japanese ancestry and putting them in internment camps, supposedly because the U.S. government feared they would side with the Japanese government against the United States. Although

there was a great deal of prejudice against those of Japanese ancestry throughout the United States at the time, Colorado Gov. Ralph Carr came to their defense, stating, "They are loyal Americans, sharing only race with the enemy." He welcomed them to the state and authorized the Amache Relocation Center, which at its peak had a population of more than 7,500. Amache was much like other Colorado towns of the time, with a school, post office, hospital, and even its own government, although its residents did not have the freedom to travel.

Colorado continued its steady growth in the 1950s, aided by tourism and the federal government. The $200-million U.S. Air Force Academy, authorized by Congress in 1954 and opened to cadets in 1958, is Colorado Springs' top tourist attraction today. There was a brief oil boom in the 1970s, followed by increasing high-tech development and even more tourism. Colorado made national news in 1967 when it became the first state to legalize medically necessary abortions,.

Weapons plants, which had seemed like a good idea when they were constructed during World War II, began to haunt Denver and the state in the 1970s and 1980s. Rocky Mountain Arsenal, originally built to produce chemical weapons, was found to be creating hazardous conditions by contaminating the land with

- **2002** One of the worst wildfire seasons in history hits Colorado, with about 1,000 fires burning some 364,000 acres across the state. The biggest fire, southwest of Denver, burns 138,000 acres and destroys 133 homes.

- **2003** Wynkoop Brewing Company owner John Hickenlooper elected mayor of Denver.
- **2006** T-REX, the biggest road and light-rail project in Denver history, completed.
- **2008** Denver hosts the 2008 Democratic National Convention.

deadly chemicals. A massive cleanup began in the early 1980s, and by the 1990s the arsenal was well on its way to accomplishing its goal of converting the 27-square-mile site into a national wildlife refuge.

The story of Rocky Flats, a nuclear weapons facility spurred on by the Cold War, is not so happy. Efforts to deal with contamination caused by nuclear waste have been largely unsuccessful. Although state and federal officials announced in 1996 that they had reached agreement on the means of removing some 14 tons of plutonium, their immediate plan calls for keeping it in Denver until at least 2010, and Department of Energy officials don't know what they'll do with it then. In the meantime, plans are underway to build storage containers that will safely hold the plutonium for up to 50 years.

In 1992, Colorado voters approved a controversial state constitutional amendment that would bar any legal measure specifically protecting homosexuals. The amendment would have nullified existing gay-rights ordinances in Denver, Boulder, and elsewhere. Enforcement was postponed pending judicial review, and in the meantime, gay-rights activists urged tourists to boycott Colorado. (Tourism did decline somewhat, although many Colorado ski resorts posted record seasons.) Then, in May 1996, the U.S. Supreme Court struck down the measure in a 6-to-3 vote, saying that, if enforced, it would have denied homosexuals constitutional protection from discrimination in housing, employment, and public accommodations.

On April 20, 1999, in a suburb of Denver, two students shook the city, state, and nation when they went on a shooting spree through Columbine High School. They killed 12 students and one teacher before turning their guns on themselves in the worst school shooting in the nation's history.

Now in the 21st century, the state's attention has turned to controlling population growth. With Colorado's growth rate well over the national average, both residents and government leaders question how this unabated influx of outsiders can continue without causing serious harm to the state's air, water, and general quality of life.

3 THE LAY OF THE LAND

First-time visitors to Colorado's Front Range are often awed by the looming wall of the Rocky Mountains, which come into sight a good 100 miles away, soon after you cross the border from Kansas. East of the Rockies, a 5,000-foot peak is considered high—yet Colorado has 1,143 mountains above 10,000 feet, including 53 over 14,000 feet! Mount Elbert, which is southwest of Leadville, is the highest of all at 14,433 feet.

The Rockies were formed some 65 million years ago by pressures that forced hard Precambrian rock to break through the earth's surface and push layers of earlier rock up on end. Millions of years of erosion then eliminated the soft surface material, producing the magnificent Rockies of calendar fame.

An almost perfect rectangle, Colorado measures some 385 miles east to west, and 275 miles north to south. The Continental Divide zigzags more or less through the center of the 104,247-square-mile state, the eighth largest in the nation.

You can visualize Colorado's basic topography by dividing the state into vertical thirds: The eastern part is plains, the midsection is high mountains, and the western third is mesa.

That's a broad simplification, of course. The central Rockies, though they cover six times the mountain area of Switzerland, are not a single vast highland but consist of a series of high ranges running roughly north to south. East of the Continental Divide, the primary river systems are the South Platte, Arkansas, and Rio Grande, all flowing toward the Gulf of Mexico. The westward-flowing Colorado River system dominates the western part of the state, with tributary networks including the Gunnison, Dolores, and Yampa-Green rivers. In most cases, these rivers are not broad bodies of water such as the Ohio or Columbia, but streams, heavy with spring and summer snowmelt, that shrink to mere trickles during much of the year under the demands of farm and ranch irrigation. Besides agricultural use, these rivers provide necessary water to wildlife and offer wonderful opportunities for rafting, fishing, and swimming.

The forested mountains are essential in that they retain precious water for the lowlands. Eleven national forests cover 15 million acres of land, with an additional 8 million acres, controlled by the Bureau of Land Management, also open for public recreation. Another half-million acres are within national parks, monuments, and recreation areas; and there are more than 40 state parks, including about 10 within an hour's drive of Denver, Boulder, or Colorado Springs.

Colorado's name, Spanish for "red," derives from the state's red soil and rocks. Some of the sandstone agglomerates have become attractions in their own right, such as Red Rocks Amphitheatre, west of Denver, and the startling Garden of the Gods, in Colorado Springs.

Of Colorado's 4.5 million people, some 80% live along the I-25 corridor, where the plains meet the mountains. Denver, the state capital, has a population of well over half a million, with over 3 million in the metropolitan area. Colorado Springs has the second largest population, with almost 380,000 residents, followed by Fort Collins (125,000), Pueblo (105,000), and Boulder (100,000). There is concern that this large and growing population threatens Colorado's natural habitat.

4 DENVER, BOULDER & COLORADO SPRINGS IN POPULAR CULTURE: BOOKS, FILM, TV & MUSIC

Those planning vacations in Denver, Boulder, and Colorado Springs and the nearby mountains can turn to a number of sources for background on the state and its major cities. Among my favorites is *A Lady's Life in the Rocky Mountains,* a fascinating compilation of Isabella L. Bird's letters to her sister; they were written in the late 1800s as she traveled alone through the Rockies, usually on horseback. Those who enjoy lengthy novels will want to get their hands on a copy of James Michener's 1,000-page *Centennial,* inspired by the northeastern plains of Colorado. For a more bohemian point of view, look no further than Jack Kerouac's classic, *On the Road.* Also engrossing is Wallace Stegner's Pulitzer Prize–winning 1971 novel, *Angle of Repose.* Horror fans will surely appreciate a pair of Stephen King classics with Colorado ties: *The Stand* is set in Boulder and *The Shining* was inspired by the writer's stay at the Stanley Hotel in Estes Park.

Travelers interested in seeing wildlife will likely be successful with help from the *Colorado Wildlife Viewing Guide,* by Mary Taylor Gray. You'll probably see a lot of historical sights here, too, so it's good to first get some background from the short, easy-to-read *Colorado: A History,* by Marshall Sprague.

Movies set on the Front Range are few and far between, although *Things to Do in Denver When You're Dead, About Schmidt,* and *WarGames* are exceptions, at least in part. Television shows in the area are more noteworthy: *Dynasty* (Denver), *Mork & Mindy* (Boulder), and *South Park* (50 miles southwest of Denver).

Musically speaking, the region has a rich heritage and a diverse current scene. John Denver; Earth, Wind & Fire; Big Head Todd and the Monsters; and the String Cheese Incident are among the bands that broke it big with strong ties to Denver or Boulder. In parts of the world, the "Denver Sound," a roots-based genre that melds Gothic and country, has been gaining notoriety, with bands like 16 Horsepower, Munly and the Lee Lewis Harlots, DeVotchKa, and Slim Cessna's Auto Club gaining an international following.

5 EATING & DRINKING IN DENVER, BOULDER & COLORADO SPRINGS

In Denver, Boulder, and Colorado Springs, restaurants tend to close no later than 10pm during the week and 11pm on weekends, although there are exceptions. Tipping is standard for the U.S. at 15% to 20%. Local delicacies include Rocky Mountain oysters (yes, they are deep-fried bull's testicles), Mexican fare, beef, and game. Boulder is on the forefront of numerous culinary trends, namely vegetarian, "localvore," and organic, as are Denver and Colorado Springs, although to a lesser degree. There are also quite a few microbreweries on the Front Range; Denver and the surrounding area have been dubbed "the Napa Valley of beer."

Planning Your Trip to Denver, Boulder & Colorado Springs

It's important to prepare for any trip, including one to Colorado's major cities. This chapter offers a variety of planning tools—information on when to go, how to get there, how to get around, and other tips.

1 VISITOR INFORMATION

Start by contacting the **Colorado Tourism Office,** 1625 Broadway, Denver, CO 80202 (© **800/COLORADO;** www.colorado.com), for a free copy of the official state vacation guide, which includes a state map and describes attractions, activities, and lodgings throughout Colorado. Another good source for Colorado information is the website of the *Denver Post,* the state's major daily newspaper, at **www.denverpost.com.**

The **Colorado Hotel and Lodging Association,** 999 18th St., Suite 1240, Denver, CO 80202 (© **303/297-8335;** www.coloradolodging.com), offers a free guide to lodging across the state. The non-profit **Bed and Breakfast Innkeepers of Colorado,** P.O. Box 38416, Colorado Springs, CO 80937 (© **800/265-7696;** www.innsofcolorado.org), distributes a free directory describing about 100 B&Bs across the state, including a number of historic inns in Denver, Boulder, and Colorado Springs.

Hostelling International-USA, 8401 Colesville Rd., Suite 600, Silver Spring, MD 20910 (© **301/495-1240;** www.hiayh.org), has a computerized system for making reservations in hostels worldwide, and also has a print directory of U.S. hostels.

A free copy of *Your Guide to Outdoor Adventure,* which contains details on the state's 40 parks, is available from state park offices at 1313 Sherman St., Suite 618, Denver, CO 80203 (© **303/866-3437;** www.parks.state.co.us). State park offices can also provide information on boating and snowmobiling.

2 ENTRY REQUIREMENTS & CUSTOMS

ENTRY REQUIREMENTS
Passports
New regulations issued by the Department of Homeland Security now require virtually every air traveler entering the U.S. to show a passport. As of January 23, 2007, all persons, including U.S. citizens, traveling by air between the United States and Canada, Mexico, Central and South America, the Caribbean, and Bermuda are required to present a valid passport. As of January 31, 2008, U.S. and Canadian citizens entering the U.S. at land and sea ports of entry from within the western hemisphere will need to

Destination: Denver, Boulder, Colorado Springs— Predeparture Checklist

- Are there any special requirements for your destination? Vaccinations? Special visas, passports, or IDs? Detailed road maps? Bug repellents? Appropriate attire? If you're flying, are you carrying a current, government-issued ID, such as a driver's license or passport?
- Did you find out your daily ATM withdrawal limit?
- Do you have your credit card PIN numbers? If you have a five- or six-digit PIN number, did you obtain a four-digit number from your bank?
- To check in at a kiosk with an e-ticket, do you have the credit card you bought your ticket with or a frequent-flier card?
- If you purchased traveler's checks, have you recorded the check numbers and stored the documentation separately from the checks?
- Did you bring your ID cards that could entitle you to discounts, such as AAA and AARP cards and student IDs?
- Did you leave a copy of your itinerary with someone at home?
- Do any theater, restaurant, or travel reservations need to be booked in advance?
- Some attractions (such as the top of the dome in the Colorado State Capitol in Denver, and the U.S. Air Force Academy and Peterson Air & Space Museum in Colorado Springs) have been closed for security reasons, or have reopened with special restrictions. Call ahead for specifics.
- If you want to attend a Denver Broncos game, call early—home games sell out months ahead.

present government-issued proof of citizenship, such as a birth certificate, along with a government issued photo ID, such as a driver's license. A passport is not required for U.S. or Canadian citizens entering by land or sea, but it is highly recommended to carry one.

For information on how to obtain a passport, go to **"Passports"** in the **"Fast Facts"** section of the appendix (p. 228).

Visas

The U.S. State Department has a **Visa Waiver Program (VWP)** allowing citizens of the following countries to enter the United States without a visa for stays of up to 90 days: Andorra, Australia, Austria, Belgium, Brunei, Denmark, Finland, France, Germany, Iceland, Ireland, Italy, Japan, Liechtenstein, Luxembourg, Monaco, the Netherlands, New Zealand, Norway, Portugal, San Marino, Singapore, Slovenia, Spain, Sweden, Switzerland, and the United Kingdom. (*Note:* This list was accurate at press time; for the most up-to-date list of countries in the VWP, consult www.travel.state.gov/visa.) Canadian citizens may enter the United States without visas; they will need to show passports (if traveling by air) and proof of residence, however. *Note:* Any passport issued on or after October 26, 2006, by a VWP country must be an **e-Passport** for VWP travelers to be eligible to enter the U.S. without a visa. Citizens of these nations also need to present a round-trip air or cruise ticket upon arrival. E-Passports contain computer chips capable of storing biometric information, such as the required digital photograph of the holder. (You can identify an e-Passport by the symbol on the bottom center cover of your passport.) If your passport doesn't have this feature, you can still travel without a visa if it is a valid passport issued before October 26, 2005, and includes a machine-readable zone, or between October 26, 2005, and October 25, 2006, and includes a digital photograph. For more information, go to **www. travel.state.gov/visa**.

Citizens of all other countries must have (1) a valid passport that expires at least 6 months later than the scheduled end of their visit to the U.S., and (2) a tourist visa, which may be obtained without charge from any U.S. consulate.

As of January 2004, many international visitors traveling on visas to the United States will be photographed and fingerprinted on arrival at Customs in airports and on cruise ships in a program created by the Department of Homeland Security called **US-VISIT**. Exempt from the extra scrutiny are visitors entering by land or those who don't require a visa for short-term visits (see above). For more information, go to the Homeland Security website at **www.dhs.gov/dhspublic**.

For specifics on how to get a visa, go to "**Visas**" in the "**Fast Facts**" section of the appendix (p. 230).

Medical Requirements

Unless you're arriving from an area known to be suffering from an epidemic (particularly cholera or yellow fever), inoculations or vaccinations are not required for entry into the United States.

CUSTOMS
What You Can Bring into the U.S.

Every visitor more than 21 years of age may bring in, free of duty, the following: (1) 1 liter of wine or hard liquor; (2) 200 cigarettes, 100 cigars (but not from Cuba), or 3 pounds of smoking tobacco; and (3) $100 worth of gifts. These exemptions are offered to travelers who spend at least 72 hours in the United States and who have not claimed them within the preceding 6 months. It is forbidden to bring into the country almost any meat products (including canned, fresh, and dried meat products such as buillion, soup mixes, etc.). Generally, condiments including vinegars, oils, spices, coffee, tea, and some cheeses and baked goods are permitted. Avoid rice products, as rice can often harbor insects. Bringing fruits and vegetables is not advised, though not prohibited. Customs will allow produce depending on where you got it and where you're going after you arrive in the U.S. Foreign tourists may carry in or out up to $10,000 in U.S. or foreign currency with no formalities; larger sums must be declared to U.S. Customs on entering or leaving, which includes filing form CM 4790. For details regarding U.S. Customs and Border Protection, consult your nearest U.S. embassy or consulate, or **U.S. Customs** (www.customs.ustreas.gov).

What You Can Take Home from the U.S.

Canadian Citizens: For a clear summary of Canadian rules, write for the booklet *I Declare*, issued by the **Canada Border Services Agency** (*C* **800/461-9999** in Canada, or 204/983-3500; **www.cbsa-asfc.gc.ca**).

Lighten Up

Denver has more days of sunshine each year than San Diego or Miami Beach.

Cut to the Front of the Airport Security Line as a Registered Traveler

In 2003, the **Transportation Security Administration** (**TSA;** www.tsa.gov) approved a pilot program to help ease the time spent in line for airport security screenings. In exchange for information and a fee, persons can be pre-screened as registered travelers, granting them a front-of-the-line position when they fly. The program is run through private firms—the largest and most well-known is Steven Brill's **Clear** (www.flyclear.com), and it works like this: travelers complete an online application providing specific points of personal information including name, addresses for the previous 5 years, birth date, social security number, driver's license number, and a valid credit card (you're not charged the **$99 fee** until your application is approved). Print out the completed form and take it, along with proper ID, with you to an "enrollment station" (this can be found in over 20 participating airports and in a growing number of American Express offices around the country, for example). It's at this point where it gets seemingly sci-fi. At the enrollment station, a Clear representative will record your biometrics necessary for clearance; in this case, your fingerprints and your irises will be digitally recorded.

Once your application has been screened against no-fly lists, outstanding warrants, and other security measures, you'll be issued a clear plastic card that holds a chip containing your information. Each time you fly through participating airports (and the numbers are steadily growing), go to the Clear Pass station located next to the standard TSA screening line. Here you'll insert your card into a slot and place your finger on a scanner to read your print—when the information matches up, you're cleared to cut to the front of the security line. You'll still have to follow all the procedures of the day like removing your shoes and walking through the x-ray machine, but Clear promises to cut 30 minutes off your wait time at the airport.

On a personal note: Each time I've used my Clear Pass, my travel companions are still waiting to go through security while I'm already sitting down, reading the paper, and sipping my overpriced smoothie. Granted, registered traveler programs are not for the infrequent traveler, but for those of us who fly on a regular basis, it's a perk I'm willing to pay for.

—David A. Lytle

U.K. Citizens: For information, contact **HM Customs & Excise** at ℂ **0845/010-9000** (from outside the U.K., 020/8929-0152), or consult their website at www.hmce.gov.uk.

Australian Citizens: A helpful brochure available from Australian consulates or Customs offices is *Know Before You Go*. For more information, call the **Australian Customs Service** at ℂ **1300/363-263,** or log on to **www.customs.gov.au**.

New Zealand Citizens: Most questions are answered in a free pamphlet available at New Zealand consulates and Customs offices: *New Zealand Customs Guide for Travellers, Notice no. 4.* For more information, contact **New Zealand Customs,** The Customhouse, 17–21 Whitmore St., Box 2218, Wellington (© **04/473-6099** or 0800/428-786; **www.customs.govt.nz**).

3 WHEN TO GO

Colorado has two tourist seasons: warm and cold. Those who want to see the state's parks and other scenic wonders, hike, mountain-bike, or raft will usually visit from May to October; those who prefer skiing, snowboarding, and snowmobiling will obviously have to wait for winter, usually from late November to March or April, depending on snow levels. Although you can visit most major museums year-round, some, especially in smaller communities, close in winter. The best way to avoid crowds at the more popular destinations is to try to visit March through May and October through mid-December.

To hear Coloradans tell it, the state has perfect weather all the time. Although they may be exaggerating just a bit, the weather is usually quite pleasant, with an abundance of sun and relatively mild temperatures in most places—just avoid those winter snowstorms that come sweeping out of the mountains.

Along the Front Range, including Denver, Boulder, and Colorado Springs, summers are hot and dry, with mild evenings and cool nights. Humidity is low, and temperatures seldom rise into the 100s. Evenings start to get cooler by mid-September, but even as late as November the days are often sunny and warm. Surprisingly, winters are milder and less snowy than those in the Great Lakes region or New England; many golf courses remain open year-round. The accompanying chart lists average temperatures and precipitation for Denver and Colorado Springs; Denver and Boulder are so close that their statistics are virtually identical.

Average Monthly High/Low Temperatures (°F & °C) & Precipitation (Inches):

		Jan	Feb	Mar	Apr	May	June	July	Aug	Sept	Oct	Nov	Dec
Denver	Temp. (°F)	43/16	47/20	52/26	62/35	71/44	82/53	88/59	86/57	77/48	66/37	52/25	45/18
	Temp. (°C)	6/–9	8/–6	11/–3	16/1	21/6	27/11	31/15	30/13	25/8	18/2	11/–3	7/–7
	Precip. (in.)	0.5	0.6	1.3	1.8	2.5	1.7	1.9	1.5	1.1	1.0	0.9	0.6
Elev. 5,280'													
Colorado Springs	Temp. (°F)	41/17	44/20	51/26	60/34	68/42	79/52	85/57	82/56	75/48	63/36	50/25	42/18
	Temp. (°C)	5/–8	6/–6	10/–3	15/1	20/5	26/11	29/13	27/13	23/8	17/2	10/–3	5/–7
	Precip. (in.)	0.3	0.4	1.2	1.4	2.8	2.5	2.5	3.3	1.1	0.9	0.6	0.5
Elev. 6,035'													

Most of Colorado is considered semi-arid, and overall the state has almost 300 sunny days a year—more sunshine than San Diego or Miami Beach. The prairies average about 16 inches of precipitation annually; the Front Range, 15 to 18 inches; the western slope, only 8 inches. Rain, when it falls, is commonly a short deluge—a summer afternoon thunderstorm.

However, if you want to see snow, simply head to the mountains, where snowfall is measured in feet instead of inches, and mountain peaks may still be white in July. Mountain temperatures can be bitterly cold, especially if it's windy, but even at the higher elevations of Colorado's top ski resorts, you'll find plenty of sunshine.

CALENDAR OF EVENTS

Below are some of the major annual events in Denver, Boulder, Colorado Springs, and the surrounding area. You'll find additional events on the Internet at **www.colorado.com** and **www.denver365.com**, as well as on each city's website. We strongly recommend, however, that if a particular event is especially important to your visit, you confirm the date by telephone before you leave home. For an exhaustive list of events beyond those listed here, check **http://events.frommers.com**, where you'll find a searchable, up-to-the-minute roster of what's happening in cities all over the world.

JANUARY

Great Fruitcake Toss, Colorado Springs. This zany event, in which contestants compete to see who can throw a fruitcake the farthest, has been covered by national media and is among the most outlandish and festive spectacles of the year. It takes place in Manitou Springs' Memorial Park, 5 miles west of downtown Colorado Springs. Call ⓒ **800/642-2567** or 719/685-5089 for more information. Early January.

Mahlerfest, Boulder. This may be the only festival celebrating the work of Gustav Mahler. Attend a full orchestra concert, free chamber concerts, or the free symposium. Call ⓒ **303/447-0513** or visit **www.mahlerfest.org** for more information. Early January.

National Western Stock Show and Rodeo, Denver. This is the world's largest livestock show and indoor rodeo, with about two dozen rodeo performances, a trade exposition, Western food and crafts booths, and livestock auctions. Call ⓒ **303/297-1166** for details. Second and third weeks in January.

Boulder Bach Festival, Boulder. Music of the master baroque composer. Call ⓒ **303/652-9101** or visit **www.boulderbachfest.org** for details. Last weekend in January.

FEBRUARY

Buffalo Bill's Birthday Celebration, Golden. Ceremonies and live entertainment that commemorate the life of the legendary scout and entertainer take place at the Buffalo Bill Memorial Museum. Call ⓒ **303/526-0744** or 303/526-0747 or check **www.buffalobill.org** for further information. Late February.

MARCH

Colorado Springs Dance Theatre Wine Festival, Colorado Springs. Sample the best wines at this 3-day benefit for the Colorado Springs Dance Theatre. Call ⓒ **719/630-7434** for information. Early March.

Pow Wow, Denver. More than 1,500 American Indians (as well as 60 drum groups), representing some 85 tribes from 32 states, perform traditional music and dances. Arts and crafts are also sold. Call ⓒ **303/934-8045** for details. Mid-March.

Saint Patrick's Day, Denver. Among the largest Irish holiday parades in the United States, with floats, marching bands, and more than 5,000 horses. Call ⓒ **303/892-1112** for further information. Saturday before March 17.

APRIL

Easter Sunrise Service, Colorado Springs and Denver. Worshipers watch the rising sun light red sandstone formations in the Garden of the Gods in Colorado Springs. For details, call ⓒ **719/634-3144.** Denver's Easter Sunrise Service takes place at Red Rocks Amphitheatre, also in the midst of stunning geological formations. Call

© 303/295-4444 or visit **www.red rocksonline.com** for further information. Easter Sunday.

MAY

Cinco de Mayo, Denver and Colorado Springs. More than 250,000 people from around the Denver metro area celebrate this annual Hispanic event, centered on north Federal Boulevard. It features mariachi bands, dancers, Mexican food, and other activities. Call © 303/534-8342 for information. Memorial Park is the site for the Colorado Springs celebration. Call © 719/635-5001 for information. May 5.

Plant and Book Sale, Denver. The largest volunteer-run plant and book sale in the nation, this event at Denver Botanic Gardens offers more than 250,000 plants, thousands of new and used books, and free gardening advice. Call © 720/865-3500 or visit **www.botanic gardens.org** for details. Early May.

Boulder Kinetic Fest, Boulder. This is a wacky event that's a real crowd pleaser. Most years an average of 70 teams race over land and water at Boulder Reservoir in a variety of imaginative, human-powered conveyances. Activities include the kinetic parade, kinetic concerts, the kinetic ball, and a hot-air balloon launch. Call © 303/444-5600 for details. Early May.

Bolder Boulder, Boulder. This footrace attracts some 40,000 entrants each year, plus numerous spectators. Participants walk, jog, or run the 10K course. Call © 303/444-RACE or visit **www.bolder boulder.com** for details. Memorial Day.

JUNE

International Buskerfest, Denver. An international street performers' festival featuring amazing shows by world-class jugglers, sword swallowers, magicians, tightrope artists, mimes, and acrobats!

Call © 303/478-7878 for more information. Mid-June.

Wool Market, Estes Park. This huge natural-fiber show boasts contests, demonstrations, a children's tent, and sale of animals as well as products made from their wool. Kids love it. Call © 970/586-5800 or go to **www.estes net.com** for details. Mid-June.

Colorado Shakespeare Festival, Boulder. This is considered among the top Shakespeare festivals in the country, with most performances in an outdoor theater. Call © 303/492-0554 for details. Late June through late August.

Garden Concerts, Denver. Jazz, blues, and folk concerts take place in the outdoor amphitheater at **Denver Botanic Gardens.** Call © 720/865-3500 or visit **www.botanicgardens.org** for information. June through September.

JULY

Pikes Peak Auto Hill Climb, Colorado Springs. This "race to the clouds," held annually since 1916, takes drivers to the top of 14,110-foot Pikes Peak. Call © 719/685-4400 for additional information. Usually the Saturday before or after July 4th.

Cherry Creek Arts Festival, Denver. This 3-day celebration of visual arts, which takes place in the chic Cherry Creek neighborhood, brings over 200 artists and 300,000 visitors. Call © 303/355-2787 or visit **www.cherryarts.org** for information. Early July.

Rooftop Rodeo & Parade, Estes Park. Features award-winning rodeos Tuesday through Sunday evenings. A grand parade kicks it all off on Tuesday morning. Call © 970/586-5800 or visit **www.estesnet.com** for details. Mid-July.

ArtFair, Boulder. Some 150 local and regional artists display their works in downtown Boulder, offering "fine art to fun art" plus live musical performances. Call ☏ **303/449-3774** or visit **www. boulderdowntown.com** for more information. Third weekend in July.

Buffalo Bill Days, Golden. A parade, kids' rides, a burro race, arts and crafts displays, a petting zoo, a car show, and a pancake breakfast mark Golden's largest event. Call ☏ **303/384-0003** or visit **www.buffalobilldays.com** for more information. Late July.

AUGUST

Pikes Peak or Bust Rodeo, Colorado Springs. Colorado's largest outdoor rodeo is a popular stop on the professional rodeo circuit. Call ☏ **719/635-3547** or visit **www.coloradosprings rodeo.com** for details. Early August.

Colorado State Fair, Pueblo. National professional rodeo, carnival rides, food booths, industrial displays, horse shows, animal exhibits, and entertainment by top-name performers. Call ☏ **800/876-4567,** ext. 2028, or visit **www.colorado statefair.com** for additional information. Mid-August through Labor Day.

SEPTEMBER

Colorado Springs Balloon Classic, Colorado Springs. More than 100 colorful hot-air balloons launch from Memorial Park, making this one of the largest balloon rallies in the country. Call ☏ **719/471-4833** or visit **www. balloonclassic.com** for more information. Labor Day weekend.

A Taste of Colorado, Denver. This is Denver's largest celebration, with an annual attendance of about 400,000. Local restaurants serve house specialties; there are also crafts exhibits and free concerts. Call ☏ **303/295-6330** or visit **www.atasteofcolorado.com** for details. Labor Day weekend.

Fall Festival, Boulder. An Oktoberfest celebration in downtown Boulder, this festival includes polka bands, food, carnival rides, and an art fair. Call

☏ **303/449-3774** or visit **www.boulder downtown.com** for more information. Late September or early October.

OCTOBER

Great American Beer Festival, Denver. Hundreds of American beers are available for sampling, and seminars are presented at what is considered the largest and most prestigious beer event in the United States. Call ☏ **303/447-0816** or visit **www.beertown.org** for information. Early October.

Pumpkin Festival, Denver. This family event, sponsored by **Denver Botanic Gardens** and held at Chatfield Nature Preserve southwest of town, includes pumpkin picking, food, crafts, hayrides, and other activities. Call ☏ **720/865-3500** or visit **www.botanic gardens.org** for details. Mid-October.

NOVEMBER

Holiday Sale, Denver. Handmade Christmas ornaments, gifts, dried-flower arrangements, and food items are among the unique merchandise at this annual sale at **Denver Botanic Gardens.** Call ☏ **720/865-3500** or visit **www.botanicgardens.org** for information. Mid-November.

DECEMBER

World's Largest Christmas Lighting Display, Denver. Some 40,000 colored floodlights illuminate the Denver City and County Building. All month.

Trail of Light, Denver. More than 12,000 sparkling lights cascade through the Botanic Gardens. Grand topiaries, nightly entertainment, "kissing spots," whimsical displays, and warm treats make for an unforgettable winter evening. Call ☏ **303/865-3500** or visit **www.botanicgardens.org** for information. All month.

Parade of Lights, Denver. A holiday parade winds through downtown Denver, with floats, balloons, and marching bands. Call ☏ **303/478-7878** or visit www.denverparadeoflights.com for information. Early December.

Festival of Lights Parade, Colorado Springs. A nighttime parade kicks off this month-long celebration of the holidays. Features include decorated live trees and holiday scenes from cultures around the world. Call © **719/649-9111** or visit **www.coloradosprings festivaloflights.org** for information. Early December.

Christmas with Cody, Golden. Buffalo Bill Cody playing Santa? He sure did,

and a reenactor continues the tradition, with gifts for the kids at the Buffalo Bill Memorial Museum. Call © **303/526-0744** or 303/526-0747 or check **www. buffalobill.org** for further information. First Sunday in December.

Pikes Peak Summit Fireworks, Colorado Springs. A wondrous fireworks display to ring in the New Year. Call © **800/888-4748** or 719/635-7506 or check out **www.experiencecolorado springs.com**. December 31.

4 GETTING THERE & GETTING AROUND

GETTING TO DENVER, BOULDER & COLORADO SPRINGS
By Plane

Those flying to Colorado will probably land at Denver International Airport or Colorado Springs Airport. Each airport is on the fringe of its respective city, so, depending on your itinerary, it can be a toss-up as to which is best. Denver certainly has the better average airfares. Both offer car rentals and shuttle services to their city's hotels.

Denver International Airport (DIA) is 23 miles northeast of downtown Denver, about a 35- to 45-minute drive. It is the sixth-busiest airport in the nation, with six runways and 93 gates. An information line (© **800/AIR-2-DEN** [247-2336] or 303/342-2000; www.flydenver.com) provides data on flight schedules and connections, parking, ground transportation, current weather conditions, and local accommodations. The local airport information and paging number is © **303/342-2300.** Airlines serving Denver include **Air Canada** (© 888/247-2262; www.aircanada.ca), **Alaska Airlines** (© 800/252-7524; www. alaskaair.com), **American** (© 800/433-

7300; www.aa.com), **Continental** (© 800/523-3273; www.continental.com), **Delta** (© 800/221-1212; www.delta.com), **Frontier** (© 800/432-1359; www.frontier airlines.com), **JetBlue Airways** (© 800/538-2583; www.jetblue.com), **Mexicana** (© 800/531-7921; www.mexicana.com), **Midwest Airlines** (© 800/452-2022; www. midwestairlines.com), **Northwest** (© 800/225-2525; www.nwa.com), **Southwest** (© 800/435-9792; www.southwest.com), **United** (© 800/241-6522; www.ual.com), and **US Airways** (© 800/428-4322; www. usair.com).

Colorado Springs Airport (COS) (© **719/550-1900**), located in the southeast corner of Colorado Springs, has nearly 100 flights each day, with connections to most major U.S. cities. **Allegiant** (© 702/505-8888; www.allegiantair.com), **American, Continental, ExpressJet** (© 888/958-9538; www.expressjet.com), **Frontier, Northwest, United,** and **US Airways** serve Colorado Springs.

Flights from the United Kingdom
British Airways (© **800/247-9297** or 0845/773-3377 in London; www.british-airways.com) offers one daily nonstop

flight between London and Denver. Travelers from the United Kingdom can also take British Airways to other U.S. cities and make connecting flights to Denver or Colorado Springs.

Immigration & Customs Clearance International visitors arriving by air, no matter what the port of entry, should cultivate patience and resignation before setting foot on U.S. soil. U.S. airports have considerably beefed up security clearances in the years since the terrorist attacks of September 11, 2001, and clearing Customs and Immigration can take as long as 2 hours.

Getting into Town from the Airport

Bus, taxi, and limousine services shuttle travelers between the airport and downtown, and most major car-rental companies have outlets at the airport. Many major hotels are some distance from the airport, so travelers should check on the availability and cost of hotel shuttle services when making reservations.

The cost of a **city bus** ride from the airport to downtown Denver is $9; from the airport to Boulder and suburban Park-n-Ride lots, it is about $11. The **SuperShuttle** (© 800/525-3177 or 303/ 370-1300; www.supershuttle.com) provides transportation to and from a number of hotels downtown and in the Denver Tech Center. The SuperShuttle has frequent scheduled service between the airport and downtown hotels for $19 each way; door-to-door service is also available. **Taxi** companies are another option, with fares generally in the $30-to-$50 range, and you can often share a cab and split the fare by calling the cab company ahead of time. For instance, **Yellow Cab** (© 303/ 777-7777) will take up to five people from DIA to most downtown hotels for a flat rate of $45. **Metro Taxi** (© 303/333-3333) is the other service in Denver.

Long-Haul Flights: How to Stay Comfortable

- Your choice of airline and airplane will definitely affect your leg room. Find more details about U.S. airlines at **www.seatguru.com**. For international airlines, the research firm Skytrax has posted a list of average seat pitches at **www.airlinequality.com**.

Tips Coping with Jet Lag

Jet lag is a pitfall of traveling across time zones. If you're flying north–south and you feel sluggish when you touch down, your symptoms will be the result of dehydration and the general stress of air travel. When you travel east–west or vice-versa, your body becomes confused about what time it is, and everything from your digestive system to your brain is knocked for a loop. Traveling east is more difficult on your internal clock than traveling west because most peoples' bodies are more inclined to stay up late than to fall asleep early.

Here are some tips for combating jet lag:

- **Reset your watch** to your destination time before you board the plane.
- **Drink lots of water** before, during, and after your flight. Avoid alcohol.
- **Exercise and sleep well** for a few days before your trip.
- If you have trouble sleeping on planes, **fly eastward on morning flights.**
- **Daylight** is the key to resetting your body clock. At the website for **Outside In** (www.bodyclock.com), you can get a customized plan of when to seek and avoid light.

Fun Facts **Take the High Road**

The world's highest automobile tunnel, the Eisenhower Tunnel, crosses the Continental Divide 65 miles west of Denver, at an elevation of 11,000 feet.

- Emergency exit seats and bulkhead seats typically have the most legroom. Emergency exit seats are usually left unassigned until the day of a flight (to ensure that someone able-bodied fills the seats); it's worth checking in online at home (if the airline offers that option) or getting to the ticket counter early to snag one of these spots for a long flight. Many passengers find that bulkhead seating offers more legroom, but keep in mind that bulkhead seats have no storage space on the floor in front of you.

- To have two seats for yourself in a three-seat row, try for an aisle seat in a center section toward the back of coach. If you're traveling with a companion, book an aisle and a window seat. Middle seats are usually booked last, so chances are good you'll end up with three seats to yourselves. And in the event that a third passenger is assigned the middle seat, he or she will probably be more than happy to trade for a window or an aisle.

- To sleep, avoid the last row of any section or the row in front of an emergency exit, as these seats are the least likely to recline. Avoid seats near highly trafficked toilet areas. Avoid seats in the back of many jets—these can be narrower than those in the rest of coach. Or reserve a window seat so you can rest your head and avoid being bumped in the aisle.

- Get up, walk around, and stretch every 60 to 90 minutes to keep your blood flowing. This helps avoid **deep vein thrombosis,** or "economy-class syndrome." See the box "Avoiding 'Economy Class Syndrome,'" p. 34.

- Drink water before, during, and after your flight to combat the lack of humidity in airplane cabins. Avoid caffeine and alcohol, which will dehydrate you.

By Car

An excellent road system, connecting to interstate highways heading in all directions, makes driving a good and economical choice. This is especially true for those planning excursions out of the Denver, Boulder, or Colorado Springs city limits. Although these cities have good public transportation within their boundaries, a car (either your own or a rental) is practically mandatory for those intent on getting out into the country.

Most major car-rental companies have locations in all three cities; metro Denver has the lion's share of them. For listings of the major car rental agencies, please see "Toll-Free Numbers & Websites," in the appendix.

Some 1,000 miles of interstate highways form a star on the map of Colorado, with its center at Denver. **I-25** crosses the state from south to north, extending from New Mexico to Wyoming; over its 300 miles, it goes through nearly every major city of the Front Range, including Pueblo, Colorado Springs, Denver, and Fort Collins. **I-70** crosses from west to east, extending from Utah to Baltimore, Maryland. It enters Colorado near Grand Junction, passes through Glenwood Springs, Vail, and Denver, and exits just east of Burlington, a distance of about 450 miles. **I-76** is an additional 190-mile spur that begins in Denver and extends northeast to Nebraska, joining I-80 just beyond Julesburg.

Denver is about 1,025 miles from Los Angeles, 780 miles from Dallas, 600 miles from Kansas City, 510 miles from Salt Lake City, 440 miles from Albuquerque, 750 miles from Las Vegas, 820 miles from Phoenix, 1,010 miles from Chicago, and 1,800 miles from New York City.

By Train

Amtrak (© 800/USA-RAIL; www. amtrak.com) has two routes through Colorado. The California Zephyr, which links San Francisco and Chicago, passes through Grand Junction, Glenwood Springs, Granby, Winter Park, Denver, and Fort Morgan en route to Omaha, Nebraska. The Southwest Chief, which runs between Los Angeles and Chicago, travels from Albuquerque, New Mexico, via Trinidad, La Junta, and Lamar before crossing the southeastern Colorado border into Kansas.

GETTING AROUND

Since most visitors to Denver, Boulder, and Colorado Springs will probably be traveling between cities and also into surrounding areas, you will most likely want to rent a car. However, you can save a bit of cash by doing your downtown city exploring, which can be done quite conveniently using public transportation, at either the beginning or the end of your stay, and only renting a car when you plan to leave town.

Each of the individual city chapters that follow contains information on car rentals and public transportation. A good stop: Denver's largest map store, **Mapsco Map and Travel Center,** 800 Lincoln St., Denver, CO 80203 (© **800/456-8703** or 303/830-2373; www.mapsco.com), offers USGS and recreation maps, state maps and travel guides, raised relief maps, and globes.

By Car

In Denver, Boulder, and Colorado Springs, the most cost-effective way to travel is by car, but all three have pedestrian- and bicycle-friendly routes and at least decent public transportation.

If you're visiting from abroad and plan to rent a car in the United States, keep in mind that foreign driver's licenses are usually recognized in the U.S., but you should get an international one if your home license is not in English.

Check out **Breezenet.com,** which offers domestic car-rental discounts with some of the most competitive rates around. Also worth visiting are Orbitz.com, Hotwire. com, Travelocity.com, and Priceline.com, all of which offer competitive online car-rental rates. For additional car rental agencies, see the "Toll-Free Numbers & Websites," in the appendix.

By Plane

Although you can fly between Denver and Colorado Springs, it's not nearly as economical as driving the 70 miles.

Overseas visitors can take advantage of the APEX (Advance Purchase Excursion) reductions offered by all major U.S. and European carriers. In addition, some large airlines offer transatlantic or transpacific passengers special discount tickets under the name **Visit USA,** which allows mostly one-way travel from one U.S. destination to another at very low prices. Unavailable in the U.S., these discount tickets must be purchased abroad in conjunction with your international fare. This system is the easiest, fastest, and cheapest way to see the country.

By Train

Although you can catch an Amtrak train from Union Station in Denver, it's not a particularly good method of travel between Denver, Boulder, and Colorado Springs—not until a light-rail build-out takes place in the next decade, at least. In Denver, existing light rail is useful for navigating certain attractions.

International visitors can buy a **USA Rail Pass,** good for 15 or 30 days of unlimited travel on **Amtrak** (© **800/USA-RAIL;** www.amtrak.com). The pass is available online or through many overseas travel agents. See Amtrak's website for the cost of travel within the western, eastern, or northwestern United States. Reservations are generally required and should be made as early as possible. Regional rail passes are also available.

By Bus

Bus travel is often the most economical form of public transit for short hops between U.S. cities, but it's certainly not an option for everyone (particularly when Amtrak, which is far more luxurious,

offers similar rates). Between Colorado Springs and Denver, the **Front Range Express** (℅ **719/636-3739;** www.front rangeexpress.com) offers bus service for $9 one-way. **Greyhound** (℅ **800/231-2222;** www.greyhound.com) is the sole nationwide bus line. International visitors can obtain information about the **Greyhound North American Discovery Pass.** The pass can be obtained from foreign travel agents or through their website (www. discoverypass.com) for unlimited travel and stopovers in the U.S. and Canada.

5 MONEY & COSTS

In general, Colorado is not particularly expensive, especially compared with destinations on the East and West coasts. In Denver, Boulder, and Colorado Springs, you'll find a wide range of prices for lodging and dining; admission to most attractions is less than $10 (it's sometimes free, especially in Boulder). Those traveling away from the major cities will discover prices in small towns are usually quite reasonable, but ski resorts such as Vail and Aspen can be rather pricey, especially during winter holidays. **Traveler's checks** and **credit cards** are accepted at almost all hotels, restaurants, shops, and attractions, plus many grocery stores.

Hotel rooms in the area are typically $100 to $200, but there are exceptions that are lower and higher—particularly higher when it comes to peak seasons. You'll find main courses for dinner typically running $10 to $20 up and down the Front Range.

In the United States, the most common bills are the $1 (a "buck"), $5, $10, and $20 denominations. There are also $2 bills (seldom encountered), $50 bills, and $100

bills (the last two are usually not welcome as payment for small purchases).

Coins come in seven denominations: 1¢ (1 cent, or a penny); 5¢ (5 cents, or a nickel); 10¢ (10 cents, or a dime); 25¢ (25 cents, or a quarter); 50¢ (50 cents, or a half dollar); the gold-colored Sacagawea coin, worth $1; and the rare silver dollar.

The easiest and best way to get cash away from home is from an **ATM (automated teller machine).** Look at the back of your bank card to see which network you're on; then call or check online for ATM locations at your destination. Be sure you know your personal identification number (PIN) and daily withdrawal limit before you depart. Also, if you have a five- or six-digit PIN, change it to a four-digit PIN before coming to Colorado.

Remember that many banks impose a fee every time you use a card at another bank's ATM, and that fee can be higher for international transactions (up to $5 or more) than for domestic ones (where they're rarely more than $2). In addition, the bank from which you withdraw cash may charge its own fee.

6 HEALTH

STAYING HEALTHY

Colorado's Front Range has its fair share of regional health concerns to be aware of before your trip, most of them relating to the altitude and the wildlife, but these can easily be avoided in most cases.

General Availability of Health Care

Contact the **International Association for Medical Assistance to Travelers** (**IAMAT;** ✆ **716/754-4883** or, in Canada, 416/652-0137; **www.iamat.org**) for tips on travel and health concerns in the countries you're visiting, and for lists of local, English-speaking doctors. The United States **Centers for Disease Control and Prevention** (✆ **800/311-3435;** www.cdc.gov) provides up-to-date information on health hazards by region or country, and offers tips on food safety. The website **www.tripprep.com**, sponsored by a consortium of travel-medicine practitioners, may also offer helpful advice on traveling abroad. You can find listings of reliable clinics overseas at the **International Society of Travel Medicine** (www.istm.org).

COMMON AILMENTS

ALTITUDE SICKNESS About two-thirds of Colorado is more than a mile above sea level, which means there is less oxygen and lower humidity than many travelers are accustomed to. This creates a unique set of problems for short-term visitors, such as the possibility of shortness of breath, fatigue, and other physical concerns.

Those not used to higher elevations should get sufficient rest, avoid large meals, and drink plenty of nonalcoholic fluids, especially water. Individuals with heart or respiratory problems should consult their personal physicians before planning a trip to the Colorado mountains. Those in generally good health need not take any special precautions, but it is best to ease the transition to high elevations by changing altitude gradually. For instance, spend a night or two in Denver (elevation 5,280 ft.) or Colorado Springs (elevation 6,035 ft.) before driving or taking the cog railway to the top of Pikes Peak (elevation 14,110 ft.).

Lowlanders can also help their bodies adjust to higher elevations by taking it easy

---

Avoiding "Economy-Class Syndrome"

Deep vein thrombosis, or as it's known in the world of flying, "economy-class syndrome," is a blood clot that develops in a deep vein. It's a potentially deadly condition that can be caused by sitting in cramped conditions—such as an airplane cabin—for too long. During a flight (especially a long-haul flight), get up, walk around, and stretch your legs every 60 to 90 minutes to keep your blood flowing. Other preventive measures include frequent flexing of the legs while sitting, drinking lots of water, and avoiding alcohol and sleeping pills. If you have a history of deep vein thrombosis, heart disease, or another condition that puts you at high risk, some experts recommend wearing compression stockings or taking anticoagulants when you fly; always ask your physician about the best course for you. Symptoms of deep vein thrombosis include leg pain or swelling, or even shortness of breath.

Colorado boasts 75% of the land in the continental United States above 10,000 feet in elevation.

for their first few days in the mountains, cutting down on cigarettes and alcohol, and avoiding sleeping pills and other drugs. Your doctor can provide prescription drugs to help prevent and relieve symptoms of altitude sickness.

Because the sun's rays are more direct in the thinner atmosphere, they cause sunburn more quickly. The potential for skin damage increases when the sun reflects off snow or water. A good sunblock is strongly recommended, as are good-quality ultraviolet-blocking sunglasses. Remember that children need more protection than adults.

HANTAVIRUS State health officials warn outdoor enthusiasts to take precautions against the Hantavirus, a rare but often fatal respiratory disease first recognized in 1993. About half of the country's confirmed cases have been reported in the Four Corners states of Colorado, New Mexico, Arizona, and Utah. The disease is usually spread by the urine and droppings of deer mice and other rodents, and health officials recommend that campers avoid areas with signs of rodent droppings. Symptoms of Hantavirus are similar to flu and lead to breathing difficulties and shock.

WEST NILE VIRUS Colorado has also had its share of cases of the West Nile virus illness. The best prevention is mosquito repellant. Though it's typically not fatal, the virus can cause death in some cases. Symptoms include fever, headache, and body aches.

WHAT TO DO IF YOU GET SICK AWAY FROM HOME

We list **hospitals** and **emergency numbers** in the "Fast Facts" section of the appendix.

If you suffer from a chronic illness, consult your doctor before your departure. Pack **prescription medications** in your carry-on luggage, and carry them in their original containers, with pharmacy labels—otherwise they won't make it through airport security. Visitors from outside the U.S. should carry generic names of prescription drugs. For U.S. travelers, most reliable health-care plans provide coverage if you get sick away from home. Foreign visitors may have to pay all medical costs up front and be reimbursed later.

7 SAFETY

While there are many reasons to visit Colorado and its major cities, two of the reasons most often cited are its historic sites and its magnificent outdoor activities. However, visiting historic sites and participating in outdoor activities can lead to accidents.

When visiting such historic sites as ghost towns, gold mines, and railroads, keep in mind that they were probably built more than 100 years ago, at a time when safety standards were extremely lax, if they existed at all. Never enter abandoned buildings, mines, or railroad equipment on your own. When you're visiting commercially operated historic tourist attractions, use common sense and don't be afraid to ask questions.

Walkways in mines are often uneven and poorly lit, and are sometimes slippery due to seeping groundwater that can also stain your clothing with its high iron content. When entering old buildings, be prepared for steep, narrow stairways, creaky floors, and low ceilings and doorways. Steam trains are a wonderful experience as long as you remember that steam is very hot, and that oil and grease can ruin your clothing.

When heading to the great outdoors, keep in mind that injuries often occur when people fail to follow instructions. Pay attention when the experts tell you to stay on established ski trails, hike only in designated areas, carry rain gear, and wear a life jacket when rafting. Mountain weather can be fickle, and many of the most beautiful spots are in remote areas. Be prepared for extreme changes in temperature at any time of year, and watch out for sudden summer-afternoon thunderstorms that can leave you drenched and shivering.

8 SPECIALIZED TRAVEL RESOURCES

TRAVELERS WITH DISABILITIES

Most disabilities shouldn't stop anyone from traveling in the U.S. Thanks to provisions in the Americans with Disabilities Act, most public places are required to comply with disability-friendly regulations. Almost all public establishments (including hotels, restaurants, museums, etc., but not including certain National Historic Landmarks), and at least some modes of public transportation provide accessible entrances and other facilities for those with disabilities.

The **America the Beautiful—National Park and Federal Recreational Lands Pass—Access Pass** (formerly the **Golden Access Passport**) gives visually impaired or permanently disabled persons (regardless of age) free lifetime entrance to federal recreation sites administered by the National Park Service, including the Fish and Wildlife Service, the Forest Service, the Bureau of Land Management, and the Bureau of Reclamation. This may include national parks, monuments, historic sites, recreation areas, and national wildlife refuges.

For more on organizations that offer resources to disabled travelers, go to Frommers.com.

GAY & LESBIAN TRAVELERS

In general, gay and lesbian travelers will find they are treated just like any other travelers in Colorado. Even cities such as Colorado Springs, home of Focus on the Family and other conservative groups, have become somewhat more open-minded about alternative lifestyles recently. Those with specific concerns can contact **Gay, Lesbian, Bisexual, and Transgender Community Services Center of Colorado** (ℂ 303/733-7743; www.glbtcolorado.org) in Denver; the organization can also provide information on events and venues of interest to gay and lesbian visitors.

The **International Gay and Lesbian Travel Association (IGLTA;** ℂ 954/776-2626; www.iglta.org) is the trade association for the gay and lesbian travel industry, and offers an online directory of gay- and lesbian-friendly travel businesses; go to its website and click on "Members."

For more gay and lesbian travel resources visit Frommers.com.

SENIOR TRAVEL

Many Colorado hotels and motels offer special rates to senior citizens, and an increasing number of restaurants, attractions, and public transportation systems offer discounts as well, some for "oldsters" as young as 55.

Members of **AARP** (formerly known as the American Association of Retired Persons), 601 E St. NW, Washington, DC 20049 (© **888/687-2277;** www.aarp.org), get discounts on hotels, airfares, and car rentals. AARP offers members a wide range of benefits, including *AARP: The Magazine* and a monthly newsletter. Anyone over 50 can join.

The U.S. National Park Service offers an **America the Beautiful—National Park and Federal Recreational Lands Pass—Senior Pass** (formerly the **Golden Age Passport**), which gives seniors 62 years or older lifetime entrance to all properties administered by the National Park Service—national parks, monuments, historic sites, recreation areas, and national wildlife refuges—for a one-time processing fee of $10. The pass must be purchased in person at any NPS facility that charges an entrance fee. Besides free entry, the America the Beautiful Senior Pass also offers a 50% discount on some federal-use fees charged for such facilities as camping, swimming, parking, boat launching, and tours. For more information, go to www.nps.gov/fees_passes.htm or call the United States Geological Survey (USGS), which issues the passes, at © **888/275-8747.**

Frommers.com offers more information and resources on travel for seniors.

FAMILY TRAVEL

Denver, Boulder, and Colorado Springs are loaded with family attractions, although their downtown dining and nightlife tends to focus more on adult pursuits. Nonetheless, such kid's landmarks as Tiny Town, Casa Bonita, Elitch Gardens, and Giuseppe's continue to thrive. To locate accommodations, restaurants, and attractions that are particularly kid-friendly, refer to the "Kids" icon throughout this guide.

If your travels are taking you to Rocky Mountain National Park, *Frommer's*

National Parks with Kids is a good resource.

For a list of more family-friendly travel resources, turn to the experts at Frommers.com.

STUDENT TRAVEL

A valid student ID will often qualify students for discounts on airfare, accommodations, and admission to museums, cultural events, movies, and more on Colorado's Front Range.

Check out the **International Student Travel Confederation (ISTC)** (www.istc.org) website for comprehensive travel services information and details on how to get an **International Student Identity Card (ISIC),** which qualifies students for substantial savings on rail passes, plane tickets, entrance fees, and more. It also provides students with basic health and life insurance and a 24-hour helpline. The card is valid for a maximum of 18 months. You can apply for the card online or in person at **STA Travel** (© **800/781-4040** in North America; 132-782 in Australia; 0871/2300-040 in the U.K.; www.statravel.com), the biggest student travel agency in the world; check out the website to locate STA Travel offices worldwide. If you're no longer a student but are still under 26, you can get an **International Youth Travel Card (IYTC)** from the same people, which entitles you to some discounts. **Travel CUTS** (© **800/592-2887;** www.travelcuts.com) offers similar services for both Canadians and U.S. residents. Irish students may prefer to turn to **USIT** (© **01/602-1904;** www.usit.ie), an Ireland-based specialist in student, youth, and independent travel.

TRAVELING WITH PETS

Many of us wouldn't dream of going on vacation without our pets. Under the right circumstances, it can be a wonderful experience for both you and your animals. Dogs and cats are accepted at many lodgings in Colorado, but not as universally in resorts and at the more expensive hotels. Throughout this book, we've tried to consistently note those lodgings that take pets. Some properties require you to pay a fee or damage deposit in advance, and most insist they be notified at check-in that you have a pet.

Be aware, however, that national parks and monuments and other federal lands administered by the National Park Service are not pet-friendly. Dogs are usually prohibited on all hiking trails, must always be leashed, and in some cases cannot be taken more than 100 feet from established roads. On the other hand, U.S. Forest Service and Bureau of Land Management areas and most state parks are pro-pet, allowing dogs on trails, and just about everywhere except inside buildings. State parks require that dogs be leashed; regulations in national forests and BLM lands are generally looser.

Aside from regulations, though, you need to be concerned with your pet's well-being. Just as people need extra water in Colorado's dry climate, so do pets. We especially like those clever spill-resistant travel water bowls sold in pet shops. And keep in mind that many trails are rough, and jagged rocks can cut the pads on your dog's feet.

For more resources about traveling with pets, go to Frommers.com.

9 SUSTAINABLE TOURISM

Sustainable tourism is conscientious travel. It means being careful with the environments you explore, and respecting the communities you visit. Two overlapping components of sustainable travel are **ecotourism** and **ethical tourism.** The **International Ecotourism Society** (TIES) defines ecotourism as responsible travel to natural areas that conserves the environment and improves the well-being of local people. TIES suggests that ecotourists follow these principles:

- Minimize environmental impact.
- Build environmental and cultural awareness and respect.
- Provide positive experiences for both visitors and hosts.
- Provide direct financial benefits for conservation and for local people.
- Raise sensitivity to host countries' political, environmental, and social climates.
- Support international human rights and labor agreements.

You can find some ecofriendly travel tips and statistics, as well as touring companies and associations—listed by destination under "Travel Choice"—at the **TIES** website, www.ecotourism.org. Also check out **Ecotravel.com**, which lets you search for sustainable touring companies in several categories (water-based, land-based, spiritually oriented, and so on).

While much of the focus of ecotourism is about reducing impacts on the natural environment, ethical tourism concentrates on ways to preserve and enhance local economies and communities, regardless of location. You can embrace ethical tourism by staying at a locally owned hotel or shopping at a store that employs local workers and sells locally produced goods.

Responsible Travel (www.responsible travel.com) is a great source of sustainable travel ideas; the site is run by a spokesperson for ethical tourism in the travel industry. **Sustainable Travel International** (www.sustainabletravelinternational.org) promotes ethical tourism practices, and manages an extensive directory of sustainable properties and tour operators around the world.

In the U.K., **Tourism Concern** (www.tourismconcern.org.uk) works to reduce

ⓘ Tips It's Easy Being Green

Here are a few simple ways you can help conserve fuel and energy when you travel:

- Each time you take a flight or drive a car greenhouse gases release into the atmosphere. You can help neutralize this danger to the planet through "carbon offsetting"—paying someone to invest your money in programs that reduce your greenhouse gas emissions by the same amount you've added. Before buying carbon offset credits, just make sure that you're using a reputable company, one with a proven program that invests in renewable energy. Reliable carbon offset companies include **Carbonfund** (www.carbonfund.org), **TerraPass** (www.terrapass.org), and **Carbon Neutral** (www.carbonneutral.org).

- Whenever possible, choose nonstop flights; they generally require less fuel than indirect flights that stop and take off again. Try to fly during the day—some scientists estimate that nighttime flights are twice as harmful to the environment. And pack light—each 15 pounds of luggage on a 5,000-mile flight adds up to 50 pounds of carbon dioxide emitted.

- Where you stay during your travels can have a major environmental impact. To determine the green credentials of a property, ask about trash disposal and recycling, water conservation, and energy use; also question if sustainable materials were used in the construction of the property. The website **www.greenhotels.com** recommends green-rated member hotels around the world that fulfill the company's stringent environmental requirements. Also consult **www.environmentallyfriendlyhotels.com** for more green accommodation ratings.

- At hotels, request that your sheets and towels not be changed daily. (Many hotels already have programs like this in place.) Turn off the lights and air-conditioner (or heater) when you leave your room.

- Use public transport where possible—trains, buses, and even taxis are more energy-efficient forms of transport than driving. Even better is to walk or cycle; you'll produce zero emissions and stay fit and healthy on your travels.

- If renting a car is necessary, ask the rental agent for a hybrid, or rent the most fuel-efficient car available. You'll use less gas and save money at the tank.

- Eat at locally owned and operated restaurants that use produce grown in the area. This contributes to the local economy and cuts down on greenhouse gas emissions by supporting restaurants where the food is not flown or trucked in across long distances. Visit **Sustain Lane** (www.sustainlane.org) to find sustainable eating and drinking choices around the U.S.; also check out **www.eatwellguide.org** for tips on eating sustainably in the U.S. and Canada.

PLANNING YOUR TRIP

3

SUSTAINABLE TOURISM

Frommers.com: The Complete Travel Resource

Planning a trip or just returned? Head to **Frommers.com**, voted Best Travel Site by *PC Magazine*. We think you'll find our site indispensable before, during, and after your travels—with expert advice and tips; independent reviews of hotels, restaurants, attractions, and preferred shopping and nightlife venues; vacation giveaways; and an online booking tool. We publish the complete contents of over 135 travel guides in our **Destinations** section, covering over 4,000 places worldwide. Each weekday, we publish original articles that report on **Deals and News** via our free **Frommers.com Newsletters.** What's more, **Arthur Frommer** himself blogs 5 days a week, with cutting opinions about the state of travel in the modern world. We're betting you'll find our **Events** listings an invaluable resource; it's an up-to-the-minute roster of what's happening in cities everywhere—including concerts, festivals, lectures, and more. We've also added weekly **podcasts, interactive maps,** and hundreds of new images across the site. Finally, don't forget to visit our **Message Boards,** where you can join in conversations with thousands of fellow Frommer's travelers and post your trip report once you return.

social and environmental problems connected to tourism. The **Association of Independent Tour Operators (AITO;** www.aito.co.uk) is a group of specialist operators leading the field in making holidays sustainable.

Volunteer travel has become increasingly popular among those who want to venture beyond the standard group-tour experience to learn languages, interact with locals, and make a positive difference while on vacation. Volunteer travel usually doesn't require special skills—just a willingness to work hard—and programs vary in length from a few days to a number of weeks. Some programs provide free housing and

food, but many require volunteers to pay for travel expenses, which can add up quickly.

For general info on volunteer travel, visit **www.volunteerabroad.org** and **www. idealist.org**.

Before you commit to a volunteer program, it's important to make sure any money you're giving is truly going back to the local community, and that the work you'll be doing will be a good fit for you. **Volunteer International** (www.volunteer international.org) has a helpful list of questions to ask to determine an organization's intentions.

10 PACKAGES FOR THE INDEPENDENT TRAVELER

Package tours are simply a way to buy the airfare, accommodations, and other elements of your trip (such as car rentals,

airport transfers, and sometimes even activities) at the same time and often at discounted prices. Many of the hotels in

Denver, Boulder, and Colorado Springs offer specific packages—for example, the Broadmoor (p. 177), in Colorado Springs, offers a golf package, while Denver's Hotel Teatro (p. 62) offers a theater package; many hotels and resorts in the region offer packages involving outdoor recreation in the Rockies.

For more information on package tours and for tips on booking your trip, see Frommers.com.

11 ESCORTED GENERAL-INTEREST TOURS

Escorted tours are structured group tours, with a group leader. The price usually includes everything from airfare to hotels, meals, tours, admission costs, and local transportation. Below are some of the better companies that offer escorted tours in the Denver, Boulder, and Colorado Springs areas.

Gray Line, 5855 E. 56th Ave. (P.O. Box 646), Denver, CO 80217 (© **303/ 289-2841;** www.coloradograyline.com), provides traditional bus and van tours to the U.S. Air Force Academy, Pikes Peak, Rocky Mountain National Park, and historic sites of Denver.

Maupintour, 2688 Rainbow Blvd., Las Vegas, NV 89146 (© **800/255-4266;** www.maupintour.com), offers a variety of tours, including well-planned multiday tours of Rocky Mountain National Park and other scenic and historic areas.

See also the "Organized Tours" section in chapter 6 for Denver and chapter 8 for Colorado Springs.

Despite the fact that escorted tours require big deposits and predetermined hotels, restaurants, and itineraries, many people derive security and peace of mind from the structure they offer. Escorted tours let travelers sit back and enjoy the trip without having to worry about details. They take you to the maximum number of sights in the minimum amount of time with the least amount of hassle. They're particularly convenient for people with limited mobility and they can be a great way to make new friends.

On the downside, you'll have little opportunity for serendipitous interactions with locals. The tours can be jampacked with activities, leaving little room for individual sightseeing or adventure—plus they often focus on the heavily touristed sights, so you miss out on many a lesser-known gem.

12 SPECIAL-INTEREST TRIPS

Hikers, bikers, and other outdoor recreationists can head into the mountains with **The World Outdoors,** 2840 Wilderness Place, Suite F, Boulder, CO 80301 (© **800/ 488-8483** or 303/413-0938; fax 303/413-0926; www.theworldoutdoors.com), which leads hiking and multisport adventures throughout the West, including trips into Rocky Mountain National Park. Most trips last 6 days and include transportation, lodging, and dining.

13 STAYING CONNECTED

TELEPHONES

The area codes for Denver and Boulder are **303** and **720**. In Colorado Springs, it's **719**. In Denver and Boulder, the full 10-digit phone number is required to make local calls, whereas the area code is not necessary in Colorado Springs. Most convenience stores and supermarkets carry calling cards for national and international calls. Pay phones still exist in the area, but their numbers have been on the decline in recent years. However, they are readily available in the downtowns of all three cities.

CELLPHONES

All major U.S. cellular networks work fine on the Front Range, but things quickly get spotty outside the urban cores. If you're not from the U.S., you'll be appalled at the poor reach of the **GSM (Global System for Mobile Communications) wireless network,** which is used by much of the rest of the world. Your phone will probably work in most major U.S. cities; it definitely won't work in many rural areas. To see where GSM phones work in the U.S., check out www.t-mobile.com/coverage. And you may or may not be able to send SMS (text messaging) home.

VOICE-OVER INTERNET PROTOCOL (VOIP)

If you have Internet access while traveling, consider a broadband-based telephone service (in technical terms, **Voice over Internet protocol,** or **VoIP**) such as Skype (www.skype.com) or Vonage (www.vonage.com), which allow you to make free international calls from your laptop or in a cybercafe. Neither service requires the people you're calling to also have that service (though there are fees if they do not). Check the websites for details.

Online Traveler's Toolbox

Veteran travelers usually carry some essential items to make their trips easier. Following is a selection of handy online tools to bookmark and use.

- **Airplane Food** (www.airlinemeals.net)
- **Airplane Seating** (www.seatguru.com and www.airlinequality.com)
- **Events** (www.denver365.com)
- **Foreign Languages for Travelers** (www.travlang.com)
- **Maps** (www.mapquest.com)
- **Ski Report** (www.coloradoski.com/snowreport)
- **Subway Navigator** (www.subwaynavigator.com)
- **Tickets (concerts and sporting events)** (www.ticketmaster.com)
- **Time and Date** (www.timeanddate.com)
- **Travel Warnings** (http://travel.state.gov, www.fco.gov.uk/travel, www.voyage.gc.ca, www.smartraveller.gov.au)
- **Universal Currency Converter** (www.oanda.com)
- **Weather** (www.intellicast.com and www.weather.com)

INTERNET & E-MAIL
With Your Own Computer

Wi-Fi is readily available at hotels, cafes, and some public places in Denver, Boulder, and Colorado Springs, including Denver's 16th Street Mall. For specific spots, check out the website **www.jiwire. com.**

Without Your Own Computer

Most major airports have **Internet kiosks** that provide basic Web access for a per-minute fee that's usually higher than cybercafe prices. Check out copy shops like **FedEx Kinkos,** which offers computer stations with fully loaded software.

14 TIPS ON ACCOMMODATIONS

Denver, Boulder, and Colorado Springs offer a variety of lodging options, from typical American chain motels to luxury hotels, cozy bed-and-breakfasts to inexpensive mom-and-pop independent motels, cabins to magnificent grande dame hotels.

The chains here are the same ones you see everywhere else in America: Best Western, Comfort, Days Inn, Embassy Suites, Hampton Inn, Hilton, Holiday Inn, Motel 6, Quality Inn, Sheraton, Super 8, Travelodge, and so on. They look just about the same as those found elsewhere, and have the same levels of service. In most cases their rooms are little more than boring boxes of various sizes, with beds and the appropriate plumbing and heating fixtures, and, if you're lucky, a decent view out the window. These chains, even the

high-end ones like Hilton and Sheraton, are fine if you just want a place to sleep, and plan to take advantage of their swimming pools, exercise rooms, and other facilities. However, they do little to enhance your vacation experience or even to let you know you're in Colorado.

To make your lodging an integral part of your Colorado experience, we suggest choosing a historic property. We discuss numerous historic bed-and-breakfast inns in the following pages, and—especially when you take into consideration the wonderful breakfasts most of them serve—the rates are fairly reasonable. Why spend $90 for a generic motel room, and then another $10 to $15 for breakfast, when for just a bit more you can sleep in a handsome, antique-decorated Victorian home and enjoy a home-cooked morning meal?

PLANNING YOUR TRIP

3

TIPS ON ACCOMMODATIONS

House-Swapping

House-swapping is becoming a more popular and viable means of travel; you stay in their place, they stay in yours, and you both get an authentic and personal view of the area, the opposite of the escapist retreat that many hotels offer. Try **HomeLink International** (Homelink.org), the largest and oldest home-swapping organization, founded in 1952, with over 11,000 listings worldwide ($75 for a yearly membership). **HomeExchange.org** ($50 for 6,000 listings) and **InterVac. com** ($69 for over 10,000 listings) are also reliable. Many travelers find great housing swaps on Craigslist (www.craigslist.org), too, though the offerings cannot be vetted or vouched for. Swap at your own risk.

This area of Colorado also has several magnificent but pricey historic hotels, including the absolutely wonderful Brown Palace in Denver and the family-friendly Broadmoor in Colorado Springs. These hotels are as much attractions as they are lodgings. Other accommodations choices here include cabins and a handful of small independent motels. Both are usually fairly inexpensive, although they often lack the facilities, such as pools, spas, and exercise equipment, that you'll find in most chains. We still prefer the cabins and independents, though, because they're often a very good value and the rooms usually have at least some personality; and the cabins, although sometimes a bit primitive, are often in beautiful settings.

For tips on surfing for hotel deals online, visit Frommers.com.

4

Suggested Itineraries in Denver, Boulder & Colorado Springs

On an 80-mile chunk of Colorado's Front Range, the three metropolitan areas covered in this guide are home to almost three-quarters of the state's population and a good deal of its attractions. Among Denver (Colorado's economic and political capital), Boulder (its intellectual one), and Colorado Springs (the first resort town in the West), there are destinations of every kind. Whereas many visitors use the area as a springboard to the resorts and national parks of the High Rockies, others find there is enough to do down below to make a 1- or 2-week vacation out of it, with the occasional foray into the great outdoors for good measure.

1 DENVER, BOULDER & COLORADO SPRINGS IN 1 WEEK

Day ❶: Arrive in Denver ★★

Whether you arrive by interstate or land at Denver International Airport, the best place to base yourself is downtown, where you can see all of the attractions on foot and by public transportation. Forgo the rental car (and parking costs) and take a taxi or shuttle to a downtown hotel. Get acquainted with the lay of the land by walking the **16th Street Mall** (p. 94) and wandering down Wynkoop Street in LoDo. Have dinner at one of the many top dining spots in the area, such as the **Wynkoop Brewing Company** (p. 74) or **Rioja** (p. 72).

Days ❷–❸: Explore Denver

From your room downtown, start the morning at **Larimer Square,** Denver's birthplace, with a self-guided walking tour of the historic sites (p. 84). Then stroll the 16th Street pedestrian mall and head toward the **State Capitol** (p. 79), just across Broadway. En route, take a 1-block detour for an early lunch or a cup of tea at the **Brown Palace Hotel** (p. 59). After seeing the capitol, explore other Civic Center sites, especially the **Denver Art Museum** (p. 79). On your third day, explore more of Denver. The city has numerous historic homes, beautiful parks, attractive shopping centers, and several highly touted museums (for example, the **Denver Museum of Nature & Science** [p. 82], the **Botanic Gardens** [p. 88], and the **Black American West Museum** [p. 85]). Take your pick of the many activities, and run with it.

Day ❹: Boulder ★★★

From Denver, rent a car and make the 30-minute trip to Boulder. Split your time between the **Pearl Street Mall** (p. 139) and an attraction or two: I'm particularly fond of the **Celestial Seasonings tour** (p. 142) and the **Boulder Museum of Contemporary Art** (p. 144). Explore a bit of the Boulder Creek Path by foot or bike (if time allows) before dinner and a show at one of the many venues—Boulder is renowned for its music.

Day ❺: Explore Rocky Mountain National Park ★★★

Boulder is about an hour's drive from Estes Park, the eastern gateway to **Rocky Mountain National Park** (p. 155). Stop for lunch in **Lyons**, if the time is right (p. 153), and then explore the park by car, parking to take a hike. Stay in Estes Park for the night. See p. 164.

Day ❻: Rocky Mountain National Park to Golden ★

Drive over **Trail Ridge Road** (p. 158) and south to Berthoud Pass to get back to I-70. This scenic drive gives you the option to further hike in the park, or else high-tail it back south to Golden for a tour of the **Coors Brewery** (p. 116) or just some time to stroll around the pleasant downtown. Either way, it's an ideal overnight stop that lets you avoid the bulk of the traffic in central Denver. See p. 113.

Day ❼: Colorado Springs ★★

Leave for the 70-mile trip in the morning and you can easily make it to downtown Colorado Springs for lunch. Spend the afternoon in Manitou Springs, or drive or take the train up to the summit of **Pikes Peak** (p. 193). In the evening, if your pocketbook allows, head to **The Broadmoor** (p. 184) for a fitting dinner to cap the trip.

2 DENVER, BOULDER & COLORADO SPRINGS IN 2 WEEKS

Build on the preceding 1-week itinerary, expanding your time in Denver to 4 nights, Boulder to 3 nights, and Rocky Mountain National Park to 2 nights. Overnight in Golden en route to Colorado Springs for the final 3 nights.

Days ❶–❹: Denver ★★

As in the itinerary above, start with a shuttle to a downtown hotel for the first 3 days, but take the extra day in Denver to explore a neighborhood by bike and foot. Get a rental and a map from **Campus Cycles** (p. 106), and then hop on one of the in-city trails that converges on Confluence Park for lunch in the vicinity. After your ride, get your rental car and head to one of the attractions that's further afield, or if the schedule allows, take in a Rockies game at Coors Field, or another sporting event in this sports-crazy city.

Days ❺–❼: Boulder ★★

As above, explore the Pearl Street Mall and a museum on your first day, but take the second day to hike some of the trails in the area (p. 162), packing a lunch before descending for dinner. On your third day in Boulder, visit the **National Center for Atmospheric Research** (p. 139) or the **Redstone Meadery** (p. 143), and take time to do more hiking, biking, or Pearl Street Mall people-watching.

Days ❽–❾: Rocky Mountain National Park ★★★

Use Estes Park as a base on night 1 and camp in the park (or stay in Grand Lake, the park's western gateway) on night 2. Spending 2 full days in the area allows for the second day to be centered on a significant day hike, like the **Mills Lake Trail** or the **Bierstadt Lake Trail.** See p. 162.

Day ❿: Rocky Mountain National Park to Golden ★

This is the same as Day 6 in the previous itinerary.

Days ⑪–⑭: Colorado Springs ★★

Instead of a rushed afternoon, take your time to explore the Pikes Peak region over 3 unhurried days. Move Pikes Peak and Manitou Springs to your second day here, and spend your entire first day and night exploring downtown and its attractions, namely the **Fine Arts Center** (p. 197) and the **Pioneers Museum** (p. 190). The following morning, head to Manitou Springs before ascending **Pikes Peak** (p. 193) by rail or car; then descend for an overnight in Manitou Springs or Old Colorado City. The final day's foci: **Garden of the Gods** (p. 191) and **The Broadmoor** (p. 177), where the trip-capping dinner from above remains my recommendation.

3 DENVER, BOULDER & COLORADO SPRINGS FOR FAMILIES

Denver, Boulder, and Colorado Springs are all great family vacation destinations, with plenty of museums, kid-friendly restaurants and accommodations, and parks to romp around in—not to mention easy access to the Rocky Mountains.

Day ❶: Arrive in Denver ★★

As with the 1-week itinerary above, start in Denver and base your time there out of downtown. However, kid-friendly destinations are more far-flung, so rent a car from the get-go. See p. 56.

Days ❷–❸: Explore Denver ★★

Start with a stop at **Confluence Park** before boarding the **Platte River Trolley** (p. 56); then hit the **Children's Museum** (p. 90) and the **Downtown Aquarium** (p. 89). For dinner, **Casa Bonita** (p. 78) is a beloved birthday place where the kids can run around while the parents soak in the kitsch. On the third day, hit the **Colorado State Capitol** (p. 79) and the **U.S. Mint** (p. 82) in the morning, and then head to the southern suburbs to **Wildlife Experience** (p. 87) or to **City Park,** home of the **Denver Zoo** (p. 89) and the **Denver Museum of Nature & Science** (p. 82).

Days ❹–❺: Explore Colorado Springs ★★

Leave Denver on the fourth morning, arriving in downtown Colorado Springs in time to have a romp in the water feature at nearby Acacia Park followed by lunch at **Meadow Muffins** (p. 190), in Old Colorado City. In the afternoon, visit **Garden of the Gods** (p. 191) before returning downtown for dinner at **Giuseppe's Old Depot Restaurant** (p. 187). Center your next day on Manitou Springs and a trip up **Pikes Peak** (p. 193) by car or rail.

Days ❻–❼: Explore Boulder ★★ & Rocky Mountain National Park ★★★

Return north on the sixth day of your trip. En route to Boulder, stop off U.S. 36 at the **Butterfly Pavilion** (p. 88) in Westminster. Visit **Pearl Street Mall** (p. 139) and **Celestial Seasonings** (p. 142) in the afternoon. On your last day, make a trip up to Estes Park for a quick taste of the Rockies. See p. 164.

4 A BEER-LOVER'S TRIP TO COLORADO'S FRONTRANGE

Some have dubbed Denver "the Napa Valley of beer" for its preponderance of microbreweries, not to mention brewer-turned-mayor John Hickenlooper. Extend the quest for suds in all directions and you'll find enough beer-related destinations to build a weeklong vacation.

Day ❶: Arrive in Denver

Stay downtown for easy access to the **Wynkoop Brewing Company** (p. 74), the mayor's flagship joint in LoDo, and to several other brewpubs. **Rock Bottom, Great Divide,** and **Breckenridge** should be high on the list. See p. 110.

Day ❷: Denver ★★

Try to time your trip so your second day coincides with a baseball game, day or night, at **Coors Field** (p. 101), and a visit to the resident microbrewery, the Sandlot, before heading out for nightcaps at **Falling Rock Tap House** (p. 109), one of the greatest beer joints on the planet, with 69 beers on tap.

Day ❸: Golden ★

Home to the world's largest single-site brewery—**Coors Brewery** (p. 116)—Golden is the natural next stop. There is plenty to do here besides the brewery tour—hiking, rafting, and riverboarding being my recommendations. See p. 113.

Day ❹: Colorado Springs ★★

Colorado Springs has its fair share of microbreweries, so pop downtown for a visit to **Phantom Canyon Brewing Co.** (p. 209) and Bristol Brewing next door to **Blue Star** (p. 185). While in the area, take in the **Garden of the Gods** (p. 191) by day, or hit the links for a round of golf. See p. 204.

Day ❺: Boulder ★★

Venture north again on Day 5 for a visit to Boulder and its numerous brewpubs—**Walnut Brewery** (p. 152) and **Mountain Sun Pub & Brewery** (p. 152) come to mind. Hit the tour at the **Rockies Brewing Company**, and, for a change of pace, visit the **Redstone Meadery** (p. 143) to see what a micromeadery is all about.

Days ❻–❼: Lyons & Rocky Mountain National Park ★★★

Stay in Boulder again on your sixth night if you'd like, but try to time your trip so you can take the free shuttle up to **Oskar Blues Grill & Brew** (p. 153), the state's largest brewpub, in Lyons. On your final day, cap your trip by working off a bit of that beer on the trails in **Rocky Mountain National Park.** See p. 155.

Settling into Denver

It's no accident that Denver is called "the Mile High City": When you climb up to the State Capitol, you're precisely 5,280 feet above sea level when you reach the 13th step. Denver's location at this altitude was purely coincidental; Denver is one of the few cities not built on an ocean, a lake, a navigable river, or even (at the time) an existing road or railroad.

In the summer of 1858, eager prospectors discovered a few flecks of gold where Cherry Creek empties into the shallow South Platte River, and a tent camp quickly sprang up on the site. (The first permanent structure was a saloon.) When militia Gen. William H. Larimer arrived in 1859, he claim-jumped the land on the east side of the Platte, laid out a city, and, hoping to gain political favors, named it after James Denver, governor of the Kansas Territory, which included this area. Larimer was not aware that Denver had recently resigned.

Larimer's was one of several settlements on the South Platte. Three others also sought recognition, but Larimer had a solution. For the price of a barrel of whiskey, he bought out the other would-be town fathers, and the name "Denver" caught on.

Although the gold found in Denver was but a teaser for much larger strikes in the nearby mountains, the community grew as a shipping and trade center, in part because it had a milder climate than the mining towns it served. A devastating fire in 1863, a deadly flash flood in 1864, and American Indian hostilities in the late 1860s created many hardships. But the establishment of rail links to the east and the influx of silver from the rich mines to the west kept Denver going. Silver from Leadville and gold from Cripple Creek made Denver a showcase city in the late 19th and early 20th centuries. The U.S. Mint, built in 1906, established Denver as a banking and financial center.

In the years following World War II, Denver mushroomed to become the largest city between the Great Plains and the Pacific Coast, with almost 600,000 residents within the city limits and over 3 million in the metropolitan area. It remains a growing city, with a booming downtown and suburbs. Denver is noted for its tree-lined boulevards, 200 city parks that cover more than 20,000 acres, and architecture ranging from Victorian to postmodern.

1 ORIENTATION

ARRIVING
By Plane
Denver International Airport (DIA) is 23 miles northeast of downtown, usually a 35- to 45-minute drive. Covering 53 square miles (twice the size of Manhattan), DIA has one of the tallest flight-control towers in the world, at 327 feet. The airport, which has 95 gates and six full-service runways, can handle around 50 million passengers annually.

Major national airlines serving Denver include American, Continental, Delta, Frontier, JetBlue, Northwest, Southwest, United, and US Airways. **International airlines** include Air Canada, British Airways, Lufthansa, and Mexicana de Aviación.

Regional and **commuter airlines** connecting Denver with other points in the Rockies and Southwest include Alaska Airlines and Great Lakes Airlines.

For airlines' national reservations phone numbers and websites, see "Getting There," in chapter 3. For other information, call the Denver International Airport **information line** (© **800/AIR-2-DEN** [247-2336] or 303/342-2000; TDD 800/688-1333; www.flydenver. com). Other important airport phone numbers include **ground transportation,** © 303/342-4059; **lost and found,** © 303/342-4062; **paging,** © 303/342-2300; **parking,** © 303/342-7275; **police,** © 303/342-4211; and **security wait times,** © 303/342-8477.

GETTING TO & FROM THE AIRPORT Bus, taxi, and limousine services shuttle travelers between the airport and downtown, and most major car-rental companies have outlets at the airport. Because many major hotels are some distance from the airport, travelers should check on the availability and cost of hotel shuttle services when making reservations.

The **city bus** fare from the airport to downtown Denver is $9; from the airport to Boulder and suburban Park-n-Ride lots, it is about $11. The **SuperShuttle** (© **800/525-3177** or 303/370-1300; www.supershuttledenver.com) provides transportation to and from a number of hotels downtown and in the Denver Tech Center. The SuperShuttle has frequent scheduled service between the airport and downtown hotels for $19 per person each way; door-to-door service is also available. **Taxi** companies (see "Getting Around," below) are another option, with fares generally in the $30-to-$50 range, and you can often share a cab and split the fare by calling the cab company ahead of time. For instance, **Yellow Cab** (© **303/777-7777;** www.yellowtrans.com) will take up to five people from DIA to most downtown hotels for a flat rate of $45.

Those who prefer a bit of luxury should call **White Dove Limousine** (© **800/910-7433** or 303/399-3683; www.whitedovelimo.com). Rates to different parts of the Denver metro area start around $70 but vary, so call for prices. The company operates sedan, stretch, and Hummer limousines, as well as a minibus. Charter services are also available.

By Car

The principal highway routes into Denver are **I-25** from the north (Fort Collins and Wyoming) and south (Colorado Springs and New Mexico), **I-70** from the east (Burlington and Kansas) and west (Grand Junction and Utah), and **I-76** from the northeast (Nebraska). If you're driving into Denver from Boulder, take **U.S. 36;** from Salida and southwest, **U.S. 285.**

By Train

Amtrak serves Union Station, 17th and Wynkoop streets (© **800/USA-RAIL** or 303/825-2583; www.amtrak.com), in the lower downtown historic district. Denver is a stop for the **California Zephyr** (Chicago to Emeryville, California); there are two trains daily in each direction.

By Bus

Greyhound, 1055 19th Street (at Arapahoe Street) (© **800/231-2222;** www.greyhound. com), is the major bus service in Colorado, with about 60 daily arrivals and departures to communities in and out of the state.

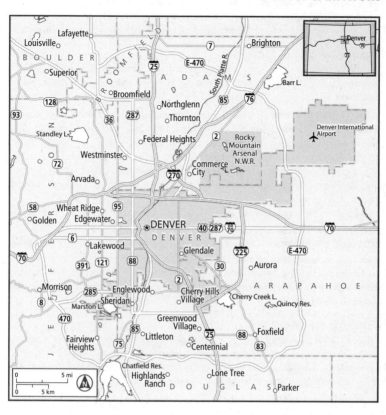

VISITOR INFORMATION

The **Denver Metro Convention and Visitors Bureau** operates a visitor center on the 16th Street Mall at 1600 California St. (© **303/892-1505**). It's open Monday through Friday from 9am to 5pm. In summer, it is open until 6pm on weekdays, as well as on Saturdays from 9am to 5pm and Sundays from 11am to 3pm. Visitor information is also available at Denver International Airport. Ask for the *Official Visitors Guide,* a 150-plus-page full-color booklet with a comprehensive listing of accommodations, restaurants, and other visitor services in Denver and surrounding areas.

For advance information, contact the Denver Metro Convention and Visitors Bureau, 1555 California St., Suite 300, Denver, CO 80202-4264 (© **800/233-6837** or 303/892-1112; www.denver.org).

CITY LAYOUT

It's tough to get lost in Denver—just remember that the mountains, nearly always visible, are to the west. Nonetheless, getting around a city of half a million people can be a challenge. One element of confusion is that Denver has both an older grid system downtown, which is oriented northeast–southwest to parallel the South Platte River, and a newer north–south grid system that surrounds the older one.

The *Official Visitors Guide,* available free of charge from the Denver Metro Convention and Visitors Bureau (see "Visitor Information," above), contains a good map.

Main Arteries & Streets

It's probably easiest to get your bearings from Civic Center Park. From here, Colfax Avenue (U.S. 40) extends east and west as far as the eye can see. The same is true for Broadway, which reaches north and south.

DOWNTOWN DENVER   North of Colfax and west of Broadway is the center of downtown, where the streets follow the old grid pattern. A mile-long pedestrian mall, **16th Street,** cuts northwest off Broadway just above this intersection. (The numbered streets parallel 16th to the northeast, extending to 44th; and to the southwest, as far as 5th.) Intersecting the numbered streets at right angles are **Lawrence Street** (which runs one-way northeast) and **Larimer Street** (which runs one-way southwest), 12 and 13 blocks north, respectively, of the Colfax–Broadway intersection.

I-25 skirts downtown Denver to the west, with access from Colfax or **Speer Boulevard,** which winds diagonally along Cherry Creek past Larimer Square.

OUTSIDE DOWNTOWN   Outside the downtown sector, the pattern is a little less confusing. But keep in mind that the numbered *avenues* that parallel Colfax to the north and south (Colfax is equivalent to 15th Ave.) have nothing in common with the numbered *streets* of the downtown grid. In fact, any byway labeled an "avenue" runs east–west, never north–south.

Finding an Address

NORTH–SOUTH ARTERIES   The thoroughfare that divides avenues into east and west is **Broadway,** which runs one-way south between 19th Street and I-25. Each block east or west adds 100 to the avenue address; thus, if you wanted to find 2115 E. 17th Ave., it would be a little more than 21 blocks east of Broadway, just beyond Vine Street.

Main thoroughfares that parallel Broadway to the east include **Downing Street** (1200 block), **York Street** (2300 block; it becomes **University Boulevard** south of 6th), **Colorado Boulevard** (4000 block), **Monaco Street Parkway** (6500 block), and **Quebec Street** (7300 block). Colorado Boulevard (Colo. 2) is the busiest street in the whole state, intersecting I-25 on the south and I-70 on the north. North–south streets that parallel Broadway to the west include **Santa Fe Drive** (U.S. 85; 1000 block); west of I-25 are **Federal Boulevard** (U.S. 287 North; 3000 block) and **Sheridan Boulevard** (Colo. 95; 5200 block), the boundary between Denver and Lakewood.

EAST–WEST ARTERIES   Denver streets are divided into north and south at **Ellsworth Avenue,** about 2 miles south of Colfax. Ellsworth is a relatively minor street, but it's a convenient dividing point because it's just a block south of **1st Avenue.** With building numbers increasing by 100 each block, that puts an address like 1710 Downing St. at the corner of East 17th Avenue. **First, 6th, Colfax** (1500 block), and **26th** avenues, and **Martin Luther King Jr. Boulevard** (3200 block) are the principal east–west thoroughfares. There are no numbered avenues south of Ellsworth. Major east–west byways south of Ellsworth are **Alameda** (Colo. 26; 300 block), **Mississippi** (1100 block), **Louisiana** (1300 block), **Evans** (2100 block), **Yale** (2700 block), and **Hampden** avenues (U.S. 285; 3500 block).

NEIGHBORHOODS IN BRIEF

Lower Downtown (LoDo) A 25-block area surrounding Union Station, and encompassing **Wynkoop Street** southeast to **Market Street** and **20th Street** southwest to **Speer Boulevard,** this delightful and busy historic district was until recently a somewhat seedy neighborhood of deteriorating Victorian houses and redbrick warehouses. A major restoration effort has brought it back to life. Today it is home to chic shops, art galleries, nightclubs, and restaurants. Listed as both a city and a county historic district, it boasts numerous National Historic Landmarks; skyscrapers are prohibited by law. Coors Field, the 50,000-seat home of the Rockies baseball team, opened here in 1995.

Central Business District This extends along **16th, 17th, and 18th streets between Lawrence Street and Broadway.** The ban on skyscrapers certainly does not apply here. In this area you'll find the Brown Palace Hotel, the Westin Hotel at Tabor Center, and other upscale lodgings; numerous restaurants and bars; plus the popular 16th Street Mall.

Far East Center Denver's Asian community is concentrated along this strip of **Federal Boulevard,** between **West Alameda** and **West Mississippi** avenues. It burgeoned in the aftermath of the Vietnam War to accommodate throngs of Southeast Asian refugees, especially Thai and Vietnamese. Look for authentic restaurants, bakeries, groceries, gift shops, and clothing stores. The Far East Center Building at Federal and Alameda is built in Japanese pagoda style.

Five Points The "five points" actually meet at 23rd Street and Broadway, but the cultural and commercial hub of Denver's black community, from **23rd** to **38th** streets, northeast of downtown, covers a much larger area and incorporates four historic districts. Restaurants offer soul food, barbecued ribs, and Caribbean cuisine, while jazz and blues musicians and contemporary dance troupes perform in theaters and nightclubs. The Black American West Museum and Heritage Center is also in this area.

Highlands Perched northwest of downtown from **32nd** to **38th** avenues between **Federal** and **Zuni** streets, the historic, increasingly chic Highlands neighborhood is the most densely populated neighborhood in the city outside of Capitol Hill. Mexican and Italian eateries brush elbows with stylish boutiques and galleries. In the neighboring West Highlands neighborhood, the eclectic retail district centered on 32nd Avenue and Lowell Boulevard is one of the most vibrant in the city.

La Alma Lincoln Park/Auraria Hispanic culture, art, food, and entertainment predominate along this strip of **Santa Fe Drive,** between **West Colfax** and **West 6th** avenues. It's notable for its Southwestern character and architecture. This neighborhood is well worth a visit for its numerous restaurants, art galleries, and crafts shops. Denver's annual Cinco de Mayo celebration takes place here.

Uptown Denver's oldest residential neighborhood, from **Broadway** east to **York Street** (City Park) and **23rd Avenue** south to **Colfax Avenue,** is best known today for two things: It's bisected by 17th Avenue, home to many of the city's finest restaurants, and several of its classic Victorian and Queen Anne–style homes have been converted to captivating bed-and-breakfasts (see "Where to Stay," below).

SETTLING INTO DENVER

5

NEIGHBORHOODS IN BRIEF

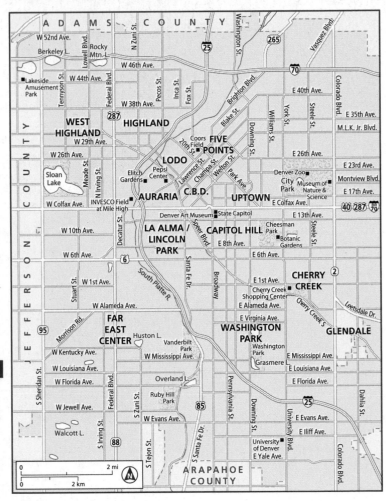

Washington Park A grand Victorian neighborhood centered on the lush park of its namesake, "Wash Park" is one of Denver's trendiest and most popular neighborhoods. Bounded by **Broadway** east to **University Boulevard,** and **Alameda Avenue** south to **Evans Avenue,** it features a good deal of dining and recreational opportunities, but little in the way of lodging. It is a

great place, however, for architecture and history buffs to drive or walk past the grand rows of houses.

Capitol Hill One of Denver's most diverse and oldest neighborhoods lies just southeast of downtown. Capitol Hill centers on the gold-domed Capitol Building, encompassing **Broadway** east to **York,** and **Colfax Avenue** south to **6th Avenue.** The north edge is improving after years of neglect and criminal activity, and now features such attractions as the Fillmore Auditorium and a lively restaurant and bar scene. There are several commercial and retail districts in the area, nestled amid Victorian houses and modern lofts and apartments. Also here are the Molly Brown House Museum (see chapter 6) and several lodging options, ranging from B&Bs to luxury hotels (see "Where to Stay," below). You'll notice that there are no old wooden buildings here. After a disastrous fire in 1863, the government forbade the construction of wooden structures, a ban that stood until after World War II.

Cherry Creek Home of the Cherry Creek Shopping Center and Denver Country Club, this area extends north from **East 1st Avenue** to **East 8th Avenue,** and from **Downing Street** east to **Steele Street.** You'll find huge,

ostentatious stone mansions here, especially around Circle Drive (southwest of 6th and University), where many of Denver's wealthiest families have lived for generations.

Glendale Denver surrounds Glendale, an incorporated city. The center of a lively entertainment district that is home to a slew of topless clubs, Glendale straddles Cherry Creek on **South Colorado Boulevard** south of **East Alameda Avenue.**

Tech Center At the southern end of the metropolitan area is the Denver Tech Center, along **I-25** between **Belleview Avenue** and **Arapahoe Road.** In this district, about a 25-minute drive from downtown, you will find the headquarters of several international and national companies, high-tech businesses, and a handful of upscale hotels heavily oriented toward business travelers.

2 GETTING AROUND

BY PUBLIC TRANSPORTATION

The **Regional Transportation District,** or **RTD** (© **800/366-7433,** 303/299-6000, or TDD 303/299-6089 for route and schedule information; 303/299-6700 for other business; www.rtd-denver.com), calls itself "The Ride." It operates bus routes and a light-rail system, with free transfer tickets available. It provides good service within Denver and its suburbs and outlying communities (including Boulder, Longmont, and Evergreen), as well as free parking at 65 Park-n-Ride locations throughout the Denver-Boulder metropolitan area. The light-rail service is designed to get buses and cars out of congested downtown Denver; many of the bus routes from outlying areas deliver passengers to light-rail stations rather than to downtown.

The local one-way fare is $1.75; seniors and passengers with disabilities pay 85¢, and children age 5 and under travel free. Regional bus fares vary (for example, Denver to Boulder costs $4). Exact change is required for buses, and train tickets can be purchased at vending machines beneath light-rail station awnings.

Depending on the route, the departure time of the last bus or train varies from 9pm to 2am. Maps for all routes are available at any time at the RTD **Civic Center Station,** 16th Street and Broadway; and the **Market Street Station,** Market and 16th streets. RTD also provides special service to Colorado Rockies (baseball) and Denver Broncos (football) games. All RTD buses and trains are completely wheelchair accessible.

Free buses run up and down the 16th Street Mall between the Civic Center and Market Street, daily from 6am to 1am.

The light rail is also useful for exploring downtown and the greater metro area. The **C Line** diverts from the main north–south **D Line** at Colfax Avenue, and it veers west and stops at Invesco Field at Mile High, the Pepsi Center, and Six Flags Elitch Gardens before chugging into Union Station at 17th and Wynkoop streets in lower downtown. The D Line continues along northeast through the east side of downtown before its terminus at 30th Avenue and Downing Street. The **E Line** runs along I-25 from Broadway to Lincoln Avenue in the south suburbs. The **F Line** connects 18th and California streets downtown with Lincoln Avenue. The **G Line** runs from Nine Mile in Aurora at I-225 and Parker Road to Lincoln; the **H Line** connects Nine Mile and 18th and California.

The open-air **Platte Valley Trolley** ((C) 303/458-6255; www.denvertrolley.org) operates year-round. From April to October between 12:30 and 4pm Friday through Sunday, there's a 25-minute "Riverfront Ride" ($3 adults, $2 seniors and children), which operates from 15th Street at Confluence Park, south to the Denver Children's Museum along the west bank of the Platte River. From Memorial Day to Labor Day, the ride is also available on Mondays. Different routes are offered at other times.

BY TAXI

The main companies are **Yellow Cab** ((C) 303/777-7777; www.yellowtrans.com) and **Metro Taxi** ((C) 303/333-3333; www.metrotaxidenver.com). Taxis can be hailed on the street, though it's preferable to telephone for a taxi or to wait for one at a taxi stand outside a major hotel. On weekends, hailing a taxi can be difficult when the bars close down for the night.

BY CAR

Because cars are not necessary downtown, visitors can save money by staying downtown while in Denver, and then renting a car to leave the area.

The Denver office of the **American Automobile Association (AAA)** is at 4100 E. Arkansas Ave., Denver, CO 80222-3405 ((C) **800/222-4357** or 303/753-8800; www. aaacolorado.com); there are several other locations in the Denver area.

CAR RENTALS Most major car-rental agencies have outlets in or near downtown Denver, as well as at Denver International Airport. These include **Alamo,** 24530 E. 78th Ave. ((C) 800/462-5266 or 303/342-7373); **Avis,** 1900 Broadway ((C) 800/331-1212 or 303/839-1280; 303/342-5500 at DIA); **Dollar,** 10343 N. Federal Blvd., Westminster ((C) 866/434-2226; 303/342-9678 at DIA); **Enterprise,** 7720 Calawba Ct. ((C) 800/ 261-7331 or 303/794-3333; 303/342-7350 at DIA); **Hertz,** 2001 Welton St. ((C) 800/ 654-3131 or 303/297-9400; 303/342-3800 at DIA); **National,** at Denver International Airport ((C) 800/227-7368 or 303/342-0717); and **Thrifty,** 8006 E. Arapahoe Ave. ((C) 800/847-4389 or 303/342-9400; 877/283-0898 at DIA). You can rent campers, travel trailers, motor homes, and motorcycles from **Cruise America** ((C) 800/671-8042; www.cruiseamerica.com).

Per-day rentals for midsize cars range from $35 to $70, although AAA and other discounts are often available, and weekend and multiday rates can also save money. Four-wheel-drive vehicles, trucks, and campers cost more.

PARKING Downtown parking-lot rates vary from 75¢ per half-hour to $20 or more per full day. Rates are higher near the 16th Street Mall, in the central business district, and in hotel lots. Keep a handful of quarters available if you plan to use on-street parking meters.

(*Fast Facts*) Denver

American Express The American Express travel agency, 555 17th St. ((℃ **303/383-5050**), is open Monday through Friday from 8am to 5pm. It offers full member services and currency exchange. To report a lost card, call ℃ **800/528-4800;** to report lost traveler's checks, call ℃ **800/221-7282.**

Area Code Area codes are **303** and **720,** and local calls require 10-digit dialing.

Babysitters Front desks at major hotels can often arrange for babysitters for their guests.

Business Hours Generally, business offices are open weekdays from 9am to 5pm and government offices are open from 8am until 4:30 or 5pm. Stores are open 6 days a week, with many also open on Sunday; department stores usually stay open until 9pm at least 1 day a week. Discount stores and supermarkets are often open later than other stores, and some supermarkets are open 24 hours a day.

 Banks are usually open weekdays from 9am to 5pm, occasionally a bit later on Friday, and sometimes on Saturday. There's 24-hour access to automated teller machines (ATMs) at most banks, plus in many shopping centers and other outlets.

Car Rentals See "Getting Around," above.

Dentists & Doctors Doctor and dentist referrals are available by calling ℃ **800/ DOCTORS. Ask-A-Nurse Centura** (℃ **800/327-6877** or 303/777-6877) provides free physician referrals and answers health questions.

Drugstores Throughout the metropolitan area, you will find Walgreens and other chain pharmacies, as well as Safeway and King Soopers grocery stores (which also have drugstores). The **Walgreens** at 2000 E. Colfax Ave. (℃ **303/331-0917**) is open 24 hours a day. For the locations of other Walgreens, call ℃ **800/925-4733.**

Emergencies Call ℃ **911.** For the **Colorado Poison Center,** call ℃ **303/739-1123.** For the **Rape Crisis and Domestic Violence Hotline,** call ℃ **303/318-9989.**

Eyeglasses One-hour replacements and repairs are available at **Pearle Vision,** 2720 S. Colorado Blvd. at Yale Avenue (℃ **303/758-1292**), and **LensCrafters,** in Cherry Creek Shopping Center (℃ **303/321-8331**).

Hospitals Among Denver-area hospitals are **St. Joseph Hospital,** 1835 Franklin St. (℃ **303/837-7111**), just east of downtown, and **Children's Hospital,** 13123 E. 16th Ave. (℃ **720/777-1234**).

Maps Denver's largest map store, **Mapsco Map and Travel Center,** 800 Lincoln St., Denver, CO 80203 (℃ **800/456-8703** or 303/830-2373; www.mapsco.com), offers USGS and recreation maps, state maps and travel guides, raised relief maps, and globes.

Newspapers & Magazines The *Denver Post* (www.denverpost.com) is Colorado's largest daily newspaper. The *Rocky Mountain News* (www.rockymountainnews. com) also covers the metropolitan area. Under a joint operating agreement, each publishes a separate weekday edition, only the *News* prints on Saturday, and only the *Post* appears on Sunday. A widely read free weekly, *Westword* (www.westword. com), is known as much for its coverage of local politicians and celebrities and its entertainment and dining listings. National newspapers such as *USA Today* and the *Wall Street Journal* can be purchased at newsstands and at major hotels.

Photographic Needs For photographic supplies, equipment, 1-hour processing, and repairs, visit **Wolf Camera** at 1 of its 18 Denver locations; the downtown branch, at 1545 California St. (✆ **303/623-1155;** www.wolfcamera.com), claims to be the biggest single-floor camera store in the world. Another good source for photo supplies and film processing is **Mike's Camera,** 759 S. Colorado Blvd. (✆ **303/733-2121;** www.mikescamera.com).

Post Office The main downtown post office, 951 20th St., is open Monday through Friday from 7am to 10:30pm, Saturday and Sunday from 8:30am to 10:30pm. For full 24-hour postal service, go to the General Mail Facility, 7500 E. 53rd Place. For other post office locations and hours, check with the U.S. Postal Service (✆ **800/ 275-8777;** www.usps.com).

Safety Although Denver is a relatively safe city, it is not crime-free. Safety is seldom a problem on the 16th Street Mall, but even streetwise Denverites avoid late-night walks along certain sections of Colfax Avenue, just a few blocks away. If you are unsure of the safety of a particular area you wish to visit, ask your hotel concierge or desk clerk.

Taxes State and local sales tax in Denver is about 7.75% (it varies slightly in neighboring counties and suburbs). The hotel tax is 10.75%, bringing the total tax on accommodations to about 18.5%.

Useful Telephone Numbers For a weather report, time, and temperature, call ✆ **303/337-2500.** Statewide road condition reports are available at ✆ **303/639-1111.** For information on possible road construction delays in the Denver area and statewide, see **www.cotrip.org**.

---

3 WHERE TO STAY

Although most hotels and motels in the Denver area do not have seasonal rates (as you'll find in many other parts of Colorado), hotels that cater to business travelers, such as the **Brown Palace** and the **Warwick** (see below), often offer substantial weekend discounts, sometimes as much as 50% off the regular rates. Rates listed below do not include the 18.5% accommodations tax.

The lodging industry is catching up with the construction of Denver International Airport, and you'll find that many of the major chains and franchises have built or are in the process of constructing facilities near the airport—there's also a proposed hotel at the terminal itself. Among those now open are **Courtyard by Marriott at DIA,** 6901 Tower Rd., Denver, CO 80249 (✆ **800/321-2211** or 303/371-0300), with rates of $219 to $249 for a double; and **Hampton Inn DIA,** 6290 Tower Rd., Denver, CO 80249 (✆ **800/426-7866** or 303/371-0200), with a rate of $139 to $179 for a double.

Reliable (and relatively inexpensive hotels) in the downtown area include **Comfort Inn,** 401 17th St., Denver, CO 80202 (✆ **800/228-5150** or 303/296-0400), with a convenient location and rates of $149 for a double and $189 to $329 for a suite; **La Quinta Inn Downtown,** 3500 Park Ave. W. (at I-25, exit 213), Denver, CO 80216

(© **800/531-5900** or 303/458-1222), charging $99 for a double; and **Hotel VQ,** 1975 Mile High Stadium Circle (at I-25, exit 210B), Denver, CO 80204 (© **800/388-5381** or 303/433-8331), with rates of $89 to $129 for a double.

These official, or "rack," rates, do not include any discounts, such as those offered to members of AAA or AARP. Be sure to ask if you qualify for a reduced rate. Because a chain hotel's national reservation service may not be able to offer discounts, your best bet may be to call the hotel directly.

DOWNTOWN

Hotels in downtown Denver, "the central business district of the Rocky Mountain West," generally cater to businesspeople, with high-tech amenities and locations convenient to the Convention Center or the financial district. These properties are more than adequate for leisure travelers, and especially enticing on weekends when they lower their rates.

Very Expensive

Brown Palace Hotel ★★ (Moments) For more than 100 years, the city's finest hotel has been the place to stay for anyone who is anyone. It combines great rooms and amenities with the intangibles: interesting history, romantic atmosphere, regional personality, and impeccable service. A National Historic Landmark, the Brown Palace has operated continuously since it opened in 1892. Designed with an odd triangular shape by the renowned architect Frank Edbrooke, it was built of Colorado red granite and Arizona sandstone. The lobby's walls are paneled with Mexican onyx, and elaborate cast-iron grillwork surrounds six tiers of balconies up to the stained-glass ceiling. Every president since 1905 (except Calvin Coolidge) has visited the hotel, and Dwight Eisenhower made the Brown his home away from the White House. His former room, now known as the Eisenhower Suite, is a vision of stately elegance, with a preserved dent in the fireplace trim that is the alleged result of an errant golf swing. There are also lavish, unique suites named after Teddy Roosevelt, Ronald Reagan, and The Beatles.

Standard rooms are also lush and comfortable, either Victorian or Art Deco in style with reproduction furnishings and fixtures. Each has a desk, a duvet, and individual climate control. The clientele is a mix of leisure travelers and businesspeople with a taste—and a budget—for luxury. The staterooms on the ninth floor are especially enticing, with cordless phones, big-screen TVs, fridges, fax/printers, and safes. The water is great here: The Brown Palace has its own artesian wells!

321 17th St., Denver, CO 80202. © **800/321-2599** or 303/297-3111. Fax 303/312-5900. www.brown palace.com. 241 units. $210–$385 double; $360–$535 suite. Lower weekend rates. AE, DC, DISC, MC, V. Valet parking $24 overnight. Pets up to 20 lb. accepted. **Amenities:** 3 restaurants (all American; see "Where to Dine," later in this chapter); 2 lounges; exercise room; concierge; courtesy car; business center; 24-hr. room service; in-room massage (for an extra charge). *In room:* A/C, cable TV w/pay movies, free Wi-Fi, hair dryer, iron.

(Fun Facts) **On the Hoof**

If you're in town for the National Western Stock Show, make sure to visit the Brown Palace Hotel for a study in contrasts—the champion steer is traditionally corralled in the lobby during one of the event's final mornings.

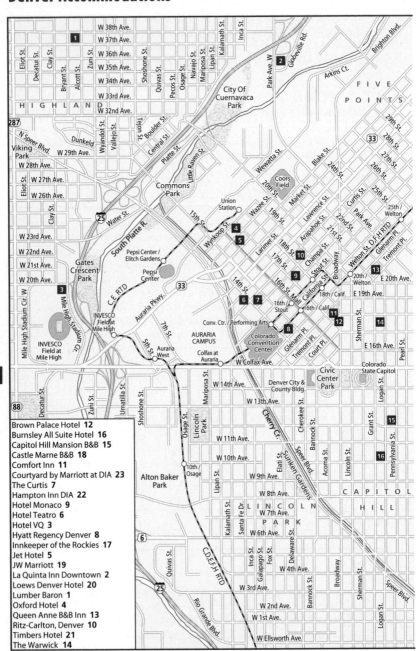

Brown Palace Hotel **12**
Burnsley All Suite Hotel **16**
Capitol Hill Mansion B&B **15**
Castle Marne B&B **18**
Comfort Inn **11**
Courtyard by Marriott at DIA **23**
The Curtis **7**
Hampton Inn DIA **22**
Hotel Monaco **9**
Hotel Teatro **6**
Hotel VQ **3**
Hyatt Regency Denver **8**
Innkeeper of the Rockies **17**
Jet Hotel **5**
JW Marriott **19**
La Quinta Inn Downtown **2**
Loews Denver Hotel **20**
Lumber Baron **1**
Oxford Hotel **4**
Queen Anne B&B Inn **13**
Ritz-Carlton, Denver **10**
Timbers Hotel **21**
The Warwick **14**

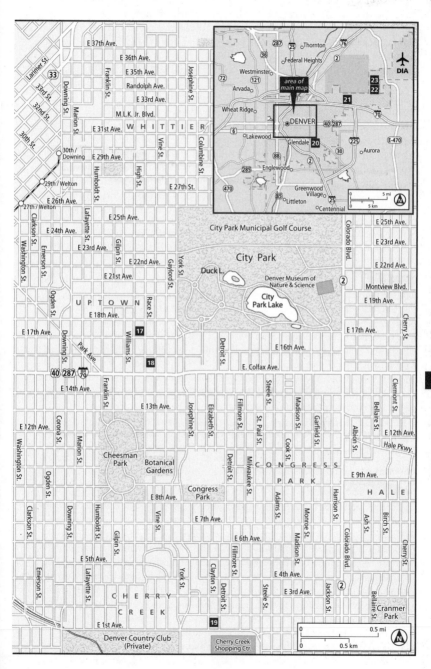

Hotel Monaco ★★ (Kids)   Billing itself as "Denver's hippest high-style luxury hotel," the Hotel Monaco is a standout for Kimpton Hotels. With eye-catching interiors inspired equally by Art Deco and French design, the hotel occupies a pair of renovated historic buildings in the heart of the central business district. This is one of the few downtown hotels that is 100% pet-friendly—the staff even delivers guests a named goldfish upon request. (The establishment also has a "Director of Pet Relations," a Jack Russell terrier named Lily Sopris.) Rooms have a rich style, equal parts sinful red and snazzy yellow, with perks such as CD stereos; plush, animal-print robes; and Starbucks coffee. With jetted tubs, wet bars, and VCRs, the generously sized suites are even more luxurious. You might bump into a celebrity here—the Monaco is a favorite of pro sports teams, rock bands, and Hollywood types, who often stay in the "music suites," named for and decorated after John Lennon, Grace Slick, and Miles Davis. Another perk is the nightly "Altitude Adjustment Hour" in the lobby, where guests enjoy complimentary wine and munchies along with 5-minute massages from the employees of the on-site Aveda Spa.

1717 Champa St. (at 17th St.), Denver, CO 80202. ✆ **800/397-5380** or 303/296-1717. Fax 303/296-1818. www.monaco-denver.com. 189 units. $329–$349 double; from $349 suite. Call for weekend rates. AE, DC, DISC, MC, V. Valet parking $21. Pets accepted. **Amenities:** Restaurant (Panzano; see "Where to Dine," later in this chapter); lounge; exercise room; spa; concierge; 24-hr. room service; in-room massage (for an extra charge); laundry service. *In room:* A/C, cable TV w/pay movies, fax, free Wi-Fi, minibar, fridge, coffeemaker, hair dryer, iron, safe.

Hotel Teatro ★★ (Finds)   Hotel Teatro is one of Denver's most luxurious hotels. It's also the most dramatic: The Denver Center for the Performing Arts (across the street) inspired the decor, which features masks, playbills, and wardrobes from past productions of its resident theater company. The hotel caters to both business and leisure travelers with exquisitely furnished guest rooms that hold Indonesian marble, cherrywood desks and fixtures, and Frette linens and towels. The nine-story building is a historic landmark, constructed as the Denver Tramway Building in 1911. Cutting-edge perks include iPod docking stations and 36-inch plasma-screen TVs in each room. All rooms also feature Aveda amenities and a rainforest shower head. Kevin Taylor, one of Denver's best-known chefs, runs both restaurants and the room service.

1100 14th St. (at Arapahoe St.), Denver, CO 80202. ✆ **303/228-1100.** Fax 303/228-1101. www.hotel teatro.com. 111 units. $269–$399 double; $469–$1,500 suite. AE, DC, DISC, MC, V. Valet parking $24 overnight. Pets accepted. **Amenities:** 2 restaurants (Italian, French); lounge; concierge; courtesy car; 24-hr. room service; massage; laundry service; dry cleaning. *In room:* A/C, cable TV w/pay movies, fax, free Wi-Fi, minibar, fridge, coffeemaker, hair dryer, iron.

Hyatt Regency Denver ★★   The 37-story Hyatt Regency is the city's crisp new convention center hotel, one of the biggest and best such properties in the Rockies and the first skyscraper to rise in downtown Denver since the early 1980s. With an ideal location—adjacent to the newly expanded Colorado Convention Center and its trademark "Blue Bear" sculpture—and a thorough, modern list of amenities, the Hyatt immediately emerged as the top convention hotel in the Rockies. Showcasing a terrific contemporary art collection with a local bent, the sleek lobby features automated check-in kiosks and the Strata bar. On the 27th floor, another bar, Peaks Lounge, offers the best views downtown. In between, the hotel's guest rooms are contemporary but comfortable, with plush furnishings and an ergonomic workstation. The suites are the biggest downtown, ranging from 500 all the way up to 3,000 square feet.

650 15th St., Denver, CO 80202. ✆ **800/233-1234** or 303/436-1234. Fax 303/436-9102. www.denver regency.hyatt.com. 1,100 units, including 60 suites. $125–$429 double; $550–$5,000 suite. AE, DC, DISC,

MC, V. Underground valet parking $24, self-parking $20. **Amenities:** Restaurant (steaks/seafood); 2
lounges; heated indoor pool; health club (weight room, cardiovascular machines); spa; outdoor Jacuzzi; sauna; concierge; car-rental desk; business center; room service (6am–midnight); dry cleaning; executive level. *In room:* A/C, cable TV w/pay movies, free Wi-Fi, fridge, coffeemaker, hair dryer, iron, safe.

Ritz-Carlton, Denver ★★

Opening in early 2008, the Ritz-Carlton is downtown Denver's only household-name luxury hotel (at least until the Four Seasons opens in late 2009). The former Embassy Suites was gutted and rebuilt to Ritz-Carlton's exacting standards and now has a distinctive style and a long list of perks for guests. The plush rooms—at 550 square feet—feature such amenities as steam-free mirrors, iPod-ready clock radios, down comforters, and combination coffee/tea/cappuccino makers. Beyond the rooms, the lavish common areas lead the way to **Elway's,** the downtown sibling to the Denver quarterbacking legend's Cherry Creek steakhouse, a spa, and a fully equipped business center.

1881 Curtis St., Denver, CO 80202. ✆ **303/312-3800.** Fax 303/312-3801. www.ritzcarlton.com. 202 units, including 48 suites. $309–$429 double; $409–$1,200 suite. Weekend rates from $209. AE, DC, DISC, MC, V. Underground valet parking $26, self-parking $15. **Amenities:** Restaurant (steaks); lounge; heated indoor lap pool; health club (weight room, cardiovascular machines, basketball court); spa; concierge; business center; 24-hr. room service; dry cleaning; executive level. *In room:* A/C, cable TV w/pay movies, high-speed Internet access (fee), fridge, coffeemaker, hair dryer, iron, safe.

Expensive

Burnsley All Suite Hotel ★★

Built as an apartment in 1963 but converted into a lodging by an ownership group that included Kirk Douglas and Ella Fitzgerald, this small, elegant hotel offers suites with private balconies and separate living, bedroom, dining, and fully stocked kitchen areas. The units are handsome, featuring marble entrance floors and antiques. The suites are expansive (averaging 700 sq. ft.) and popular with travelers who prefer to be a bit away from the hubbub of downtown. The hotel sits on a relatively quiet one-way street a few blocks southeast of the State Capitol. The restaurant serves breakfast, lunch, and dinner on weekdays, and breakfast and dinner on weekends. The lounge is a local favorite, a swank space with live jazz Friday and Saturday. The hotel is conveniently situated near the Cherry Creek shopping areas and is only 5 blocks from downtown.

1000 Grant St. (at E. 10th Ave.), Denver, CO 80203. ✆ **800/231-3915** or 303/830-1000. Fax 303/830-7676. www.burnsley.com. 80 suites. $179–$389 double. Lower weekend rates available. AE, DC, MC, V. Free covered parking. **Amenities:** Restaurant (Continental); lounge; seasonal outdoor pool; courtesy car; business center; room service until 10pm; laundry service. *In room:* A/C, cable TV, free Wi-Fi, kitchen, coffeemaker, hair dryer, iron.

The Curtis ★ (Finds)

A convention center lodging reimagined as a pop-culture-themed hotel, the Curtis reopened in 2007, with nostalgic boardgames in the lobby, floors with various themes (from "The Big Hair Floor" with art of oversized hairdos to "The 13th Floor," the hallway graced by Jack Nicholson's leering mug from *The Shining*), and wakeup calls by Darth Vader and Austin Powers sound-alikes. Featuring a toned-down version of the theme in the hallway, the rooms are modern and outfitted with techie perks like iPod-friendly speaker systems and flatscreen TVs. The staff has a sense of humor and there is a "5 & Dime" store selling toys and candy in the lobby. Corner rooms have fridges and great downtown views.

1405 Curtis St., Denver, CO 80202. ✆ **800/525-6651** or 303/572-3300. Fax 303/825-4301. www.thecurtis. com. 336 units, including 2 suites. $229–$425 double; suites from $450. AE, DC, DISC, MC, V. Valet parking $24, self-parking $15. **Amenities:** Restaurant (seafood); lounge; limited room service; indoor heated pool (large); exercise room; concierge. *In room:* A/C, TV w/DVD player, free Wi-Fi, coffeemaker, hair dryer, iron.

Jet Hotel ★   This contemporary boutique hotel is one of the few lodging options in the lively LoDo neighborhood. Located in a historic redbrick, the property has undergone a metamorphosis in the new millennium: It was first transformed from the LoDo Inn to the Luna Hotel, and then in 2008 it was renovated and became the Jet. It's sleek and smart, combining the personal service of a B&B with the conveniences of a full-service hotel. The guest rooms are spare studies in efficiency, with perks like CD and DVD players, unique art prints, and large armoires. Some rooms have private balconies and others have jetted tubs; the suite has a copper-topped table and a small kitchen. On weekend nights, the lobby morphs into a popular nightspot. The hotel is entirely non-smoking.

1612 Wazee St., Denver, CO 80202. ℂ 303/572-3300. Fax 303/623-0773. www.thejethotel.com. 18 units. $169–$199 double; $211–$299 suite. Rates include complimentary continental breakfast. AE, DC, DISC, MC, V. Parking $10. **Amenities:** 2 restaurants (cafe, eclectic); lounge; exercise room; concierge; limited room service. In room: A/C, TV w/DVD player, free Wi-Fi, kitchenette, coffeemaker, hair dryer, iron.

Oxford Hotel ★ (Finds)   Designed by the architect Frank Edbrooke and listed on the National Register of Historic Places, this is one of Denver's few hotels to have survived from the 19th century (another being the Brown Palace, described above). The facade is simple red sandstone, but the interior boasts marble walls, stained-glass windows, frescoes, and silver chandeliers, all of which were restored between 1979 and 1983 using Edbrooke's original drawings.

Antique pieces imported from England and France furnish the large rooms, which were created by combining smaller rooms during the restoration. No two units are alike (they're either Art Deco or Western Victorian in style), but all are equipped with one king or queen bed, individual thermostats, dressing tables, and large closets.

An Art Deco gem, the Cruise Room Bar boasts perhaps the swankest cocktail atmosphere in Denver, and the spa is the largest in the area.

1600 17th St. (at Wazee St.), Denver, CO 80202. ℂ 800/228-5838 or 303/628-5400. Fax 303/628-5413. www.theoxfordhotel.com. 80 units. $230–$300 double; $370–$500 suite. AE, DC, DISC, MC, V. Valet parking $21. **Amenities:** Restaurant (McCormick's Fish House & Bar; see "Where to Dine," later in this chapter); 2 lounges; exercise room; spa (w/Jacuzzi and sauna); concierge; courtesy car; salon; 24-hr. room service; massage; laundry service; dry cleaning. In room: A/C, TV, free Wi-Fi, minibar, hair dryer, iron.

The Warwick ★★   One of five Warwicks in the United States (the others are in New York, San Francisco, Dallas, and Seattle), this handsome midsize choice boasts an exterior and rooms reminiscent of hotels in Paris, where the corporate office is located. In contrast, the earth-tone lobby stylishly reflects the region, with classic European design, contemporary Western furnishings, and slate and red-stone stonework.

Similarly stylish, every room features a full private balcony with a great city view, and most are equipped with a fridge and wet bar. Each has one king- or two full-size beds, contemporary mahogany furniture, floral prints on the walls, cable TV (with pay-per-view movies), and two incoming phone lines. The standard rooms are very spacious, averaging 450 square feet each, and the 60 suites, which range from two-room parlor suites to grand luxury suites, are even more so.

1776 Grant St. (at E. 18th Ave.), Denver, CO 80203. ℂ 800/525-2888 or 303/861-2000. Fax 303/832-0320. www.warwickdenver.com. 220 units, including 60 suites. $189–$379 double; $269–$1,000 suite. Weekend rates $139–$209 double; from $195 suite. Children under 18 stay free in parent's room. AE, DC, DISC, MC, V. Valet parking $15 per day, self-parking $12 per day, both underground. **Amenities:** Restaurant (contemporary); lounge; rooftop heated pool; exercise room; concierge; courtesy town car; business center; 24-hr. room service; laundry service. In room: A/C, cable TV w/pay movies, coffeemaker, hair dryer, iron, safe.

Bed & Breakfasts
Bed & Breakfasts

Those seeking an alternative to a hotel or motel might consider one of Denver's many bed-and-breakfast inns. Often located in historic 19th-century homes, bed-and-breakfasts offer a more personalized lodging experience than you could expect in all but the very best hotels, because you rarely find more than 10 rooms in a B&B, and you are, literally, a guest in someone's home.

Capitol Hill Mansion Bed & Breakfast ★★ Located on Denver's "Mansion Row" just southeast of downtown and the State Capitol, this turreted B&B exemplifies Richardsonian Romanesque design with its ruby sandstone exterior and curving front porch. Built in 1891 the mansion is listed on the National Register of Historic Places and has the original woodwork and stained glass.

The inn is outfitted for the 21st century, with refrigerators, color TVs, and wireless Internet access. Each individually decorated room is named after a Colorado wildflower; some feature two-person Jacuzzi tubs, fireplaces, and private balconies. The elegant Elk Thistle Suite, on the third floor, features a panoramic view of the Rockies, a claw-foot tub, and a kitchen. Honeymooners might enjoy the second floor Shooting Star Balcony Room, which has a separate whirlpool tub and shower, and a private balcony with a city view.

Breakfasts include such items as crème brûlée French toast and pecan bread pudding. Smoking is not permitted inside the inn.

1207 Pennsylvania St., Denver, CO 80203. © **800/839-9329** outside 303 and 720 area codes or 303/839-5221. www.capitolhillmansion.com. 8 units. $114–$179 double; $159–$199 suite. Rates include full breakfast and evening wine and refreshments. AE, DC, DISC, MC, V. Free off-street parking. *In room:* A/C, cable TV, free Wi-Fi, fridge, coffeemaker, hair dryer, iron.

Castle Marne Bed & Breakfast ★★ A National Historic Landmark, Castle Marne is an impressive stone fortress designed and built in 1889 by the renowned architect William Lang for a contemporary silver baron. It was so named because a subsequent owner's son fought in the Battle of the Marne during World War I.

The inn is furnished with antiques, fine reproductions, and family heirlooms. Three rooms have private balconies with hot tubs. Three rooms have old-fashioned bathrooms with pedestal sinks and cast-iron clawfoot tubs. A gourmet breakfast (two seatings) is served in the original formal dining room, and a proper afternoon tea is served daily in the parlor. There is also a computer and printer for guest use. Smoking is not permitted, but well-behaved kids over 10 are welcome.

1572 Race St., Denver, CO 80206. © **800/92-MARNE** (800/926-2763) or 303/331-0621 for reservations. Fax 303/331-0623. www.castlemarne.com. 9 units. $95–$235 double; $210–$270 suite. Rates include full breakfast and afternoon tea. AE, DC, DISC, MC, V. Free off-street parking. *In room:* A/C, free Wi-Fi.

Lumber Baron ★ (Finds) After buying this turreted mansion in Denver's Highlands neighborhood on April Fool's Day 1991, Walt Keller began a 4-year, $1.5-million renovation. Built in 1890 by lumber baron John Mouat (hence the name), the 8,500-square-foot house held many surprises: a myriad of ornate wood fixtures (cherry, poplar, maple, and oak, to name a few) and a once-hidden third-story ballroom under an ornate pyramidal dome. Featuring flatscreen TVs and jetted tubs, the rooms have antique furnishings from around the world and unique themes: The Honeymoon Suite has a neoclassical bent, a four-poster mahogany queen bed, and a gargantuan mirror; and the Mary Ann Keller Suite (named for Walt's mother) has a garden motif with historic photos and intricate Anglo-Japanese wallpapering. For those seeking entertainment, the Lumber Baron hosts 50 "murder mystery parties" annually for $37 (dinner included;

SETTLING INTO DENVER

5

WHERE TO STAY

Family-Friendly Hotels

Hotel Monaco (p. 62)   Kids get a kick out of the colorful decor, the complimentary goldfish, and the house mascot, a Jack Russell terrier named Lily Sopris.

JW Marriott (see below)   This Cherry Creek hostelry is right in the vicinity of the bike trail, the mall, and other kid-friendly attractions, and has plenty of perks to keep the kids occupied when they're in their rooms.

Loews Denver Hotel (p. 67)   Kids get a teddy bear and coloring books when they arrive; the Tuscany Restaurant has a special children's menu.

two-for-one pricing for guests), comedic events with a handful of actors among the 50 to 100 partygoers.

2555 W. 37th Ave., Denver, CO 80211. ✆ **303/477-8205.** Fax 303/477-0269. www.lumberbaron.com. 5 units. $149 double; $199–$239 suite. Much lower weekday rates. Rates include full breakfast. AE, DISC, MC, V. *In room:* A/C, hair dryer, iron.

Queen Anne Bed & Breakfast Inn ★★   A favorite of both business travelers and couples, the Queen Anne might be considered the perfect bed-and-breakfast in the perfect home. It consists of two Victorian houses: one built by the well-known architect Frank Edbrooke in 1879, and the other built in 1886, now featuring piped-in chamber music, fresh flowers, and wireless Internet access. Each of the 10 double rooms in the 1879 Pierce-Tabor House is decorated with period antiques. Three rooms have original murals: All four walls of the Aspen Room are filled with (what else?) aspen trees; the third-floor Park Room overlooks a park and has a mural depicting the view that visitors would have seen in 1879; and the Rooftop Room has an outdoor hot-tub deck with a superb skyline view. Each of the four two-room suites in the adjacent 1886 Roberts house is dedicated to a famous artist (Norman Rockwell, Frederic Remington, John Audubon, and Alexander Calder). The suites have deep soaking tubs, and the Remington suite has a hot tub. Half of the rooms have cable television. Located in the Clements Historic District, the Queen Anne borders downtown Denver and is within easy walking distance of the major attractions. Smoking is not permitted.

2147–51 Tremont Place, Denver, CO 80205. ✆ **800/432-4667** or 303/296-6666. Fax 303/296-2151. www.queenannebnb.com. 14 units. $135–$185 double; $215 suite. Rates include hot breakfast and Colorado wine each evening. AE, DC, DISC, MC, V. Free off-street parking. *In room:* A/C, free Wi-Fi.

OUTSIDE DOWNTOWN
Very Expensive
JW Marriott ★★   Opened in 2004, the high-end JW Marriott was the first hotel in the Cherry Creek neighborhood, and it was well worth the wait. Sumptuous interiors and bold primary colors make for a distinctive ambience, and the attention to detail is excellent. The little touches are what this hotel is all about: jumbo flatscreen, high-definition TVs with DVD players, spectacular views, big bathrooms with granite aplenty, user-friendly thermostats, and excellent service. For shoppers, it's beyond ideal, a block from the Cherry Creek Mall and surrounded by chic retailers of all stripes. The

standout amenities: Second Home Kitchen and Bar, a sleek eatery; a huge exercise room; a 9,300-square-foot day spa; and an upscale shopping arcade. The hotel is also very close to the Cherry Creek bike path.

150 Clayton Lane, Denver, CO 80206. ✆ **866/706-7814** or 303/316-2700. Fax 303/316-4697. www. jwmarriottdenver.com. 196 units. $309–$379 double; $599–$1,200 suite; weekend rates from $199. AE, DC, DISC, MC, V. Pets accepted. **Amenities:** Restaurant; lounge; exercise room; spa; 2 outdoor Jacuzzis; concierge; courtesy car; business center; shopping arcade; salon; 24-hr. room service; massage; coin-op washers and dryers; dry cleaning; executive level. *In room:* A/C, cable TV w/pay movies and DVD player, high-speed Internet access, minibar, coffeemaker, hair dryer, iron, safe.

Expensive

Loews Denver Hotel ★★ (Kids)   Located just east of Colorado Boulevard and south of Cherry Creek, the Loews Denver's sleek, towering exterior is black steel with a reflecting glass tower. Inside, it's bella Italia, with columns finished in imitation marble, and Renaissance-style murals and paintings that look 500 years old. The location, about a 15-minute drive from downtown, is good for those who want access to scattered attractions or the Denver Tech Center. Throughout the hotel, much use has been made of floral patterns, Italian silk wall coverings, and marble-top furnishings. All the spacious rooms have elegant decor, and they include all the business perks any traveler could want: at least three phones, wireless Internet access, and a fax machine. The resident eatery, The Tuscany, is excellent.

4150 E. Mississippi Ave., Denver, CO 80246. ✆ **800/345-9172** or 303/782-9300. Fax 303/758-6542. www. loewshotels.com. 200 units, including 18 suites. $119–$239 double; $239–$389 suite; weekend rates from $99. Children under 18 stay free in parent's room. AE, DC, DISC, MC, V. Free valet and self-parking. Pets accepted. **Amenities:** Restaurant (Mediterranean); lounge; exercise room; access to nearby health club; concierge; courtesy van; business center; secretarial services; 24-hr. room service; massage; laundry service; dry cleaning; business-traveler rooms. *In room:* A/C, cable TV w/pay movies, free Wi-Fi, minibar, coffeemaker, hair dryer, iron, safe.

Moderate

The Timbers Hotel ★ (Value)   About midway between the Colorado State Capitol and Denver International Airport, The Timbers is my pick for a slick place to hang your hat east of downtown. That means the rates are lower than in central Denver, but the style is just as high: The place exudes contemporary Western ambience, hitting the right notes between colorful and comfortable. Each room is dubbed a suite, but only the one-bedroom suites actually have separate bedrooms and living areas. Done up in earth tones and plenty of hardwood, the executive studio suites have kitchens, but they are smaller one-room units without a separate bedroom; the studio suites are one-room units with one king or two queens and a fridge and a microwave. Most rooms have private patios or balconies.

4411 Peoria St., Denver, CO 80239. ✆ **800/844-9404** or 303/373-1444. Fax 303/373-1975. www.timbers denver.com. 127 units. $119–$209 studio suite; $159–$259 1-bedroom suite. Lower weekend and off-season rates. Rates include complimentary continental breakfast. AE, DISC, MC, V. Free self-parking. **Amenities:** Restaurant (American); lounge; indoor and outdoor pools; exercise room; 2 Jacuzzis; sauna; courtesy airport shuttle; business center; 24-hr. room service; complimentary washers and dryers; dry cleaning. *In room:* A/C, cable TV w/pay movies, free Wi-Fi, kitchens, minibar, coffeemaker, hair dryer, iron.

Inexpensive

Innkeeper of the Rockies (Value)   This centrally located hostel moved to spiffy new digs in 2005, about 2 miles east of downtown. Now housed in a converted 1905 apartment building—along with private rooms at a nearby house—the hostel is a clean and convenient choice. Facilities include a community kitchen, laundry machines, Internet access, and barbecue grills. There are two men's rooms, two women's rooms, and two co-ed rooms, each with six bunks.

1717 Race St., Denver, CO 80206. ✆ **303/861-7777.** Fax 720/225-9321. www.innkeeperrockies.com. 36 beds, 4 private units. $20 per person; $43 private double. AE, DISC, MC, V. Free street parking. **Amenities:** Free Internet access; coin-op laundry. *In room:* No phone.

CAMPING

Chatfield State Park ★   On the south side of Denver, 1 mile south of the intersection of Colo. 121 (Wadsworth) and Colo. 470, Chatfield has a 1,550-acre reservoir with ample opportunities for boating, water-skiing, fishing, and swimming, plus around 20 miles of trails for horseback riding, mountain biking, and hiking. Facilities include hot showers, picnic areas, a dump station, boat ramps and rentals, and full hookups.

11500 N. Roxborough Park Rd., Littleton, CO 80125. ✆ **303/791-7275,** or 800/678-2267 for state park reservation service (outside Denver) or 303/4170-1144. www.parks.state.co.us. 197 sites. $18–$22, plus $8 reservation fee and $7 day-use fee. MC, V only for advance reservations.

Chief Hosa Campground   Those seeking the amenities and easy accessibility of a commercial campground close to Denver will find a nice (but often quite busy) campground at this long-standing establishment 20 miles west of Denver. There are tent and RV sites, and most of the latter have electric and water hookups. When it opened in 1913, the south campground here was dubbed "America's First Motor-Camping Area." The campground is open year-round. The amenities include showers, grills, and a volleyball court.

27661 Genessee Dr., Golden, CO 80401. ✆ **303/526-1324.** www.chiefhosa.org. 61 sites. $22–$26. AE, DC, DISC, MC, V. Just off I-70, exit 253, 20 miles west of Denver.

4 WHERE TO DINE

Denver abounds with Mexican hole-in-the-walls, chain eateries, steak joints, and even a few bison joints, and the restaurants in LoDo and Cherry Creek become more like those in Los Angeles and Manhattan every year. Below, I've primarily listed independent restaurants, unique to this area and a cut above others in their price ranges.

DOWNTOWN
Very Expensive
Buckhorn Exchange ★★ ROCKY MOUNTAIN   In the same rickety premises where it was established in 1893, this landmark restaurant displays its Colorado Liquor License No. 1 above the 140-year-old bar in the upstairs saloon. On the first level, the densely decorated dining room, dominated by a daunting menagerie of taxidermy, will alarm vegetarians, but meat lovers will not be disappointed. The Buckhorn's game dishes (slow-roasted buffalo prime rib, lean and served medium rare; elk, and quail) are the best in the city. The beefsteaks, ranging from 8-ounce tenderloins to 64-ounce table steaks for five, are also quite good. With fried alligator tail, Rocky Mountain oysters, and smoked buffalo sausage among the options, the appetizers will surely broaden one's palate. My recommendation: rattlesnake, served in cream cheese–chipotle dip with tricolor tortilla chips. For dessert, try a slab of hot Dutch apple pie—if you have room. Lunch is lighter and more affordable, with an assortment of charbroiled meat entrees, sandwiches, and

Family-Friendly Restaurants

Casa Bonita (p. 78)   If the kids aren't concentrating on the tacos, the puppet shows, high divers, fun house, and video arcade will enthrall them.

Wynkoop Brewing Company (p. 74)   With a dining area separate from the bar, this pub and restaurant has a loud, bustling atmosphere and plenty of kid-friendly menu options.

hearty homemade soups. A mile southwest of the State Capitol, the Buckhorn has its own light-rail stop, making it a fun and easy trip from downtown.

1000 Osage St. (at W. 10th Ave.). (✆ **303/534-9505.** www.buckhorn.com. Reservations recommended. Main courses $8–$16 lunch, $18–$44 dinner. AE, DC, DISC, MC, V. Mon–Fri 11am–2pm; Mon–Thurs 5:30–9pm; Fri–Sat 5–10pm; Sun 5–9pm. Bar open all day. Light rail: Osage.

Palace Arms ★★ CONTINENTAL/REGIONAL   Despite its dramatic Napoleonic decor—antiques dating from 1700s include a dispatch case and a pair of dueling pistols that may have belonged to Napoleon—the Palace Arms' cuisine is a combination of traditional American, contemporary regional, Mediterranean, and Japanese influences. To begin, the Caesar salad is superb, prepared tableside for two. For an excellent main course try the Wagyu Master premium Japanese beef ($20 an ounce), lobster with ravioli and vegetables, or truffled Colorado bison. The wine list has received *Wine Spectator's* "Best of" award.

In the Brown Palace Hotel (p. 59), 321 17th St. (✆ **303/297-3111.** www.brownpalace.com. Reservations recommended. Main courses $40–$100 dinner. AE, DC, DISC, MC, V. Daily 6–10pm.

Expensive

Bistro Vendome ★★ FRENCH BISTRO   Across the street from sister eatery Rioja (see below), Bistro Vendome serves up splendid interpretations of Gallic standbys (dubbed "French soul food") in an intimate space on Larimer Square. The house interpretations of lamb, poultry, and veal dishes mix tradition and invention, and there is always a vegetarian plate on the menu. The pomme frites (aka french fries) are also beloved by locals, and the side dishes and desserts don't disappoint. Brunch brings crepes, quiches, and eggs Benedict. The patio is one of the best in Denver.

1424-H Larimer Sq. (✆ **303/825-3232.** www.bistrovendome.com. Reservations accepted. Main courses $7–$13 brunch, $16–$23 dinner. AE, DC, DISC, MC, V. Mon–Thurs 5–10pm; Fri–Sat 5–11pm; Sun 5–9pm; brunch Sat–Sun 10am–2pm.

Denver ChopHouse & Brewery ★ STEAKS   A LoDo mainstay since it opened alongside Coors Field in 1995, this is one of the Mile High City's best places for carnivores. Set in the steeped brick-and-wood atmosphere of a restored early-19th-century train depot, the ChopHouse does classic meat and potatoes (not to mention microbrews) as well as anybody in town. My picks are always juicy steaks, from filet mignon to New York strip, and the other hearty classics, such as huge, cheese-stuffed pork chops and herb-crusted racks of lamb; white cheddar mashers are my side of choice. The restaurant also serves a nice selection of fresh seafood and some less-expensive sandwiches and pizzas, and even a few vegetarian items.

SETTLING INTO DENVER

5

WHERE TO DINE

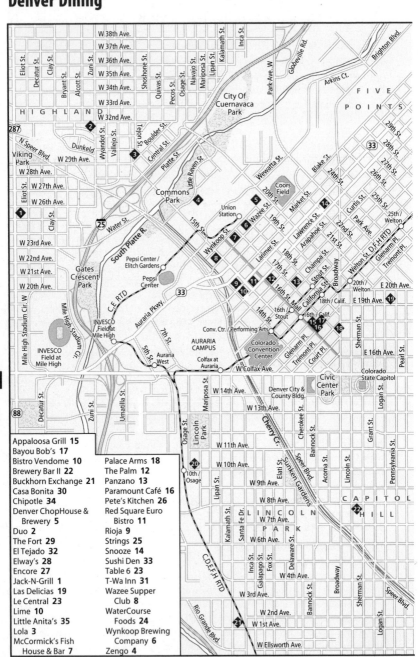

SETTLING INTO DENVER

5

WHERE TO DINE

Appaloosa Grill **15**
Bayou Bob's **17**
Bistro Vendome **10**
Brewery Bar II **22**
Buckhorn Exchange **21**
Casa Bonita **30**
Chipotle **34**
Denver ChopHouse & Brewery **5**
Duo **2**
The Fort **29**
El Tejado **32**
Elway's **28**
Encore **27**
Jack-N-Grill **1**
Las Delicias **19**
Le Central **23**
Lime **10**
Little Anita's **35**
Lola **3**
McCormick's Fish House & Bar **7**
Palace Arms **18**
The Palm **12**
Panzano **13**
Paramount Café **16**
Pete's Kitchen **26**
Red Square Euro Bistro **11**
Rioja **9**
Strings **25**
Snooze **14**
Sushi Den **33**
Table 6 **23**
T-Wa Inn **31**
Wazee Supper Club **8**
WaterCourse Foods **24**
Wynkoop Brewing Company **6**
Zengo **4**

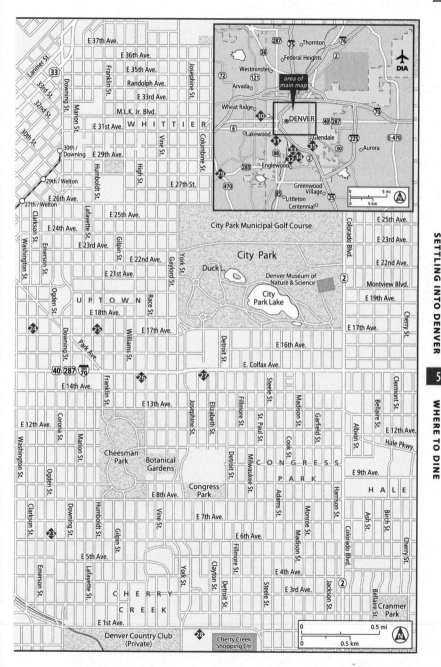

1735 19th St. ✆ **303/296-0800.** www.chophouse.com. Reservations recommended for dinner. Main courses $11–$36. AE, DC, MC, V. Mon–Thurs 11am–11pm; Fri–Sat 11am–midnight; Sun 11am–10pm.

The Palm ★ ITALIAN/STEAK/SEAFOOD   Pio Bozzi and John Ganzi opened the first Palm restaurant in New York City in 1926. It originally specialized in cuisine from their hometown of Parma, Italy, but whenever a customer requested steak, Ganzi ran to a nearby butcher shop, bought a steak, and cooked it to order. This eventually led to The Palm's having its own meat wholesale company to ensure the quality of its steaks. The current third-generation owners introduced seafood to the menu and expanded the business by opening a dozen more restaurants across the country. Most famous for its prime cuts of beef and live Nova Scotia lobsters, The Palm celebrates tradition, with some of Ganzi's original Italian dishes still popular (and cheaper) items on the menu. The dining room is plastered with caricatures of local celebrities; customers are seated at either booths or tables.

In the Westin at Tabor Center, 1672 Lawrence St. ✆ **303/825-7256.** www.thepalm.com. Reservations recommended. Main courses $9–$22 lunch, $20–$55 dinner. AE, DC, DISC, MC, V. Mon–Fri 11am–11pm; Sat 5–11pm; Sun 5–10pm.

Panzano ★★ CONTEMPORARY ITALIAN   The Hotel Monaco's resident eatery is one of the best Italian restaurants in town. Served in a densely decorated dining room with a busy open kitchen, Chef Elise Wiggins's menu changes regularly but employs both traditional preparations and inventive variations of Italian plates. You'll likely find the signature *buridda,* a Genovese seafood stew with mussels, calamari, and shrimp in a savory lobster broth; *capesante,* scallops with citrus-fennel-cheese ravioli; and an array of pastas prepared fresh in-house daily. There are also innovative variations on steak, poultry, soups, and salads, which change according to available ingredients: In the summer, for example, a sweet-corn soup appears on the menu. For dessert, don't pass on the tiramisu, which manages to be heavenly and sinful at once. With lighter, similar fare (including killer salads), lunch attracts power meetings. Happy hours are good for getting small portions of the dinner specialties.

In Hotel Monaco (p. 62), 909 17th St. ✆ **303/296-3525.** www.panzano-denver.com. Reservations recommended. Main courses $6–$20 breakfast and brunch, $9–$23 lunch, $17–$30 dinner. AE, DC, DISC, MC, V. Mon–Fri 7–10am and 11am–2:30pm; Mon–Thurs 5–10pm; Fri–Sat 5–11pm; Sat–Sun 8am–2:30pm; Sun 4:30–9:30pm. Closed Thanksgiving and Dec 25.

Rioja ★★★ CONTEMPORARY MEDITERRANEAN   Chef-owner Jennifer Jasinski emerged as Denver's most creatively inspired restaurateur since opening Rioja in 2004. In the time since, the slick Larimer Square eatery has become a national standout, a critical darling, and my pick for dinner in downtown Denver. With a copper-topped bar and an atmosphere that's formal without being stuffy, Rioja is the perfect vehicle for Jasinski's menu of contrasting flavors and textures. Offerings range from fresh bacon and cardamom-spiced pork belly to curried cauliflower soup served with fresh apple salad to grilled Colorado lamb. Jasinski keeps the menu fresh, but you'll always get a selection of her delectable handmade pastas for dinner—the artichoke tortellini is my pick—and truly transcendent beignets for dessert.

1431 Larimer Sq. ✆ **303/820-2282.** www.riojadenver.com. Reservations recommended. Main courses $10–$20 brunch and lunch, $16–$30 dinner. AE, DISC, MC, V. Wed–Fri 11:30am–2:30pm; Sat–Sun 10am–2:30pm; Sun–Thurs 5–10pm; Fri–Sat 5–11pm.

Strings ★★ CONTEMPORARY   Open for 20 years in Denver's Uptown neighborhood, Strings attracts a hip crowd of loyal locals, as well as visiting celebrities who contribute to a wall of autographed photos. Popular and typically crowded, the restaurant welcomes guests in T-shirts as well as tuxedos; it's especially busy during the before- and after-theater hours. The menu focuses on "New American" cuisine, creative noodle dishes, and fresh seafood—such as cashew-crusted sea bass with saffron couscous and vanilla bean butter. Lunch and dinner specials change weekly to match the season and the mood of the chef. Strings has an outdoor patio for summer dining.

1700 Humboldt St. (at E. 17th Ave.). © 303/831-7310. www.stringsrestaurant.com. Reservations recommended. Main courses $9–$25 lunch, $14–$35 dinner. AE, DISC, MC, V. Mon–Fri 11am–10pm; Sat 5–10:30pm; Sun 5–9pm.

Zengo ★ LATIN/ASIAN   With a menu that runs the gamut from dim sum and sushi to empanadas and ceviche, Zengo—Japanese for "give and take"—is the standout eatery in the booming Riverfront area just west of LoDo. Under the guidance of Chef Richard Sandoval (who also owns restaurants in New York, San Francisco, Las Vegas, and elsewhere, as well as Tamayo in Denver), the restaurant is a favorite of the young and hip, and just the place to see and be seen. The colorful contemporary decor matches the lively social scene and the vibrant dishes. Entrees are often Latin-Asian fusions, such as miso-chipotle soup, achiote barbecue salmon, and Szechuan-grilled pork loin with sweet corn salsa. Lunch includes dim sum, sushi, ensaladas, and tortas. There are also numerous vegetarian options.

1610 Little Raven St. © **720/904-0965.** www.modernmexican.com. Reservations recommended. Main courses $16–$28. AE, DISC, MC, V. Sun–Thurs 5–10pm; Fri–Sat 5–11pm; Sat–Sun 11am–3pm. Bar open later.

Moderate

Appaloosa Grill CONTEMPORARY/ECLECTIC   The employee-owned Appaloosa features an eclectic menu, merging Asian, Southwestern, and bar grub. The ribs are a good bet, as are the tamales, and the all-natural Highland Heritage steaks, originating in the Rockies. The lunch menu includes salads, sandwiches, and assorted lighter entrees. With a casual, semi-intimate atmosphere and a handsome antique bar, this is a good place for dinner to morph into a night on the town. The bar menu is available until 1am and there is live musical entertainment nightly.

535 16th St. Mall (at Welton St.). © 720/932-1700. www.appaloosagrill.com. Main courses $9–$12 lunch, $9–$32 dinner. AE, DISC, MC, V. Daily 11am–1am. Bar open later.

Le Central ★ (Value) FRENCH   Seven blocks south of the Colorado State Capitol, Le Central is a romantic restaurant that since 1980 has prided itself on creating French dishes that are both top-quality and affordable. Housed in an aged urban structure with a distinctive European vibe, the restaurant changes its menus daily, but you can always expect to find a selection of fresh chicken, pork, beef, lamb, and seafood. They're available grilled, sautéed, or roasted, and finished with some of the tastiest sauces this side of Provence. Bouillabaisse and paella are usually available, and every menu features a vegetarian dish. Shellfish fanatics, take note: Le Central's mussel menu is legendary, and served with all the french fries you can eat.

112 E. 8th Ave. (at Lincoln St.). © 303/863-8094. www.lecentral.com. Reservations recommended. Main courses $7–$14 lunch, $14–$22 dinner. AE, DC, DISC, MC, V. Mon–Fri 11:30am–2:15pm; Sat–Sun 11am–2pm; Mon–Thurs 5:30–10pm; Fri–Sat 5–10pm; Sun 5–9pm.

McCormick's Fish House & Bar ★ SEAFOOD   In lower downtown's historic Oxford Hotel, McCormick's maintains a late-19th-century feel with stained-glass windows, oak booths, and a fine polished-wood bar. Come here for the best seafood in town—it's flown in daily, and might include Alaskan salmon and halibut, mussels from Florida, lobsters from Maine, Hawaiian mahimahi, red rockfish from Oregon, and trout from Idaho. The menu also offers pasta, chicken, and a full line of prime beef. Across the hall, the Corner Bar's happy hour (served 3–6pm every day and 10pm–midnight on Fri and Sat) is legendary, featuring $1.95 to $4.95 crab cakes, cheeseburgers, and steamed mussels. There is breakfast service from the same kitchen at the adjacent bar from 7am until 10:30am daily.

In the Oxford Hotel (p. 64), 1659 Wazee St. ☎ **303/825-1107.** www.msmg.com. Reservations recommended. Lunch and light dishes $7–$17; dinner $17–$35. AE, DC, DISC, MC, V. Mon–Fri 11am–2pm; Sun–Thurs 5–10pm; Fri–Sat 5–11pm.

Red Square Euro Bistro ★★ RUSSIAN/CONTEMPORARY After the Little Russian Café closed in 2003, its all-Russian staff reunited under owner Steve Ryan and opened Red Square. They did their old place one better, with a rich red interior, tucked-away patio, contemporary Russian art, and a vodka bar stocked with infusions made in-house (ranging from raspberry to garlic) and about 100 brands from 17 countries, including Russia, Holland, Poland, Sweden, and even Mexico. The excellent entrees are not purely Russian: The steak stroganoff has a salmon counterpart, the menu has Asian and French influences, and the appetizers include pâté and Dungeness crab ravioli. But there is borscht (cold in summer, hot in winter), a roasted Russian wild boar chop, and, of course, the vodka—lots and lots of vodka.

1512 Larimer St. at Writer Square. ☎ **303/595-8600.** www.redsquarebistro.com. Main courses $16–$23. AE, DC, DISC, MC, V. Daily 5–10pm. Bar open later.

Wynkoop Brewing Company ★ **Kids** REGIONAL AMERICAN/PUB Denver's biggest and best brewpub took on an even more esteemed significance in 2003 when founder John Hickenlooper took office as the mayor of Denver. ("Hick" sold his restaurants to an employee group after taking office.) Occupying a renovated warehouse across from Union Station and close to Coors Field, the Wynkoop is one of the country's model microbreweries, and even served as a catalyst for the rebirth of surrounding LoDo. The menu offers pub fare, sandwiches, soups, and salads, plus dinners of steak, chicken burritos, bangers and mash, and buffalo meatloaf—not to mention a nice variety of beers on tap, including a spicy standout in Patty's Chile Beer. See also "Denver After Dark," in chapter 6.

1634 18th St. (at Wynkoop St.). ☎ **303/297-2700.** www.wynkoop.com. Reservations recommended for large parties. Main courses $9–$22. AE, DC, DISC, MC, V. Mon–Thurs 11am–11pm; Fri–Sat 11am–midnight; Sun 11am–10pm. Bar open later.

Inexpensive

In addition to the options listed below, there are a number of great breakfast spots in the downtown area. **Snooze,** 2262 Larimer St. (☎ **303/297-0700**), is a great new breakfast and lunch spot in the Ballpark neighborhood, serving delicacies like pineapple upside-down pancakes and bison meatball subs. Established in 1942, **Pete's Kitchen,** 1962 E. Colfax Ave. (☎ **303/321-3139**), is a prototypical urban diner, with checkerboard floors, a breakfast bar, booths, plenty of local color, and killer breakfast burritos. Pete's is open 24 hours on weekends, making it a favorite of the barhopping crowd. For burrito aficionados, the world's first **Chipotle** is located near the University of Denver, at 1644 E. Evans Ave. (☎ **303/777-4121**).

Bayou Bob's (Finds) CAJUN   Fishnets, street signs, and Southern-tinged bric-a-brac cover the walls of Bayou Bob's, which serves Denverites reasonably priced Cajun food in its bar and dining room. Gumbo, red beans and rice, fresh crawfish étouffée, and jambalaya are all favorites, as are the huge Mardi Gras–style Hurricanes. The spicy fried alligator is a great starter, and the many combination plates are a good bet for almost any taste. Catfish, po' boys, and hamburgers are also available.

1635 Glenarm St. (in the Paramount Theatre Building). © **303/573-6828.** Main courses $6–$14. AE, DC, DISC, MC, V. Mon 11am–9pm; Tues–Sat 11am–10pm.

Paramount Cafe AMERICAN   Housed in the restored lobby of Denver's historic Paramount Theatre on the 16th Street Mall, this bar and grill is popular, lively, and a bit noisy. A plethora of televisions, a poolroom with five tables plus satellite trivia games, and a year-round patio on the mall make this a good choice for people-watching. The menu features exotic subs, excellent burgers, large salads, and some Tex-Mex fare.

519 16th St. (at Glenarm St.). © **303/893-2000.** Main courses $6–$10. AE, DC, DISC, MC, V. Daily 11am–1am. Bar open until 2am.

Wazee Supper Club ★ (Finds) PIZZA/SANDWICHES   A former plumbing-supply store in lower downtown, the Wazee is a Depression-era relic with a black-and-white tile floor and a bleached mahogany burl bar—a magnificent example of 1930s Art Deco. It's been popular for more than 30 years with artists, architects, theatergoers, entertainers, businesspeople, and just about everybody else. Pizza lovers throng to the place (some believe the pizza here is the best in town, if not the world), but you'll also find an array of overstuffed sandwiches, from New York Reubens to Philly cheese steaks, plus buffalo burgers, and more than 20 draft beers. Don't miss the dumbwaiter used to shuttle food and drinks to the mezzanine floor—it's a converted 1937 garage-door opener.

1600 15th St. (at Wazee St.). © **303/623-9518.** Most menu items $7.50–$10; pizzas $8.50–$21. AE, MC, V. Mon–Sat 11am–midnight; Sun noon–11pm. Bar open until 2am.

OUTSIDE DOWNTOWN
Very Expensive

Elway's ★★ STEAKS/SEAFOOD   Owned by retired Denver Broncos quarterback John Elway, this popular Cherry Creek eatery—unlike many celebrity restaurants—is no flash in the pan. Dim but lively, the restaurant is a model of "New West" design, with a menu that melds swank and comfortable. On the swank side: crab cakes, hand-cut USDA prime steaks, Alaskan halibut, and veggies served a la carte. And the comfy: burgers, enchiladas, and mac and cheese. But it's the little details, such as buttonholes in the napkins, milk bottles full of water, and delectable desserts, that won me over in the end. Service is smooth and business is brisk, in both the cavernous dining room and the bustling bar. If you're lucky, you might bump into Elway himself here—he's not just the owner, but a regular, too. There is also an **Elway's Downtown** in the Ritz-Carlton Denver, 1881 Curtis St. (© **303/312-3107**) that opened in 2007.

2500 E. 1st Ave. (immediately west of the Cherry Creek Shopping Center). © **303/399-5353.** www. elways.com. Reservations recommended. Main courses $10–$33 lunch and brunch, $16–$50 dinner. AE, DC, DISC, MC, V. Mon–Thurs 11am–10pm; Fri–Sat 11am–11pm; Sun 11am–9pm.

The Fort ★★★ (Moments) ROCKY MOUNTAIN   There are several reasons to drive 18 miles southwest (and 800 ft. up) from downtown to The Fort in Denver's foothills. First: the atmosphere. The building was hand-constructed of adobe bricks in 1962 as a

> ## (Tips) A Good City for Green Chile Fiends
>
> **Green chile** (green *chil*-ay) *n.* a fiery-sweet stew made of chile peppers and other ingredients, often but not always including chunks of pork, tomato, and onion. Denver's eateries serve bowl after bowl of good green chile, stuff that ranges from merely spicy to flat-out nuclear. If you have a serious weakness for a bowl of green (as I do), here are six hot spots in the Mile High City, in no particular order:
>
> 1. **Las Delicias,** 439 E. 19th Ave. ((C) **303/839-5675**): A Denver tradition, Las Delicias serves up some of the city's best green chile from its downtown location among its four metro-area eateries.
> 2. **Brewery Bar II,** 150 Kalamath St. ((C) **303/893-0971**): Inconspicuously nestled in a warehouse district, the Brewery Bar serves up some of the hottest green chile in Denver. It also happens to be some of the tastiest.
> 3. **Jack-N-Grill,** 2524 N. Federal Blvd. ((C) **303/964-9544**): Sweet and typically served in a bowl with beans, Jack Martinez's green chile is excellent, as is his red.
> 4. **Little Anita's,** 1550 S. Colorado Blvd. ((C) **303/691-3337**): Relatively new in Denver, this longtime Albuquerque eatery cooks up wicked green chile from a strip mall in southeast Denver.
> 5. **Lime,** 1414 Larimer St. ((C) **303/893-5463**): Almost too hip for its own good, Larimer Square's Lime eschews pork for chicken and dresses up the bowl with tortilla strips. Defying tradition tastes pretty good.
> 6. **El Tejado,** 2651 S. Broadway ((C) **303/722-3987**): This locals' favorite in the southern reaches of the city serves a unique thick green chile plate as well as some of the best authentic Mexican dishes in the Rockies.

full-scale reproduction of Bent's Fort, Colorado's first fur-trading post. The equally authentic interior boasts striking views of Denver's city lights. Second: The Fort's impeccable, gracious service, which might just be the finest in town. The third and best reason to go is the food. The Fort built its reputation on high-quality, low-cholesterol buffalo, of which it claims to serve the largest variety and greatest quantity of any restaurant in the world. There's steak, roast marrow, tongue, and even "bison eggs"—hard-boiled quail eggs wrapped in buffalo sausage. My pick is the game plate, with elk chop, teriyaki-style quail, and buffalo filet, served with a salad (and extraordinary homemade dressings), rice, and vegetables. Other house specialties include Rocky Mountain Oysters and elk medallions with wild-huckleberry sauce. Die-hards can get good ol' beefsteak.

19192 Colo. 8 (just north of the intersection of Colo. 8 and W. Hampden Ave./U.S. 285), Morrison. (C) **303/697-4771.** www.thefort.com. Reservations recommended. Main courses $22–$52. AE, DC, DISC, MC, V. Mon–Fri 5:30–9:30pm; Sat 5–9:30pm; Sun 5–9pm. Call for special holiday hours.

Moderate to Expensive

Duo ★★ (Finds) CONTEMPORARY AMERICAN Nestled in the back of a very homey and warm room with brick, worn wood, and a wall of suspended old window frames, Duo's open kitchen plates up a variety of dishes that start with tradition but exude creativity in terms of both presentation and flavor. The menu changes seasonally, but you might find expertly grilled pork chops, buttery buttermilk-fried chicken, or an artful tower of vegetarian gratin. Appetizers are similarly remarkable, my favorite being the leek tart, topped with the transcendental contrast of creamy goat cheese and salty pancetta. For dessert, the housemade ice cream will leave you wanting more.

2413 W. 32nd Ave. © **303/477-4141.** www.duodenver.com. Reservations recommended. Main courses $17–$25 dinner, $8–$12 brunch. AE, DISC, MC, V. Mon–Sat 5–10pm; Sun 5–9pm; Sat–Sun 10am–2pm.

Encore ★ CONTEMPORARY MEDITERRANEAN   This smart and hip eatery adjoins the Tattered Cover bookstore and an art cinema, and is a good pick for lunch or dinner east of downtown. With black-and-white tiled floors, great happy-hour deals, and excellent service, Encore is a nice fit for a variety of options, from vegetarian (falafel burgers) to carnivorous (black-pepper crusted rib-eye). In between are great appetizers, wood-fired pizzas, mussels, pastas, and big salads. To finish, the house carrot cake is a delectable dessert in a pumpkin pie–like guise.

2250 E. Colfax Ave. © **303/355-1112.** www.encoreoncolfax.com. Reservations accepted. Main courses $9–$27. AE, DISC, MC, V. Daily 11am–10pm. Bar open later.

Lola ★★ COASTAL MEXICAN   Moving from south Denver to the hip Highlands neighborhood in 2006 quadrupled this popular eatery's floor space, and it still fills to the rafters. It's easy to see why: Lola has oodles of pizzazz, in terms of both its art and airy design—complete with a killer patio with an indoor/outdoor bar and great city views—and the savory dishes on its menu. Start off with some guacamole, prepared fresh tableside, before moving on to a bowl of shellfish of some kind or perhaps an inventively prepared grouper. Most entrees use creative Mexican preparations on fresh seafood with terrific results. Served Saturdays and Sundays from 10am to 2pm, the brunch favorite is steak and eggs served with sweet potato hash and chorizo gravy. Lola's margaritas and caipirinhas, sweet Brazilian cocktails with entire quartered limes, are also hard to beat. Below the restaurant is a hip, aptly named lounge, Belola.

1575 Boulder St. © **720/570-8686.** www.loladenver.com. Main courses $18–$26. AE, DC, MC, V. Mon–Thurs 4–10pm; Fri 4–11pm; Sat 10am–11pm; Sun 10am–9pm.

Sushi Den ★★ SUSHI/JAPANESE   The long-standing Sushi Den is not only the best sushi restaurant in Denver; it's on the short list of the top sushi restaurants in the country. Owned by three Kizaki brothers—one of whom is based in Japan and sends a daily shipment of ingredients—the Sushi Den's landlocked location is incidental: This is some of the freshest fish you'll find anywhere. The formidable sushi menu, running the gamut from squid and salmon to smoked trout, is complemented by lunch and dinner menus with a wide variety of Japanese fare and sushi and sashimi combination plates. Located in south Denver in the charming Old South Pearl Street retail district, the Sushi Den is one of two locations worldwide—its sister restaurant is in Fukuoka, Japan.

1487 S. Pearl St. © **303/777-0826.** www.sushiden.net. Main courses $8–$18 lunch, $9–$28 dinner; sushi rolls $4.50–$14. AE, DC, MC, V. Mon–Fri 11am–2:30pm; Mon–Thurs 4:45–10:30pm; Fri–Sat 4:30pm–midnight; Sun 5–10:30pm.

Table 6 ★★ (Finds) CONTEMPORARY MEDITERRANEAN   A bistro with a bit of southern comfort, Table 6 balances a hip but unpretentious sensibility, great food, and one of the best wine lists in town, offered on a tableside stand in an antique photo album. Directed by Chef Scott Parker, the open kitchen plates up such tantalizing dishes as mushroom risotto, crisp duck confit, and spaghetti and meatballs in citrus marinara. The atmosphere is lived-in and homey, with rough hardwood floors, brick walls, and ceiling fans, with a blackboard showcasing the day's specials. The desserts are hard to turn down, especially the Nutella beignets and margarita nachos.

609 Corona St. ℂ **303/831-8800.** www.table6denver.com. Reservations recommended. Main courses $16–$26. AE, MC, V. Daily 5–10pm.

Inexpensive

Casa Bonita (Kids) MEXICAN/AMERICAN   A west Denver landmark, Casa Bonita is more of a theme park than a restaurant. A pink Spanish cathedral-type bell tower greets visitors, who discover nonstop action inside: divers plummeting into a pool below a 30-foot waterfall, puppet shows, a video arcade, "Black Bart's Cave," and strolling mariachi bands. The 52,000-square-foot restaurant is said to be the largest restaurant in the Western Hemisphere. There's standard Mexican fare—enchiladas, tacos, and fajitas—along with country-fried steak and fried chicken dinners. Although the food is average at best, many plates are all-you-can-eat, and patrons need only raise a miniature flag to get another round of tacos. Meals include hot sopaipillas (deep-fried sweet dough), served with honey.

In the JCRS Shopping Center, 6715 W. Colfax Ave., Lakewood. ℂ **303/232-5115.** www.casabonitadenver. com. Reservations not accepted. All-you-can-eat dinners $10–$20; children's meals around $4. DISC, MC, V. Mon–Thurs 11am–9:30pm; Fri–Sat 11am–10pm.

Jack-N-Grill ★ (Finds) NEW MEXICAN   "WE ARE NOT FAST FOOD," reads a sign at Jack-N-Grill, and it's spot on: This is clearly a restaurant that takes its time, and its food is worth the wait. Named for Jack Martinez and his ever-present grill, the food reflects Jack's father's motto: *"Comida sin chile, no es comida,"* or "A meal without chile is not a meal." Not surprisingly, just about everything at Jack-N-Grill has chiles in it, roasted onsite by the Martinez family. Both the green and the red chile are top-notch, as are the Mexican dishes and the fresh homemade salsa. Also popular: Frito pies and calabasitas, bowls with squash, zucchini, corn, green chiles, and onions. Don't expect Jack to add any chile-free dishes to the menu. "What's the use?" he says.

2524 N. Federal Blvd. ℂ **303/964-9544.** www.jackngrill.com. Plates $6–$14, a la carte dishes $2–$6. AE, MC, V. Sun–Thurs 7am–9pm; Fri–Sat 7am–10pm.

T-Wa Inn (Finds) VIETNAMESE   Denver's oldest Vietnamese restaurant is still the best. With simple, pleasant decor and relics from the Far East on display, it looks the part, but the food is what makes it work. Everything is excellent, but I especially like the succulent shrimp, the spicy pork tenderloin, and the attention to authentic Vietnamese flavors. T-Wa also serves several spicy Thai dishes, as well as Asian beers and a whole rainbow of neon-colored specialty drinks.

555 S. Federal Blvd. (2 blocks south of Alameda Ave.). ℂ **303/922-2378.** www.twainn.com. Most main courses$6–$13. AE, DISC, MC, V. Sun–Thurs 11am–9pm; Fri–Sat 11am–10pm.

WaterCourse Foods ★ (Finds) VEGETARIAN   Beloved by local vegetarians and vegans, WaterCourse is a bustling restaurant that recently relocated to the Uptown neighborhood after outgrowing its old Capitol Hill digs. Breakfast is served all day—the menu includes scrambles (cage-free eggs or tofu with tomatoes, chiles, cheese, and other ingredients), meatless tamales, and banana-bread French toast—and there is also a selection of sandwiches, pasta dishes, salads, and other uniformly tasty vegetarian and vegan specialties for lunch and dinner. Beer and wine are available.

837 E. 17th Ave. ℂ **303/832-7313.** www.watercoursefoods.com. Main courses $5–$9 breakfast, $7–$10 lunch and dinner. AE, DISC, MC, V. Mon–Fri 7am–10pm; Mon–Sat 8am–10pm.

What to See & Do in Denver

Denver, an intriguing combina- tion of modern American city and overgrown Old West town, offers a wide variety of attractions, activities, and events. Thanks to its geographic isolation, it's a true cultural hub for a significant chunk of the country: You'll discover art, history, sports, recreation, shopping, and plenty of nightlife. It is quite easy to spend an entire week of vacation in the city, but Denver also makes a convenient base for trips to Boulder, Colorado Springs, or the mountains.

1 THE TOP ATTRACTIONS

Colorado State Capitol ★★ Built to last 1,000 years, the capitol was constructed in 1886 of granite from a Colorado quarry. The dome, which rises 272 feet above the ground, was first sheathed in copper and then replaced with gold leaf after a public outcry: Copper was not a Colorado product.

Murals depicting the history of water in the state adorn the walls of the first-floor rotunda, which offers a splendid view upward to the underside of the dome. The rotunda resembles the layout of the U.S. Capitol in Washington, D.C. South of the rotunda is the governor's office, paneled in walnut and lit by a massive chandelier.

On the first floor, the west lobby hosts revolving temporary exhibits. To the right of the main lobby is the governor's reception room. The second floor has main entrances to the House, Senate, and old Supreme Court chambers. On the third floor are entrances to the public and visitor galleries for the House and Senate (open to the public during legislative session from Jan to early May).

Lincoln St. and Colfax Ave. ℂ **303/866-2604.** Free admission. 45-min. tours offered year-round (more frequently in summer), Memorial Day to Labor Day Mon–Fri 9am–3:30pm; rest of year Mon–Fri 9:15am–2:30pm. Bus: 0, 2, 7, 12, 15, or 50.

Denver Art Museum ★★ Kids Founded in 1893, this seven-story museum has two distinct buildings. The main 1972 building, designed by Gio Ponti, is wrapped by a thin 28-sided wall faced with 1 million sparkling tiles. The second, a jagged, avant-garde addition, designed by renowned architect Daniel Libeskind, opened in fall 2006, doubling the size of the museum and giving Denver a unique architectural highlight in the process.

The museum's collection of Western and regional works is its cornerstone. Included are Frederic Remington's bronze *The Cheyenne,* Charles Russell's painting *In the Enemy's Country,* plus 19th-century photography, historical pieces, and works by Georgia O'Keeffe. In 2001, Dorothy and William Harmsen, longtime Colorado residents and founders of the Jolly Rancher Candy Company, donated their prestigious Western art collection to the museum. Assembled over 40 years, the collection immediately made the museum's inventory of Western art one of the most impressive in the nation. The

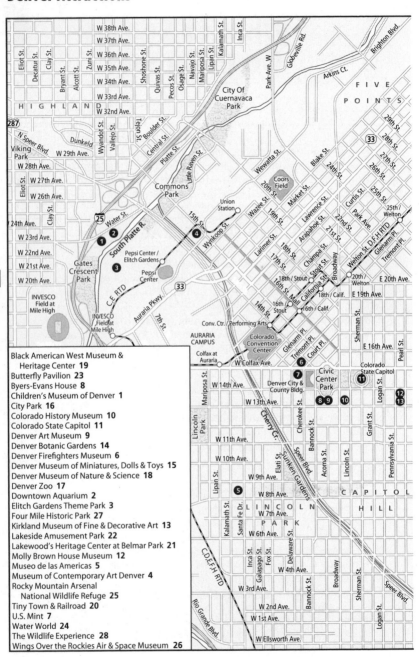

Black American West Museum &
  Heritage Center **19**
Butterfly Pavilion **23**
Byers-Evans House **8**
Children's Museum of Denver **1**
City Park **16**
Colorado History Museum **10**
Colorado State Capitol **11**
Denver Art Museum **9**
Denver Botanic Gardens **14**
Denver Firefighters Museum **6**
Denver Museum of Miniatures, Dolls & Toys **15**
Denver Museum of Nature & Science **18**
Denver Zoo **17**
Downtown Aquarium **2**
Elitch Gardens Theme Park **3**
Four Mile Historic Park **27**
Kirkland Museum of Fine & Decorative Art **13**
Lakeside Amusement Park **22**
Lakewood's Heritage Center at Belmar Park **21**
Molly Brown House Museum **12**
Museo de las Americas **5**
Museum of Contemporary Art Denver **4**
Rocky Mountain Arsenal
  National Wildlife Refuge **25**
Tiny Town & Railroad **20**
U.S. Mint **7**
Water World **24**
The Wildlife Experience **28**
Wings Over the Rockies Air & Space Museum **26**

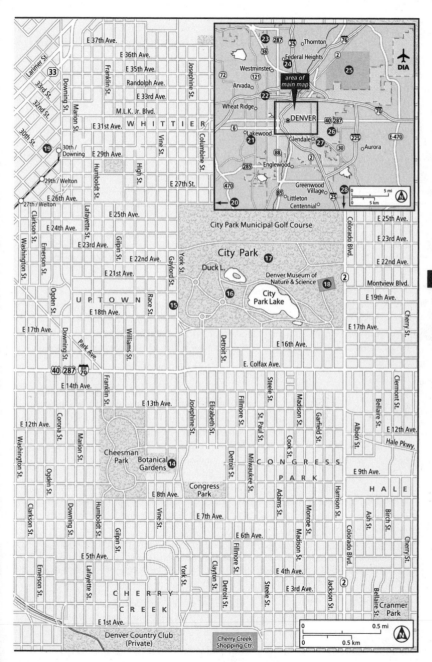

Impressions

. . . Cash! Why, they create it here.
—Walt Whitman, on Denver in *Specimen Days,* 1881

American Indian collection is also excellent, consisting of more than 18,000 pieces from 150 tribes of North America, and spanning nearly 2,000 years. The collection is growing through the acquisition of historic pieces as well as the commissioning of works by contemporary artists. Other collections include architecture and design; graphics; Asian, African, Oceanic, European, and American painting and sculpture; and modern, contemporary, pre-Columbian, Spanish Colonial, and textile art.

Overview tours are available Tuesday through Sunday at 1:30pm, as well as at 11am on Saturday; an in-depth tour of a different area of the museum is offered each Wednesday and Friday at noon and 1pm; and a variety of child-oriented and family programs are scheduled regularly. There are gift shops in both buildings. Allow 2 to 3 hours.

100 W. 14th Ave. Pkwy. (at Civic Center Park). ℂ **720/865-5000.** www.denverartmuseum.org. Admission $13 adults, $10 college students and seniors 65 and over, free for children under 6; free for Colorado residents the first Sat of each month. Tues–Thurs and Sat 10am–5pm, Fri 10am–10pm; Sun noon–5pm. Bus: 0, 2, 7, 12, 15, or 50.

Denver Museum of Nature & Science ★★ (Kids)   The largest museum of its kind in the Rocky Mountain region, the Denver Museum of Nature & Science features scores of world-renowned dioramas, an extensive gems and minerals display, a pair of Egyptian mummies, a terrific fossil collection, and several other award-winning exhibitions. The museum focuses on six areas of science: anthropology, health science, geology, paleontology, space science, and zoology.

At "Space Odyssey," visitors experience a carefully crafted mix of exhibits, live programming, digital multimedia, and interactive modules that engage them in contemporary stories of space exploration. The state-of-the-art Gates Planetarium has an advanced computer graphics and video system, unlike any other in the world. "Prehistoric Journey" traces the history of life on earth through 3.5 billion years with dinosaur skeletons, fossils, interactive exhibits, and dioramas of ancient ecologies. New in 2009, "Expedition Health" is a state-of-the-art exhibit that allows visitors an eye-opening look at the workings of their own bodies, gathering information on themselves as they move through the exhibits, and getting a printout about their own physical condition at the end.

An **IMAX theater** (ℂ **303/322-7009**) presents science, nature, or technology-oriented films with surround sound on a screen that measures four and a half stories tall. Allow 2 to 4 hours.

City Park, 2001 Colorado Blvd. ℂ **800/925-2250** outside Metro Denver, or 303/322-7009; 303/370-8257 for those with hearing impairment. www.dmns.org. Admission to museum $11 adults, $6 children 3–18 and seniors 65 and older, free for children under 3; IMAX $8 adults, $6 children and seniors; planetarium $5 subsequent adults, $4 subsequent children and seniors. Daily 9am–5pm. Closed Dec 25. Bus: 32 or 40.

U.S. Mint ★★ (Kids)   Whether we worship it or simply consider money a necessary commodity, we all have to admit a certain fascination with the coins and bills that seem to make the world turn. There are four mints in the United States, but the Denver Mint is one of only two (the other is the Philadelphia Mint) where we can actually see the process of turning lumps of metal into shiny coins.

(Fun Facts) Robbery at the Mint

A daring armed robbery took place at the Denver Mint in 1922, just 1 week before Christmas, and although police were certain they knew who the culprits were, no one ever served a day in jail for the crime. The most secure building in Denver, the Mint seemed an unlikely target for a robbery. In fact, the thieves did not rob the Mint itself—they simply waited for guards to carry the money out the front door.

A Federal Reserve Bank truck was parked outside the Mint on West Colfax Avenue at about 10:30am on December 18. It was being loaded with $200,000 worth of brand-new $5 bills, which were to be taken to a bank about 12 blocks away, when a black Buick touring car pulled up. Two men jumped out and began firing sawed-off shotguns, killing one guard and spraying the Mint and nearby buildings, while a third robber grabbed the bags of money. Guards inside the Mint quickly pulled their guns and returned fire, but within a minute and a half the robbers were gone—$200,000 richer.

Mint guards were certain they had hit one of the thieves, and 4 weeks later the Buick turned up in a dusty Denver garage. Lying in the front seat was the frozen, bloody body of Nick Trainor, a convicted criminal who had recently been released on parole from the Nebraska State Penitentiary. Trainor had been shot several times.

Secret Service agents recovered $80,000 of the missing loot the following year in St. Paul, Minnesota, but no arrests were made, and little more was mentioned until 1934, when Denver police announced that they knew the identities of the other men involved. Still, no charges were filed. Two of the suspects were already serving life sentences for other crimes.

At the time, police said a Midwest gang had pulled off the robbery and immediately fled to the Minneapolis–St. Paul area. The robbers gave the money to a prominent Minneapolis attorney, who also was never charged.

Opened in 1863, the Mint originally melted gold dust and nuggets into bars. In 1904 the office moved to this site, and 2 years later began making gold and silver coins. Copper pennies were added a few years later. The last silver dollars (containing 90% silver) were coined in 1935. In 1970, all silver was eliminated from dollars and half dollars (today they're made of a copper-nickel alloy). The Denver Mint stamps billions of coins each year, and each has a small D on it.

Although visitors today don't get as close as they once did, a self-guided tour along the visitors' gallery provides a good look at the process, with a bird's-eye view from the mezzanine of the actual coin-minting process. A variety of displays help explain the minting process, and an adjacent **gift shop** on Cherokee Street (© **303/572-9500**) offers a variety of souvenirs. Allow 1 hour.

320 W. Colfax Ave. (between Cherokee and Delaware sts.). © **303/405-4757** or 303/405-4761; 303/572-9500 for gift shop. www.usmint.gov. Free admission. Tours Mon–Fri 8am–2pm. Gift shop 8am–3:30pm. Reservations recommended; online reservations available. Closed 1–2 weeks in summer for audit; call for exact date. Bus: 7.

2 MORE ATTRACTIONS

HISTORIC BUILDINGS

Denver encompasses 17 recognized historic districts, including Capitol Hill, the Clements District (around 21st St. and Tremont St., just east of downtown), and 9th Street Park in Auraria (off 9th St. and West Colfax Ave.). **Historic Denver** (📞 303/534-5288; www.historicdenver.org) offers publications covering many of these areas and organizes several annual events. For additional information on some of Denver's historic areas, see the "Neighborhoods in Brief" section in chapter 5.

Byers-Evans House   This elaborate Victorian home, built by *Rocky Mountain News* founding editor William Byers in 1883, has been restored to its appearance of 1912–24, when it was owned by William Gray Evans, son of Colorado's second territorial governor. (The Evans family continued to reside here until 1981.) Guided tours describe the architecture and explain the fascinating lives of these prominent Denver families. There is a gift shop. Allow 45 minutes.

1310 Bannock St. (in front of the Denver Art Museum). 📞 303/620-4933. Admission $5 adults, $4 seniors, $3 children 6–16, free for children under 6. Tues–Sun 11am–3pm. Closed state holidays. Bus: 7.

Larimer Square ★   This is where Denver began. Larimer Street between 14th and 15th streets was the entire community of Denver City in 1858, with false-fronted stores, hotels, and saloons to serve gold-seekers and other pioneers. In the mid-1870s it was the main street of the city and the site of Denver's first post office, bank, theater, and streetcar line. By the 1930s, however, this part of Larimer Street had deteriorated so much that it had become a skid row of pawnshops, gin mills, and flophouses. Plans had been made to tear these structures down, when a group of investors purchased the entire block in 1965.

The Larimer Square project became Denver's first major historic preservation effort. All 16 of the block's commercial buildings, constructed in the 1870s and 1880s, were renovated, providing space for street-level retail shops, restaurants, and nightclubs, as well as upper-story offices. A series of courtyards and open spaces was created, and in 1973 it was added to the National Register of Historic Places. Allow at least a half-hour—but this is a great spot for a meal if you have more time. In June, Larimer Square hosts La Piazza dell'Arte, featuring hundreds of artists creating pastel masterpieces on the street.

1400 block of Larimer St. 📞 303/534-2367 or 303/685-8143 (events line). www.larimersquare.com. Bus: 2, 12, 15, 28, 31, 32, 38, or 44.

Molly Brown House Museum ★★   Built in 1889 of Colorado rhyolite with sandstone trim, this was the residence of J. J. and Margaret (Molly) Brown from 1894 to 1932. The "unsinkable" Molly Brown became a national heroine in 1912 when the *Titanic* sank. She took charge of a group of immigrant women in a lifeboat and later raised money for their benefit.

Restored to its 1910 appearance, the Molly Brown House has a large collection of early-20th-century furnishings and art objects, many of which belonged to the Brown family. There are also temporary exhibits (recent ones detailed the lives of servants in Brown's day and trends in Victorian undergarments), and a carriage house with a museum store at the rear is open to visitors. The house can be seen on guided tours. Allow 1 hour.

1340 Pennsylvania St. 📞 303/832-4092. www.mollybrown.org. Guided tour $6.50 adults, $5 seniors over 65, $3 children 6–12, free for children under 6. June–Aug Mon–Sat 10am–4pm, Sun noon–4pm;

Sept–May Tues–Sat 10am–4pm, Sun noon–4pm. Guided tours every 30 min.; last tour of the day begins at 3:30pm. Closed major holidays. Bus: 2 on Logan St. to E. 13th, and then 1 block east to Pennsylvania.

85

MUSEUMS & GALLERIES

Black American West Museum & Heritage Center ★

Nearly one-third of the cowboys in the Old West were black, and this museum chronicles their little-known history, along with that of black doctors, teachers, miners, farmers, newspaper reporters, and state legislators. The extensive collection occupies the Victorian home of Dr. Justina Ford, the first black woman licensed to practice medicine in Denver. Known locally as the "Lady Doctor," Ford (1871–1951) delivered more than 7,000 babies—most of them at home because she was denied hospital privileges—and consistently served the disadvantaged and underprivileged of Denver.

The museum's founder and curator emeritus, Paul Stewart, loved to play cowboys and Indians as a boy, but his playmates always chose him to be an Indian because "There was no such thing as a black cowboy." He began researching the history of blacks in the West after meeting a black cowboy who had led cattle drives in the early 20th century. Stewart explored almost every corner of the American West, gathering artifacts, memorabilia, photographs, oral histories—anything to document the existence of black cowboys—and his collection served as the nucleus for this museum when it opened in 1971. Allow 1 hour.

3091 California St. (at 31st St.). ℂ 303/482-2242. www.blackamericanwestmuseum.com. Admission $8 adults, $7 seniors, $6 children under 13. June–Aug Tues–Sat 10am–5pm; Sept–May Tues–Sat 10am–2pm. Light rail: 30th and Downing.

Colorado History Museum ★ (Kids)

The Colorado Historical Society's permanent exhibits include "The Colorado Chronicle," an 1800-to-1949 timeline that uses biographical plaques and a remarkable collection of photographs, news clippings, and paraphernalia to illustrate Colorado's past. Dozens of dioramas portray episodes in state history, including an intricate re-creation of 19th-century Denver. Among the other standouts, "Ancient Voices" and "Confluence of Cultures" are slickly produced multimedia exhibits dedicated to the history of Colorado's native tribes and the state's Pioneer era, respectively. The museum offers a series of lectures and statewide historical and archaeological tours. Allow 1 hour.

1300 Broadway. ℂ 303/866-3682. www.coloradohistory.org. Admission $7 adults, $6 seniors and students, $5 children 6–12, free for children under 6. Mon–Sat 10am–5pm; Sun noon–5pm. Bus: 0, 2, 7, 12, 15, or 50.

Denver Firefighters Museum (Kids)

The history of the Denver Fire Department is preserved and displayed here, in historic Fire Station No. 1. Built in 1909 for Engine Company No. 1, it was one of the largest firehouses in Denver, occupying 11,000 square feet on two floors. In its early years, it lodged men, fire engines, and horses. Motorized equipment replaced horse-drawn engines by 1923, and in 1932 the firehouse was "modernized." Concrete replaced the wooden floor, the stables and hayloft were removed, and the plumbing was improved. Visitors today see firefighting equipment dating to 1866, as well as historic photos and newspaper clippings. Allow 45 minutes.

1326 Tremont Place. ℂ 303/892-1436. www.denverfirefightersmuseum.org. Admission $6 adults, $5 students and seniors, $4 children under 13. Mon–Sat 10am–4pm. Closed major holidays. Located 2 blocks west of Civic Center Park on the north side of Colfax.

Denver Museum of Miniatures, Dolls & Toys (Kids) (Finds)

This late-19th-century property is home to an intriguing collection of antique and collectible dolls, from rag and wood to exquisite German and French bisque. Also on display are dollhouses, from a

Santa Fe adobe with hand-carved furniture to a replica of a 16-room home in Newport, Rhode Island. The museum also displays wonderful old toys, from teddy bears to model cars, and temporary exhibits that change every 3 months. The gift shop is equally delightful. Allow 45 to 60 minutes.

1880 Gaylord St. (just west of City Park). ℂ **303/322-1053.** www.dmmdt.org. Admission $6 adults, $5 seniors, $4 children 5–16, free for children under 5. Wed–Sat 10am–4pm; Sun 1–4pm.

Four Mile Historic Park ★ (Kids Four miles southeast of downtown Denver—thus the name—the city's oldest extant log home (1859) serves as the centerpiece for this 12-acre open-air museum. Everything is authentic to the period from 1859 to 1883, including the house (a former stagecoach stop), its furnishings, outbuildings, and farm equipment. There are draft horses and chickens in the barn, and crops in the garden. Weekend visitors can enjoy horse-drawn carriage rides ($2), weather permitting. Seasonal "Heritage Events" feature pioneer-era musicians and actors as well as many food and craft demonstrations. Big events include July 4th and an outdoor theater series. Allow 1 hour.

715 S. Forest St. (at Exposition Ave.). ℂ **303/399-1859.** www.fourmilepark.org. Free admission; museum tours $3.50 adults, $2 seniors and children 6–15, free for children under 6. Apr–Sept Wed–Fri noon–4pm, Sat–Sun 10am–4pm; Oct–Mar Sat–Sun noon–4pm.

Kirkland Museum of Fine & Decorative Art ★★ (Finds This terrific museum covers Colorado's most illustrious artist, Vance Kirkland (1904–81), in grand fashion, while also presenting a world-class collection of decorative arts. Kirkland was a watercolor painter focused on Western landscapes when he started experimenting, combining oils and watercolors on one canvas. The Denver arts establishment discounted his modern ideas, but Kirkland later won accolades for creating his own artistic universe in his stunning paintings, about 60 of which are on display here. First built in 1911, his preserved brick studio has an unusual harness he used for painting on flat canvases facedown (dating from his "dot" period). The museum's decorative-arts collection, located here and in a separate gallery across the street, includes more than 3,300 pieces ranging from teacups to armchairs, and there are also more than 700 works by notable Colorado artists other than Kirkland.

1311 Pearl St. ℂ **303/832-8576.** www.kirklandmuseum.org. Admission $6 adults, $5 students, teachers, and seniors. No one under 13 permitted due to the fragile nature of the collection. Children 13 to 17 must be accompanied by an adult. Tues–Sun 1–5pm. Guided tour Wed–Sat at 1:30pm. Closed major holidays.

Lakewood's Heritage Center at Belmar Park In Denver's early days, many wealthy residents maintained summer estates in the rural Lakewood area, and this historic village tells their story as well as that of others who lived and worked here. For an introduction to the museum, your first stop should be the visitor center; you can begin a personalized guided or self-guided tour here. The village includes an 1870s farmhouse, a 1920s one-room school, a 1950s variety store, and the Barn Gallery. There's an exhibit on "Lakewood People and Places," antique and vintage farm machinery, self-guided history walks through the surrounding 127-acre park, changing art exhibits, and a picnic area. Also on-site are an amphitheater and festival area, which hosts a summer concert series and a slate of seasonal fairs and celebrations. Allow 1 to 2 hours.

Another worthwhile attraction in the area is the **Lab at Belmar,** 404 S. Upham St., Lakewood (ℂ **303/934-1777;** www.belmarlab.org), an art museum–public forum that opened in 2006; it features weekly lectures and seminars as well as a regularly rotating gallery.

801 S. Yarrow Blvd. (near Wadsworth and Ohio), Lakewood. © **303/987-7850.** Free admission; guided tours $5 adults, $4 seniors, $3 children 4–18, free for children under 4. Tues–Sat 10am–4pm; guided tours on the hour until 3pm. Closed Sun & Mon.

Museo de las Americas ★ (Finds)

Billed as the only museum in the Rocky Mountains focusing exclusively on the art, culture, and history of Latinos, the Museo is worth a stop, as is a stroll through the colorful surrounding gallery- and *taquería*-laden neighborhood. The exhibits here change regularly, and a semipermanent exhibit tells the story of pre-Columbian Latin America, with a replica of an ornate sunstone and exhibits on Tenochtitlan, the Aztec metropolis (on the site of present-day Mexico City) destroyed by invading Spaniards in the 16th century. Allow 1 to 2 hours.

861 Santa Fe Dr. © **303/571-4401.** www.museo.org. Admission $4 adults, $3 seniors and students, free for children under 13. Tues–Fri 10am–5pm; Sat–Sun noon–5pm.

Museum of Contemporary Art Denver ★

Having moved in 2007 into a translucent new LEED-certified structure in LoDo (actually three buildings wrapped in glass), this is a stark canvas for the artists who are on center stage here. Five galleries are dedicated to five different disciplines (photography, paper works, large works, new media, and projects), and only one artist at a time occupies a given gallery; most works were created for their exhibition or are a year or two old. An interesting library showcases influences of the artists currently on display. There is also a small gift shop full of books and oddball knickknacks. Allow 1 hour.

1485 Delgany St. © **303/298-7554.** www.mcadenver.org. Admission $10 adults, $5 seniors and students, free for children under 6. $1 discount for those who come by public transportation, foot, or bike. Tues–Sun 10am–6pm; Sun noon–5:30pm.

The Wildlife Experience ★ (Kids)

Located near the Denver Technological Center, this impressive museum has three focuses: natural history, nature films, and wildlife art, with nine galleries of paintings, sculptures, and photography. The museum's aim is to educate visitors about conservation and the delicate balance between people and the environment, and to do it in an aesthetically pleasing fashion. It accomplishes the task with such highlights as a National Geographic Channel screening room and an interactive Children's Gallery. Also here are a 315-seat Iwerks Extreme Screen Theater, a restaurant, and a gift shop. Allow 1 hour.

10035 S. Peoria St. © **720/488-3300.** www.thewildlifeexperience.org. Admission or theater tickets $7.95 adults, $6.95 seniors, $4.95 children; combination museum/theater tickets $12 adults, $11 seniors, $6.95 children. Tues–Sun 9am–5pm. Closed major holidays and non-holiday Mon. Located 1 mile east of I-25 via Lincoln Ave. (exit 193).

Wings Over the Rockies Air & Space Museum ★ (Kids)

More than 40 planes and spacecraft occupy cavernous Hangar No. 1, which became a museum when Lowry Air Force Base closed in 1995; now it's a burgeoning residential area about 6 miles southeast of downtown. On display are antique biplanes, a search-and-rescue helicopter, an F-14 Tomcat, a massive B-1A bomber—one of only two in existence—and most of the F-100 fighter series. You can also see a World War II uniform collection, a Norden bombsight, U3A Blue Canoe, and the Freedom space module, plus seasonal exhibits. On each month's second Saturday the museum hosts "Demo Cockpit Day," when visitors get to climb into the planes' cockpits from 10am to 2pm. Sci-fi fans take note: A full-size X-Wing prop used in the filming of *Star Wars* is on permanent display. The store is filled with aviation- and space-oriented souvenirs. Allow 1 1/2 hours.

7711 E. Academy Blvd., Hangar No. 1. ℂ **303/360-5360**. www.wingsmuseum.org. Admission $9 adults, $8 seniors, $6 children 4–12, free for children under 4. Mon–Sat 10am–5pm; Sun noon–5pm. Bus: 65.

PARKS, GARDENS & ZOOS

Butterfly Pavilion ★★ (Kids)   A walk through the butterfly conservatory introduces the visitor to a world of grace and beauty. The constant mist creates a hazy habitat to support the lush green plants that are both food and home to the 1,200 butterfly inhabitants representing 50 species at any given time. If you stand still for a few minutes, a butterfly might land on you, but don't try to pick up the butterflies—the oils on your hands contaminate their senses, interfering with their ability to find food. One display describes the differences among butterflies, moths, and skippers, and color charts help with identification.

In the "Crawl-A-See-Um," meet arthropods (the scientific name for insects) that are native to Colorado, and see exotic species from around the world. A fascinating "touch cart" allows you to get up close to a cockroach or tarantula, assuming that you really want to. "Shrunk!" features giant animatronic insects (it can be scary for little ones) and nifty interactive exhibits about the biomechanics of bugs. Also on the premises are a large gift shop and a snack bar. Outside, a .5-mile nature trail meanders amid cactuses and other desert-friendly plants. Allow 2 to 3 hours.

6252 W. 104th Ave., Westminster. ℂ **303/469-5441**. www.butterflies.org. Admission $7.95 adults, $5.95 seniors, $4.95 children 3–12, free for children under 3. Daily 9am–5pm. Take the Denver–Boulder Turnpike (U.S. 36) to W. 104th Ave. and go east for about a block. The pavilion is on your right.

City Park   Denver's largest urban park covers 330 acres on the east side of uptown. Established in 1881, it retains Victorian touches. The park encompasses two lakes (with boat rentals and fishing), athletic fields, jogging and walking trails, a free children's water feature, playgrounds, tennis courts, picnic areas, and an 18-hole municipal golf course. In summer, there are concerts. The park is also the site of the Denver Zoo (see below) and the Denver Museum of Nature & Science (p. 82), including its IMAX Theater.

E. 17th to E. 26th aves., between York St. and Colorado Blvd. Free admission to park. Separate admission to zoo, museum, golf course, and other sites. Bus: 24 or 32.

Denver Botanic Gardens ★★   Twenty-three acres of outstanding outdoor and indoor gardens display plants native to the desert, plains, mountain foothills, and alpine zones. There's also a traditional Japanese garden, an herb garden, a water garden, a fragrance garden, and a garden inspired by the art of Monet. Even in the cold of winter, the dome-shaped, concrete-and-Plexiglas Tropical Conservatory houses thousands of species of tropical and subtropical plants. Huge, colorful orchids and bromeliads share space with a collection of plants used for food, fibers, dyes, building materials, and medicines. The Botanic Gardens also have a gift shop, a library, and an auditorium. Special events, scheduled throughout the year, range from garden concerts in summer to a spring plant sale to a cornfield maze southwest of Denver in the fall. Allow 1 to 2 hours.

1005 York St. ℂ **720/865-3500**. www.botanicgardens.org. Admission $11 adults, $7.50 seniors, $6 children 4–15 and students with ID, and free for children under 4. May to mid-Sept Sat–Tues 9am–8pm; Wed–Fri 9am–5pm; mid-Sept to Apr daily 9am–5pm. Bus: 2 or 10.

Denver Mountain Parks ★★   Formally established in August 1913, the city's Mountain Parks system immediately began acquiring land in the mountains near Denver to be set aside for recreational use. Today it includes more than 14,000 acres, with 31 developed mountain parks and 16 unnamed wilderness areas that are wonderful places for hiking, picnicking, bird-watching, golfing, or lazing in the grass and sun.

The first and largest, **Genesee Park,** is 20 miles west of Denver off I-70, exit 254; its 2,341 acres contain the Chief Hosa Lodge and Campground (the only overnight camping available in the system), picnic areas with fireplaces, a softball field, a scenic overlook, and an elk-and-buffalo enclosure.

Among the system's other parks is **Echo Lake,** about 45 minutes from downtown Denver on Colo. 103. At 10,600 feet elevation on Mount Evans, the park has good fishing, hiking, and picnicking, plus a restaurant and curio shop. Other parks include 1,000-acre **Daniels Park** (23 miles south of Denver; take I-25 to Castle Pines Parkway, and then go west to the park), which offers picnic areas, a bison enclosure, and a scenic overlook; **Red Rocks Park,** just southwest of Denver in Morrison, featuring the famed amphitheatre, a trading post, a museum that covers both natural history and rock and roll, and hiking trails amid the red sandstone formations (see www.redrocksonline.com); and **Dedisse Park** (2 miles west of Evergreen on Colo. 74), which provides picnic facilities, a golf course, a restaurant, a clubhouse, and opportunities for ice-skating, fishing, and volleyball.

Dept. of Parks and Recreation. ℂ **303/697-4545.** www.denvergov.org. Free admission.

Denver Zoo ★★ (Kids) More than 700 species of animals (nearly 4,000 individuals) live in this spacious zoological park, home to the rare deerlike okapi as well as to Siberian tigers, Komodo dragons, and western lowland gorillas. The newest (and most ambitious) habitat here is Predator Ridge, a re-created African savanna with lions, hyenas, and other African predators. The exhibit is modeled after a Kenyan preserve, complete with artificial termite mounds that dispense insects for the banded mongoose that live here. The zoo has long been an innovator in re-creating realistic habitats: Bear Mountain, built in 1918, was the first animal exhibit in the United States constructed of simulated concrete rockwork.

The zoo is home to the nation's first natural gas–powered train ($2). The electric Safari Shuttle ($2.50 adults, $1.50 children) tours all zoo paths spring through fall. An especially kid-friendly attraction is the Conversation Carousel ($2), featuring wood-carved renditions of such endangered species as okapi, polar bears, Komodo dragons, and hippos. The Hungry Elephant, a cafeteria with an outdoor eating area, serves full meals, and picnicking is popular, too. Feeding times are posted near the zoo entrance so you can time your visit to see the animals when they are most active. Allow from 2 hours to a whole day.

City Park, 2300 Steele St. (main entrance between Colorado Blvd. and York St. on 23rd Ave.). ℂ **303/376-4800.** www.denverzoo.org. Admission $12 adults summer, $9 adults winter; $9 seniors 62 and over summer, $7 seniors winter; $7 children 3–12 (accompanied by an adult) summer, $5 children winter; free for children under 3. Apr–Sept daily 9am–5pm; Oct–Mar daily 10am–4pm. Bus: 24 or 32.

Downtown Aquarium (Kids) Denver's state-of-the-art aquarium—the largest between Chicago and Monterey, California—opened in 1999 as a nonprofit, went belly-up, and in 2003 was sold to the for-profit Landry's seafood restaurant chain. The sale brought the aquarium stability, not to mention new exhibits and a theme restaurant and lounge on-site. Residents include greenback cutthroat trout (the Colorado state fish), river otters, tigers, nurse sharks, sea turtles, and moray eels. Among the other exhibits: a flash-flood simulation, a gold-panning and mining display, "Stingray Reef" (visitors can pet and feed the slippery denizens), and a lifelike animatronic orangutan. On Saturdays, licensed divers and novice snorkelers can swim in the big tanks for a fee (about $175 for divers, $75 for snorkelers). Allow 2 hours.

700 Water St., just east of I-25 via 23rd Ave. (exit 211). (🕐 **303/561-4444.** www.aquariumrestaurants.com. Admission before 6pm $14 adults, $13 seniors, $8.25 children 3–11, free for children under 3. Discounts available after 6pm or with receipt from restaurant. Sun–Thurs 10am–9pm; Fri–Sat 10am–9:30pm. Closed Dec 25. Bus: 28.

Rocky Mountain Arsenal National Wildlife Refuge   Once a site where the U.S. Army manufactured chemical weapons such as mustard gas and GB nerve agent, and later leased to a private enterprise to produce pesticides, the Rocky Mountain Arsenal has become an environmental success story. The 27-square-mile Superfund cleanup site, an area of open grasslands and wetlands just west of Denver International Airport, is home to more than 330 species, including deer, coyotes, prairie dogs, and birds of prey. This is one of the country's largest eagle-roosting locales during the winter.

The Rocky Mountain Arsenal Wildlife Society Bookstore is at the visitor center, and there are about 15 miles of hiking trails as well as catch-and-release fishing. Allow at least an hour.

56th Ave. at Quebec St. (🕐 **303/289-0930.** www.fws.gov/rockymountainarsenal. Free admission. Tues–Sun 6am–6pm. Bus: 88.

3 AMUSEMENT PARKS & PLACES ESPECIALLY FOR KIDS

Denver abounds in child-oriented activities, and the listings below will probably appeal to young travelers of any age. In addition, some sights listed in the previous sections may appeal to families. They include the Butterfly Pavilion and Insect Center, Colorado History Museum, Downtown Aquarium, Denver Art Museum, Denver Museum of Miniatures Dolls & Toys, Denver Museum of Nature and Science, Denver Zoo, Four Mile Historic Park, and the U.S. Mint.

Children's Museum of Denver ★ (Kids)   Denver's best hands-on experience for children, this intriguing museum is both educational and just plain fun. Focusing on children 8 years old and younger, the museum uses educational "playscapes" to entertain and activate young minds. These exhibits include "CMD Fire Station No. 1," which teaches fire safety, and "My Market," a faux supermarket that allows kids to role-play as shoppers and clerks. There are several other playscapes with themes ranging from biology to engineering. There's also a resource center that provides parenting information to adults, and a cafe that serves sandwiches, snacks, and beverages. Allow at least 2 hours.

2121 Children's Museum Dr. (🕐 **303/433-7444.** www.mychildsmuseum.org. Admission $7 ages 1–59, $5 seniors 60 and over, free for children under 1. Mon–Fri 9am–4pm; Sat–Sun 10am–5pm. Take exit 211 (23rd Ave.) east off I-25; turn right on 7th St., and again on Children's Museum Dr. Bus: 28.

Elitch Gardens Theme Park ★ (Kids)   A Denver tradition established in 1889, this amusement park moved to its present downtown site in 1995. The 45-plus rides include Twister II, an unbelievable 10-story roller coaster with a 90-foot drop and dark tunnel; the Flying Coaster, a one-of-a-kind "hang gliding" experience in which passengers lie facedown; the Halfpipe, a snowboarding-themed thrill ride that involves 16 passengers on a 39-foot board; the 220-foot, free-fall Tower of Doom; and a fully restored 1925 carousel with 67 hand-carved horses and chariots. Patrons of all ages can enjoy the Island Kingdom Water Park while the little ones have fun on pint-sized rides in StarToon

---

Fun Facts   The Big Blue Bear

Denver has a new face to the world, and it's peering into the second floor of the Colorado Convention Center. Known popularly as "The Big Blue Bear," the 40-foot blue ursine immediately became Denver's most photogenic piece of public art when it was installed in 2005. Sculptor Lawrence Argent designed the big fella—officially named *I See What You Mean*—and then a California-based fabricator shaped him out of 5 tons of steel, fiberglass, and cement; transported him to Colorado in sections; and bolted him into place.

The sculpture is located right by the convention center's 14th Street entrance, and can be photographed from inside or out. For a Denver souvenir, it's hard to beat the little blue bear replicas available at the Denver Art Museum, inside the Colorado Convention Center, and at the visitor information center at 16th and California streets.

Studios. There are also musical revues and stunt shows, games and arcades, food, shopping, and beautiful flower gardens. Allow 3 hours.

Speer Blvd., at I-25, exit 212A. (C) **303/595-4386.** www.elitchgardens.com. Gate admission with unlimited rides $35 for those taller than 4 ft., $20 for those 4 ft. and under, free for children under 4 and seniors over 69. Online ticket specials available. Parking $10. Memorial Day to Labor Day daily 10am–9pm; Apr–late May and early Sept–Oct weekends (call for hours). Light rail: C Line, Pepsi Center/Elitch Gardens.

Lakeside Amusement Park (Kids)   Among the largest and most historic amusement parks in the Rocky Mountains, Lakeside has about 40 rides, including a Cyclone roller coaster, a midway with carnival and arcade games, and a rare steam-powered miniature train from the early 20th century that circles the lake. There are also food stands and picnic facilities, plus a separate Kiddie's Playland with 15 rides. Allow 3 hours.

4601 Sheridan Blvd. (just south of I-70, exit 271). (C) **303/477-1621.** www.lakesideamusementpark.com. Admission $2.50. Ride coupons 50¢ (rides require 1–4 coupons each); unlimited rides $14 Mon–Fri, $20 Sat–Sun and holidays. May Sat–Sun and holidays noon–10pm; June to Labor Day Mon–Fri 6–10pm, Sat–Sun and holidays noon–10pm. Kiddie's Playland Mon–Fri 1–10pm, Sat–Sun and holidays noon–10pm. Closed from the day after Labor Day to Apr.

Tiny Town and Railroad (Kids) (Finds)   Originally built in 1915 at the site of a Denver–Leadville stagecoach stop, Tiny Town is exactly what its name implies—a one-sixth–scale Western village. Nestled in a scenic mountain canyon about 20 miles southeast of downtown Denver, Tiny Town is made up of 100 colorful buildings and a steam-powered locomotive that visitors can ride for an additional $1. Allow 1 hour.

6249 S. Turkey Creek Rd., Tiny Town. (C) **303/697-6829.** www.tinytownrailroad.com. Admission $5 adults, $3 children 2–12, free for children under 2. Memorial Day to Labor Day daily 10am–5pm; May and Sept Sat–Sun 10am–5pm. Closed Oct–Apr. Located 20 miles southeast of downtown via U.S. 285 (Hampden Ave.).

Water World ★ (Kids)   This 64-acre complex, billed as America's largest family water park, has two ocean-like wave pools, river rapids for inner tubing, twisting water slides, several kids' play areas, a gondola to the country's first water-based funhouse, plus other attractions—more than 40 in all—as well as food service and other amenities. Allow at least 4 hours.

88th Ave. and Pecos St., Federal Heights. © **303/427-SURF [7873]**. www.waterworldcolorado.com. Admission $34 for those 48 in. and taller, $29 for those 40–48 in., free for seniors and children under 40 in. Memorial Day to Labor Day daily 10am–6pm. Closed rest of year and some school days in Aug. Take the Thornton exit (exit 219, 84th Ave.) off I-25 north.

| WALKING TOUR | DOWNTOWN DENVER |

START:	**Denver Information Center, Civic Center Park.**
FINISH:	**State Capitol, Civic Center Park.**
TIME:	**2 to 8 hours, depending on how much time you spend shopping, eating, and sightseeing.**
BEST TIMES:	**Any Tuesday through Friday in late spring.**
WORST TIMES:	**Monday and holidays, when the museums are closed.**

Start your tour of the downtown area at Civic Center Park, on West Colfax Avenue at 14th Street.

❶ Civic Center Park

This 2-square-block oasis features a Greek amphitheater, fountains, statues, flower gardens, and 30 different species of trees, 2 of which (it is said) were originally planted by Abraham Lincoln at his Illinois home.

Overlooking the park on its east side is the State Capitol. On its south side is the:

❷ Colorado History Museum

The staircase-like building houses exhibits that make the state's colorful history come to life.

Also on the south side of the park are the Denver Public Library and the:

❸ Denver Art Museum

With buildings designed by Gio Ponti of Italy and Daniel Libeskind of Germany, the art museum is an architectural wonder. Inside are more than 35,000 works of art, including renowned Western and American Indian collections.

On the west side of Civic Center Park is the:

❹ City & County Building

During the Christmas season, a rainbow of colored lights decorates it in spectacular fashion.

A block farther west is the:

❺ U.S. Mint

Modeled in Italian Renaissance style, the building resembles the Palazzo Riccardi in Florence. More than 60,000 cubic feet of granite and 1,000 tons of steel went into its construction in 1904.

Cross over Colfax and go diagonally northwest up Court Place. Two blocks ahead is the:

❻ Denver Pavilions

The city's newest retail hot spot sits at the south end of the 16th Street Mall, featuring a Hard Rock Cafe, a 15-screen movie theater, and a Barnes & Noble Superstore.

Three blocks up the 16th Street Mall, head southwest 2 blocks on California Street past the Colorado Convention Center and turn right on 14th Street. Walk 2 blocks to the:

❼ Denver Performing Arts Complex

The complex covers 4 square blocks between 14th Street and Cherry Creek, Champa Street, and Arapahoe Street. The entrance is under a block-long, 80-foot-high glass archway. The center includes seven theaters, a symphony hall in the round, a voice research laboratory, and a smoking solar fountain. Free tours are offered.

Two more blocks up 14th Street, past the arts center is:

❽ Larimer Square

This is Denver's oldest commercial district. Restored late-19th-century Victorian

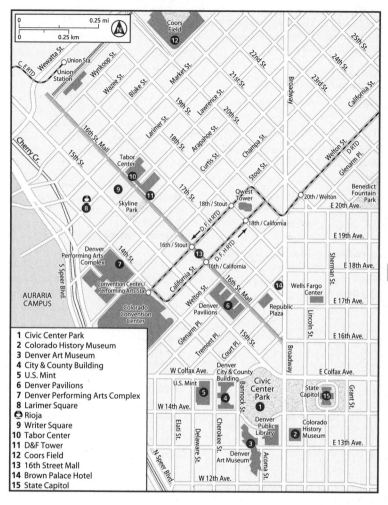

1 Civic Center Park
2 Colorado History Museum
3 Denver Art Museum
4 City & County Building
5 U.S. Mint
6 Denver Pavilions
7 Denver Performing Arts Complex
8 Larimer Square
● Rioja
9 Writer Square
10 Tabor Center
11 D&F Tower
12 Coors Field
13 16th Street Mall
14 Brown Palace Hotel
15 State Capitol

buildings accommodate more than 30 shops and a dozen restaurants and clubs. Colorful awnings, hanging flower baskets, and quiet open courtyards accent the square, once home to such notables as Buffalo Bill Cody and Bat Masterson. Horse-drawn carriage rides originate here for trips up the 16th Street Mall or through lower downtown.

 TAKE A BREAK
Stop at **Rioja**, 1431 Larimer St., between 14th and 15th sts. (✆ **303/820-2282**), or one of the patios on Larimer Square for a drink and people-watching. (See review on p. 72.)

A walkway at the east corner of Larimer and 15th leads through:

❾ Writer Square

Quaint gas lamps, brick walkways, and outdoor cafes dot this shopping-and-dining complex.

At 16th Street, cross to the:

❿ Tabor Center

The glass-enclosed shopping and entertainment complex spreads over three levels, in effect a 2-block-long greenhouse.

To the east, the Tabor Center is anchored by the:

⓫ D&F Tower

The city landmark was patterned after the campanile of St. Mark's Basilica in Venice, Italy, in 1910. In the basement is a performing arts venue, Lannie's Clocktower Cabaret.

Head northwest along 16th Street, then turn right on Wynkoop Street and go 4 blocks to LoDo's centerpiece:

⓬ Coors Field

The anchor of the vital LoDo ("Lower Downtown") neighborhood and the home of baseball's Colorado Rockies, the stadium is right at home amid the Victorian redbricks. There are plenty of eateries and bars in the area, as well as transportation hubs in Union Station and Market Street Station, plus a few shops.

Here, head southeast to 16th Street and begin a leisurely stroll down the:

⓭ 16th Street Mall

The $76-million pedestrian path affords the finest people-watching spot in the city.

You'll see everyone from street entertainers to lunching office workers to travelers like yourself. Built of red and gray granite, it is lined with 200 red oak trees, a dozen fountains, and a lighting system straight out of *Star Wars*. You'll also see outdoor cafes, restored Victorian buildings, modern skyscrapers, and hundreds of shops—with an emphasis on sports—plus restaurants and department stores. If you are done with walking, sleek European-built shuttle buses run through, offering free transportation up and down the mall as often as every 90 seconds.

You'll walk 7 blocks down 16th Street from the Tabor Center before reaching Tremont Place. Turn left, go 1 block farther, and across the street, on your right, you'll see the:

⓮ Brown Palace Hotel

One of the most beautiful grande dame hotels in the United States, it was built in 1892 and features a nine-story atrium lobby topped by a Tiffany stained-glass ceiling. Step into the lobby for a look.

Continue across Broadway on East 17th Avenue. Go 2 blocks to Sherman Street, turn right, and proceed 2 blocks south on Sherman to East Colfax Avenue. You're back overlooking Civic Center Park, but this time you're at the:

⓯ State Capitol

If you stand on the 13th step on the west side of the building, you're exactly 5,280 feet (1 mile) above sea level. Architects modeled the Colorado capitol after the U.S. Capitol in Washington, D.C., and used the world's entire known supply of rare rose onyx in its interior wainscoting.

4 ORGANIZED TOURS

Visitors who want to be personally guided to the attractions of Denver and the surrounding areas by those in the know have a variety of choices. In addition to the following, see "Escorted General-Interest Tours" and "Special-Interest Trips," in chapter 3.

Half- and full-day bus tours of Denver and the nearby Rockies are offered by the ubiquitous **Gray Line**, P.O. Box 17646, Denver, CO 80217 (© **800/348-6877** for information only; 303/289-2841 for reservations and information; www.coloradograyline. com). Fares for children under 13 are half the adult prices listed below. Prices include entry fees but usually no food. Tours depart from the Cherry Creek Shopping Center at 1st Avenue and Milwaukee Street, as well as from local hotels and hostels on a reservation basis.

A 4-hour tour (no. 27), leaving at 1:30pm, takes in Denver's mountain parks: Red Rocks Park, Bergen Park, and Buffalo Bill's grave atop Lookout Mountain. It costs $40 for adults. The Denver city tour (no. 28), which departs daily at 8:30am and takes about $3^{1}/_{2}$ hours, gives you a taste of both old Denver—through Larimer Square and other historic buildings—and the modern-day city. It's $35 for adults. The city tour combined with the mountain-parks tour costs $70. Gray Line also offers tours of Rocky Mountain National Park, Golden and Morrison, and the Colorado Springs area; call or check the website for information.

The Colorado Sightseer, 6780 W. 84th Circle, Suite 60, Arvada, CO 80003 (© 303/423-8200; www.coloradosightseer.com), offers guided tours of Denver and environs. The Historic Denver tour includes a visit to LoDo and some of the city's earliest buildings, the State Capitol, the Molly Brown House, and Four Mile Historic Park. It lasts about 4 hours and costs $45 for adults, $35 for children 5 to 12, and it's free for children under 5. A Rocky Mountain National Park tour, lasting about $9^{1}/_{2}$ hours, costs $85 for adults and $65 for children 5 to 12 (free for children under 5), including a box lunch. The $4^{1}/_{2}$-hour Foothills Tour includes stops at Coors Brewery, the Buffalo Bill memorial, and scenic Red Rocks Park. The costs are $45 for adults, $35 for children 5 to 12, and free for children under 5.

The LoDo District (© 303/628-5428; www.lodo.org) leads guided walking tours of the storied area June to October. Tours depart from Union Station (17th and Wynkoop sts.) on Tuesdays at 10am and Saturdays at 1pm; the cost is $10 adults, $5 students, and free for those under 13. They also offer different walking tours on Thursday and Saturday afternoons. Take advantage of your cellphone with Rocky Mountain Audio Guides (© 303/898-7073; www.rmaguides.com), which delivers 40- and 80-minute walking tours of downtown Denver. Call 24 hours before your tour to purchase; then you simply dial a number and walk around town, guided via satellite.

BICYCLING & MULTISPORT TOURS

The World Outdoors (© 800/488-8483 or 303/413-0938; www.theworldoutdoors.com) offers a 6-day, 5-night multisport hut-to-hut tour that begins and ends in Vail (100 miles west of Denver). The huts, described by *Mountain Bike Magazine* as "luxurious backcountry accommodations," serve as recreational headquarters for guests, who have plenty of hiking, rafting, and sightseeing opportunities between mountain-biking treks. The trips aren't cheap, costing around $1,500 per person, but this might be the best way for the outdoors enthusiast to enjoy the Rockies west of Denver. Available in June and August, tours include meals but not biking and camping gear.

Colorado Mountain Expeditions (© 888/CME-HIKE [263-4453]; www.coloradotrailhiking.com) offers supported weeklong treks on the Colorado Trail (which runs 483 miles from Denver to Durango) for $925 per person, all meals included. The beauty of these trips: You only carry a day pack. A support crew sets up your camp and makes your meals while you focus on the trail, not the campsite.

Another company that offers weeklong tours in the area is Bicycle Tour of Colorado (© 303/985-1180; www.bicycletourcolorado.com). For $300 to $400, a biker can join a tour involving more than 1,000 riders and 70 volunteers—including medical and bike-tech support as well as guiding services—on a 400-mile journey that hits six different cities each year, crossing the Continental Divide several times in the process. Although accommodations can be prearranged at hotels, most riders elect to stay at facilities provided by the city (for example, the local high school). All meals are provided for the one fee for the week.

A good resource for bicyclists is the **Denver Bicycle Touring Club** (www.dbtc.org), which organizes local rides and publishes a monthly newsletter. See also "Bicycling & Skateboarding," below.

5 OUTDOOR ACTIVITIES

Denver's proximity to the Rocky Mountains makes it possible to spend a day skiing, snowmobiling, horseback riding, hiking, river running, sailing, fishing, hunting, mountain climbing, or rockhounding and return to the city by nightfall. Within the city limits and nearby, visitors will find more than 200 miles of jogging and bicycle paths, more than 100 free tennis courts, and several dozen public golf courses.

The city has an excellent system of **Mountain Parks** (℃ 303/697-4545), covering more than 14,000 acres, which are discussed earlier in this chapter in the "Parks, Gardens & Zoos" section.

Campsites are easy to reach from Denver, as are suitable sites for hang gliding and hot-air ballooning. Sailing is popular within the city at Sloan's Lake and in Washington Park (both Denver City Parks), and the Platte River is clear for many miles of river running in rafts, kayaks, and canoes.

The Denver Metro Convention and Visitors Bureau (see "Visitor Information," in chapter 5) can supply detailed information about activities in the city. Information on nearby outdoor activities is available from **Colorado State Parks,** 1313 Sherman St., Suite 618, Denver, CO 80203 (℃ 303/866-3437; www.parks.state.co.us); the **U.S. Forest Service,** Rocky Mountain Region, 740 Simms St., Golden, CO 80401 (℃ 303/275-5350; www.fs.fed.us/r2); the **U.S. Bureau of Land Management,** 2850 Youngfield St., Lakewood, CO 80215 (℃ 303/239-3600; www.co.blm.gov); and the **National Park Service's** Intermountain Region headquarters, 12795 W. Alameda Pkwy., Lakewood, CO 80228 (℃ 303/969-2000; www.nps.gov).

Visitors who don't bring the necessary equipment should hit the **REI Flagship** store, 1416 Platte St. (℃ 303/756-3100); its rental department is stocked with tents, backpacks, stoves, mountaineering equipment, kayaks, and other gear.

BALLOONING   You can't beat a hot-air balloon ride for viewing the magnificent Rocky Mountain scenery. **Life Cycle Balloon Adventures, Ltd.** (℃ 800/980-9272 or 303/216-1990; www.lifecycleballoons.com), and **Colorado Rocky Ballooning** (℃ 888/468-9280 or 970/468-9280; www.coloradoballoonrides.com) both offer sunrise flights daily. The cost at both companies is usually $195 to $250 per person.

BICYCLING & SKATEBOARDING   The paved bicycle paths that crisscross Denver include a 12-mile scenic stretch along the bank of the South Platte River and along Cherry Creek beside Speer Boulevard. All told, the city has more than 85 miles of off-road trails for bikers and runners. Bike paths link the city's 205 parks, and many streets have bike lanes. In all, the city has more than 130 miles of designated bike paths and lanes. Mountain bikers will take delight in the foothills; one option is **Waterton Canyon,** where singletrack connects metro Denver and Deckers. For more information, contact **Bike Denver** (www.bikedenver.org) or **Bicycle Colorado** (℃ 303/417-1544;

388-1630; www.cherrycreekbikerack.com), offers rentals, service, and free parking for
bikes.

Denver also has the largest free skateboarding park (3 acres) in the country, the **Denver Skatepark,** 19th and Little Raven sts. (℃ **720/913-1311;** www.denverskatepark.com). It is quite popular and open between the hours of 5am and 11pm.

BOATING   A quiet way to view some of downtown Denver is from a punt on scenic Cherry Creek. **Venice on the Creek** (℃ 303/893-0750; www.veniceonthecreek.com) operates from June to August, Thursday to Sunday from 5 to 10pm. On weekdays it accommodates only groups of 12 or more; smaller groups are taken on weekends. Guides describe the history of the city while pointing out landmarks. Tickets are available at the kiosk at Creekfront Plaza, at the intersection of Speer Boulevard and Larimer Street. A 1-hour trip costs $25 to $30 per bench (each accommodates two) or $75 for a private boat. Also downtown, you can rent a kayak ($50 a day) and take kayaking classes ($49 per session) at **Confluence Kayaks,** 1615 Platte St. (℃ 303/433-3676).

In the outlying areas, you'll find powerboat marinas at **Cherry Creek State Park,** 4201 S. Parker Rd., Aurora (℃ **303/699-3860**), 11 miles from downtown off I-225; and **Chatfield State Park,** 11500 N. Roxborough Park Rd., Littleton (℃ **303/791-7275**), 16 miles south of downtown Denver. Jet-skiing and sailboarding are also permitted at both parks. Sailboarding, canoeing, and other wakeless boating are popular at **Barr Lake State Park,** 13401 Picadilly Rd., Brighton (℃ **303/659-6005**), 21 miles northeast of downtown on I-76.

For a different watersports experience, try riverboarding with **RipBoard** (℃ **866/311-2627** or 303/904-8367; www.ripboard.com), which entails going down Clear Creek face-first with flippers on your feet and a helmet on your head. It's exciting and exhausting, but can be a lot of fun in the right water. Lessons (including equipment) are $75 for 4 hours; rentals and sales are also available.

For information on other boating opportunities, contact Colorado State Parks, the National Park Service, or the U.S. Forest Service (see above).

FISHING   A couple of good bets in the metropolitan area are Chatfield State Park, with trout, bass, and panfish, and Cherry Creek State Park, which boasts trout, walleye pike, bass, and crappie (see "Boating," above). In all, there are more than 7,100 miles of streams and 2,000 reservoirs and lakes in Colorado. For information, contact Colorado State Parks, the Colorado Division of Wildlife (℃ 303/297-1192), or the U.S. Fish and Wildlife Service (℃ 303/236-7917). Within Denver city limits, the **Denver Department of Parks and Recreation** (℃ 720/913-1311) stocks a number of lakes with fish.

A number of sporting-goods stores can provide more detailed information. The skilled and experienced staff at **Anglers All,** 5211 S. Santa Fe Dr. (℃ **303/794-1104;** www.anglersall.com), can help with equipment choices and recommendations for where to go. Anglers All also offers lessons, seminars, clinics, and guided wade and float trips (about $400 a day for two people).

GOLF   Throughout the Front Range, it's often said that you can play golf at least 320 days a year, because the sun always seems to be shining, and even when it snows, the little snow that sticks melts quickly. There are more than 50 courses in the Denver area, including 7 municipal golf courses, with nonresident greens fees up to $24 for 18 holes. City courses are **City Park Golf Course,** East 25th Avenue and York Street (℃ 303/295-2096);

WHAT TO SEE & DO IN DENVER

6

OUTDOOR ACTIVITIES

Evergreen Golf Course, 29614 Upper Bear Creek Rd., Evergreen (℃ 303/674-4128); the par-3 **Harvard Gulch Golf Course,** East Iliff Avenue and South Clarkson Street (℃ 303/698-4078); **Kennedy Golf Course,** 10500 E. Hampden Ave. (℃ 303/751-0311); **Overland Park Golf Course,** South Santa Fe Drive and West Jewell Avenue (℃ 303/698-4975); **Wellshire Golf Course,** 3333 S. Colorado Blvd. (℃ 303/692-5636); and **Willis Case Golf Course,** 4999 Vrain St. near West 50th Avenue (℃ 303/458-4877). Wellshire is the best overall course, but I prefer Willis Case for its spectacular mountain views.

You can make same-day reservations by calling the course; otherwise, nonresident golfers must purchase a $10 card at City Park, Wellshire, or Willis Case, and then make reservations through the **automated phone system** (℃ 303/784-4000). The one exception to this policy is Evergreen Golf Course, where you can call the starter for reservations 3 days in advance. For information on any course, you can also call the **Department of Parks and Recreation** (℃ 720/913-1311).

An 18-hole Frisbee golf course is located at Lakewood Gulch, near Federal Boulevard and 12th Street. Call the **Department of Parks and Recreation** (℃ 720/913-1311) for more information.

HIKING & BACKPACKING The **Colorado Trail ★★** is a hiking, horse, and mountain-biking route stretching 500 miles from Denver to Durango. The trail is also open to cross-country skiing, snowshoeing, and llama-pack hiking. Opened in 1988, the trail is still being fine-tuned. It took 15 years to establish, using volunteer labor, and crosses eight mountain ranges and five river systems, winding from rugged terrain to pristine meadows. For information, contact the **Colorado Trail Foundation,** 710 10th St., Room 210, Golden, CO 80401-1022 (℃ **303/384-3729;** www.coloradotrail.org). Beyond being a source of information, the foundation maintains and improves the trail, publishes relevant guidebooks, and offers supported treks (see "Bicycling & Multisport Tours," above) and accredited courses.

For hikes in the Denver area, contact the city **Department of Parks and Recreation** (℃ **720/913-1311)** for information on Denver's park system. Or contact any of the following agencies: Colorado State Parks, Colorado Division of Wildlife, National Park Service, U.S. Bureau of Land Management, or U.S. Forest Service (see the introduction to this section and "Fishing," above). A good source for the many published area maps and hiking guides is **Mapsco Map and Travel Center,** 800 Lincoln St., Denver (℃ **303/830-2373**).

Above Red Rocks Park, **Mount Falcon Park ★** (℃ 303/271-5925) offers excellent trails that are easy to moderate in difficulty, making this a good place for families with children. There are also picnic areas, shelters, and ruins of an old castlelike home. From Denver, go west on U.S. 285, north on Parmalee Gulch Road, and follow the signs; the park is open daily from dawn to dusk, and admission is free. Mountain bikes and horseback riding are permitted, as are leashed dogs.

Other relatively easy trails near Denver are in **Roxborough State Park** (℃ 303/973-3959), 10 miles south of Littleton—the 1-mile **Willow Creek Trail** and the 2.3-mile **Fountain Valley Trail ★**. There are several more strenuous trails at Roxborough, which are worth the effort if you

---

The Skinny on Denver

According to the statisticians, Denver has the highest proportion of thin people of any city in the country. A 2008 study showed Colorado to be the state with the lowest percentage of the population to be overweight.

> **(Tips) Denver's Dog Parks**
>
> In 2004, Denver began to allow canines to roam free at five parks within city limits, and there are dozens of off-leash parks in the metropolitan area as a whole. Contact the Department of Parks and Recreation (© **720/913-1311**) for more information or visit **www.denvergov.org**.

enjoy beautiful red rocks and the chance to see wildlife. To get to Roxborough Park, exit Colo. 470 south onto U.S. 85, turn west onto Titan Road, and then go south again at Roxborough Park Road to the main entrance. Admission is $6 per passenger vehicle. The park is open daily from 8am to 8pm in summer, with shorter hours the rest of the year. Dogs, bikes, and horseback riding are not permitted.

HORSEBACK RIDING Equestrians can find a mount year-round at **Stockton's Plum Creek Stables,** 7479 W. Titan Rd., Littleton (© **303/791-1966;** www.stocktonsplum creek.com), near Chatfield State Park, 15 miles south of downtown. Stockton's offers hayrides and barbecue picnics, as well as lessons. **Paint Horse Stables,** 4201 S. Parker Rd., Aurora (© **303/690-8235;** www.painthorsestables.net), at Cherry Creek State Park, also rents horses, boards horses, and provides riding lessons, trail rides, hayrides, and pony rides for kids.

RECREATION CENTERS The **Denver Department of Parks and Recreation** (© **720/913-1311**) operates about 30 recreation centers around the city, several of which have facilities oriented to seniors. Daily guest passes for all facilities, including swimming pools, cost $5 for adults, $2 for children under 18. Facilities vary but may include basketball courts, indoor or outdoor pools, gyms, and weight rooms. The centers offer fitness classes and other recreation programs, including programs for those with special needs. Call © **720/913-0693** for current program information.

Among the city's recreation centers are the following: **Scheitler Recreation Center,** 5031 W. 46th Ave. (© **303/458-4898**), which has an indoor pool and a weight room; **Martin Luther King, Jr., Recreation Center,** 3880 Newport St. (© **303/331-4034**), which is the nearest full-service center to Denver International Airport and has an indoor pool, a large gym, and a racquetball court; **20th Street Recreation Center,** downtown at 1011 20th St., between Arapahoe and Curtis streets (© **303/295-4430**), with an indoor pool and a weight room; and **Washington Park Recreation Center,** 701 S. Franklin St. (© **303/698-4962**), with an indoor pool, an advanced weight room, a large gym, and walking and jogging trails.

SKIING Several ski resorts close to the Front Range target primarily locals. They include **Eldora Mountain Resort,** 45 miles west (© **303/440-8700;** www.eldora.com), which covers almost 700 acres and has 53 trails, with skiing rated 20% beginner, 50% intermediate, and 30% advanced. **Loveland Basin and Valley,** 56 miles west on I-70, exit 216 (© **800/736-3754** or 303/569-3203; www.skiloveland.com), covers 1,365 acres and has 70 trails, rated 13% beginner, 41% intermediate, and 46% advanced. **Winter Park Resort** ★, 67 miles west of Denver on I-70 and U.S. 40 (© **970/726-5514** or 303/316-1564; www.winterparkresort.com), boasts 2,762 ski-able acres with 134 trails, rated 8% beginner, 17% intermediate, and 75% advanced. Winter Park is

WHAT TO SEE & DO IN DENVER

6

OUTDOOR ACTIVITIES

accessible by car and via the **Ski Train** (☏ **303/294-4754;** www.skitrain.com) from Union Station in downtown Denver. Fares are about $50 to $75 per person round-trip; packages including lift tickets are also available. Eldora and Winter Park offer Nordic as well as alpine terrain.

Full information on statewide skiing is available from **Colorado Ski Country USA** (☏ **303/837-0793;** www.coloradoski.com) and the **Colorado Cross Country Ski Association** (www.colorado-xc.org).

Some useful Denver telephone numbers for skiers include **ski-area information and snow report** (☏ 303/825-7669), **weather report** (☏ 303/337-2500), and **road conditions** (☏ 303/639-1111).

SWIMMING   The Denver Department of Parks and Recreation (☏ **720/913-1311**) operates 16 outdoor swimming pools (open daily mid-June to mid-Aug) and 12 indoor pools (open Mon–Sat year-round). Nonresident fees are $3 for adults and $2 for children. See "Recreation Centers," above.

TENNIS   The Denver Department of Parks and Recreation (☏ **720/913-1311**) manages or owns close to 150 tennis courts, more than one-third of them lit for night play. Among the most popular courts are those in City Park (York St. and E. 17th Ave.), Berkeley Park (Tennyson St. and W. 17th Ave.), Green Valley East Ranch Park (Jebel St. and E. 45th Ave.), Washington Park (S. Downing St. and E. Louisiana Ave.), and Sloan's Lake Park (Sheridan Blvd. and W. 17th Ave.). The public courts are free. For more information, contact the **Colorado Tennis Association** (☏ **303/695-4116;** www.coloradotennis. com).

GREAT NEARBY STATE PARKS

Colorado has a number of excellent state parks offering a wide range of activities and scenery. Information on the state's parks is available at **www.parks.state.co.us**.

BARR LAKE STATE PARK   About 25 miles northeast of Denver on I-76 in Brighton, this wildlife sanctuary of almost 2,800 acres comprises a prairie reservoir and surrounding wetlands and uplands. Boats with motors exceeding 10 horsepower are not allowed, but you can sail, paddle, row, and fish. A 9-mile hiking and biking trail circles the lake. A boardwalk from the nature center at the south parking lot leads to a good view of a heron rookery, and bird blinds along this trail allow wildlife observation and photography. Three picnic areas provide tables and grills; there's a commercial campground opposite the park on the west side. The entrance is at 13401 Picadilly Rd. Admission costs $6 per vehicle. Call ☏ **303/659-6005** for more information.

CASTLEWOOD CANYON STATE PARK ★   Steep canyons, a meandering stream, a waterfall, lush vegetation, and considerable wildlife distinguish this 2,000-acre park. You can see the remains of Castlewood Canyon Dam, which was built for irrigation in 1890; it collapsed in 1933, killing two people and flooding the streets of Denver. The park, 30 miles south of Denver on Colo. 83, east of Castle Rock in Franktown, provides picnic facilities and hiking trails. The entrance is at 2989 S. State Hwy. 83; admission is $6 per vehicle. Call ☏ **303/688-5242** for more information.

CHATFIELD STATE PARK ★   Sixteen miles south of downtown Denver on U.S. 85 in Littleton, this park occupies 5,600 acres of prairie against a backdrop of the steeply rising Rocky Mountains. Chatfield Reservoir, with a 26-mile shoreline, invites swimming, boating, fishing, and other watersports. The area also has 18 miles of paved bicycle trails, plus hiking and horseback-riding paths. In winter, there's ice fishing and cross-country skiing. The park also has a hot-air-balloon launch pad, a radio-controlled model aircraft field, and a 21-acre man-made wetlands area.

Facilities include 197 pull-through campsites, showers, laundry, and a dump station. Admission is $7 per vehicle; the camping fee is $18 to $22 daily. The entrance is 1 mile south of C-470 on Wadsworth Boulevard (© **303/791-7275**).

CHERRY CREEK STATE PARK The 880-acre Cherry Creek Reservoir, created for flood control by the construction of a dam in 1950, is the central attraction of this popular park, which draws 1.5 million visitors each year. Located at the southeast Denver city limits (off Parker Rd. and I-225) about 12 miles from downtown, the park encompasses 4,200 acres in all.

Watersports include swimming, water-skiing, boating, and fishing. There's a nature trail, dog-training area, model-airplane field with paved runways, jet-ski rental facility, rifle range, pistol range, and trap-shooting area. Twelve miles of paved bicycle paths and 12 miles of bridle trails circle the reservoir (horse rentals are available). Rangers offer guided walks by appointment, as well as evening campfire programs in an amphitheater. In winter, there's skating, ice fishing, and ice boating.

Each of the park's 102 campsites has access to showers, laundry, and a dump station. Most sites have full hookups with water and electric. Many lakeshore day-use sites have picnic tables and grills.

Admission is $7 to $8 per vehicle; campsites are $14 to $22 daily. Campgrounds are open year-round. The entrance is at 4201 S. Parker Rd. in Aurora. Call © **303/690-1166** for general information or © **800/678-2267** for camping reservations.

GOLDEN GATE STATE PARK ★ About 30 miles west of Denver, this 12,000-acre park ranges in elevation from 7,400 to 10,400 feet and offers camping, picnicking, hiking, biking, fishing, hunting, and horseback-riding opportunities. A daily vehicle pass costs $6, and camping fees range from $14 to $18 in developed campgrounds, $8 for backcountry camping. There are around 160 developed campsites, with a limited number of electrical hookups. Reverend's Ridge, the park's largest campground, has coin-operated showers and laundry facilities.

To get to Golden Gate, take Colo. 93 north from Golden 1 mile to Golden Gate Canyon Road. Turn left and continue 13 miles to the park. For more information, call © **303/582-3707.**

6 SPECTATOR SPORTS

Tickets to many sporting events can be obtained from **Ticketmaster** (© **303/830-TIXS** [**8497**]; www.ticketmaster.com), which has several outlets in the Denver area.

AUTO RACING For drag racing and other motorsports, head to **Bandimere Speedway**, 3051 S. Rooney Rd., Morrison (© **303/697-6001**, or 303/697-4870 for a 24-hr. recording; www.bandimere.com), with races scheduled April through October. There are motorcycles, pickup trucks, street cars, and sports cars, plus car shows, swap meets, and other special events.

BASEBALL The **Colorado Rockies** (© **800/388-7625** or 303/762-5437; www.coloradorockies.com) of Major League Baseball's National League West initially enjoyed record-breaking fan support, but attendance has fallen recently, a 2007 run to the World Series notwithstanding. The team plays at the attractive Coors Field, located at 20th and Blake streets in historic Lower Downtown. The 50,000-seat stadium, with a redbrick exterior and on-site microbrewery, was designed in the style of baseball stadiums of old. Tickets are easy to come by, from either the box office or the scalpers on the street. Craigslist (www.craigslist.org) is another good place to find tickets.

BASKETBALL   The **Denver Nuggets** (𝄞 303/405-1111 for ticket information; www. nuggets.com) of the National Basketball Association have gained fans thanks to young superstar Carmelo Anthony. The Nuggets play their home games at the handsome Pepsi Center (downtown at Speer Blvd. and Auraria Pkwy.). There are 41 home games a year between November and April, with playoffs continuing into June.

The **University of Denver** (𝄞 303/871-2336 for ticket office or 303/830-2497; www.denverpioneers.com) plays a competitive college basketball schedule from late November to March.

FOOTBALL   The **Denver Broncos** (𝄞 720/258-3333 for tickets; www.denverbroncos. com) of the National Football League make their home at Invesco Field at Mile High. Home games are sold out months in advance, so call early; there are also a few tickets sold on game day. Your best bet may be to find someone hawking tickets outside the stadium entrance on game day. Pricing tickets above face value is technically illegal, but the law is rarely enforced. Craigslist (www.craigslist.org) is another good place to look for tickets.

You might have better luck getting into a college game. The **University of Colorado Buffaloes** (𝄞 303/492-8337; www.cubuffs.com), of the Big 12 Conference, play in Boulder. Other top college football teams in the area are Colorado State University in Fort Collins and the Air Force Academy in Colorado Springs.

HOCKEY   Denver's National Hockey League team, the **Colorado Avalanche** (𝄞 303/405-1111 for ticket information; www.coloradoavalanche.com), plays in front of sellout crowds at the Pepsi Center (Speer Blvd. and Auraria Pkwy.). The season runs from October to April.

For a cheaper ticket (and a fun atmosphere), the **University of Denver** men's hockey team (𝄞 303/871-2336 for ticket office or 303/830-2497; www.denverpioneers.com) is consistently top tier and plays a competitive schedule between October and mid-March at the Ritchie Center.

HORSE RACING   **Arapahoe Park,** 26000 E. Quincy Ave., Aurora (𝄞 303/690-2400; www.milehiracing.com), offers horse racing May to August, with simulcast wagering the rest of the year. Admission varies.

RODEO   The **National Western Stock Show, Rodeo, and Horse Show** (𝄞 303/297-1166; www.nationalwestern.com) is held the second and third weeks of January. While a move to the plains near Denver International Airport is on the drawing board, the rodeo takes place at the Denver Coliseum, and other activities are at the National Western Complex and the Event Center. With more than $500,000 available in prize money and 700,000 people in attendance, this is one of the world's richest and largest rodeos.

SOCCER   The **Colorado Rapids** (𝄞 303/405-1100; www.coloradorapids.com), of Major League Soccer, play home games at Dick's Sporting Goods Park, a new, soccer-only stadium at Quebec Street and 60th Avenue in Commerce City.

If you're in Denver on foot, you'll find that most visitors do their shopping along the **16th Street Mall** (the mile-long pedestrian walkway between Market St. and Tremont Place) and adjacent areas, including **Larimer Square, The Shops at Tabor Center, Writer Square,** and the newest retail development downtown, **Denver Pavilions.**

Outside the downtown area there are more options, primarily the huge **Cherry Creek Shopping Center**—a shopper's dream—south of downtown. There are also numerous funky urban retail areas within the city limits, as well as suburban shopping malls.

Business hours vary from store to store and from mall to mall. Generally, stores are open 6 days a week, with many open on Sunday, too; department stores usually stay open until 9pm at least 1 evening a week. Discount stores and supermarkets are often open later than other stores, and some supermarkets are open 24 hours a day.

SHOPPING A TO Z
Antiques
Denver's main antiques area is **Antique Row** (www.antique-row.com) along **South Broadway,** between Mississippi and Iowa streets, with hundreds of dealers selling all sorts of fine antiques, collectibles, and junk. Wandering through the wide variety of stores, where each dealer has his or her own unique bent, is great fun. Just remember that prices are often negotiable; unless you're quite knowledgeable about antiques, it wouldn't hurt to do some comparison shopping before making a major purchase.

Art & Fine Crafts
The preeminent arts destination in Denver is the **ArtDistrict on Santa Fe.** In recent years, Santa Fe Drive has emerged as home to about 40 galleries and studios between 5th and 11th avenues. Most of the galleries are contemporary or Latin American and there is a popular First Friday Art Walk here from 6 to 9pm the first Friday of every month. For additional information, visit **www.artdistrictonsantafe.com.**

Also, the renaissance of Denver's lower downtown (LoDo) has resulted in the creation of the **Lower Downtown Arts District,** where you can explore a number of galleries. The district runs from Larimer to Wynkoop streets between 14th and 20th streets. Call *©* **303/628-5428** or browse **www.lodo.org** for additional information.

A mile to the southeast, the Golden Triangle neighborhood, bordered by Lincoln Street, Speer Boulevard, and Colfax Avenue, has more than 25 galleries and a number of museums. The **Golden Triangle Museum District** (*©* **303/534-0771;** www.gtmd.org) puts together an open gallery event the first Friday night of every month, complete with a free shuttle.

Andenken   Open weekends, this hip gallery shows the work of contemporary young artists working in every medium under the sun, usually outside the boundaries of tradition. 2990 Larimer St. *©* **303/941-2458.**

Camera Obscura (Finds)   This highly respected gallery exhibits vintage and contemporary photographs, including works by internationally renowned photographers. Closed Monday. 1309 Bannock St. *©* **303/623-4059.**

Dori Quilts & Lodge Furniture   This 10,000-square-foot gallery, which calls itself the largest quilt gallery in America, has some 3,000 to 5,000 handmade quilts on display at any given time. It also sells handmade red cedar log and dried cactus furniture and accessories. Colorado Mills Mall, 14500 W. Colfax Ave., Lakewood. © 303/590-1490.

Native American Trading Company   Older weavings, pottery, baskets, jewelry, and other American Indian works from the Rocky Mountain region are the focus at this fine gallery. It's located in a 1906 Mission Revival building across the street from the Denver Art Museum. Closed Monday. 213 W. 13th Ave. © 303/534-0771.

Pirate   Denver's oldest arts co-op, Pirate has showcased the work of cutting-edge contemporary artists of all kinds for more than 20 years. It's in a funky north Denver neighborhood with several eateries and a theater. 3655 Navajo St. © 303/458-6058.

Pismo Contemporary Art Glass   Nationally renowned glass artists, as well as emerging stars, are represented in this gallery, located in Cherry Creek North. 2770 E. 2nd Ave. © 303/333-2879.

Sandy Carson Gallery   Established regional artists are represented at this respected gallery in the arts district on Santa Fe Drive, which is known for showing contemporary works in traditional media. Closed Sunday and Monday. 760 Santa Fe Dr. © 303/573-8585.

Books

Barnes & Noble   This two-story location is in the Denver Pavilions retail area on the south side of downtown Denver. There's a particularly good travel section, where you'll find local and regional maps. 500 16th St. (in the Denver Pavilions). © 303/825-9166.

Mile High Comics Megastore (Kids)   One of five Mile High Comics locations in the Denver area, this is the largest comic-book store in the nation. Its 11,000 square feet are packed with comics of all descriptions, plus games, toys, posters, and other books. 9201 N. Washington St., Thornton (10 miles north of downtown Denver). © 303/457-2612.

Tattered Cover ★★   One of the country's largest bookstores, the locally beloved Tattered Cover moved to new digs on East Colfax Avenue in 2006 after more than 30 years in Cherry Creek. Taking over the old Lowenstein Theater, the store remains a bibliophile's paradise, with comprehensive selections on every subject and a design that incorporates elements of the old theater. Also in the development: Twist & Shout, Denver's top independent record store; an art-house movie theater with its own cocktail lounge; a restaurant, Encore; and a coffee shop. 2526 E. Colfax Ave. (opposite East High School). © 303/322-7727. www.tatteredcover.com. There are also locations at Denver's LoDo at 16th and Wynkoop sts. (© 303/436-1070) and in the Town Center development in Highlands Ranch (© 303/470-7050).

Fashion

Eddie Bauer   This is the place to come for good deals on the famous Eddie Bauer line of upscale outdoor clothing. This extralarge store features a wide variety of men's and women's fashions alongside outdoor-oriented gadgetry. 3000 E. Cherry Creek Ave. (in the Cherry Creek Mall). © 303/377-2100.

Lawrence Covell   This renowned upscale shop, established in 1967 by Lawrence and Cathy Covell, offers the finest men's and women's fashions, including designer clothing by Kiton, John Lobb, Etro, and Paul Smith. 225 Steele St. (in Cherry Creek N.). © 303/320-1023.

Rockmount Ranch Wear ★★   Founded in 1946 by Jack A. Weil—who is well into his 100s and still serves as CEO—Rockmount is one of the last real Western landmarks in town. The three-generation family business—which was the first company to put a snap on a shirt!—recently turned its landmark warehouse into a retail store, and it's even got a small museum of Western wear and memorabilia. The place sells hats, shirts, scarves, and everything else anyone might need to dud up like a cowboy or cowgirl. Rock bands and movie stars love the brand, and even stop by the store on a regular basis. 1626 Wazee St. ✆ 303/629-7777. www.rockmount.com.

Food & Drink

King Soopers, Safeway, and **Albertson's** are the main grocery-store chains.

Applejack Wine & Spirits (Value)   This huge store, which covers some 40,000 square feet and is one of America's largest beer, wine, and liquor supermarkets, offers some of the best prices in the area. It also delivers. The store has a wide choice of single-malt scotches; an extensive wine section, which includes a number of Colorado wines; and a good selection of cigars. 3320 Youngfield St. (in the Applewood Shopping Center), Wheat Ridge (I-70, exit 264). ✆ 303/233-3331.

Corks/Wine Complements   Side by side near Confluence Park, these two stores offer oenophiles a nice selection of reasonably priced bottles (Corks) and every wine gadget and edible wine accompaniment imaginable (Wine Complements). 1620 Platte St. ✆ 303/477-5799 or 303/480-9463.

The Market at Larimer Square   A combination deli/gourmet market/coffee shop right downtown, the Market is something of a community hub for all of downtown Denver. Its location on Larimer Square is ideal for people-watching and convenience. 1445 Larimer Sq. ✆ 303/534-5140.

Whole Foods   This enormous store helps perpetuate Coloradans' healthy lifestyles. No food sold here contains artificial flavoring or preservatives, nor was any grown using pesticides, chemicals, or other additives. There's sushi, a salad bar, and many to-go lunch and dinner offerings as well. This Cherry Creek–area store, part of the national chain, is one of several locations scattered throughout the metropolitan area. 2375 E. 1st Ave. (at University Blvd.). ✆ 720/941-4100.

Gifts & Souvenirs

Colorado History Museum Store   This museum shop carries unique made-in-Colorado gifts and souvenirs, including American Indian jewelry and sand paintings, plus an excellent selection of books on Colorado. 1300 Broadway. ✆ 303/866-4993.

Where the Buffalo Roam   Here you'll find the gamut of traditional Denver and Colorado souvenirs, from T-shirts to buttons to hats to mugs. 535 16th St. ✆ 303/260-7347.

Jewelry

Jeweler's Center at the University Building   Here you'll find about a dozen retail and wholesale outlets in what is billed as Denver's largest concentration of jewelers. 910 16th St. ✆ 303/534-6270.

John Atencio   A highly regarded Colorado artist, John Atencio has received several awards for his unique jewelry designs. Located on historic Larimer Square, his store offers 14- and 18-karat gold jewelry accented with high-quality stones, plus special collections such as "Elements," which features unusual combinations of gold, sterling silver, and stones. 1440 Larimer St. (on Larimer Sq.). ✆ 303/534-4277.

Malls & Shopping Centers

Cherry Creek Shopping Center   Saks Fifth Avenue, Neiman Marcus, and Nordstrom anchor this deluxe million-square-foot mall, with more than 160 shops, restaurants, and services, including an eight-screen movie theater. Across the street is Cherry Creek North, an upscale retail neighborhood. The mall is open Monday through Friday from 10am to 9pm, Saturday from 10am to 8pm, and Sunday from 11am to 6pm. 3000 E. 1st Ave. (between University Blvd. and Steele St.). ✆ 303/388-3900.

Colorado Mills   This relatively new mall, on the western fringe of metro Denver, has over 200 stores and outlet centers, as well as theaters, restaurants, and a skatepark. Stores include Super Target, Eddie Bauer Outlet, and Sports Authority. I-70 and W. Colfax Ave., Lakewood. ✆ 303/384-3000.

Denver Pavilions   Located on the southern end of the 16th Street Mall, this three-level complex jammed with entertainment and dining options features Denver's Hard Rock Cafe, a movie-plex, Niketown, a bowling alley, Virgin Records, and Barnes & Noble megastores (see "Books," above). Store hours are Monday to Saturday from 10am to 9pm and Sunday from 11am to 6pm; the restaurants and movie theaters are open later. 500 16th St. (between Welton and Tremont sts.). ✆ 303/260-6000.

Larimer Square   This restored quarter of old Denver (see "More Attractions," earlier in this chapter) includes numerous art galleries, boutiques, restaurants, and nightclubs. Most shops are open Monday through Thursday from 10am to 7pm, Friday and Saturday from 10am to 6pm, and Sunday from noon to 5pm. Restaurant and nightclub hours vary, and hours are slightly shorter during the winter. 1400 block of Larimer St. ✆ 303/534-2367.

Mile High Flea Market   Just 10 minutes northeast of downtown Denver, this huge market attracts more than 1.5 million shoppers a year to 2,000 vendors on more than 80 paved acres. Besides closeouts, garage sales, and seasonal merchandise, it has more than a dozen places to eat and snack, plus family rides. It's open year-round on Friday, Saturday, and Sunday from 7am to 5pm. Admission is $2 Friday, $3 Saturday and Sunday, and always free for children under 12. 7007 E. 88th Ave. (at I-76), Henderson. ✆ 303/289-4656.

The Outlets at Castle Rock   This outlet mall between Denver and Colorado Springs, about 30 minutes south of Denver, has about 100 stores, including Levi's/Dockers, Van Heusen, Eddie Bauer, Bass, Nike, Big Dog, Gap, Borders, and Coleman, plus a food court. Open Monday through Saturday from 10am to 8pm and Sunday from 11am to 6pm. I-25, exit 184. ✆ 303/688-4494.

Park Meadows Retail Resort   Located at the C-470/I-25 interchange south of Denver, this is the largest shopping center in Colorado, and now the heart of a mind-boggling retail area. Very posh and upscale—the interior is reminiscent of a luxurious mountain lodge—Park Meadows features Nordstrom, Dillard's, Macy's, and 160 specialty shops and restaurants. Stores are open Monday through Saturday from 10am to 9pm, Sunday from 11am to 6pm. 8401 Park Meadows Center Dr. (south of C-470 on Yosemite St.), Littleton. ✆ 303/792-2533.

Sporting Goods

Those in need of a bike should talk to the experts at **Campus Cycles,** 2102 S. Washington St. (✆ 303/698-2811), which carries the Gary Fisher, Trek, and Giant brands. Sports fans looking for that Rockies cap or Broncos shirt will have no trouble finding it at the appropriately named **Sportsfan,** 1962 Blake St., across from Coors Field (✆ 303/295-3460). There are several other locations in the Denver area, and mail orders are accepted.

For information on where to rent sporting-goods equipment, see the "Outdoor Activities" section, earlier in this chapter.

REI ★★   Although the Seattle-based co-op has several stores in the metro area, its flag-ship store, a beautifully restored redbrick just west of downtown, is one of the country's best and biggest outdoor-oriented retailers. (It is one of only three flagship stores; the others are in Seattle and the Minneapolis area.) This is the place to go before heading for an excursion in the Rockies. The gargantuan store features a 45-foot climbing wall, an outdoor bike-testing area, a kayaking area on adjacent Cherry Creek, and a "cold room" to try out outerwear and sleeping bags. 1416 Platte St. ✆ 303/756-3100.

Sports Authority Sportscastle   Active travelers will be pleased to discover that Denver has sporting-goods stores that match the scale of the outdoor opportunities in Colorado—namely, this five-story monster. With everything from footballs to golf clubs to tents, the selection is comprehensive. Extras include a driving cage for golfers, ball courts on the roof, and the annual Sniagrab (that's *bargains* spelled backward), featuring rock-bottom prices on ski equipment every Labor Day weekend. 1000 Broadway. ✆ 303/863-2260.

Toys & Hobbies

Caboose Hobbies   Model-train buffs should plan to spend at least half a day here. Billed as the world's largest train store, it stocks electric trains, accessories, books, and so much train-related stuff (over 100,000 items on nearly 20,000 square feet of floor space) that it's hard to know where to start. The knowledgeable employees seem just as happy to talk about trains as to sell them. Naturally, there are model trains of every scale winding through the store, as well as test tracks so that you can check out a locomotive before purchasing it. There are also mugs, patches, and decals from just about every railroad line that ever existed in North America. 500 S. Broadway. ✆ 303/777-6766. www.caboosehobbies.com.

Wizard's Chest (Kids)   This store's magical design—a castle with drawbridge and moat—and legendary wizard out front are worth the trip alone, but be sure to go inside. The Wizard's Chest is paradise for kids of all ages, specializing in games, toys, and puzzles. The costume department is fully stocked with attire, wigs, masks, and professional makeup. 230 Fillmore St. in Cherry Creek N. ✆ 303/321-4304. www.wizardschest.com.

8 DENVER AFTER DARK

The anchor of Denver's performing arts scene, an important part of this increasingly sophisticated city, is the 4-square-block **Denver Performing Arts Complex,** located downtown just a few blocks from major hotels. The complex houses nine theaters, a concert hall, and what may be the nation's first symphony hall in the round. It is home to the Colorado Symphony, Colorado Ballet, Opera Colorado, and Denver Center for the Performing Arts (an umbrella organization for resident and touring theater companies). In all, Denver has some 30 theaters, more than 100 cinemas, and dozens of concert halls, nightclubs, discos, and bars. Clubs offer country-and-western music, jazz, rock, and comedy.

Current entertainment listings appear in special Friday-morning sections of the two daily newspapers, the *Denver Post* and *Rocky Mountain News. Westword,* a weekly newspaper distributed free throughout the city every Wednesday evening, has perhaps the best listings: It focuses on the arts, entertainment, and local politics.

You can get tickets for nearly all major entertainment and sporting events from **Ticketmaster** (✆ 303/830-TIXS [8497]), which has several outlets in the Denver area.

Rock, Jazz & Blues

Bluebird Theater   This historic theater, built in 1913 to show silent movies, has been restored and now offers a diverse selection of rock, alternative, and other live music, as well as films. The performers generally target teens and 20-somethings. Tickets usually run $7 to $20. 3317 E. Colfax Ave. (at Adams St.). *Ⓒ* **303/377-1666.** www.bluebirdtheater.net.

The Church   Located just a few blocks southeast of downtown, this cavernous and historic former church features three dance floors and several bars, including wine and sushi bars. One of Denver's most popular dance clubs, it attracts celebrity DJs and a throng of beautiful people on a regular basis. The semireligious decor and diverse crowd, in conjunction with the loud music, make for near sensory overload. 1160 Lincoln St. *Ⓒ* **303/832-3528.** www.the-church.com.

El Chapultepec   Denver's oldest jazz club, the "Pec" offers live jazz nightly in a noisy, friendly atmosphere. You'll often find standing-room only, not to mention a hearty helping of local color—young and old, poor and rich, in equal measure. A small burrito kitchen and poolroom adjoin the club. There is never a cover. 1962 Market St. *Ⓒ* **303/295-9126.**

Gothic Theatre   One of metro Denver's best-looking (and best-sounding) midsize venues, the Gothic is light-years beyond the heavy-metal dive it was in the 1980s. Both local and national acts play the stage here. Tickets usually cost $7 to $30. 3263 S. Broadway, Englewood. *Ⓒ* **303/788-0984.** www.gothictheatre.com.

hi-dive   A standout for indie rock and experimental music, the hi-dive is popular with young and in-the-know hipsters and features an adjoining no-cover bar, **Sputnik,** with a kitchen in the back. 7 S. Broadway. *Ⓒ* **303/570-4500.** www.hi-dive.com.

Larimer Lounge   This bar on old Larimer Street has been serving drinks since 1892 and serving loud punk rock and alternative music since 2003. The place is out of the hustle and bustle of LoDo, in an old neighborhood east of Broadway, and has seen such national acts as the Arcade Fire and Mudhoney take the stage. The average patron is young, tattooed, and a bit rough around the edges. 2721 Larimer St. *Ⓒ* **303/291-1007.** www. larimerlounge.com.

Mercury Cafe   It's hard to classify the Mercury as specializing in any genre of music, but there's always something exciting happening, even on poetry night. It attracts a casual, eclectic clientele. Offerings usually range from tango lessons to avant-garde jazz to classical violin to tarot readings to progressive rock. A healthful-oriented restaurant is also here. 2199 California St. (at 22nd St.). *Ⓒ* **303/294-9258.** www.mercurycafe.com.

3 Kings Tavern   A relatively new venue in the Baker neighborhood, 3 Kings offers a hip vibe and interesting decor (Elvis paraphernalia, pop culture bric-a-brac, comic-book wallpapering, and a big "Sanatorium" sign above the bar) to go with the touring and local rockabilly, punk, metal, and country acts that grace the stage. 60 S. Broadway. *Ⓒ* **303/777-7352.** www.3kingstavern.com.

Country Music

Grizzly Rose   Known to locals as "the Griz" or "the Rose," its 5,000-square-foot dance floor beneath a 1-acre roof has drawn such national acts as Garth Brooks, Willie Nelson, LeAnn Rimes, and Johnny Paycheck. There's live music Tuesday through Saturday; Sunday is family night. Dance lessons are available Wednesday night. 5450 N. Valley Hwy., at I-25, exit 215. *Ⓒ* **303/295-1330.**

Stampede This colossal nightclub offers free country-western dance lessons on Friday and Saturday, a huge solid-oak dance floor, pool tables, a restaurant, and seven bars. Its Wednesday ladies' nights are notoriously rowdy. Closed Sunday through Tuesday. 2430 S. Havana St. (at Parker Rd.), Aurora. ☎ **303/696-7686.** www.stampedeclub.net.

The Bar Scene

The first permanent structure on the site of modern Denver was supposedly a saloon, and the city has built on that tradition ever since. Today, there are sports bars, dance bars, lots of brewpubs, outdoor cafe bars, English pubs, Old West saloons, city-overlook bars, Art Deco bars, gay bars, and a few bars we don't want to discuss here.

Appropriately, the newest Denver "in" spot for barhopping is also the oldest part of the city—LoDo—which has been renovated and upgraded, and now attracts all the young partiers and upwardly mobile professionals. Its trendy nightspots are often noisy and crowded, but if you're looking for action, this is where you'll find it.

Other popular "strips" are along Broadway (centered on 10th and Ellsworth aves., respectively), and along East Colfax Avenue from about Ogden to Monroe streets.

> ### Bottoms Up!
>
> More beer is brewed in metropolitan Denver than in any other city in the United States

For those who prefer caffeine to alcohol, there are also a number of good coffee bars throughout downtown Denver, as well as in the Capitol Hill and Uptown neighborhoods.

The following are among the popular bars and pubs, but there are plenty more, so be sure to check out the publications mentioned at the beginning of this section.

Bull & Bush Pub & Brewery A neighborhood hangout in Cherry Creek, this recreation of a famous London pub always has about 10 of its own award-winning beers on tap. On Sunday evening, there's traditional jazz by regional groups. A full brew-house menu is available. 4700 Cherry Creek Dr. S., Glendale. ☎ **303/759-0333.** www.bullandbush.com.

Charlie Brown's Just south of downtown, Charlie Brown's is a piano bar, some version of which has been in existence since 1927. The atmosphere is casual, with a baby grand piano and a diverse crowd. The grill serves three meals a day, inside and outside on a great patio. 980 Grant St. (at 10th Ave.). ☎ **303/860-1655.**

Churchill Bar You'll find an excellent selection of fine cigars, single-malt Scotches, and after-dinner drinks at this refined lounge, which caters to older, well-to-do professional types. In the Brown Palace Hotel, 321 17th St. ☎ **303/297-3111.**

Cruise Room Bar Modeled after a 1930s-era bar aboard the *Queen Mary,* the Cruise Room opened in 1933 on the day Prohibition ended. Restored to its Art Deco best, the very red room features decorative panels depicting toasts around the world and mixes one of the best martinis in town. In the Oxford Hotel, 1600 17th St. (at Wazee St.). ☎ **303/825-1107.**

Falling Rock Tap House Comfy, woody, and just down the street from Coors Field, this LoDo pub has 69 beers on tap—the best selection of good beer in Denver. You'll also find darts and pool, happy hours, and occasional live music. 1919 Blake St. ☎ **303/293-8338.** www.fallingrocktaphouse.com.

(Finds) **Brewery Tours**

Whether or not you drink beer, it can be fun to look behind the scenes and see how beer is made. Denver's first modern microbrewery, the **Wynkoop Brewing Co.,** 1634 18th St., at Wynkoop Street (℃ **303/297-2700;** www.wynkoop. com), offers tours every Saturday between 1 and 5pm. Housed in the renovated 1898 J. S. Brown Mercantile Building across from Union Station, the Wynkoop is also a popular restaurant (see "Where to Dine," in chapter 5). At least 10 beers are always on tap, including a few exotic recipes—the spicy chile beer is my favorite. If you can't decide which one to try, the "taster set" provides a nice sampling: nine 4-ounce glasses of different brews. For non–beer drinkers, the Wynkoop offers some of the best root beer in town. On the second floor is a top-notch pool hall with billiards, snooker, and darts.

Also downtown, **Great Divide Brewing Co.,** 2201 Arapahoe St. (℃ **303/296-9460, ext. 26;** www.greatdivide.com), has a terrific taproom and free samples. Tours are offered Monday through Friday at 3pm and on the hour on Saturdays from 2 to 7pm. Great Divide is known for being a beer-lover's brewery, crafting such favorites as the rice-based Samurai and the aptly named Yeti Imperial Stout.

Since it opened in 1991, **Rock Bottom Brewery,** 1001 16th St. (℃ **303/534-7616;** www.rockbottom.com), has been one of the leading brewpubs in the area. Tours, which are given upon request, offer great views of the brewing process, plus a sampling of the product.

A mile south of downtown, **Breckenridge Brewery,** 471 Kalamath St. (℃ **303/623-BREW [2739];** www.breckenridgebrewery.com) also lets you see the brewing process. Free brewery tours are given by appointment. In addition to its award-winning ales, the brewery serves traditional pub fare.

East of downtown in the Uptown neighborhood, the same folks behind Mountain Sun in Boulder opened **Vine Street Pub & Brewery** in 2008; it's at 1700 Vine St. (℃ **303/388-2337**) and has a fun and funky neighborhood vibe with a healthful bent to its menu. In Cherry Creek, **Bull & Bush Pub & Brewery,** 4700 Cherry Creek Dr. S. (℃ **303/759-0333;** www.bullandbush.com), produces about 10 handcrafted ales and will give tours of its facilities upon request.

For a look at the other side of the coin, take a trip to nearby Golden for a look at **Coors,** one of the world's largest breweries (see "A Side Trip to Colorado's Gold Circle Towns," below).

JR's   A cavernous gay bar with a little bit of country, JR's is centered on a horseshoe-shaped bar and known for its drink specials and busy dance floor. 777 E. 17th Ave. ℃ 303/831-0459. www.myjrs.com.

Meadowlark   This dim, hip subterranean bar oozes style, featuring plenty of industrial chic, great margaritas and other mixed drinks, and an eclectic music calendar both live and prerecorded. 2721 Larimer St. ℃ 303/293-0251.

My Brother's Bar A Platte Valley fixture since the Beat Generation (this was one of **111** Jack Kerouac's favorite Denver hangouts), this is the locals' choice for big, juicy burgers, wrapped in wax paper and served with an array of condiments and a side helping of friendly, unpretentious vibes. 2376 15th St. ☎ **303/455-9991.**

Old Curtis Street Bar A classic family-owned bar, complete with vinyl booths and a Mexican menu, Old Curtis Street is my pick for a low-key evening downtown. There is an eclectic entertainment calendar featuring punk bands, DJs, and stand-up comedy nights. 2100 Curtis St. ☎ **303/292-2083.** www.oldcurtis.com.

Samba Room The atmosphere at the Samba Room—Cuban murals, booming Latin music, a fashionable young clientele—is right up there with Denver's flashiest nightclubs. The menu of Latin-Caribbean fusion, albeit a bit pricey and uneven, adds to the theme. 1460 Larimer St. ☎ **720/956-1701.**

Sing Sing A noisy, eclectic crowd dominates the scene at this LoDo hot spot, located beneath the Denver ChopHouse & Brewery (see "Where to Dine," in chapter 5). You'll often find low-priced beer specials, which encourage the hard-partying college types to sing along (loudly and badly) with the dueling pianos. A fun place, but hang on tight. Closed Sunday. 1735 19th St. ☎ **303/291-0880.** www.singsing.com.

Wynkoop Brewing Company Owned by Denver Mayor John Hickenlooper, Denver's first modern brewpub is still the city's best. Among its most interesting offerings are India pale ale, chile beer, and Scotch ale, but you really can't go wrong with any of the selections. Added attractions: a large upstairs pool hall, which generally draws a more party-hearty crowd than the restaurant and bar, and an improv and comedy theater in the basement. 1634 18th St. (at Wynkoop St.). ☎ **303/297-2700.** www.wynkoop.com.

THE PERFORMING ARTS
Classical Music & Opera
Colorado Symphony Orchestra This international-caliber orchestra performs more than 100 classical, pops, and family concerts each year at locations throughout the metropolitan area, mostly at the Denver Center for the Performing Arts. Most tickets run $20 to $80. 1000 14th St., #15. ☎ **303/623-7876.** www.coloradosymphony.org.

Opera Colorado Every season, the company stages three operas (four performances each), with English supertitles, at the stunning Ellie Caulkins Opera House at the Denver Performing Arts Complex. Internationally renowned singers and local favorites sing the lead roles. The typical schedule is three evening performances and one matinee each week from February to May. Tickets usually cost $30 to $125. 695 S. Colorado Blvd., #20. ☎ **303/357-2787** for tickets or 303/778-1500. www.operacolorado.org.

Theater & Comedy
Buntport Theater Injecting a fresh dose of creativity and zaniness into the Denver theater scene, the Buntport plays host to a number of original productions and adaptations (including "live sit-coms") as well as improv and open mics at its black-box–style theater south of downtown. 717 Lipan St. ☎ **720/946-1388.** www.buntport.com.

Comedy Works Considered one of the region's top comedy clubs for more than 20 years, this is your best bet for seeing America's hot comics at work—Bob Saget and *Last Comic Standing* winner (and Denver local) Josh Blue recently took the stage. Admission is $7 to $10 on weekdays, more on weekends and for marquee performers. A second

Comedy Works opened at Belleview and I-25 in the Denver Tech Center. 1226 15th St. (C) 303/595-3637. www.comedyworks.com.

Denver Center for the Performing Arts   An umbrella organization for resident and touring theater, youth outreach, and conservatory training, the DCPA includes the **Denver Center Theatre Company,** the largest professional resident theater company in the Rockies. With 40 artists on its payroll, the troupe performs about 10 plays in repertory from October to June, including classical and contemporary dramas, musicals, and premieres of new plays. Tickets cost roughly $30 to $60. **Denver Center Attractions** brings in more than 10 touring Broadway productions annually. Tickets run $25 to $80. For both companies, many shows sell out well in advance. 14th and Curtis sts. (C) 800/641-1222 or 303/893-4100. www.denvercenter.org.

Denver Civic Theatre   A restored 1921 gem, the Denver Civic Theatre is a new outlet for touring productions, typically a bit edgy. Tickets usually cost $30 to $50. 721 Santa Fe Dr. (C) 303/309-3773. www.denvercivic.com.

El Centro Su Teatro   A Hispanic theater and cultural center, El Centro presents bilingual productions on a regular basis. Tickets cost $10 to $20. 4725 High St. (C) 303/296-0219. www.suteatro.org.

Lannie's Clocktower Cabaret   In the basement of the landmark D&F Tower on the 16th Street Mall, Lannie's is a funky bordello-inspired theater that sees a wide variety of entertainers on its stage, including hostess/singer Lannie Garrett (known for her portrayal of "Patsy DeCline") as well as burlesque, comedy, and music. In the D&F Tower, 1601 Arapahoe St. (C) 303/293-0075. www.lannies.com.

Dance
Cleo Parker Robinson Dance   A highly acclaimed multicultural modern-dance ensemble and school, the Cleo Parker Robinson group performs a varied selection of programs each year, both on tour around the world and at several Denver locations. Tickets usually run $20 to $35. 119 Park Ave. W. (C) 303/295-1759. www.cleoparkerdance.org.

Colorado Ballet   The state's premier professional resident ballet company performs at the Ellie Caulkins Opera House and other venues. The company presents five productions during its fall-through-spring season—a balance of classical and contemporary works that always includes *The Nutcracker* at Christmastime. Tickets range from $25 to $150. 1278 Lincoln St. (C) 303/837-8888. www.coloradoballet.org.

MAJOR CONCERT HALLS & AUDITORIUMS
Arvada Center for the Arts & Humanities   This multidisciplinary arts center is in use almost every day of the year for performances by internationally known artists and its own theater companies, its historical museum and art gallery exhibitions, and its hands-on education programs for all ages. In addition, the children's theater program performs in front of an annual audience of 60,000. A new, fully accessible playground features a 343-foot sea creature by the name of Squiggles. 6901 Wadsworth Blvd., Arvada (2¹/₂ miles north of I-70). (C) 720/898-7200. www.arvadacenter.org.

Denver Performing Arts Complex   Covering 4 square downtown blocks, from Speer Boulevard to 14th Street and Champa to Arapahoe streets, the Center for the Performing Arts (called the "Plex" by locals) is impressive even to those not attending a performance. Its numerous theaters seat from 157 to 2,800, and there's also a restaurant. 14th and Curtis sts. (C) 800/641-1222 or 303/893-4100. www.denvercenter.org.

Fiddler's Green Amphitheatre   The alfresco summer concerts here feature national and international stars of rock, jazz, classical, and country music. The amphitheater has about 6,500 reserved seats and room for 10,000 more on its spacious lawn. Located in the southwestern section of the metropolitan area, just west of I-25 between Arapahoe and Orchard roads, it's open from May to September. The surrounding streets are a gallery for the Museum of Outdoor Arts featuring numerous characters from *Alice in Wonderland.* 6350 Greenwood Plaza Blvd., Englewood. ✆ 303/220-7000.

Fillmore Auditorium   The 3,600-seat Fillmore is the former Mammoth Gardens, which was renovated by proprietors of the legendary Fillmore in San Francisco. The slickly remodeled venue is now one of Denver's best, loaded with bars and countless vintage rock photos. It attracts national rock acts from Ween to Bob Dylan. Tickets generally cost $20 to $100. 1510 Clarkson St. ✆ 303/837-0360. www.fillmoreauditorium.com.

Paramount Theatre   A performing-arts center since 1929, this restored 2,000-seat downtown theater is a wonderful place to enjoy jazz, pop, and folk performances, as well as comedy, lectures, and theater. Recent bookings have included Foreigner and Chelsea Handler. 1621 Glenarm Place. ✆ 303/623-0106. www.paramountdenver.com.

Red Rocks Amphitheatre ★★★   Quite possibly the country's best and most beautiful venue for top-name outdoor summer concerts, Red Rocks is in the foothills of the Rocky Mountains, 15 miles southwest of the city. Four-hundred-foot-high red sandstone rocks flank the 9,000-seat amphitheater, a product of the Civilian Conservation Corps. At night, with the lights of Denver spread across the horizon, the atmosphere is magical. The Beatles performed here, as have Jimi Hendrix, Paul Simon, the Grateful Dead, Sting, Bonnie Raitt, Lyle Lovett, Willie Nelson, and top symphony orchestras from around the world. The venue has a sparkling new **visitor center** at the amphitheater's apex, which affords amazing views and displays detailing the varied performances that have taken place here since it opened in 1941. There's also a restaurant, a network of hiking trails, and the **trading post,** carrying a good selection of American-Indian jewelry and pottery, plus a variety of other curios and souvenirs. I-70, exit 259 S., 16351 County Rd. 93, Morrison. ✆ 720/865-2494. www.redrocksonline.com.

9 A SIDE TRIP TO COLORADO'S GOLD CIRCLE TOWNS

Golden, Idaho Springs, and **Georgetown** make up most of the fabled Gold Circle—those towns that boomed with the first strikes of the gold rush in 1859. Central City, once the richest of the four towns but now the least attractive, completes the circle. Central City is trying to relive its glory days with a return to gambling, largely supported by locals from Denver, and although the exteriors of its historic buildings remain appealing, the rows of electronic slot machines and other gambling devices inside are a turnoff. Visitors to the area might like to make a brief stop and then move on to Idaho Springs.

GOLDEN ★★

Golden, 15 miles west of downtown Denver by way of U.S. 6 or Colo. 58 off I-70, is better known for the Coors Brewery (founded in 1873) and the Colorado School of Mines (established in 1874) than for its years as territorial capital. For tourist information, contact the **Greater Golden Area Chamber of Commerce,** 1010 Washington Ave., Golden, CO 80402 (℃ **303/279-3113;** www.goldencochamber.org).

What to See & Do

Historic downtown Golden centers on the **Territorial Capitol** in the **Loveland Building,** 12th Street and Washington Avenue. Built in 1861, it housed the first state legislature from 1862 to 1867, when the capital was moved to Denver. Today it contains offices and a restaurant. The **Armory,** 13th and Arapahoe streets, is probably the largest cobblestone structure in the United States; 3,300 wagonloads of stone and quartz went into its construction. **The Rock Flour Mill Warehouse,** 8th and Cheyenne streets, dates from 1863; it was built with red granite from nearby Golden Gate Canyon and still has its original cedar beams and wooden floors.

In addition to the attractions listed below, see the section on Golden Gate State Park, in the Denver "Outdoor Activities" section, and RipBoard, in the "Boating" section, earlier in this chapter.

Astor House Museum   This handsome native stone structure, believed to be the first stone hotel built west of the Mississippi River, was constructed in 1867 to house legislators when Golden was the territorial capital. Scheduled for demolition to make space for a parking lot, the Astor House was instead restored in the 1970s and is now listed on the National Register of Historic Places. Today the Western-style Victorian hotel offers glimpses into life in Golden during the town's heyday in the late 19th century. Allow 30 to 60 minutes. While there, you can obtain a walking-tour guide for the 12th Street Historic District or visit the Victorian Gift Shop, whose proceeds benefit the museum.

822 12th St. ℃ **303/278-3557.** www.astorhousemuseum.org. Admission $3 adults ($4.50 for combo ticket that also includes Clear Creek History Park), $2 children under 13 ($3 combo ticket). Tues–Sat 10am–4:30pm; June–Aug also Sun 11am–3pm.

Boettcher Mansion   This historic Jefferson County estate was built by Charles Boettcher in 1917 as a summer home and hunting lodge. It contains displays of furnishings and other items from the American Arts and Crafts period of the late 1800s and early 1900s. Other exhibits explore the history of Golden and the Boettcher family. Allow 1 hour.

900 Colorow Rd. (on Lookout Mountain). ℃ **720/497-7630.** http://jeffco.us/boettcher/index.htm. Free admission, donations accepted. Mon–Fri 8am–4pm, or by appointment.

Bradford Washburn American Mountaineering Museum   Named for pioneering mountaineer and cartographer Bradford Washburn, this museum, which opened in 2008, takes on the daunting task of telling the story of conquering the world's toughest mountains in an indoor facility and does a remarkable job of keeping the epic scale. Exhibits cover mountain and rock-climbing history, technique, and technology, and showcase the contributions of the legends of the sport. The scale model of Mount Everest is a highlight. Allow 1 hour.

710 10th St. ℃ **303/996-2755.** www.bwamm.org. Admission $6.50 adults, $4.50 children. Tues–Sat 10am–6pm (Thurs until 7pm).

Buffalo Bill Museum & Grave ★ (**Kids**)   William Frederick "Buffalo Bill" Cody, the famous Western scout, is buried atop Lookout Mountain, south of Golden. (Some folks claim that friends stole Cody's body after his sister sold it to the City of Denver and the *Denver Post,* hightailed it north, and buried it in Wyoming, but I was assured that this

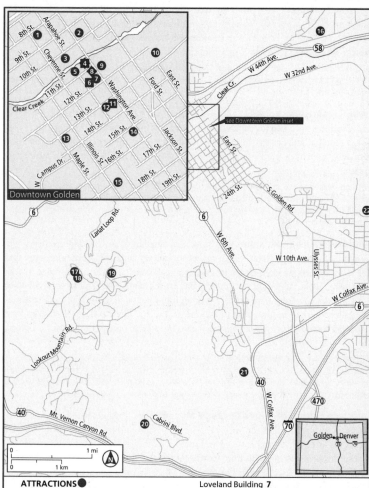

Downtown Golden

see Downtown Golden inset

Golden • Denver

ATTRACTIONS ●
Armory **12**
Astor House Museum **7**
Boettcher Mansion **17**
Bradford Washburn American
  Mountaineering Museum **2**
Buffalo Bill Museum & Grave **19**
Clear Creek History Park **5**
Colorado Railroad Museum **16**
Colorado School of Mines
  Geology Museum **13**
Coors Brewing Company **10**
Foothills Art Center **14**
Golden Pioneer Museum **3**
Heritage Square **21**
Lookout Mountain Nature Center **18**

Loveland Building **7**
Mother Cabrini Shrine **20**
National Earthquake Information Center **15**
National Renewable Energy Laboratory
  Visitor Center **22**
Rock Flour Mill Warehouse **1**
Rocky Mountain Quilt Museum **9**

ACCOMMODATIONS ■
Golden Hotel **4**
La Quinta Inn–Golden **6**
Table Mountain Inn **11**

DINING ◆
The Bridgewater Grill **4**
Old Capitol Grill **8**

was the real McCoy.) The museum contains memorabilia from the life and legend of Buffalo Bill, who rode for the Pony Express, organized buffalo hunts for foreign royalty, and toured the world with his Wild West Show. There are also displays of American Indian artifacts, guns, and Western art; an observation deck provides a great view of Denver. The museum is in 66-acre **Lookout Mountain Park,** a Denver municipal park popular for picnicking. Allow 1 to 1¹/₂ hours.

987¹/₂ Lookout Mountain Rd. (C) 303/526-0747. www.buffalobill.org. Admission $3 adults, $2 seniors, $1 children 6–15, free for children under 6. May–Oct daily 9am–5pm; Nov–Apr Tues–Sun 9am–4pm. Closed Dec 25. I-70, exit 256.

Clear Creek History Park   This 3-acre creekside park illustrates the history of the area's ranching, with two log cabins, several animal barns, a blacksmith's shop, and a one-room schoolhouse from the 1870s. The buildings were moved to this site to save them from development in nearby Golden Gate Canyon, their original location. Allow about an hour.

11th and Arapahoe sts. in downtown Golden. (C) **303/278-3557.** www.clearcreekhistorypark.org. Admission $3 adults ($4.50 for combo ticket that also includes the Astor House Museum), $2 children under 13 ($3 combo ticket). June–Aug Tues–Sat 10am–4:30pm, Sun 1–4pm; May and Sept Sat 10am–4:30pm. Closed Oct–Apr.

Colorado Railroad Museum ★   Housed in a replica of an 1880 railroad depot, this museum 2 miles east of Golden is a must-see for railroad buffs. On display are more than 100 narrow- and standard-gauge locomotives, cabooses, and cars, plus other historic equipment, artifacts, photos, documents, and model trains. The exhibits cover 12 acres, including the two-story depot and a working roundhouse. You can climb into many of the old locomotives and wander through the parlor cars. The excellent gift-and-souvenir shop sells hundreds of railroad-related items, from coffee mugs to posters to T-shirts. Allow 1 to 2 hours.

17155 W. 44th Ave. (C) **800/365-6263** or 303/279-4591. www.coloradorailroadmuseum.org. Admission $8 adults, $7 seniors over 60, $5 children under 16, free for children under 2, $18 families. Open daily 9am–5pm. Closed Jan 1, Thanksgiving, and Dec 25. Follow signs from I-70, exit 265, westbound; exit 266, eastbound.

Colorado School of Mines Geology Museum ★   Exhibits here help explain the history of mining in Colorado with a replica of a uranium mine and other displays. On exhibit are some 50,000 minerals, gems, fossils, and artifacts from around the world, plus displays on geology, earth history, and paleontology. The Colorado School of Mines, founded in 1874, has an enrollment of about 3,000. Allow 1 hour.

13th and Maple sts. (C) **303/273-3815** or 303/273-3823. Free admission. School year Mon–Sat 9am–4pm, Sun 1–4pm; summer Mon–Sat 9am–4pm. Closed Colorado School of Mines holidays.

Coors Brewing Company   Reputedly the world's largest single-site brewery, this facility produces 1.5 million gallons of beer each day. Coors conducts free public tours, followed by free samples of the various beers produced. The entire presentation lasts about 1¹/₂ hours. Tours leave a central parking lot at 13th and Ford streets, where visitors board a bus for a short drive through historic Golden before arriving at the brewery. There, a 30-minute prerecorded walking tour covers the history of the Coors family and company, the barley malting process, the 13,640-gallon gleaming copper kettles, and the entire production process all the way to packaging. Children are welcome, and arrangements can be made for visitors with disabilities. There's also a gift shop and an interactive timeline in the reception area. Allow about 2 hours—unless you take the "short tour"

which actually skips the tour altogether and heads straight to the hospitality lounge.
Note: Visitors under 18 must be accompanied by an adult.

13th and Ford sts. ☎ **866/812-2337** or 303/277-2337. www.coors.com. Free admission. Tours Thurs–Sat and Mon 10am–4pm; Sun noon–4pm. Closed Tues, Wed, and holidays. Visitors under 18 must be accompanied by an adult.

Foothills Art Center   Housed in an 1872 Gothic-style Presbyterian church (which is on the National Register of Historic Places), this exhibition center evolved from the annual Golden Sidewalk Art Show and features changing national and regional exhibits. A gift shop sells crafts by local artisans. Allow 30 minutes.

809 15th St. ☎ **303/279-3922.** www.foothillsartcenter.org. Admission $5 adults, $3 seniors. Mon–Sat 10am–5pm; Sun 1–5pm.

Golden Pioneer Museum   This museum exhibits an impressive collection of furniture, household articles, photographs, and other items, including a re-created 19th-century parlor and boudoir. Especially impressive is its collection of 200 American-Indian dolls, representing 39 different groups from all around North America. There are also a genealogical and historic research library and a gift shop. Allow 1 hour.

923 10th St. ☎ **303/278-7151.** www.goldenpioneermuseum.com. Admission $3 adults, $2 seniors and children 6–18, free for children under 6, $10 families. Mon–Sat 10am–4:30pm. Closed major holidays.

Heritage Square (Kids   A family-oriented shopping, dining, and entertainment village with a Wild West theme, Heritage Square features some Victorian specialty shops, a Ferris wheel, a stocked fishing pond, and a dinner theater. Warm-weather activities include go-carts, bumper boats, and a 2,350-foot alpine slide with bobsled-style carts. Heritage Square Music Hall offers shows for adults and children, and there's a nostalgic ice-cream parlor. Allow 1 to 2 hours.

18301 Colfax Ave. (U.S. 40). ☎ **303/279-2789.** www.heritagesquare.info. Free admission; separate charges for individual activities. Memorial Day to Labor Day Mon–Sat 10am–8pm, Sun noon–8pm; rest of year Mon–Sat 10am–6pm, Sun noon–6pm. I-70, exit 259.

Lookout Mountain Nature Center (Kids   A 1.5-mile self-guided nature trail winds through this 110-acre preserve among ponderosa pines and pretty mountain meadows. A free trail guide is available at the Nature Center when it's open, and a map is on display at a kiosk for those walking the trail at other times. The nonprofit Nature Center has displays on the pine beetle, pollination, and Colorado wildlife, plus an interactive exhibit on the ponderosa pine forest. The building is also worth a look—it's constructed of used and recycled materials such as ground-up plastic soda containers and the pulp of aspen trees. The center schedules free naturalist-guided environmental education activities year-round. Topics vary, but could include the flowers, butterflies, or wildlife of the area, or a look at the night sky. Advance registration is required for most programs, and age restrictions may apply. Call for details. Allow at least 1 hour.

910 Colorow Rd. (on Lookout Mountain). ☎ **720/497-7600.** Free admission. Trail daily 8am–dusk; Nature Center Tues–Sun 10am–4pm; also open 9am–5pm Sat–Sun in winter.

Mother Cabrini Shrine   A 22-foot statue of Jesus stands at the top of a 373-step stairway adorned by carvings representing the stations of the cross and mysteries of the rosary. Terra-cotta benches provide rest stops along the way. The shrine is dedicated to the country's first citizen saint, St. Frances Xavier Cabrini, who founded the Order of the Missionary Sisters of the Sacred Heart. The order has a convent here with a gift shop that's open from 9am to 5pm daily. Allow 45 to 90 minutes.

20189 Cabrini Blvd. (I-70, exit 259), Lookout Mountain. (✆ **303/526-0758.** www.den-cabrini-shrine.org. Free admission, donations welcome. Summer daily 7am–7pm; winter daily 7am–5:30pm; masses daily 7:30am, Sun also 11am.

National Earthquake Information Center The U.S. Geological Survey operates this facility to collect rapid earthquake information, transmit warnings over the Earthquake Early Alerting Service, and publish and disseminate earthquake data. Tours of 30 to 45 minutes can be scheduled by appointment when a guide is available. They include information about the NEIC, the Earthquake Early Alerting Service, and earthquakes in general.

1711 Illinois St. (✆ **303/273-8500** or 303/273-8420. http://neic.usgs.gov. Free admission. Tues–Thurs 9–11am and 1–3pm, by appointment only.

National Renewable Energy Laboratory Visitor Center This federal lab's public face features interactive exhibits covering all things renewable, from solar to biomass. The structure is a model for efficient design, with state-of-the-art heating, lighting, cooling, and insulation. Allow 1 hour.

15013 Denver West Pkwy. (✆ **303/384-6565.** www.nrel.gov/visitors_center. Free admission. Mon–Fri 9am–5pm.

Rocky Mountain Quilt Museum This museum presents changing exhibits, including works from its permanent collection of more than 350 quilts. Consigned works are for sale in the gift shop. Allow 30 minutes.

1111 Washington Ave. (✆ **303/277-0377.** www.rmqm.org. Admission $6 adults, $4 seniors, $3 children 6–12, free for children under 6. Mon–Sat 10am–4pm; mid-May to Aug also Sun noon–4pm.

Where to Stay & Dine

La Quinta Inn–Golden, just off I-70, exit 264, at 3301 Youngfield Service Rd. (✆ **800/531-5900** or 303/279-5565), is a dependable choice, with 129 units and rates of $79 to $99 for a double room. **Table Mountain Inn,** 1310 Washington Ave. (✆ **800/762-9898** or 303/277-9898; www.tablemountaininn.com), is a smaller, slightly more expensive alternative. Rates are $149 to $189 double, $189 to $234 suite. Completely renovated in 2004, the **Golden Hotel,** 800 11th St. (✆ **800/233-7214** or 303/279-0100; www.thegoldenhotel.com), offers the best of the West, old and new, in its attractive guest rooms. Doubles run $159 to $179, suites $259 to $299.

For a good meal in a historic setting, try the **Old Capitol Grill** in downtown Golden, 1122 Washington Ave. at 12th Street (✆ **303/279-6390**), which offers steak and burgers plus a good selection of sandwiches. Located in the Territorial Capitol Building constructed in 1862, the restaurant is open daily for lunch and dinner, with dinner prices in the $10-to-$20 range. A more upscale dinner choice is **The Bridgewater Grill,** in the Golden Hotel, 800 11th St. (✆ **303/279-2010**). It serves creative regional fare in the $15-to-$25 range.

IDAHO SPRINGS ★

For visitor information, contact the **Idaho Springs Chamber of Commerce,** P.O. Box 97, Idaho Springs, CO 80452 (✆ **303/567-4382;** www.idahospringschamber.org). Information on Idaho Springs and the nearby towns of Empire, Georgetown, and Silver Plume is available from the **Clear Creek County Tourism Bureau,** P.O. Box 100, Idaho Springs, CO 80452 (✆ **866/674-9237** or 303/567-4660; www.clearcreekcounty.org).

What to See & Do

The scenic "Oh My God" dirt road, a steep, winding thoroughfare, runs from Central City through Virginia Canyon to Idaho Springs, although most visitors prefer to take I-70 directly to this community 35 miles west of Denver. Site of a major gold strike in 1859, Idaho Springs today beckons visitors to try their luck at panning for any gold that may remain. The quaint Victorian downtown is worth a look; don't miss the Bridal Veil Falls tumbling through the largest waterwheel in Colorado across from City Hall.

The **Argo Gold Mine, Mill, and Museum,** 2350 Riverside Dr. (© 303/567-2421; www.historicargotours.com), is listed on the National Register of Historic Places, and offers tours daily from mid-April to October from 9am to 6pm. Visitors can see the Double Eagle Gold Mine, relatively unchanged since the early miners first worked it more than 100 years ago, and the mill, where ore was processed into gold. Everyone is welcome to take part in gold- and gemstone-panning. Admission is $15 for adults, $7.50 for children 7 to 12, and free for kids under 7. Allow at least 45 minutes.

At the **Phoenix Gold Mine ★**, on Trail Creek Road (© 303/567-0422; www.phoenix goldmine.com), you can don a hard hat and follow a working miner through narrow tunnels to see what mining 100 years ago was all about. You can also pan for gold on the property and relax in the picnic area. Weather permitting, the mine is open daily from 10am to 5pm in the summer (until 4pm in the winter); the tours are informal and entertaining. Cost is $10 for adults, $8 for seniors, $5 for children 6 to 11, and free for children under 6. Panning only is $5. Allow about 1 hour.

Just outside Idaho Springs is **Indian Springs Resort,** 302 Soda Creek Rd. (© 303/989-6666; www.indianspringsresort.com), a fine spot for a relaxing soak in the hot springs after a long day of skiing or hiking. The resort has a covered swimming pool, indoor and outdoor private baths, and a vapor cave with soaking pools. Rates are $18 to $24 per person for an hour in the private baths or all-day use of the vapor cave, $14 to $16 for all-day use of the pool, and $10 for a mud bath in "Club Mud." Lodging is in rooms and cabins ($63–$119 for two) or a campground ($24 nightly); meals and weekend entertainment are also offered. The resort is open daily from 7:30am to 10:30pm year-round.

Idaho Springs is the starting point for a 28-mile drive to the summit of 14,260-foot **Mount Evans ★★**. From I-70, exit 240, follow Colo. 103—also called Mt. Evans Highway—as it winds along Chicago Creek through Arapahoe National Forest to **Echo Lake Park,** another Denver mountain park with fireplaces, hiking trails, and fishing. From here, Colo. 5—the highest paved auto road in North America—climbs to the Mount Evans summit. Views along this highway are of spectacular snowcapped peaks even in June, and you're likely to see mountain goats, bighorn sheep, marmots, eagles, and other wildlife. The road is generally open from Memorial Day to Labor Day. Allow at least 4 hours.

Another way to see this area's great scenery is by horseback. **A&A Historical Trails Stables,** 5 miles up Virginia Canyon from Idaho Springs (© 303/567-4808; www. aastables.com), offers a variety of trail rides, including breakfast and moonlight rides. Rides are usually offered May through November, weather permitting. A 1-hour ride costs $30 per person, and a 2-hour ride costs $70.

Where to Stay & Dine

H&H Motor Lodge, 2445 Colorado Blvd. (P.O. Box 1359), Idaho Springs, CO 80452 (© 800/445-2893 or 303/567-2838), is a mom-and-pop motel on the east side of town. It offers bright and cheery rooms, TVs with HBO, a hot tub, and a sauna. The 34 rooms and suites include several larger family units. Rates are $59 for a standard double, kitchenettes $69 to $109 extra; two-bedroom suites start at $69.

Beau Jo's Colorado Style Pizza, 1517 Miner St. (℃ **303/567-4376;** www.beaujos. com), offers a wide variety of so-called mountain pizzas, including standard pepperoni; "Skier Mike's," with Canadian bacon, green peppers, and chicken breast; and a roasted-garlic and veggie combo. Sandwiches are also available, plus a salad bar set up in a pair of old claw-foot bathtubs. The bill usually comes out to $10 to $20 per person.

GEORGETOWN ★

A pretty village of Victorian-era houses and stores, Georgetown, 45 miles west of Denver on I-70 at an elevation of 8,500 feet, is named for an 1860 gold camp. Among the best preserved of the foothill mining towns, Georgetown is one of the few that didn't suffer a major fire during its formative years. Perhaps to acknowledge their blessings, townspeople built eye-catching steeples on top of their firehouses, not their churches.

For information on attractions and travel services, drop by or contact the **Georgetown Visitors Center,** 613 6th St. (P.O. Box 444), Georgetown, CO 80444 (℃ **800/472-8230** or 303/569-2888), which runs a visitor information center at 6th and Argentine streets across from the Georgetown post office; or **Historic Georgetown, Inc.,** 15th and Argentine streets, P.O. Box 667, Georgetown, CO 80444 (℃ **303/569-2840;** www. historicgeorgetown.org).

What to See & Do

The Georgetown–Silver Plume Mining Area was declared a National Historic Landmark District in 1966, and more than 200 of its buildings have been restored.

A convenient place to begin a **walking tour** is the Old County Courthouse, at 6th and Argentine streets. Now the community center and tourist information office, it was built in 1867. Across Argentine Street is the Old Stone Jail (1868); 3 blocks south, at 3rd and Argentine, is the Hamill House (see below).

Sixth Street is Georgetown's main commercial strip. Walk east from the Old Courthouse. On your left are the Masonic Hall (1891), the Fish Block (1886), the Monti and Guanella Building (1868), and the Cushman Block (1874); on your right, the Hamill Block (1881) and the Kneisel & Anderson Building (1893). The Hotel de Paris (see below) is at the corner of 6th and Taos. Nearly opposite, at 6th and Griffith, is the Star Hook and Ladder Building (1886), along with the town hall and marshal's office.

If you turn south on Taos Street, you'll find Grace Episcopal Church (1869) at 5th Street, and the Maxwell House (1890) a couple of steps east on 4th. Glance west on 5th to see Alpine Hose Company No. 2 (1874) and the Courier Building (1875). North on Taos Street from the Hotel de Paris are the Old Georgetown School (1874), at 8th Street; First Presbyterian Church (1874), at 9th Street; Our Lady of Lourdes Catholic Church (1918), at 9th Street; and the Old Missouri Firehouse (1870), at 10th Street and Taos.

If you turn west on 9th at the Catholic church, you'll find two more historic structures: the Bowman-White House (1892), at Rose and 9th, and the Tucker-Rutherford House (ca. 1860), a miner's log cabin with four small rooms and a trapper's cabin in back, on 9th Street at Clear Creek.

Georgetown Energy Museum This small museum is dedicated to educating people about the history of hydropower in Georgetown and Colorado. Located at Georgetown's power plant—built in 1900 and still operating—the museum allows visitors an up-close look at a pair of hydroelectric-generating units in action. The museum also features photographic and text displays detailing the history of similar plants in the region, as well as a collection of antiques: washing machines, stoves, and generator meters. Allow 30 minutes.

Hamill House   Built in Country Gothic Revival style, this house dates from 1867, when silver speculator William Hamill owned it. When Historic Georgetown, Inc., acquired it in 1971, the house had its original woodwork, fireplaces, and wallpaper. A delicately carved outhouse had two sections: one with walnut seats for the family, the other with pine seats for servants. Allow 30 to 60 minutes.

305 Argentine St. ℭ **303/569-2840.** Admission $4 adults, $3 seniors 60 and older and students, free for children under 10. Memorial Day to Sept daily 10am–4pm; Oct–Dec Sat–Sun noon–4pm. Closed Jan–late May except for prearranged tours.

Hotel de Paris ★   The builder of the hotel, Louis Dupuy, once explained his desire to build a French inn so far away from his homeland: "I love these mountains and I love America, but you will pardon me if I bring into this community a remembrance of my youth and my country." The hotel opened in 1875 and soon became famous for its French Provincial luxury.

Today it's a historic museum run by the National Society of Colonial Dames of America, embellished with many of its original furnishings, including Haviland china, a big pendulum clock, paintings and etchings, photographs by William Henry Jackson, and carved walnut furniture. The kitchen contains an antique stove and other cooking equipment, and the wine cellar houses early wine barrels, with their labels still in place. Allow 45 to 60 minutes.

409 6th St. (at Taos St.). ℭ **303/569-2311.** www.hoteldeparismuseum.org. Admission $4 adults, $3 seniors 60 and older, $2 children 6–16, free for children under 6. Memorial Day to Labor Day daily 10am–4:30pm; early Sept–Dec and May Sat–Sun noon–4pm, weather permitting. Closed Jan–Apr and major holidays.

Where to Stay & Dine

Colorado's oldest continuously operating hotel, about 5 minutes from Georgetown, is the **Peck House Hotel and Restaurant,** 83 Sunny Ave. (P.O. Box 428), on U.S. 40 off I-70, exit 232, Empire, CO 80438 (ℭ **303/569-9870;** www.thepeckhouse.com). Established in 1862 as a stagecoach stop for travelers and immigrants from the East Coast, the hotel has an antiques-filled parlor lined with photos of the Peck family and their late-19th- and early-20th-century guests and a panoramic view of the Empire Valley afforded by the wide veranda. The rooms are comfortable and quaint (claw-foot tubs grace many bathrooms). There are 11 rooms (9 with private bathroom), and rates for two are in the $65-to-$140 range. The hotel's excellent **restaurant** serves fish and steak entrees and seriously delicious hot-fudge cake and raspberries Romanoff. The restaurant serves dinner daily year-round; prices for entrees are $13 to $30.

Back in Georgetown, **The Happy Cooker,** 412 6th St. (ℭ **303/569-3166**), serves unusual soups, sandwiches on homemade breads, crepes, quiches, and more substantial fare such as frittatas and eggs Benedict, in a converted home in Georgetown's historic business district. It's open Monday through Friday from 7am to 4pm, Saturday and Sunday from 7am to 5pm. Prices are in the $4-to-$8 range, and breakfast is served all day. For a beer, a burger, and a dose of local color, head to the **Red Ram Restaurant & Saloon,** 606 6th St. (ℭ **303/569-2300**). The menu also has Mexican plates and slow-cooked baby back ribs; prices run $7 to $17 for a main course, and the Red Ram has two family suites for rent to overnight guests.

Boulder

Although Boulder is known primarily as a college town (the University of Colorado is here), it would be inaccurate to begin and end the description there. Sophisticated and artsy, Boulder is home to numerous high-tech companies and research concerns; it also attracts countless outdoor sports enthusiasts with its delightful climate, vast open spaces, and proximity to Rocky Mountain National Park.

Set at the foot of the Flatirons of the Rocky Mountains, just 30 miles northwest of downtown Denver and only 74 feet higher than the Mile High City, Boulder was settled by hopeful miners in 1858 and named for the large rocks in the area. Welcomed by Chief Niwot and the resident southern Arapaho, the miners struck gold in the nearby hills the following year. By the 1870s, Boulder had become a regional rail and trade center for mining and farming. The university, founded in 1877, became the economic mainstay of the community after mining collapsed around the beginning of the 20th century.

In the 1950s, Boulder emerged as a national hub for scientific and environmental research. The National Center for Atmospheric Research and the National Institute of Standards and Technology are located here, as are dozens of high-tech and aerospace companies. Alongside the ongoing high-tech boom, the university and attendant vibrant culture have attracted a diverse mix of intellectuals, individualists, and eccentrics. Writers William S. Burroughs, Jr., Stephen King, and Allen Ginsberg, co-founder of the city's Naropa Institute, all called Boulder home at one time or another.

Today's residents are a mix of students attending the University of Colorado (called CU by locals); employees of the many computer, biotech, and research firms; and others attracted by the casual, bohemian, environmentally aware, and otherwise hip lifestyles that prevail here. Whatever differences exist among the residents, they are united by a common love of the outdoors. Boulder has 43,000 acres of open space within its city limits, 56 parks, and 200 miles of trails. On any given day, seemingly three-quarters of the population is outside making great use of this land, generally from the vantage point of a bicycle seat, the preferred mode of transport—there are about 100,000 bicycles in Boulder, one for each of the city's 100,000 residents.

1 ORIENTATION

ARRIVING
By Plane
Boulder doesn't have a commercial airport. Air travelers must fly into Denver International Airport and then make ground connections to Boulder, a trip of about an hour.

GETTING TO & FROM THE AIRPORT The **SuperShuttle Boulder** (© **303/227-0000;** www.supershuttle.com) leaves Denver International Airport hourly from 5:10am to 12:10am, and Boulder hourly between 3:30am and 9:30pm, with fewer departures on holidays. Scheduled pickups in Boulder are at the University of Colorado campus and area hotels; pickups from other locations are made on call. The one-way fare from a scheduled pickup point to the airport is $25 per person, or $28 for residential pickup service from other points; round trips run $46.

Boulder Yellow Cab (℃ **303/777-7777;** www.yellowtrans.com) charges $70 one-way to the airport for up to five passengers.

Buses operated by the **Regional Transportation District,** known locally as **RTD** (℃ **800/366-7433** or 303/299-6000; www.rtd-denver.com), charge $11 for a one-way trip to the airport (exact change required); those under 16 ride free. Buses leave from, and return to, the main terminal at 14th and Walnut streets daily every hour from before 4am to after midnight.

Boulder Limousine Service (℃ **303/449-5466**) charges $108 and up (plus any high-way tolls) to take up to three people from DIA to Boulder (or vice versa) in a limousine.

By Car

The Boulder Turnpike (U.S. 36) branches off I-25 north of Denver and passes through the suburbs of Westminster, Broomfield, and Louisville before reaching Boulder. The trip takes about 30 minutes. If you are coming from Denver International Airport, take E-470 west, which becomes the Northwest Parkway (both are toll roads; $6 for two axles) to U.S. 36. If you're arriving from the north, take the Longmont exit from I-25 and follow Colo. 119 all the way. Longmont is 7 miles due west of the freeway; Boulder is another 15 miles southwest on the Longmont Diagonal Highway.

VISITOR INFORMATION

The **Boulder Convention and Visitors Bureau,** 2440 Pearl St. (at Folsom St.), Boulder, CO 80302 (℃ **800/444-0447** or 303/442-2911; www.bouldercoloradousa.com), is open Monday through Friday from 8:30am to 5pm, and can provide excellent maps, brochures, and general information on the city. There are also visitor information kiosks on **Pearl Street Mall** and at the **Davidson Mesa overlook,** several miles southeast of Boulder on U.S. 36. Brochures are available at both sites year-round.

CITY LAYOUT

The north–south streets increase in number going from west to east, beginning with 3rd Street. (The eastern city limit is at 61st St., although the numbers continue to the Boulder County line at 124th St. in Broomfield.) Where U.S. 36 enters Boulder (and does a 45-degree turn to the north), it becomes 28th Street, a major commercial artery. The Longmont Diagonal Highway (Colo. 119) enters Boulder from the northeast and intersects 28th Street at the north end of the city.

To reach downtown Boulder from U.S. 36, turn west on Canyon Boulevard (Colo. 119 west) and north on Broadway, which would be 12th Street if it had a number. It's 2 blocks to the Pearl Street Mall, a 4-block, east–west pedestrian-only strip from 11th to 15th streets that constitutes the historic downtown district. Boulder's few one-way streets circle the mall: 13th and 15th streets are one-way north, 11th and 14th one-way south, Walnut Street (a block south of the mall) one-way east, and Spruce Street (a block north) one-way west.

Broadway continues across the mall, eventually joining U.S. 36 north of the city. South of Arapahoe Avenue, Broadway turns southeast, skirting the University of Colorado campus and becoming Colo. 93 (the Foothills Hwy. to Golden) after crossing

Baseline Road. Baseline follows a straight line from east Boulder, across U.S. 36 and Broadway, past Chautauqua Park and up the mountain slopes. To the south, Table Mesa Drive takes a similar course.

The Foothills Parkway (not to be confused with the Foothills Hwy.) is the principal north–south route on the east side of Boulder, extending from U.S. 36 at Table Mesa Drive to the Longmont Diagonal; Arapahoe Avenue, a block south of Canyon Boulevard, continues east across 28th Street as Arapahoe Road.

---

2 GETTING AROUND

BY PUBLIC TRANSPORTATION

The **Regional Transportation District,** known as the **RTD** (℃ **800/366-7433** or 303/299-6000; www.rtd-denver.com), provides bus service throughout Boulder as well as the Denver greater metropolitan area. The Boulder Transit Center, 14th and Walnut streets, is open Monday through Friday from 5am to midnight and Saturday and Sunday from 6am to midnight. Fares within the city are $1.75 for adults and children (85¢ for seniors and passengers with disabilities; children under 6 ride free). Schedules are available at the Transit Center, the Chamber of Commerce, and other locations. Buses are wheelchair accessible.

The city of Boulder runs a shuttle bus service called the **HOP** (℃ **303/447-8282**), connecting downtown, University Hill, the University of Colorado, and 30th and Pearl. The HOP operates Monday through Thursday from 7am to 10pm, Friday and Saturday from 9am to 11:30pm, and Sunday from 10am to 6pm. While the University of Colorado is in session, the night HOP runs Friday and Saturday from 10pm to 3am. Buses run about every 8 to 15 minutes during the day, every 15 to 20 minutes at night; the fare is $1.75 (85¢ for seniors; children under 6 ride free).

The RTD runs a complementary local shuttle, the **SKIP,** Monday through Friday from 5:08am to 12:30am, Saturday from 7am to 12:30am, and Sunday from 7am to 11pm. Buses run north and south along Broadway, with a loop through the west Table Mesa neighborhood, every 6 to 10 minutes during peak weekday times and less frequently in the evenings and on weekends.

BY CAR

The **American Automobile Association (AAA)** has an office at 1933 28th St., #200 (℃ **303/753-8800**). It's open Monday through Friday from 8:30am to 5:30pm, Saturday from 9am to 1pm.

CAR RENTALS Most people who fly to Colorado land at Denver International Airport and rent a car there. To rent a car in Boulder, contact **Avis** (℃ 800/331-1212), **Dollar** (℃ 800/800-4000), **Enterprise** (℃ 800/736-8222), **Hertz** (℃ 800/654-3131), or **National** (℃ 888/227-7368).

PARKING Most downtown streets have parking meters, with rates of about 25¢ per 20 minutes. Downtown parking lots cost $1 to $3 for 3 hours. Parking can be hard to find around the Pearl Street Mall, but new lots have eased the pain. Outside downtown, free parking is generally available on side streets.

Boulder is a wonderful place for bicycling; there are bike paths throughout the city and an extensive trail system leading for miles beyond Boulder's borders (see "Bicycling" under "Sports & Outdoor Activities," later in this chapter).

You can rent and repair mountain bikes and buy trail and city maps at **University Bicycles,** 839 Pearl St., about 2 blocks west of the Pearl Street Mall (© **303/444-4196;** www.ubikes.com), and **Full Cycle,** 1211 13th St., near the campus (© **303/440-7771;** www.fullcyclebikes.com). Bike rentals cost $20 to $40 (or $85 for a luxury model) daily. Maps and other information are also available at the **Boulder Convention and Visitors Bureau,** 2440 Pearl St. (© **303/442-2911**).

BY TAXI

Boulder Yellow Cab (© **303/777-7777**) operates 24 hours, but you need to call for service—there are no taxi stands, and taxis won't stop for you on the street. Another company that serves Boulder is **Metro Taxi** (© **303/333-3333**).

ON FOOT

You can walk to most of what's worth seeing in downtown Boulder, especially around the Pearl Street Mall and University of Colorado campus. **Historic Boulder, Inc.,** 4735 Walnut St. (© **303/444-5192;** www.historicboulder.org), can provide advice about exploring the city's historic neighborhoods on foot. Books and brochures covering historic walking tours are available at the Convention and Visitors Bureau, 2440 Pearl St.

(FastFacts) Boulder

Area Code Area codes are **303** and **720,** and local calls require 10-digit dialing.

Babysitters The front desk at a major hotel often can make arrangements on your behalf. Boulder's **Child Care Referral Service** (© **303/441-3180**) can also help if you call in advance.

Business Hours Most banks are open Monday through Friday from 9am to 5pm, and some have Saturday hours, too. Major stores are open Monday through Saturday from 9 or 10am until 5 or 6pm, and often Sunday from noon to 5pm. Department and discount stores often have later closing times.

Car Rentals See "Getting Around," above.

Drugstores Reliable prescription services are available at the Medical Center Pharmacy in the **Boulder Medical Center,** 2750 N. Broadway (© **303/440-3111**). The pharmacy at **King Soopers Supermarket,** 1650 30th St., in Sunrise Plaza (© **303/444-0164**), is open from 8am to 9pm weekdays, 9am to 6pm Saturdays, and 10am to 6pm Sundays.

Emergencies For police, fire, or medical emergencies, call © **911.** For the **Poison Control Center,** call © **303/739-1123.** For the **Rape Crisis Hotline,** call © **303/443-7300.**

Eyeglasses You can get fast repair or replacement of your glasses at **Visions Optical,** 1933 28th St. (© **303/442-4521**).

Hospitals Full medical services, including 24-hour emergency treatment, are available at **Boulder Community Hospital,** 1100 Balsam Ave., at North Broadway (✆ **303/440-2273**).

Newspapers & Magazines Newspaper options include the *Daily Camera* and the *Boulder Weekly*. Many Boulderites also read the campus paper, the *Colorado Daily*, available all over town. Both Denver dailies—the *Denver Post* and *Rocky Mountain News*—are available at newsstands throughout the city. You can also find the *New York Times* and *Wall Street Journal*.

Photographic Needs For standard processing requirements (including 2-hr. slide processing), as well as custom lab work, contact **Photo Craft**, 3550 Arapahoe Ave. (✆ **303/442-6410**). For equipment, supplies, and repairs, visit **Mike's Camera,** 2500 Pearl St. (✆ **303/443-1715;** www.mikescamera.com).

Post Office The main downtown post office is at 15th and Walnut streets. Contact the U.S. Postal Service (✆ **800/275-8777;** www.usps.com) for hours and other locations.

Safety Although Boulder is generally a safe city, it is not crime-free. Be aware of your surroundings, especially if walking alone at night.

Taxes State and city sales taxes total about 7%.

Useful Telephone Numbers Call ✆ **303/639-1111** for **road conditions;** ✆ **303/ 825-7669** for **ski reports;** and ✆ **303/494-4221** for **weather reports.**

3 WHERE TO STAY

You'll find a good selection of comfortable lodgings in Boulder, with a wide range of rates to suit almost every budget. Be aware, though, that the town literally fills up during the popular summer season, making advance reservations essential. It's also almost impossible to find a place to sleep during any major event at the University of Colorado, particularly graduation. Those who do find themselves in Boulder without lodging can check with the Boulder Convention and Visitors Bureau (see "Visitor Information," under "Orientation," above), which keeps track of availability. You can usually find a room in Denver, a half-hour or so away. Rates listed below do not include the 10.25% accommodations tax. Parking is free unless otherwise specified.

Major chains and franchises that provide reasonably priced lodging in Boulder include **Best Western Boulder Inn,** 770 28th St., Boulder, CO 80303 (✆ **800/780-7234** or 303/449-3800), with rates of $89 to $149 double; **Boulder Creek Quality Inn and Suites,** 2020 Arapahoe Ave., Boulder, CO 80302 (✆ **800228-5151** or 303/449-7550; www.qualityinnboulder.com), with rates of $79 to $149 double; and **Days Inn,** 5397 S. Boulder Rd., Boulder, CO 80303 (✆ **800/329-7466** or 303/499-4422), with rates of $89 to $129 double. Among the nonchains, **Boulder University Inn,** just south of downtown at 1632 Broadway (✆ **303/417-1700;** www.boulderuniversityinn.com), is a solid option, with reasonable double rates of $69 to $119.

VERY EXPENSIVE

St Julien ★★★   The first new hotel in downtown Boulder since the Boulderado debuted in 1909, the swank St Julien instantly raised the bar for lodging in Boulder when it opened in 2005. The flagstone and Norman brick exterior, accented by patina copper and red roof tiles, sheaths a sumptuous lobby and exquisite guest rooms, averaging a healthy 400 square feet each. Everything from the walnut floors to the luxurious linens to the premium bath amenities to the artistic Boulder photographs on the wall is first rate. Honeyed tones and French doors accent the guest rooms, which feature either one California king or two queens. The bathrooms are the best in town; there are separate tubs and showers in every granite-laden one. Perks include live music Tuesday through Saturday in the lobby or picture-perfect back terrace, a two-lane lap pool, complimentary yoga classes on summer weekend mornings, and a spa that offers "indigenous therapies" using local minerals and plants. Expect to be wowed.

900 Walnut St., Boulder, CO 80302. © **877/303-0900** or 720/406-9696. Fax 720/406-9697. www.stjulien. com. 201 units, including 15 suites. $239–$329 double; $399–$489 suite. AE, DC, DISC, MC, V. Valet parking $15 per night. **Amenities:** Restaurant (American); lounge; indoor heated pool; indoor Jacuzzi; fitness center; spa, salon; complimentary bikes; concierge; business center; dry cleaning. *In room:* A/C, cable TV w/pay movies, free Wi-Fi, coffeemaker, hair dryer, iron, safe.

EXPENSIVE

The Alps ★ (Finds)   A stage stop in the late 1800s, this historic log lodge sits on a mountainside about a 7-minute drive (3 miles) west of downtown Boulder. Converted into a beautiful bed-and-breakfast decorated with Arts and Crafts and Mission furnishings by owners Jeannine and John Vanderhart, the Alps is ideal for travelers planning to split time between Boulder and its outlying wilderness and scenery. Each room here is different and named after a Colorado mining town, including Magnolia, Salina, and Wall Street. All have functional fireplaces with Victorian mantels, king or queen beds with down comforters, and individual thermostats. Most are spacious, with a claw-foot or double whirlpool tub plus a double shower, and many have private porches. Shared spaces include a beautiful lounge with a huge rock fireplace, plus delightful gardens and patio areas. The entrance is the original log cabin built in the 1870s. Smoking is not permitted.

38619 Boulder Canyon Dr., Boulder, CO 80302. © **800/414-2577** or 303/444-5445. Fax 303/444-5522. www.alpsinn.com. 12 units. $149–$269 double. Rates include full breakfast. AE, DC, DISC, MC, V. **Amenities:** Jacuzzi; concierge; activities desk; in-room massage. *In room:* A/C, cable TV, hair dryer, iron.

Boulder Marriott ★   Until the St Julien came along (see above), the Marriott was the newest full-service hotel in the city. It is conveniently located just a block off 28th Street (U.S. 36), providing great access to everything in town. Furnished with Southwestern touches, the rooms are geared to the business traveler, with multiline phones, large work desks, and ergonomic chairs. Local and toll-free calls cost $1. The concierge level has a private lounge, and rates include continental breakfast, happy hour, and hors d'oeuvres. Three-quarters of the rooms feature mountain views.

2660 Canyon Blvd., Boulder, CO 80302 (1 block west of Canyon and 28th St.). © **303/440-8877.** Fax 303/440-3377. www.marriott.com/denbo. 157 units. $159–$239 double; $279–$299 suite. AE, DC, DISC, MC, V. Free valet and self-parking. **Amenities:** Restaurant (steakhouse); lounge; indoor heated pool; exercise room; spa; Jacuzzi; 24-hr. business center; shopping arcade; limited room service; massage; laundry service; dry cleaning; executive level. *In room:* A/C, cable TV w/pay movies, free Wi-Fi, coffeemaker, hair dryer, iron, safe.

Boulder Accommodations & Dining

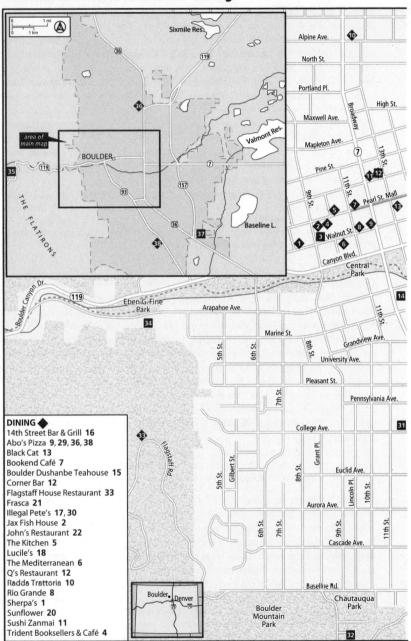

Alpine Ave. **10**
North St.
Portland Pl.
High St.
Maxwell Ave.
Broadway
Mapleton Ave. **7**
Pine St. **11** **12**
Pearl St. Mall
5 **7** **13**
2 **4** **8** **9**
3 Walnut St.
1 **6**
Canyon Blvd.
Central Park

Sixmile Res.
36
119
36
area of main map
Valmont Res.
BOULDER
35 **119** **7**
93 **157**
Baseline L.
36 **37**
38

Boulder Canyon Dr.
119
Eben G. Fine Park
Arapahoe Ave.
34
Marine St.
Grandview Ave.
5th St. 6th St. 8th St.
University Ave.
Pleasant St.
7th St.
Pennsylvania Ave.
33
Flagstaff Rd.
College Ave. **31**
Gilbert St. Grant Pl.
Euclid Ave.
5th St. 8th St. Lincoln Pl. 10th St.
Aurora Ave.
6th St. 7th St. 9th St. 11th St.
Cascade Ave.

Boulder Denver
Baseline Rd.
Chautauqua Park
Boulder Mountain Park
32

DINING ◆

14th Street Bar & Grill **16**
Abo's Pizza **9, 29, 36, 38**
Black Cat **13**
Bookend Café **7**
Boulder Dushanbe Teahouse **15**
Corner Bar **12**
Flagstaff House Restaurant **33**
Frasca **21**
Illegal Pete's **17, 30**
Jax Fish House **2**
John's Restaurant **22**
The Kitchen **5**
Lucile's **18**
The Mediterranean **6**
Q's Restaurant **12**
Radda Trattoria **10**
Rio Grande **8**
Sherpa's **1**
Sunflower **20**
Sushi Zanmai **11**
Trident Booksellers & Café **4**

THE FLATIRONS

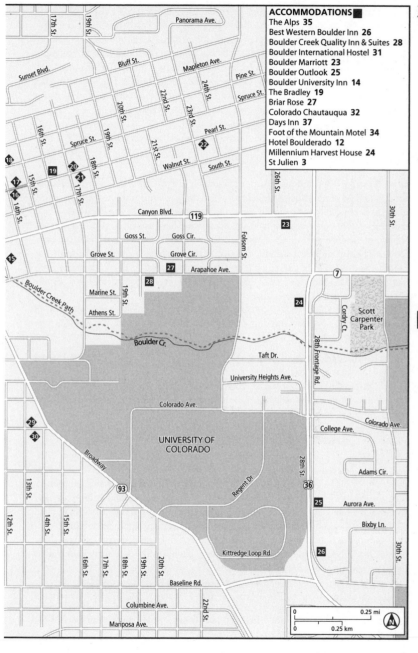

ACCOMMODATIONS
The Alps **35**
Best Western Boulder Inn **26**
Boulder Creek Quality Inn & Suites **28**
Boulder International Hostel **31**
Boulder Marriott **23**
Boulder Outlook **25**
Boulder University Inn **14**
The Bradley **19**
Briar Rose **27**
Colorado Chautauqua **32**
Days Inn **37**
Foot of the Mountain Motel **34**
Hotel Boulderado **12**
Millennium Harvest House **24**
St Julien **3**

The Bradley ★★ Built as an upscale inn in the 1990s, the Bradley nicely blends into the surrounding historic neighborhood, just northeast of the Pearl Street Mall. The striking Great Room and uniquely decorated guest rooms are all adorned with bold contemporary art from local galleries, and it's all for sale. Some of the rooms have hot tubs and balconies; all have standout Bob Timberlake furnishings from North Carolina, rainforest shower heads, and tiny sleeping cat sculptures at the foot of the bed. The eclectic inn has a very homey feel, and the breakfasts—featuring huge fresh fruit salads and bread that is baked on-site—and the nightly wine and cheese are big events.

2040 16th St., Boulder, CO 80302. ℂ 800/858-5811 or 303/545-5200. Fax 303/440-6740. www.the bradleyboulder.com. 12 units. $175–$245 double. Rates include full breakfast. AE, DC, DISC, MC, V. **Amenities:** Complimentary access to a nearby health club; concierge; business center; dry cleaning. *In room:* A/C, cable TV w/DVD player, free Wi-Fi, hair dryer, iron.

Briar Rose ★ A country-style brick home built in the 1890s, this midcity bed-and-breakfast might remind you of Grandma's place. Every room is furnished with antiques, from the bedrooms to the parlor to the sunny back porch, and the lovely gardens offer a quiet escape. Two of the six units in the main house have fireplaces; two in a separate carriage house come with either a patio or a balcony. All are furnished with feather comforters. The full organic breakfast is gourmet quality: homemade granola, fresh nut breads, yogurt with fruit, and much more. Refreshments are available in the lobby from 8am to 9pm. There are two guest computers off of the sitting room. Smoking is permitted only in the outside garden areas.

2151 Arapahoe Ave., Boulder, CO 80302. ℂ 303/442-3007. Fax 303/786-8440. www.briarrosebb.com. 10 units (6 with shower only). $149–$189 double. Rates include full breakfast. AE, MC, V. *In room:* A/C, cable TV, free Wi-Fi, hair dryer.

Hotel Boulderado ★★ Opened on January 1, 1909, this elegant and historic hotel still has the same Otis elevator that wowed visiting dignitaries that day. The colorful stained-glass ceiling and cantilevered cherrywood staircase are other reminders of days past, along with the rich woodwork of the balusters around the mezzanine and the handsome armchairs and settees in the main-floor lobby. The hotel's Christmas tree, a 28-footer with more than 1,000 white lights, is a Boulder tradition, and the setting for afternoon tea on the mezzanine in December.

Five stories tall and just a block off the Pearl Street Mall, this contemporary of Denver's Brown Palace has 42 original guest rooms, all bright and cozy, individually decorated with panache. Although the rooms are continuously renovated and refurbished, they retain a Victorian flavor, with lush floral wallpapering, custom bedspreads, and furnishings alternately stately and plush. The construction of a spacious North Wing in 1989 almost quadrupled the number of rooms; although these are larger and more typical of a modern hotel, they also embody the early-20th-century theme. All have a few high-tech touches: electronic locks and two-line phones with voice mail; most rooms have refrigerators, and a few have jetted tubs.

2115 13th St. (at Spruce St.), Boulder, CO 80302. ℂ 800/433-4344 or 303/442-4344. Fax 303/442-4370. www.boulderado.com. 160 units. $174–$304 double; $274–$394 suite. AE, DC, DISC, MC, V. **Amenities:** 2 restaurants (contemporary American; see "Where to Dine," below); 3 lounges; access to nearby health club; business center; laundry service. *In room:* A/C, cable TV w/pay movies, free Wi-Fi, coffeemaker, hair dryer, iron.

Millennium Harvest House (Kids) The Harvest House is a full-service hotel with spacious and lovely grounds. Located on 16 acres just west of U.S. 36 in south Boulder,

Family-Friendly Hotels

Millennium Harvest House (p. 130) A good place to stay with the kids, especially in the summer. The Harvest House has a nice swimming pool and lots of nearby green space; it's also next to the Boulder Creek Path and within walking distance of 29th Street.

Foot of the Mountain Motel (p. 132) There's lots of space here where the kids can expend their energy. Across the street is a lovely park with a playground, as well as the Boulder Creek Path.

Boulder Outlook (p. 131) At this eco-friendly motel, kids can use the pool and play inside even when the weather is bad, and the diversions are many (bouldering rocks, game room, dog park).

the former Regal Harvest House looks like almost any other four-story hotel from the front—but its backyard melts into a park that surrounds the east end of the 10-mile Boulder Creek Path (see "Attractions," later in this chapter), where bike rentals are available. All rooms hold one king-size or two double beds, a lounge chair and ottoman, remote-control cable TV, and direct-dial phone. My favorite rooms here are those that look out on the Boulder Creek Path.

1345 28th St., Boulder, CO 80302. ℂ **800/545-6285** or 303/443-3850. Fax 303/443-1480. www.millenniumhotels.com/boulder. 269 units. $129–$299 double; $229–$499 suite. AE, DC, DISC, MC, V. **Amenities:** Restaurant (American); 2 lounges (sports bar/cigar bar); indoor lap pool; outdoor heated swimming pool; 15 tennis courts (5 indoor); fitness center; 2 Jacuzzis (indoor and outdoor); bike rental; courtesy shuttle (local); Internet-access kiosks (fee); 24-hr. room service; on-call masseur; valet and self-service laundry. *In room:* A/C, cable TV w/pay movies, coffeemaker, hair dryer, iron.

MODERATE

Boulder Outlook ★★ (Kids) (Value The proprietors of this former Holidome have outdone every chain motel in town. The Outlook is fun, fresh, and definitively Boulder, with such unique perks as two bouldering rocks (one is 11 ft. high, the other 4 ft.), a fenced 4,000-square-foot dog run, and an ecologically conscious approach and comprehensive recycling program. The brightly painted motel has 40 rooms that have an outdoor entrance; the rest are accessed indoors. Overall, the rooms are contemporary and larger than average; the baths are nicely tiled. In-room recycling containers and all-natural bath amenities are two more distinctly Boulder touches. The indoor pool is superb, complete with a waterfall and a mural of a cloud-speckled sky, and the bar and grill here features live music Thursday, Saturday, and Sunday nights, as well as Wednesdays during the school year.

800 28th St., Boulder, CO 80303. ℂ **800/542-0304** or 303/443-3322. Fax 303/449-5130. www.boulderoutlook.com. 162 units. $109–$159 double. Rates include continental breakfast. AE, DC, DISC, MC, V. Pets accepted, $10 per night. **Amenities:** Restaurant (American); lounge; indoor heated pool; exercise room; Jacuzzi; men's and women's saunas; game room; activities desk; 24-hr. business center; limited room service; massage; coin-op washers and dryers; dry cleaning; executive level. *In room:* A/C, cable TV, coffeemaker, hair dryer, iron, safe.

Colorado Chautauqua ★★ (Finds)   During the late 19th and early 20th centuries, more than 400 Chautauquas—adult education and cultural entertainment centers—sprang up around the United States. This 26-acre park, a peaceful world apart at the foot of the Flatiron Mountains, is one of the few remaining and a National Historic Landmark. In summer, it hosts a wide-ranging arts program, including the Colorado Music Festival (see "Boulder After Dark," p. 151).

Lodging is in attractive cottages and in rooms and apartments in two historic lodges. All units were outfitted with new furnishings in recent years and come with linens and towels. They have balconies or porches, and either private or shared kitchens. The trim and tidy cottages range from efficiencies to three-bedroom, two-bathroom units. Larger groups might take the newly restored Mission House, which has eight bedrooms, a kitchen, and a screened-in porch and rents for $1,143 a night. From September to May, many cottages and apartments are rented by the month or longer, but nightly accommodations are generally available.

Guests have access to the park's playgrounds, picnic grounds, and hiking trail heads. The historic Chautauqua Dining Hall, which opened on July 4th, 1898, serves three moderately priced meals a day year-round.

900 Baseline Rd. (at 9th St.), Boulder, CO 80302. ℂ **303/952-1611** for lodging, 303/440-3776 for restaurant. Fax 303/449-0790. www.chautauqua.com. 87 units. $71–$118 lodge room; $104–$147 efficiency cottage; $126–$162 1-bedroom cottage; $152–$275 2- or 3-bedroom cottage. AE, MC, V. Bus: 203. Pets accepted in cottages, $10 night. Pets not accepted in lodges. **Amenities:** Restaurant (creative American); 4 tennis courts; children's programs during summer; self-service laundry. *In room:* Kitchen, coffeemaker, no phone.

Foot of the Mountain Motel (Kids) (Value)   This nicely preserved motel, a series of connected, cabin-style units with bright red trim near the east gate of Boulder Canyon, dates from the 1930s, but has kept up with the times. The location is inspiring, on the west edge of town where city meets mountains, and right across the street is the top end of the Boulder Creek Path and the trail head that leads to the summit of Flagstaff Mountain. The pleasant pine-walled cabins are furnished with queen or double beds and individual water heaters; two suites are big enough for families and outfitted with full kitchens and a shared hot tub.

200 Arapahoe Ave., Boulder, CO 80302. ℂ **866/773-5489** or 303/442-5688. www.footofthemountain motel.com. 20 units (2 with shower only), including 2 suites. $90 double; $115–$185 suite. Rates include complimentary continental breakfast. AE, DISC, MC, V. Pets accepted for $5 nightly fee and a $50 refundable deposit. *In room:* Cable TV, free Wi-Fi, kitchen, fridge.

INEXPENSIVE

Boulder International Hostel ★ (Value)   Established in 1961, this hostel, spread over 12 buildings with a maximum occupancy of 400, has a little something for everybody: communal dorm rooms, private rooms, and even extended-stay apartments. Wonderfully international, the hostel has a social and intellectual vibe you won't find at the hotels. The toilets, showers, kitchen, laundry, and TV room are communal. Just 2 blocks from the University of Colorado campus, the hostel is open for registration daily from 8am to 11pm. To stay in a bunk, you must present identification proving you are not a resident of Colorado.

1107 12th St., Boulder, CO 80302-7029. ℂ **888/442-0522** or 303/442-0522. Fax 303/442-0523. www.boulderhostel.com. 250 units. $27 dorm bed; $49–$55 private unit. AE, DISC, MC, V. **Amenities:** Coin-op washers and dryers; free Wi-Fi. *In room:* No phone.

4 WHERE TO DINE

Partly because Boulder is a young, hip community, it has attracted a variety of small, with-it restaurants. At these chef-owned-and-operated establishments, innovative and often-changing cuisine is the rule. You'll find a lot of California influences here, as well as a number of top-notch chefs doing their own thing.

A Boulder city ordinance prohibits smoking inside restaurants.

VERY EXPENSIVE

Flagstaff House Restaurant ★★ (Moments) NEW AMERICAN/REGIONAL

Named for its perch on Flagstaff Mountain, this restaurant attracts patrons from across the state and nation with excellent cuisine and service, and the spectacular nighttime view of the lights of Boulder spread out 1,000 feet below. The Monette family has owned and operated this restaurant, a local institution, since 1951 and kept ahead of the curve by sticking with tradition in an elegant, candlelit dining room with glass walls that maximize the view. The prices aren't for the budget-minded, but those seeking a romantic setting and superlative food can't miss with the Flagstaff House.

The menu, which changes daily, offers an excellent selection of fresh fish, flown in from the source, and Rocky Mountain game, all prepared with a creative flair. Typical appetizers include pancetta-wrapped rabbit loin or pheasant breast, calamari, black trumpet mushrooms, and caviar. Entrees, many of which are seasonal, might include Colorado rack of lamb, Maine lobster, veal cheeks, and mahimahi. The restaurant also has dessert soufflés, a world-renowned wine cellar (at, 20,000 bottles, perhaps the best in Colorado), and an impressive selection of after-dinner drinks.

1138 Flagstaff Rd. (west up Baseline Rd.). (✆) 303/442-4640. www.flagstaffhouse.com. Reservations recommended. Main courses $32–$56. AE, DC, MC, V. Sun–Fri 6–10pm; Sat 5–10pm.

EXPENSIVE

Black Cat ★★ (Finds) CONTEMPORARY/ECLECTIC One of the smallest restaurants in Boulder, the Black Cat is also one of the best. In the intimate space with contrasting walls of cloth, metal, and glass owner-chef Eric Skokan changes the menu nightly, using herbs and vegetables he harvests from his own half-acre garden in Boulder. Skokan's zero-inventory approach makes for some of the freshest food on the Front Range, but it's his creativity that shines through. The menu might include starters like warm mozzarella with rosemary coulis, inventively prepared seafood, garlic-polenta gratin, and anything else that is in season or strikes the kitchen staff's fancy. One of the few places where the menu might have a "Study of Rabbit" or "Juxtaposition of Duck," the Black Cat is a restaurant where the proprietor's passion is visible on every plate. For a special evening, the Black Cat offers a tasting menu for $62 for five courses, $99 with wine pairings.

1964 13th St. (✆) 303/444-5500. www.blackcatboulder.com. Reservations recommended. Main courses $15–$30. AE, DISC, MC, V. Daily 5:30–11pm.

Frasca ★★★ ITALIAN Winning raves since its 2004 opening, Frasca is the critical darling in Boulder for its upscale atmosphere, impeccable service, and peerless cuisine, drawn exclusively from the culinary traditions of Friuli-Venezia Giulia, a subalpine region in northeastern Italy. Using fresh ingredients, with a special emphasis on terrific seafood, cheese, and wine, the masterful kitchen delivers some of the best fare in the West. The menu changes daily, but always includes a vast selection of small plates leading

BOULDER

7

WHERE TO DINE

134 up to pasta, seafood, pork loin, and other specialties of the region. Every year the staff takes a trip to Italy for a refresher course in Italian culinary appreciation, and it shows.

1738 Pearl St. (C) **303/442-6966.** www.frascafoodandwine.com. Reservations recommended. Main courses $20–$30, $60–$70 for four-course dinner. AE, DISC, MC, V. Mon–Thurs 5:30–9pm, Fri–Sat 5:30–10pm. Closed Sun and 2 weeks in early June.

John's Restaurant ★★ (Finds) CONTINENTAL/MEDITERRANEAN This funky but elegant converted house has set the pace for the Boulder dining scene for nearly 30 years. The emphasis here is squarely on the food. Owners and siblings Chef Corey Buck and Ashley Maxwell (who bought the place from founder John Bizzarro in 2003) start with the classic cuisine of southern Europe, but Buck adds his own creative signature spin to each dish; compared to Bizzarro, Buck prepares bigger plates and is more fond of game dishes. For starters, apple Stilton pecan salad and ricotta-and-spinach gnocchi verde set the stage for the continually changing main-course offerings. Menu mainstays include filet mignon with Stilton ale sauce, surrounded by grilled Bermuda onions; phyllo-wrapped pork tenderloin with garlic whipped potatoes; and a variety of fresh seafood dishes. The menu also includes a few vegetarian items, and near-transcendent homemade desserts.

2328 Pearl St. (C) **303/444-5232.** www.johnsrestaurantboulder.com. Reservations recommended. Main courses $20–$40. AE, DISC, MC, V. Tues–Sat from 5:30pm.

The Kitchen ★★ ECLECTIC Since it opened in 2004, The Kitchen has emerged as a standout in a competitive dining market. Locals flock here for the fresh, often organic food, the expert service, and the casual atmosphere that melds metropolitan flair with Boulder funkiness. The lunch menu changes seasonally, often depending on what ingredients are locally available, but the buttery, melt-in-your mouth slow-roasted pork sandwich, topped with a mellow salsa verde, and lamb burger are always available. The daily-evolving dinner slate might include chargrilled pork chops, gnocchi, Maine oysters, and a vegetarian selection or two, once again with an emphasis on local and organic ingredients. On Monday "Community Nights," food is presented family-style for $35; reservations are necessary. Upstairs is the aptly named [Upstairs], a swank wine bar that serves a light menu and libations from the 4,500-bottle cellar, staying open into the wee hours.

1039 Pearl St. (C) **303/544-5973.** www.thekitchencafe.com. Reservations recommended. Main courses $4–$14 breakfast, $9–$16 lunch, $20–$36 dinner. AE, MC, V. Mon–Fri 8am–2pm; Sat–Sun 9am–2pm; Mon–Wed 5:30–9:30pm; Thurs–Sat 5:30–10pm; Sun 5:30–9pm. Bar open later.

Q's Restaurant ★★ CONTEMPORARY AMERICAN The historic ambience that makes the Hotel Boulderado such a delightful place to stay also makes its way into Q's, the hotel's main restaurant. The dining room combines the old—rich polished wood and stained glass—with the comfortable, casually elegant feel of today. Of course, the important thing is the food, and chef-owner John Platt does an excellent job, using locally grown organic vegetables whenever possible.

Platt, who claims seafood as his specialty after years on Cape Cod, always includes several fresh fish selections on the menu, such as seared Hawaiian ono with fresh hearts of palm and artichoke puree. Other meat dishes often include Nebraskan buffalo rib-eye, served with posole and seared greens, shoestring onions, and chile jus. Other specialties: seared scallops, gnocchi in parmesan broth, and Caesar salad.

In the Hotel Boulderado, 2115 13th St. (at Spruce St.). (C) **303/442-4880.** www.qsboulder.com. Reservations recommended. Main courses $6–$11 breakfast, $8–$16 lunch, $16–$28 dinner. AE, DC, DISC, MC, V. Mon–Fri 6:30–11am and 11:30am–2pm; Sat–Sun 6:30am–2pm; daily 5–10pm.

Sushi Zanmai ★★ (Kids) SUSHI/JAPANESE   Boulder is a hot spot for great sushi: Zanmai is a go-to stalwart but faces stiff competition from a number of like-minded upstarts. I still prefer the place for its festive atmosphere, impeccable service, and traditional sushi. Prepared while you watch—at the sushi bar or tableside—the options include everything from tuna and trout to sea urchin and octopus, with such exotic rolls as Colorado (raw filet mignon), Z-No. 9 (shrimp tempura, avocado, salmon, and eel sauce), and Two Dragon (shrimp tempura and eel). There are lunch specials as well as sushi happy-hour specials during lunch and dinner. Karaoke singalong takes place every Saturday from 10pm to midnight. Under the same ownership next door is **Amu** (© 303/440-0807), a traditional sake bar with its own menu of artfully prepared sashimi and other Japanese staples. Amu, which translates approximately as "to have nothingness," requires patrons to leave their shoes at the door.

1221 Spruce St. (at Broadway). © **303/440-0733.** www.sushizanmai.com. Reservations recommended for groups of 4 or more. Main courses $7.50–$13 lunch, $15–$26 dinner; sushi rolls $2–$12. AE, DC, MC, V. Mon–Fri 11:30am–2pm; Sun–Fri 5–10pm; Sat 5pm–midnight.

MODERATE

Boulder Dushanbe Teahouse ★ (Finds) ETHNIC WORLD CUISINE   In 1990, 200 crates were shipped to Colorado as a gift from Dushanbe, Tajikistan, Boulder's sister city. From the ornately hand-carved and -painted pieces of a Persian teahouse in the crates, the building was assembled at its present site with help from four Tajik artisans. It's the only teahouse of its kind in the Western Hemisphere. Lavishly and authentically decorated, the teahouse holds 14 pillars carved from Siberian cedar, and a grand central fountain. The cuisine includes traditional ethnic dishes from the Middle East, Asia, and elsewhere, including several noodle and vegetarian options. There are even a few Tajik specialties, often a lamb dish, and cuisine prepared with specialty tea. Pastries, coffees, and more than 70 teas are also available. There is a full bar on-site as well.

1770 13th St. © **303/442-4993.** Main courses $5–$9 breakfast, $9–$16 lunch, $11–$19 dinner. www.boulderteahouse.com. AE, DISC, MC, V. Mon–Fri 8–10:30am and 11am–3pm; Sat–Sun 8am–3pm; daily 5–10pm. Tea and coffee bar daily 8am–10pm.

14th Street Bar & Grill ★ CONTEMPORARY AMERICAN   An open restaurant with large windows facing the street, this is a great spot for people-watching as well as dining. The open wood grill and pizza oven, the long, crowded full-service bar, and a changing display of abstract art let you know that this is a fun place. The menu centers on what chef-owner Kathy Andrade calls "American grill" cuisine, which includes grilled sandwiches, Southwestern chicken salads, and unusual homemade pizzas, such as a pie topped with prosciutto, poached egg, charred green chiles, and radish sprouts. A seafood

(Kids) Family-Friendly Restaurants

Sushi Zanmai (p. 135)   Flashing knives and tableside cooking keep kids fully entertained.

Rio Grande (p. 137)   The busy atmosphere is a great match for kids' energy level and potential mood swings.

stew is also offered, plus fantastic food and drink specials during the daily social hour (3–6pm).

1400 Pearl St. (at 14th St.). $\mathcal{C}$ **303/444-5854.** www.14thstreetboulder.com. Main courses $10–$26. AE, MC, V. Daily 11:30am–10pm.

Jax Fish House ★ SEAFOOD   Fresh seafood is flown in daily from the East and West coasts to supply this restaurant, a lively space with colored chalk graffiti and oceanic art on its brick walls, social patrons, and a great happy hour. At patio, bar, and table seating, you can order one of the house specialties—the Mississippi catfish skillet is a good bet—or simply slurp down raw oysters and martinis to your heart's content. Entrees usually include scallops, New Zealand bluenose, wild King salmon, and halibut, along with soft-shell crab when in season. Or try a seafood po' boy, with slaw or fresh mussels or clams in mango-lemongrass broth or white wine and garlic. Those who prefer beef can choose from a filet and all-natural burgers.

928 Pearl St. (1 block west of the mall). $\mathcal{C}$ **303/444-1811.** www.jaxfishhouseboulder.com. Main courses $10–$35. AE, MC, V. Mon–Thurs 4–10pm; Fri–Sat 4–11pm; Sun 4–9pm.

The Mediterranean ★ MEDITERRANEAN/TAPAS   Known as "The Med," this local favorite is designed as an homage to the casual eateries of Spain and Italy. With a multihued tile interior and an enjoyable breezy patio, the Med draws a bustling after-work drinking crowd for its weekday tapas hour (3–6:30pm), which includes such reasonably priced delicacies as fried artichoke hearts, Moroccan spiced BBQ pork, and hummus. For a full dinner, the selection is extensive, ranging from pasta to poultry, steaks to gourmet wood-fired pizzas, with several vegetarian dishes to please the health-conscious Boulder crowd. The lunch menu is similar, with a nice selection of panini sandwiches (including lamb, salmon, and vegetarian). There are also several daily specials.

1002 Walnut St. $\mathcal{C}$ **303/444-5335.** www.themedboulder.com. Main courses $9–$26; most tapas $3–$5. AE, DC, DISC, MC, V. Sun–Wed 11am–10pm; Thurs–Sat 11am–11pm.

Radda Trattoria ★★ (Finds) ITALIAN   A popular neighborhood eatery north of downtown, Radda Trattoria has a social atmosphere and a terrific sense of invention in the kitchen. In a room that belies its shopping-center location next to a supermarket—centered on a large rectangular bar—the well-oiled operation serves plates of Northern Italian cuisine, such as gnocchi, *cinghiale* (wild boar), and pizzas, as well as fantastic soups and salads. The vibe is casual and smart, with more young professionals and CU faculty than the student hangouts downtown. Radda's older and more formal sister restaurant is **Mateo,** 1837 Pearl St. ($\mathcal{C}$ **303/443-7766**).

1265 Alpine Ave. $\mathcal{C}$ **303/442-6200.** www.raddatrattoria.com. Reservations not accepted. Main courses $9–$16. AE, DISC, MC, V. Mon–Fri 7am–10pm; Sat–Sun 9am–10pm.

Sunflower ★ (Finds) CONTEMPORARY/ORGANIC   This pleasant contemporary eatery, eclectically decorated with murals, rotating local art, and a flagstone floor, touts its menu as healthy and environmentally-friendly. The ingredients include certified organic produce, fresh seafood, and free-range, hormone-free poultry and game. The kitchen takes a multicultural approach: Sunflower features a diverse selection of dinner entrees, including sesame-crusted ahi tuna served with coconut-scallion basmati; buffalo sirloin tenderloin with gorgonzola crust; and tempeh korma with spinach, potatoes, raisins, and cashews. Lunch includes fresh variations on sandwiches—such as a blackened salmon burger—as well as specialties like pad Thai and vegetarian Malay fried rice. An all-you-can-eat organic salad buffet is served daily until 4pm, organic juices and wines **137** are available, and there's a popular weekend brunch.

1701 Pearl St. (2 blocks east of the mall). ✆ **303/440-0220.** www.sunflowerrestaurant.net. Main courses $9–$19 lunch and brunch, $19–$31 dinner. AE, DISC, MC, V. Tues–Fri 11am–2:30pm; Tues–Sat 5–10pm; Sun 5–9pm; Sat–Sun brunch 10am–3pm.

INEXPENSIVE

In addition to the choices below, try a slice of Boulder's best New York–style pie at any **Abo's Pizza** location: 1110 13th St. (✆ **303/443-3199**), 1911 Broadway (✆ **303/443-9113**), 2761 Iris Ave. (✆ **303/443-1921**), and 637 S. Broadway (✆ **303/494-1274**). **Lucile's,** 2124 14th St. (✆ **303/442-4743**), is a Boulder breakfast mainstay, serving beignets, buttermilk biscuits, and other morning delicacies that take inspiration from the Big Easy.

Corner Bar ★ CONTEMPORARY AMERICAN With the same kitchen as the highly rated Q's Restaurant (see above), the Hotel Boulderado's Corner Bar is far above your average sandwich shop, although sandwiches and burgers are on the menu, too. Here you can savor a grilled-salmon sandwich, served with red-onion marmalade, spinach, and horseradish aioli. Or you might try a roast turkey BLT with herbed mayo, a grilled Angus sirloin, or pan-roasted halibut with sweet corn-shiitake chowder and zucchini-scallion confit. Those not in search of a full meal can opt for an appetizer, such as fried oysters or chipotle-tomato soup.

In the Hotel Boulderado, 2115 13th St. (at Spruce St.). ✆ **303/442-4560.** Main courses $9–$17. AE, DC, DISC, MC, V. Daily 11:30am–11:45pm.

Illegal Pete's Ⓥⓐⓛⓤⓔ MEXICAN Located at the far east end of the Pearl Street Mall, Illegal Pete's is renowned locally for its creative, healthy burritos packed with chicken, steak, veggies, or fish. The menu also includes a similar range of tacos, as well as salads, quesadillas, and chile. There's a full bar you can belly up to in the back, and a patio out front. Another Illegal Pete's is on the Hill at 1320 College Ave. (✆ **303/444-3055**).

1447 Pearl St. ✆ **303/440-3955.** www.illegalpetes.com. Menu items $5–$7. AE, DISC, MC, V. Sun–Thurs 11am–10pm; Fri–Sat 11am–2:30am.

Rio Grande MEXICAN This popular neighborhood restaurant and bar, just south of the Pearl Street Mall, is probably best known for its huge, award-winning margaritas—so potent that the staff enforces a strict limit of three. Frequented by college students and Boulder's under-30 crowd, the Rio is bustling for reasons beyond its alcoholic concoctions—the loud, social atmosphere and the food, a good variety of oversize Mexican entrees and combos. My favorites are hearty fajitas (steak or veggie, with handmade tortillas), zesty Yucatan shrimp, and creative chiles rellenos.

1101 Walnut St. ✆ **303/444-3690.** www.riograndemexican.com. Meals $7–$15. AE, MC, V. Mon–Thurs 11am–2pm; Mon–Wed 5–10pm; Thurs 5–10:30pm; Fri–Sun 11am–10:30pm.

Sherpa's ★ Ⓕⓘⓝⓓⓢ TIBETAN/NEPALI Owned by Pemba Sherpa—a native of Nepal who in fact is a Sherpa, or Himalayan mountain guide—Sherpa's is located in a converted Victorian house just southwest of the Pearl Street Mall. Decorated with Himalayan relics and photography of the peaks of Nepal and Tibet, the restaurant serves up food to match: Tibetan dishes like *thupka* (noodle bowls) and sherpa stew as well as spicier Nepali and Indian cuisine, including *saag* (creamed spinach with garlic, cumin, ginger, and your choice of veggie or meat) and curry dishes. There are lunch specials daily, as well as a comfortable bar with a library full of climbing tomes.

825 Walnut St. ☎ **303/440-7151.** Reservations accepted. Main courses $5–$10 lunch, $9–$15 dinner. AE, DISC, MC, V. Daily 11am–3pm; Sun–Thurs 5–9:30pm; Fri–Sat 5–10pm.

ESPRESSO BARS, COFFEEHOUSES & RELATED ESTABLISHMENTS

Espresso fans will have no problem finding a decent espresso, cappuccino, or latte: Boulder has a number of **Starbucks** establishments, as well as many more-interesting independent coffeehouses. Many of the independents, located near the Pearl Street Mall, provide outdoor seating in nice weather. Attached to the Boulder Book Store, the **Bookend Cafe,** 1115 Pearl St. (☎ **303/440-6699**), offers a variety of coffee drinks and a delightful array of baked goods, soups, and pies. **Trident Booksellers & Café,** 940 Pearl St. (☎ **303/443-3133**), features indoor and outdoor seating as well as a comprehensive selection of used books. The **Boulder Dushanbe Teahouse,** 1770 13th St. (☎ **303/442-4993;** p. 135), offers an authentic Persian setting for quaffing more than 70 varieties of tea and a good selection of coffees from 8am to 10pm daily. Homemade baked goods are also available.

5 ATTRACTIONS

THE TOP ATTRACTIONS

Boulder Creek Path ★★ (Kids) Following Boulder Creek, this nature corridor provides about a 16-mile-long oasis and recreation area through the city and west into the mountains. With no street crossings (there are bridges and underpasses instead), the path is popular with Boulder residents, especially on weekends, when you'll see numerous walkers, runners, bicyclists, and in-line skaters. (Walkers should stay to the right; the left lane is for faster traffic.) The path links the CU campus, several city parks, and office buildings. Near the east end, watch for deer, prairie-dog colonies, and wetlands, where some 150 species of birds have been spotted. You might see Canada geese, mallard ducks, spotted sandpipers, owls, and woodpeckers.

At 30th Street, south of Arapahoe Road, the path cuts through **Scott Carpenter Park** (named for the astronaut and Colorado native), where you can enjoy swimming in summer and sledding in winter. Just west of Scott Carpenter Park, you'll find **Boulder Creek Stream Observatory,** which is adjacent to the Millennium Harvest House. In addition to observing trout and other aquatic wildlife, you're invited to feed the fish with trout food purchased from a vending machine (25¢). **Central Park,** at Broadway and Canyon Boulevard, preserves some of Boulder's history with a restored steam locomotive. The **Boulder Public Library** is also in this area.

Traveling west, watch for the **Charles A. Heartling Sculpture Garden** (with the stone image of local Indian Chief Niwot) and the **Kids' Fishing Ponds;** the Boulder Fish and Game Club stocks the ponds, which are open only to children under 12, who can fish for free and keep what they catch. Near 3rd Street and Canyon Boulevard, you'll find the **Xeriscape Garden,** where drought-tolerant plants are tested for reduced water intake.

The **Eben G. Fine Park** is named for the Boulder pharmacist who discovered Arapaho Glacier on nearby Arapaho Peak. To the west, **Red Rocks Settlers' Park** marks the beginning of the **Boulder Canyon Pioneer Trail,** which leads to a continuation of Boulder Creek Path. The park is named for Missouri gold-seekers who camped at this spot in

Impressions

If heaven has a college town, it's probably as beautiful as Boulder.

—*Sunset Magazine*

1858 and later found gold about 12 miles farther west. Watch for explanatory signs along the 1.3-mile path. The **Whitewater Kayak Course** has 20 slalom gates for kayakers and canoeists to use free; to the west, **Elephant Buttresses** is one of Boulder's more popular rock-climbing areas. The path ends at **Four Mile Canyon,** the old town site of Orodell.

55th St. and Pearl Pkwy., to the mouth of Boulder Canyon. ✆ **303/413-7200.** Free admission. Daily 24 hr. Bus: HOP.

National Center for Atmospheric Research ★ (Finds) Inspired by the cliff dwellings at Mesa Verde National Park, I. M. Pei designed this striking pink-sandstone building, which overlooks Boulder from high atop Table Mesa in the southwestern foothills. (You might recognize the center from Woody Allen's *Sleeper;* scenes were shot here.) Scientists study such phenomena as the greenhouse effect, wind shear, and ozone depletion to gain a better understanding of the earth's atmosphere. Among the technological tools on display are satellites, weather balloons, interactive computer monitors, robots, and supercomputers that can simulate the world's climate. There are also hands-on, weather-oriented exhibits and a theater. The **Walter Orr Roberts Weather Trail** outside the building's west doors takes visitors on a .4-mile, wheelchair-accessible loop along a path with interpretive signs describing various aspects of weather and climate plus the plants and animals of the area. The center also houses a changing art exhibit and a science-oriented gift shop. Allow 1 to 2 hours.

1850 Table Mesa Dr. ✆ **303/497-1174.** www.ncar.ucar.edu. Free admission. Self-guided tours weekdays 8am–5pm; weekends and holidays 9am–4pm. 1-hr. guided tours daily at noon; there is also a self-guided audio tour. Take Broadway heading southwest out of town to Table Mesa Dr., and follow it west to the center.

Pearl Street Mall ★★ (Kids) This 4-block-long tree-lined pedestrian mall marks Boulder's downtown core and its center for dining, shopping, strolling, and people-watching. Musicians, mimes, jugglers, and other street entertainers hold court on the landscaped mall day and night, year-round. Buy your lunch from one of the many vendors and sprawl on the grass in front of the courthouse to relax and eat. Locally owned businesses and galleries share the mall with trendy boutiques, sidewalk cafes, and major chains including Peppercorn, Banana Republic, and Abercrombie & Fitch. There's a wonderful play area for youngsters, with climbable boulders set in gravel. Don't miss the bronze bust of Chief Niwot (of the southern Arapaho) in front of the Boulder County Courthouse between 13th and 14th streets. Niwot, who welcomed the first Boulder settlers, was killed in southeastern Colorado during the Sand Creek Massacre of 1864.

Pearl St. from 11th to 15th sts. Bus: HOP.

University of Colorado ★ The largest university in the state, with nearly 29,000 students (including about 4,600 graduate students), "CU" dominates the city. Its student population, cultural and sports events, and intellectual atmosphere have helped shape Boulder into the city it is today. The school boasts 16 alumni astronauts who have flown in space and three Nobel laureates on the faculty.

Boulder Attractions

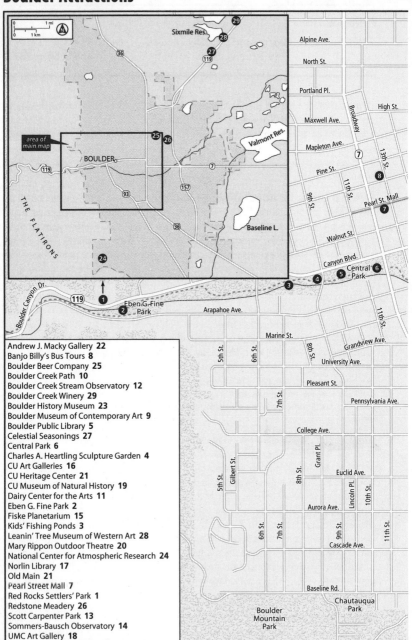

Andrew J. Macky Gallery **22**
Banjo Billy's Bus Tours **8**
Boulder Beer Company **25**
Boulder Creek Path **10**
Boulder Creek Stream Observatory **12**
Boulder Creek Winery **29**
Boulder History Museum **23**
Boulder Museum of Contemporary Art **9**
Boulder Public Library **5**
Celestial Seasonings **27**
Central Park **6**
Charles A. Heartling Sculpture Garden **4**
CU Art Galleries **16**
CU Heritage Center **21**
CU Museum of Natural History **19**
Dairy Center for the Arts **11**
Eben G. Fine Park **2**
Fiske Planetarium **15**
Kids' Fishing Ponds **3**
Leanin' Tree Museum of Western Art **28**
Mary Rippon Outdoor Theatre **20**
National Center for Atmospheric Research **24**
Norlin Library **17**
Old Main **21**
Pearl Street Mall **7**
Red Rocks Settlers' Park **1**
Redstone Meadery **26**
Scott Carpenter Park **13**
Sommers-Bausch Observatory **14**
UMC Art Gallery **18**

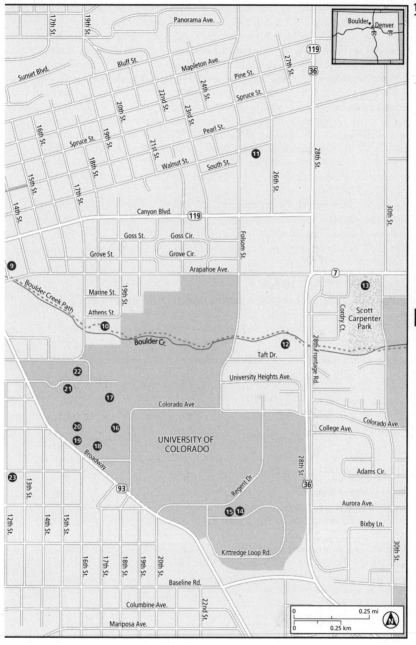

Old Main, on the Norlin Quadrangle, was the first building erected after the university was established in 1876; at that time, it housed the entire school. Later, pink-sandstone Italian Renaissance–style buildings came to dominate the campus. Visitors may want to take in the university's **Heritage Center,** on the third floor of Old Main; the **University of Colorado Museum** (see "More Attractions," below), a natural-history museum in the Henderson Building on Broadway; the **Mary Rippon Outdoor Theatre,** behind the Henderson Building, site of the annual Colorado Shakespeare Festival; **Fiske Planetarium,** between Kittredge Loop Drive and Regent Drive on the south side of campus; and the **Norlin Library,** on the Norlin Quadrangle, the largest research library in the state, with extensive holdings of American and English literature. Other attractions include the CU Art Museum, University Memorial Center (the student center), and the Integrated Teaching and Learning Laboratory in the College of Engineering. Prospective students and their parents can arrange campus tours by contacting the admissions office (© **303/492-6301**).

The **Sommers-Bausch Observatory** (© **303/492-6732** during the day, 303/492-2020 at night) offers tours and Friday-evening open houses. Among the telescopes there are 16-, 18-, and 24-inch Cassegrain reflectors and a 10-inch aperture heliostat.

East side of Broadway, between Arapahoe Ave. and Baseline Rd. © **303/492-1411.** www.colorado.edu. Bus: HOP, SKIP, STAMPEDE, and Denver buses.

MORE ATTRACTIONS

Beyond the attractions listed below, the **Boulder Creek Winery,** 6440 Odell Place (© **303/516-9031;** www.bouldercreekwine.com), offers a complimentary tasting Thursday through Sunday from 1 to 5:30pm in summer and 1 to 5pm Friday to Sunday fall through spring.

Banjo Billy's Bus Tours   A rollicking journey through Boulder and its storied history, Banjo Billy's Bus Tours utilize one of the funkiest vehicles you've ever seen. Featuring armchairs for guests inside, the exterior looks like the offspring of a log cabin and a school bus—and features 13 disco balls, five saddles, and a rubber chicken! The 90-minute tours delve into ghost stories and lurid tales of crime, but the tone is tongue-in-cheek and entertaining.

Tours depart from the Hotel Boulderado (p. 130). © **720/771-0087.** www.banjobilly.com. Tickets $16 adult, $14 seniors, $10 children 5–12, and free for children under 5. Tours depart Tues–Sun 2pm and 4pm in the summer, less frequently at other times of year.

Boulder Beer Company   From the grinding of the grain to the bottling of the beer, the 25-minute tour of Colorado's original microbrewery ends as all brewery tours should: in the pub. Tours pass by glistening copper vats that turn out hundreds of kegs of Boulder Beer a day. The pub overlooks the bottling area, so even if you visit without taking a tour, you still get a good view of the brewing process. The menu includes burgers, burritos, salads, and appetizers; most entrees run $6 to $9.

2880 Wilderness Place. © **303/444-8448.** www.boulderbeer.com. Free admission. Tours Mon–Fri 2pm (or by appt.); pub Mon–Fri 11am–9pm. Take U.S. 36 north to Valmont Rd.; then head east to Wilderness Place.

Celestial Seasonings ★ (**Value**)   The nation's leading producer of herbal teas, housed in a modern building in northeastern Boulder, offers tours that are an experience for the senses. The company began in a Boulder garage in 1969 and now produces more than 90 varieties of tea from more than 75 different herbs and spices imported from 35 countries. You'll understand why the company invites you to "see, taste, and smell the world of Celestial Seasonings" as you move from a consumer taste test in the lobby to their famed tea-box art, and finally into the production plant where nine million tea bags roll off the line daily. The exhilaratingly aromatic "Mint Room" is a highlight. The tour lasts 45 minutes, and there is a cafe and gift shop on-site.

4600 Sleepytime Dr. ℂ **303/581-1202** or 303/530-5300. www.celestialseasonings.com. Free admission. Mon–Fri 10am–4pm; Sat 10am–3pm; Sun 11am–3pm; tours on the hour. Reservations required for groups of 8 or more. Exit Colo. 119, Longmont Diagonal, at Jay Rd. go east to Spine, and then north to Sleepytime. Bus: J.

Redstone Meadery ★ (Finds Drunk by Beowulf and Shakespeare, mead is the original fermented beverage. There are about 60 active meaderies in the United States, including this standout in Boulder. Founded by David Myers in 2000, the meadery crafts several beverages (ranging from sparkling to portlike) that quickly demonstrate why this amateur mead maker turned pro. The meadery offers free 30-minute tours and tasting, and sells its wares ($17–$25 a bottle) and other regional foods and gifts.

4700 Old Pearl St., #2A. ℂ **720/406-1215.** www.redstonemeadery.com. Free admission. Tours Mon–Fri 1 and 3pm, Sat 12:30pm; tasting room Mon–Fri noon–6:30pm, Sat noon–5pm. Located 1 block northeast of the Pearl St. exit off Foothills Pkwy.

Museums & Galleries

There are three art galleries on the University of Colorado campus, all with free admission. The **CU Art Museum** (ℂ **303/492-8300**) displays the work of CU students and faculty as well as pieces from the Colorado Collection, about 5,000 works by international artists including Warhol, Dürer, Rembrandt, Tiepolo, Hogarth, Hiroshige, Matisse, and Picasso. There are also rotating exhibits. *Note:* The museum is closed until fall 2009 and will reopen at that time in the new Visual Arts Complex.

At the University Memorial Center, the **UMC Art Gallery** (ℂ **303/492-7465**) organizes and hosts a variety of exhibitions featuring regional and national artists. In the music-listening rooms, visitors can peruse current periodicals while listening to modern and classical music. The gallery is on the second floor of the center, just left of the information desk; it's open Monday to Friday from 9am to 6pm (bus: HOP, SKIP, STAMPEDE).

The **Andrew J. Macky Gallery** (ℂ **303/492-8423**), at the main entrance of Macky Auditorium, shows touring exhibits and works by local artists. It's open Wednesday from 9am to 4pm (bus: HOP, SKIP, STAMPEDE).

There are also studios and a gallery at the **Dairy Center for the Arts,** 2590 Walnut St. (ℂ **303/440-7826;** www.thedairy.org), which also houses two theaters, classrooms, and several dance, theater, and arts organizations. See "Theater & Dance," later in this chapter.

Boulder History Museum ★ Enscoced on University Hill in the 1899–1900 Harbeck-Bergheim House, a Victorian mansion with a Dutch-style front door and Italian tile fireplaces, the museum houses one of the most comprehensive local-history collections in the region. There are more than 35,000 artifacts (from snake oil to sidesaddles), plus hundreds of thousands of photographs and historical documents from Colorado's early days to the present.

Permanent exhibits include "Storymakers: A Boulder History," featuring a rich collection of oral histories and late-19th-to-early-20th-century photographs. There are also rotating exhibits that stay up for 6 to 10 months. The museum also hosts numerous lectures, programs, tours, and community events. Allow 1 to 2 hours.

1206 Euclid Ave. ☎ **303/449-3464.** www.boulderhistorymuseum.org. Admission $5 adults, $3 seniors, $2 children and students, free for children under 5. Tues–Fri 10am–5pm; Sat–Sun noon–4pm. Guided tours by appointment. Closed Mon and major holidays. Bus: HOP.

Boulder Museum of Contemporary Art   This multidisciplinary art museum, created in 1972 to exhibit the work of contemporary artists, has evolved into an exciting venue where one can expect to see almost anything art-related, from the lighthearted to the elegant, political to religious, by regional and international contemporary artists. There are special programs for young children and a variety of other events throughout the year. Performing arts—from poetry and dance to music and drama—are occasionally presented in the museum's "black box" performance venue. There are free tours during Farmer's Market (summer Saturdays) at 11am and kid's programs. Allow 30 to 45 minutes.

In addition, a separate organization puts on Saturday evening movie screenings in the adjacent parking lot in summer; classic movies such as *Citizen Kane* and cult classics are shown outside ($5 suggested donation per person; see **www.boulderoutdoorcinema. com** for information). Take a lawn chair or blanket.

1750 13th St. ☎ **303/443-2122.** www.bmoca.org. Admission $5 adults, $4 students and seniors, free for children under 12. Tues–Sat 11am–5pm (Sat 9am–4pm and until 8pm Wed in summer); Sun noon–3pm. Hours change seasonally; call ahead for current information. Closed Sun–Mon and major holidays. Bus: HOP, SKIP.

CU Heritage Center   Located in the oldest building on campus, this museum reflects the history of the university. Its seven galleries hold exhibits on early student life (together with a complete set of yearbooks), CU's contributions to space exploration, campus architecture, distinguished alumni, and an overview of the university's history. Allow 30 minutes—or a lot more if you're an alum.

3rd floor of Old Main, University of Colorado. ☎ **303/492-6329.** Free admission. Mon–Fri 10am–4pm. Bus: HOP, SKIP, STAMPEDE.

CU Museum of Natural History ★ (Kids)   The natural history and anthropology of the Rocky Mountains and Southwest are the focus of this campus museum, founded in 1902 and one of the best of its kind. Featured exhibits include Ancestral Puebloan pottery and collections pertaining to dinosaurs, geology, paleontology, botany, entomology, and zoology. A children's area has interactive exhibits, and one gallery is devoted to special displays that change throughout the year. Allow 1 to 3 hours.

University of Colorado, Henderson Bldg., just east of Broadway between 15th and 16th sts. ☎ **303/492-6892.** www.cumuseum.colorado.edu. Admission $3 adults, $1 seniors and children 6–18, free for children under 6. Mon–Fri 9am–5pm; Sat 9am–4pm; Sun 10am–4pm. Bus: HOP.

Leanin' Tree Museum of Western Art   You may know Leanin' Tree as the world's largest publisher of Western-art greeting cards. What's not so well known is that the company's headquarters houses an outstanding 400-plus-piece collection of original paintings and bronze sculptures by contemporary artists. All depict scenes from the Old or New West, including a collection of humorous cowboy art. There is also an outdoor sculpture garden of likenesses of human and animal Western icons. Free guided tours are available. Allow 1 hour.

6055 Longbow Dr. (exit Jay Rd. and Longmont Diagonal). ☎ **800/777-8716** or 303/530-1442, ext. 4299. www.leanintreemuseum.com. Free admission; donations suggested. Mon–Fri 8am–5pm; Sat–Sun 10am–5pm. Closed major holidays. Bus: 205.

City parks (see "Sports & Outdoor Activities," below) offer the best diversions for children.

On the **Boulder Creek Path** (see "The Top Attractions," earlier in this chapter), the underwater fish observatory behind the Millennium Harvest House fascinates youngsters. They can feed the huge trout swimming behind a glass barrier on the creek (machines cough up handfuls of fish food for 25¢). Farther up the path, on the south bank around 6th Street, Kids' Fishing Ponds, stocked by the Boulder Fish and Game Club, are open to children under 12. There's no charge for either activity.

The **Fiske Planetarium** (© 303/492-5001; www.fiske.colorado.edu) offers visitors a walk through the solar system. Dedicated to the memory of CU alumnus Ellison Onizuka and the six other astronauts who died in the space shuttle *Challenger* explosion, the outdoor scale model begins at the entrance to the planetarium with the sun and inner planets, and continues across Regent Drive to the outer planets, located along the walkway to the Engineering Center. Admission is free; allow at least a half-hour. The planetarium offers kids' after-school and summer discovery programs, star shows, and other programs in which you get a chance to look at the sky through the planetarium's telescopes. Admission for these events is usually around $5; call for the latest schedule (bus: HOP).

6 SPORTS & OUTDOOR ACTIVITIES

Boulder is one of the leading spots for outdoor sports in North America. The city manages more than 38,000 acres of parklands, including more than 200 miles of hiking trails and bicycle paths. Several canyons lead down from the Rockies directly into Boulder, attracting mountaineers and rock climbers. Families enjoy picnicking and camping in the beautiful surroundings. It seems that everywhere you look, people of all ages are running, walking, biking, skiing, or engaged in other active sports.

The **Boulder Parks and Recreation Department** (© 303/413-7200; www.ci. boulder.co.us/parks-recreation) manages many of the outdoor facilities and schedules a variety of year-round activities for children as well as adults. Seasonal booklets on activities and city parks are available free from the Chamber of Commerce office and through the parks and recreation department's website (see above). Although many of the programs last for several weeks or months, some are half- or full-day activities that visiting children can join, usually at a slightly higher price than that for city residents. The department sponsors hikes, fitness programs, ski trips, watersports, special holiday events, and performances in local parks, and even operates a skate park and a pottery lab. (TV trivia buffs, take note: Mork, of *Mork and Mindy,* first touched down on Planet Earth in Chautauqua Park, on the city's south side, and the house used as their residence's exterior is at 1619 Pine St.)

One destination where you can enjoy several kinds of outdoor activities is **Eldorado Canyon State Park** ★. This mountain park, just 5 miles southwest of Boulder in Eldorado Springs, is a favorite of technical rock climbers, but the 850-foot-high canyon's beauty makes it just as popular with hikers, picnickers, and others who want to get away from it all. The 1,448-acre park features 9 miles of hiking and horseback-riding trails, plus 7.5 miles of trails suitable for mountain bikes; fishing is permitted, but camping is not. An exhibit at the brand-new visitor center describes the history of the park; there's also a bookstore and rotating displays covering topics from wildflowers to climbing.

Impressions

This is Mork from Ork signing off from Boulder, Colorado. Nanu, Nanu!
—Mork from Ork (Robin Williams), on TV's *Mork & Mindy*, 1978–82

Admission is $6 to $7 per vehicle and $3 per pedestrian; the park is open daily from dawn to dusk. For further information, contact Eldorado Canyon State Park, Box B, Eldorado Springs, CO 80025 (© **303/494-3943;** parks.state.co.us).

BALLOONING   Float above the majestic Rocky Mountains in a hot-air balloon, watching as the early-morning light gradually brightens to full day. Flights often include champagne and an elaborate continental breakfast or brunch. **Fair Winds Hot Air Balloon Flights** (© **303/939-9323;** www.fairwindsinc.com) flies 7 days a week year-round, weather permitting. Prices are $195 to $275 per person, and include a certificate, T-shirt, and photograph.

BICYCLING   On some days, you see more bikes than cars in Boulder. Paths run along many of the city's major arteries, and local racing and touring events are scheduled year-round. Bicyclists riding at night are required to have lights; perhaps because of the large number of bicyclists in Boulder, the local police actively enforce traffic regulations that apply to them. Generally, bicyclists must obey the same laws that apply to operators of motor vehicles.

For current information on biking events, maps of the city's trails, tips on the best places to ride, and equipment sales and repairs, check with **University Bicycles,** 839 Pearl St., about 2 blocks west of the Pearl Street Mall (© **303/444-4196;** www.ubikes. com), and **Full Cycle,** 1211 13th St., near the campus (© **303/440-7771;** www.full cyclebikes.com). Daily bike rentals cost $20 to $40 (or $85 for a luxury model). See also "By Bicycle," under "Getting Around," earlier in this chapter.

CLIMBING & BOULDERING   If you want to tackle the nearby mountains and cliffs with ropes and pitons, contact **Boulder Mountaineering,** 1335-B Broadway (© **303/442-8355;** www.bouldermountaineering.com), which sells clothing and technical equipment, and can also provide maps and advice on climbing and trail running. Other good information sources are **Colorado Athletic Training School,** 2800 30th St. (© **303/939-9699;** www.catsgym.com), and **Total Climbing,** 2829 Mapleton Ave. (© **800/447-4008;** www.totalclimbing.com). The latter is home to the Boulder Rock Club, featuring 10,000 square feet of indoor climbing surfaces and offers guiding services.

Boulderers (those who climb without ropes) flock to **The Spot,** billed as the country's largest bouldering gym, at 3240 Prairie Ave. (© **303/379-8806;** www.thespotgym.com). Lessons and guide service are available, and there is a cafe and a yoga studio on-site.

The Flatiron Range (easily visible from downtown Boulder) and nearby Eldorado Canyon are two favorite destinations for expert rock scalers. The Third Flatiron is 1,400 feet high, taller than the Empire State Building, and has been climbed by people without using their hands, on roller skates, naked, and in a record 8 minutes (by separate climbers). For bouldering, Carter Lake (30 miles north on U.S. 36) and Boulder Canyon (west of the city on Canyon Blvd.) are two of the top spots.

FISHING   Favored fishing areas near Boulder include **Boulder Reservoir,** North 51st Street, northeast of the city off the Longmont Diagonal, where you can try your luck at walleye, catfish, largemouth bass, bluegill, crappie, and carp. The Boulder Parks and Recreation Department (📞 **303/441-3461**) manages the reservoir. Other favorite fishing holes include **Lagerman Reservoir,** west of North 73rd Street off Pike Road, about 15 miles northeast of the city, where only nonmotorized boats can be used; **Barker Reservoir,** just east of Nederland on the Boulder Canyon Drive (Colo. 119), for bank fishing; and **Walden Ponds Wildlife Habitat,** about 6 miles east of downtown on North 75th Street. Fly-fishing is also popular in the area; guide service is available through **Kinsley Outfitters,** 2070 Broadway (📞 **800/442-7420** or 303/442-6204; www.kinsley outfitters.com), for $250 for one person for a full day or $350 for two. Kinsley's fly shop offers a good selection of supplies.

GLIDER FLYING & SOARING The atmospheric conditions generated by the peaks of the Front Range are ideal for year-round soaring and gliding. **Mile High Gliding,** 5534 Independence Rd. (📞 **303/527-1122;** www.milehighgliding.com), offers rides and lessons on the north side of Boulder Municipal Airport, 2 miles northeast of downtown. Rides for one person range from $79 to $259 and last from 15 minutes to an hour or more; a 40-minute ride for two costs $219.

GOLF Local courses include the 18-hole **Flatirons Golf Course** (run by Boulder Parks and Recreation), 5706 E. Arapahoe Ave. (📞 **303/442-7851;** www.flatironsgolf.com), and the 9-hole **Haystack Mountain Golf Course,** 5877 Niwot Rd. in Niwot, 5 miles north of Boulder (📞 **303/530-1400;** www.golfhaystack.com). Nonresident greens fees range from $13 to $32.

HIKING & BACKPACKING There are plenty of opportunities in the Boulder area— the Boulder Mountain Parks system includes 4,625 acres bordering the city limits, including the Flatirons and Flagstaff Mountain. You can obtain a map with descriptions of more than 60 trails from the **Boulder Convention and Visitors Bureau,** 2440 Pearl St. (📞 **303/442-2911**).

Numerous Roosevelt National Forest trail heads leave the Peak-to-Peak Scenic Byway (Colo. 72) west of Boulder. Check with the **U.S. Forest Service,** Boulder Ranger District, 2140 Yarmouth Ave. (📞 **303/541-2500**), for hiking and backpacking information. During dry weather, check on possible fire and smoking restrictions before heading into the forest. The trail heads leading to Long, Mitchell, and Brainard lakes are among the most popular, as is the 2-mile hike to Isabel Glacier.

About 70 miles west of Boulder, on the Continental Divide, is the **Indian Peaks Wilderness Area** (📞 **303/541-2500**). More than half of the area is fragile alpine tundra; a $5 permit is required for camping from June 1 to September 15. North of Boulder, via Estes Park, is **Rocky Mountain National Park** (📞 **970/586-1206**), one of the state's prime destinations for hikers and those seeking beautiful mountain scenery. The 2.5-mile **Mills Lake Trail** ★, one of my favorites, is here; see "A Side Trip to Rocky Mountain National Park," later in this chapter. Another good hike is the 6-mile Mesa Trail, which departs from the Bluebell Shelter in Chautauqua Park.

RUNNING The Boulder Creek Path (see "The Top Attractions," earlier in this chapter) is one of the most popular routes for runners in Boulder. A good resource for the traveling runner is **Boulder Road Runners (www.boulderroadrunners.org).** They organize group runs in the area and can provide information. The **Bolder Boulder** (📞 **303/444- RACE;** www.bolderboulder.com), held every Memorial Day, attracts about 50,000 runners who circle its 6.3-mile course. The **Boulder Running Company,** 2775 Pearl St. (📞 **303/786-9255;** www.boulderrunningcompany.com), sells a wide variety of running shoes and gear, going as far as analyzing customers' strides on a treadmill to find the perfect shoe.

SKIING Friendly **Eldora Mountain Resort,** P.O. Box 1697, Nederland, CO 80466 (© **888/235-3672** or 303/440-8700; fax 303/440-8797; www.eldora.com), is just 21 miles west of downtown Boulder. It's about a 40-minute drive on Colo. 119 through Nederland. RTD buses leave Boulder for Eldora four times daily during ski season. For downhill skiers and snowboarders, Eldora has 53 trails, rated 30% novice, 50% intermediate, and 20% expert terrain on 680 acres. It has snowmaking on 320 acres and a terrain park with a 600-foot superpipe. The area has two quad lifts, two triple and four double chairlifts, four surface lifts, and a vertical rise of 1,500 feet. Lift tickets (2007–08 rates) were $59 for adults, $37 for seniors 65 to 74 or children 6 to 15, and just $7 for those under 6 and over 74. There are also discount packages that include lessons and rental equipment for both skiers and snowboarders. Snowshoeing is also gaining popularity in the area. The season runs from mid-November to mid-April, snow permitting.

For cross-country skiers, Eldora has 25 miles of groomed and backcountry trails, and an overnight hut available by reservation. About 15% of the trails are rated easy, 50% intermediate, and 35% difficult. The trail fee is $18, $10 for children 6 to 15 and seniors 65 to 74, and $2 for those under 6 and over 74.

You can rent all your ski, snowboard, and snowshoeing equipment at the ski-rental center, and Nordic equipment at the Eldora Nordic Center. A free base-area shuttle runs throughout the day from the lodge to the Little Hawk area and the Nordic Center.

In Boulder, you can rent or buy telemark and alpine touring equipment from **Eldora Mountain Sports,** 2775 Canyon Blvd. (© **303/447-2017**).

SWIMMING Five public pools are located within the city. Indoor pools, all open daily year-round, are at the newly renovated **North Boulder Recreation Center,** 3170 N. Broadway (© **303/413-7260**); the **East Boulder Community Center,** 5660 Sioux Dr. (© **303/441-4400**); and the **South Boulder Recreation Center,** 1360 Gillaspie Dr. (© **303/441-3448**). The two outdoor pools (both open daily from Memorial Day to Labor Day) are **Scott Carpenter Pool,** 30th Street and Arapahoe Avenue (© **303/441-3427**), and **Spruce Pool,** 2102 Spruce St. (© **303/441-3426**). Swimming fees for all municipal pools are $6 adults, $4 seniors, $3.50 teens, $3 children 3 to 12, and free for children under 3.

TENNIS There are more than 30 public courts in the city. The North and South Boulder Recreation centers (see "Swimming," above) each have four lighted courts and accept reservations ($8 an hour). The North Boulder Recreation Center also has two platform tennis courts. Play is free if you arrive and there's no one using the courts, or with a reservation. For locations of other public tennis courts, contact the Boulder Parks and Recreation Department (© **303/413-7200**).

WATERSPORTS For both motorboating and human-powered boating, sailboard instruction, or swimming at a sandy beach, head for the square-mile **Boulder Reservoir** (© **303/441-3461**), on North 51st Street off the Longmont Diagonal northeast of the city. Human-powered boats and canoes (no personal watercraft) can be rented at the **boathouse** (© **303/441-3468**). Rates start at $8 per hour, with sailboards at $20 per hour. There's also a boat ramp and other facilities.

SPECTATOR SPORTS

The major attractions are **University of Colorado football, women's volleyball,** and **men's and women's basketball.** For tickets, contact the Ticket Office, Campus Box 372,

Boulder, CO 80309 (© **303/49-BUFFS** [492-8337]; www.cubuffs.com). Football
tickets sometimes sell out early, particularly for homecoming and games against Nebraska
and Oklahoma.

7 SHOPPING

For the best shopping in Boulder, head to the **Pearl Street Mall** (see "The Top Attractions," earlier in this chapter), where you'll find not only shops and galleries galore but also street entertainers.

Twenty Ninth Street, centered on the former site of the Crossroads Mall at the intersection of Canyon Boulevard and 29th Street (© **303/449-1189;** www.twentyninth street.com), is a major new multiuse development featuring an outdoor shopping center. Open since 2006, tenants include Eddie Bauer, Ruby's Diner, MontBell, Borders Books & Music, Apple, and Century Theatres. Hours are 10am to 9pm Monday through Saturday and 11am to 6pm on Sunday.

The indoor-outdoor, 1.5-million-square-foot **FlatIron Crossing** (© **720/887-7467;** www.flatironcrossing.com), an upscale mall featuring Nordstrom, Dillard's, and Brookstone among its 200 shops, is a more comprehensive option for the devout shopper. It's 9 miles southeast of Boulder off U.S. 36 in Broomfield. Hours are 10am to 9pm Monday through Saturday and 11am to 6pm on Sunday.

SHOPPING A TO Z
Arts & Crafts
Art Source International   Natural-history prints, maps, and other items relevant to Western Americana, mainly from the 18th and 19th centuries, are the specialty here, along with collections of 100-year-old Colorado photographs, maps, and prints. The store also features a great selection of new globes, as well as a few reproductions. 1237 Pearl St. © 303/444-4079. www.rare-maps.com.

Boulder Arts & Crafts Cooperative   This is a good place to find a unique gift or souvenir. The shop, owned and operated by its artist members since 1971, features a wide variety of original handcrafted works. Pieces range from watercolors, serigraphs, and other fine art to top-quality crafts, including blown glass, stained glass, handmade jewelry, and functional pottery. Many of the items are made in Colorado or the Rocky Mountain region. 1421 Pearl St. © 303/443-3683. www.boulderartsandcrafts.com.

Niwot Antiques (Finds)   With dozens of dealers (including New England antiques specialist Elysian Fields), this antiques mall, in business since the 1950s, is the area's best, and a good excuse to make a trip to Niwot, 5 miles north of Boulder on the Longmont Diagonal. 136 2nd Ave., Niwot. © 303/652-2587. www.niwotantiques.com.

Books
Being a college town, Boulder is one of the best cities in the world for a browsing bookworm. It reportedly has more used-book stores per capita than any other U.S. city. Chain outlets include **Barnes & Noble,** 2915 Pearl St. (© **303/442-1665**). The independents run the gamut from the Kerouac and Burroughs specialists at **Beat Bookshop,** 1717 Pearl St. (© **303/444-7111**), to the lesbian/feminist/gay selection at **Word Is Out,** 2015 10th St. (© **303/449-1415**). **Trident Booksellers,** 940 Pearl St. (© **303/443-3133**), is a good used-book shop with a coffeehouse attached.

Boulder Book Store This meandering, four-story, 20,000-square-foot bookstore has been locally owned and operated since the 1970s. It attracts students, bohemians, and businesspeople alike with its homey vibe, and features great selections of Buddhism tomes and travel guides. Attached is The Bookend Cafe, a coffeehouse with patio seating on the Pearl Street Mall (see "Espresso Bars, Coffeehouses & Related Establishments," earlier in this chapter). 1107 Pearl St. (℃ **303/447-2074.** www.boulderbookstore.com.

Fashion

Alpaca Connection Come here for natural-fiber clothing from around the world, including alpaca-and-wool sweaters from South America. 1326 Pearl St. (℃ **303/447-2047.**

Rocky Mountain Kids (Kids Offering clothing for newborns to 12-year-olds, this bright store specializes in quality brands and is known for its kid-friendliness: complimentary animal crackers and plenty of toys in the box. 2525 Arapahoe Ave. (℃ **303/447-2267.**

Weekends The selection of men's and women's fashions is somewhat pricey but chosen for comfort and style—and it shows. 1200 Pearl St. (℃ **303/444-4231.** www.weekends boulder.com.

Food & Drink

Boulder Wine Merchant This store has a solid selection of wines from around the world, plus knowledgeable salespeople (and more than one master sommelier) who can help you make the right choice. 2690 Broadway. (℃ **303/443-6761.**

Liquor Mart Here you'll find a huge choice of discounted wine and liquor, with more than 5,000 wines and 900 beers, including a wide selection of imported and microbrewed beers. 1750 15th St. (at Canyon Blvd.). (℃ **303/449-3374.**

Whole Foods The latest and greatest of Boulder's organic supermarkets, this huge store—part of the national chain—has a wide-ranging, fresh inventory, and is a favorite lunch spot of locals. Offerings include a deli, soup and salad bar, sushi, and more free samples than you could possibly eat. 2905 Pearl St. (℃ **303/545-6611.**

Gifts & Souvenirs

The best stops for T-shirts, University of Colorado paraphernalia, and other Boulder souvenirs are **Jackalope and Company,** 1126 Pearl St. ((℃ **303/939-8434);** **Where the Buffalo Roam,** 1320 Pearl St. ((℃ **303/938-1424);** and the **CU Bookstore,** 1111 Broadway ((℃ **303/442-5051).** Long a hub for Eastern religion, Boulder also has a plethora of Tibetan gift shops—**Old Tibet,** 948 Pearl St. ((℃ **303/440-0323),** is the longest standing.

Hardware

McGuckin Hardware McGuckin claims to have the world's largest hardware selection, with more than 200,000 items in stock. In addition to the nuts, bolts, brackets, paints, tools, and assorted whatchamacallits that most hardware stores carry, you'll also find sporting goods, kitchen gizmos, automotive supplies, stationery, some clothing, electronics, outdoor furniture, fresh flowers, and a whole lot of other stuff. 2525 Arapahoe Ave. (℃ **303/443-1822** or 86-MCGUCKIN. www.mcguckin.com.

Jewelry

Angie Star Jewelry A gallery for some of the area's top jewelry designers, Angie Star's store is a showcase for one-of-a-kind pieces. 1807 Pearl St. (℃ **720/565-0288.**

El Loro   Distinctively Boulder, this bohemian jewelry shop has been a Pearl Street Mall resident for more than 25 years. Aside from a nice selection of sterling silver items with semiprecious stones, El Loro also sells clogs and incense. 1416 Pearl St. ℭ **303/449-3162.**

Kitchenware

Peppercorn   From cookbooks to pasta makers, you can find anything and everything for the kitchen here at "the Smithsonian of cookstores." In business since 1977, this vast store (12,000 sq. ft.!) has hundreds of kitchen gadgets and appliances—everything you might need to prepare, serve, and consume the simplest or most exotic meal. 1235 Pearl St. ℭ **800/447-6905** or 303/449-5847. www.peppercorn.com.

Sporting Goods

Sports Authority, 3320 N. 28th St. (ℭ **303/449-9021**), is a good all-purpose source, while the following are more specialized—and interesting—retail outlets.

Boulder Army Store   Just east of the Pearl Street Mall, this shop has the best inventory of camping gear in the city, along with a limited amount of fishing equipment. There is also a good supply of outdoor clothing and military surplus items such as fatigues, helmets, and that disarmed hand grenade you've always wanted. 1545 Pearl St. ℭ **303/442-7616.**

Boulder Mountaineering   This shop specializes in equipment, clothing, and accessories for backpacking, camping, rock and ice climbing, mountaineering, backcountry skiing, and snowshoeing. Equipment rentals include sleeping bags, tents, backpacks, and snowshoes; backcountry and telemark ski packages are available. Eldora Mountain Sports (see above) also sells maps and guidebooks, and the knowledgeable staff—which includes several trained guides—can help you plan your trip. 1335 Broadway. ℭ **303/442-8355.**

---

8 BOULDER AFTER DARK

As a cultured and well-educated community (59% of adult residents have at least one college degree), Boulder is especially noted for its summer music, dance, and Shakespeare festivals. Major entertainment events take place year-round, both downtown and on the University of Colorado campus. There's also a wide choice of nightclubs and bars, but it hasn't always been so: Boulder was dry for 60 years, from 1907 (13 years before national Prohibition) to 1967. The first new bar in the city opened in 1969, in the Hotel Boulderado. The notoriously healthy city banned smoking in 1995, 11 years before the state did the same thing.

Entertainment schedules can be found in the *Daily Camera's* weekly *Friday Magazine;* in either of the Denver dailies, the *Denver Post* or the *Rocky Mountain News;* in *Westword,* the Denver weekly; or in the free *Boulder Weekly.*

THE CLUB & MUSIC SCENE

Boulder Theater Ⓕⓘⓝⓓⓢ   Rock, folk, bluegrass, jazz, hip-hop, comedy, and who knows what else—performed by notables such as Lou Reed, Bill Maher, Herbie Hancock, and Norah Jones—take the stage here. During the week, you'll also find independent and otherwise alternative films; there are also annual film festivals here. 2032 14th St. ℭ **303/786-7030.** www.bouldertheater.com.

The Catacombs   This popular bar books live blues and jazz by local and regional performers. The loud, somewhat raucous atmosphere (and smoking room) draws a crowd of CU students and an eclectic mix of locals and traveling businesspeople. A limited pub menu is served. In the basement of the Hotel Boulderado, 13th and Spruce sts. ℂ 303/443-0486.

Fox Theatre and Cafe (Finds)   A variety of live music (including, but not limited to, bluegrass, funk, blues, hip-hop, reggae, and punk) is presented here 5 or 6 nights a week, featuring a mix of local, regional, and national talent. You'll find three bars at this converted movie theater, which is revered for its great acoustics. 1135 13th St. ℂ 303/443-3399 or 303/447-0095. www.foxtheatre.com.

'Round Midnight   A hip basement joint on the Pearl Street Mall, 'Round Midnight specializes in malt scotch, good beer, and dancing. An eclectic array of performers (hip-hop, techno, jazz, rock) take the stage here on weekends and there are DJs during the week. 1005 Pearl St. ℂ 303/442-2176. www.roundmidnight.tv.

THE BAR SCENE

Conor O'Neill's (Finds)   Everything in this pub—from the bar to the art to the timber floors—was designed and built in Ireland. The atmosphere is rich, with a "shop pub" up front and two back rooms centered on a pair of fireplaces that were constructed by visiting Irish stonemasons. There are more than a dozen beers on tap, primarily from (where else?) Ireland, and the pub menu features fish and chips, burgers, and a mean shepherd's pie. There is regular live music (surf to Celtic), and an Irish jam session Sunday afternoons. 1922 13th St. ℂ 303/449-1922. www.conoroneills.com.

Lazy Dog   With a great rooftop deck and a plethora of TVs tuned into games of all kinds, the Lazy Dog has emerged as the best sports bar in Boulder, especially after its recent relocation to the Pearl Street Mall. 1346 Pearl St. ℂ 303/440-3355. www.thelazydog.com.

Mountain Sun Pub & Brewery   An English-style neighborhood pub and microbrewery, Mountain Sun produces dozens of barrels of beer each week and provides tours on request during the day. The mostly made-from-scratch menu features soups, salads, burgers, sandwiches, and a few Mexican dishes. There's live folk, acoustic, and bluegrass music on Sunday night. There is also the **Southern Sun** in south Boulder at 627 S. Broadway (ℂ 303/543-0886). 1535 Pearl St. (east of the mall). ℂ 303/546-0886. www.mountainsunpub.com.

The Sink (Finds)   This off-campus establishment opened in 1923 (CU dropout Robert Redford was once the janitor) but has been updated with new spacy wall murals that help make it one of Boulder's funniest—and most fun—nightspots. There's a full bar with more than a dozen regional microbrews, live music, and fare such as Sinkburgers and "ugly crust" pizza. 1165 13th St. ℂ 303/444-SINK [7465]. www.thesink.com.

Sundown Saloon   This raucous dive is a CU institution. In a spacious basement on the west end of the Pearl Street Mall, pool is the pastime of choice and the drinks are reasonably priced. 1136 Pearl St. ℂ 303/449-4987. www.thesundownsaloon.com.

Walnut Brewery   In a historic brick warehouse a block from the Pearl Street Mall, this large restaurant/bar/microbrewery is popular with the after-work crowd, both young and old. 1123 Walnut St. (near Broadway). ℂ 303/447-1345. www.walnutbrewery.com.

Lyons: On the Beaten Path

Most tourists driving U.S. 36 to Rocky Mountain National Park from Boulder or Denver blaze through the dinky town of Lyons without even bothering to slow down. They're missing some top-drawer diversions in the process. For beer and music aficionados, **Oskar Blues Grill & Brew,** 303 Main St. (© **303/823-6685;** www.oskarblues.com), is a fun and—to say the least—eclectically decorated place for lunch and a beer, or a blues, rock, or rockabilly show come nighttime. Oskar Blues was the first craft brewery in the country to can its beer (Dale's Pale Ale, Old Chub, Gordon, and Ten-Fidy). The canning now happens in nearby Longmont, but the restaurant is still open daily from 11am to 10pm; the bar is open until midnight Sunday through Thursday and until 2am on Friday and Saturday. Also worth a look is the **Lyons Pinball Arcade,** 339-A Main St. (© **303/823-6100;** www.lyonspinball.com), with 30 pinball machines dating from the 1970s and more recent decades, including Kiss, Black Knight, and Addams Family. For silverball fiends, it's a trip down memory lane.

Downtown Lyons is a historic district marked by 16 Victorian sandstones, and just outside of town, the fishing and hiking are excellent. For additional information, contact the **Lyons Chamber of Commerce,** 350 Broadway (P.O. Box 426), Lyons, CO 80540 (© **877/LYONS-CO [596-6726]** or 303/823-5215; www.lyons-colorado.com).

West End Tavern A 2004 makeover of this popular neighborhood bar left the brick walls and the classic bar intact, but gave the rest of the joint a contemporary shot in the arm and a slick look. Beyond the 48 bourbons stocked by the bar, fare includes a different specialty burger every day, barbecue, and more upscale items. The tavern's roof garden is an ideal spot to unwind and enjoy some of the best views in town and outdoor cinema on certain summer nights. 926 Pearl St. © 303/444-3535. www.thewestendtavern.com.

THE PERFORMING ARTS

Music, dance, and theater are important aspects of life for Boulder residents. Many of these activities take place at **Macky Auditorium** at the University of Colorado (© **303/ 492-8008;** www.colorado.edu/music) and other campus venues, as well as the **Chautauqua Auditorium,** 900 Baseline Rd. (© **303/442-3282;** www.chautauqua.com), and the **Dairy Center for the Arts,** 2590 Walnut St. (© **303/440-7826;** www.thedairy.org).

Classical Music & Opera

Boulder Bach Festival First presented in 1981, this celebration of the music of Johann Sebastian Bach includes not only a late-January festival but also concerts and other events year-round. Tickets run about $15 to $30. Series tickets are also available. P.O. Box 1896, Boulder, CO 80306. © 303/776-9666. www.boulderbachfest.org.

Boulder Philharmonic Orchestra This acclaimed community orchestra performs an annual fall-to-spring season, primarily at Macky Auditorium, with world-class artists who have included singer Marilyn Horne, guitarist Carlos Montoya, cellist Yo-Yo Ma, and violinist Itzhak Perlman. Tickets cost $10 to $70, more for concerts that feature premier performers. 2995 Wilderness Place, Suite 100, Boulder, CO 80301. © **303/449-1343.** www.boulderphil.org.

Colorado MahlerFest   Begun in 1988, this international festival is the only one of its kind in the world. For a week each January it celebrates the work of Gustav Mahler with a performance of one of his symphonies as well as chamber concerts, films, discussions, seminars, and other musical programs. Most events are free; admission to symphony concerts ranges from $10 to $40. P.O. Box 1314, Boulder, CO 80306. © **303/447-0513.** www.mahlerfest.org.

Colorado Music Festival (Finds)   Begun in 1976, this series is the single biggest annual arts event in Boulder, with visiting musicians from around the world performing in the acoustically revered Chautauqua Auditorium. The festival presents works by composers of the classical through modern eras, such as Bach, Beethoven, Mozart, Dvorak, and Gershwin, plus living composers. It usually runs from mid-June to mid-August, with symphony orchestra performances Thursday and Friday, chamber-orchestra concerts Sunday, and a chamber-music series Tuesday; all shows start at 7:30pm. There's also a children's concert in late June and a free Independence Day concert at CU's Folsom Field. Adult ticket prices range from $12 to $47. 900 Baseline Rd., Cottage 100, Boulder, CO 80302. © **303/449-1397** for general information, 303/440-7666, or visit website for tickets. www.coloradomusicfest.org.

CU Concerts   The university's College of Music presents the Artist Series, Music, Theatre, University of Colorado Summer Opera, Takács String Quartet Series, and Holiday Festival at Macky Auditorium and Grusin Music Hall. The Artist Series features an outstanding lineup of classical soloists, jazz artists, dance companies, and multidisciplinary events. Call early for tickets for performances of the renowned Takács String Quartet. The annual Holiday Festival includes the University Symphony Orchestra, university choirs, several smaller ensembles, and soloists from the College of Music's student body and faculty. General admission tickets usually cost between $10 and $40. University of Colorado. © **303/492-8008.** www.cuconcerts.org.

Theater

Colorado Shakespeare Festival (Moments)   Considered one of the top three Shakespearean festivals in the United States, this 2-month annual event attracts more than 40,000 theatergoers between late June and late August. Held since 1958 in the University of Colorado's Mary Rippon Outdoor Theatre, and indoors at the University Theatre Main Stage, it offers more than a dozen performances of each of four plays. Actors, directors, designers, and everyone associated with the productions are fully schooled Shakespearean professionals. Tickets run from $7 to $54 for single performances, with series packages also available. Campus Box 277, University of Colorado, Boulder, CO 80309. © **303/492-0554** for information and the box office. www.coloradoshakes.org.

Upstart Crow Theatre Company   Specializing in Shakespeare and more contemporary classics, the Upstart Crow is the resident theater company at the Dairy Center for the Arts. They perform on two stages: a 99-seat theater (where no seat is more than three rows from the stage) and an 86-seat proscenium theater. Tickets are $16 to $19; there are also "name-your-price nights." Dairy Center for the Arts, 2590 Walnut St. © **303/442-1415.** www.theupstartcrow.org.

9 A SIDE TRIP TO ROCKY MOUNTAIN NATIONAL PARK

44 miles NW of Boulder, 71 miles NW of Denver

The northern half of the Colorado Rockies is the country's ultimate mountain wilderness, the crown on the head of the great range that dominates the American West. This is rugged beauty at its best, extending on either side of the meandering Continental Divide down sawtooth ridgelines, through precipitous river canyons, and across broad alpine plains. Here, snowfall is measured in feet, not inches, and when spring's sun finally melts away the frost, amazing arrays of alpine wildflowers herald the new beginning. There's no better place to experience this spectacular scenery than at Rocky Mountain National Park. Although it can be a fairly easy day trip from Boulder or Denver, I highly recommend spending at least 2 or 3 days here, perhaps making the gateway community of Estes Park your base of operations while exploring the trails and spectacular views of the national park.

ROCKY MOUNTAIN NATIONAL PARK ★★★

Snow-covered peaks—17 mountains above 13,000 feet—stand over lush valleys and shimmering alpine lakes in the 415 square miles (265,600 acres) of Rocky Mountain National Park. The highest, at 14,259 feet, is Longs Peak.

What really sets the park apart (after all, this sort of eye-popping beauty is not unusual in the Rockies) is its variety of distinct ecological zones. As you rise and descend in altitude, the landscape of the park changes dramatically. In relatively low areas, from about 7,500 to 9,000 feet, a lush forest of ponderosa pine and juniper cloaks the sunny southern slopes, with Douglas fir on the cooler northern slopes. Thirstier blue spruce and lodgepole pine cling to stream sides, with occasional groves of aspen. Elk and mule deer thrive. On higher slopes, a subalpine ecosystem exists, dominated by forests of Engelmann spruce and subalpine fir, but interspersed with wide meadows alive with wildflowers during spring and summer. This is also home to bighorn sheep, which have become unofficial mascots of the park. Above 11,500 feet, the trees become increasingly gnarled and stunted, until they disappear altogether and alpine tundra predominates. Fully one-third of the park is at this altitude; in this bleak, rocky world, many of the plants are identical to those found in the Arctic.

Trail Ridge Road, which cuts west through the middle of the park from Estes Park and then south down its western boundary to Grand Lake, is one of America's great alpine highways. Climbing to 12,183 feet near Fall River Pass, it's the highest continuous paved highway in the United States. The road is usually open from Memorial Day into October, depending on the snowfall. The 48-mile scenic drive from Estes Park to Grand Lake takes about 3 hours, allowing for stops at numerous scenic outlooks. Exhibits at the **Alpine Visitor Center** at Fall River Pass, 11,796 feet above sea level, explain life on the alpine tundra.

Fall River Road, the original park road, leads to Fall River Pass from Estes Park via Horseshoe Park Junction. West of the Endovalley picnic area, the road is one-way uphill, and closed to trailers and motor homes. As you negotiate its gravelly switchbacks, you get a clear idea of what early auto travel was like in the West. This road, too, is closed in winter.

One of the few paved roads in the Rockies that leads into a high mountain basin is **Bear Lake Road;** it is open year-round, with occasional half-day closings to clear snow. Numerous trails converge at Bear Lake, southwest of the Beaver Meadows Visitor Center, on the other side of Moraine Park.

Just the Facts

GETTING THERE   By Car   The most direct route to Estes Park (and Rocky Mountain National Park) is U.S. 36 from Denver and Boulder. At Estes Park, U.S. 36 joins U.S. 34, which runs up the Big Thompson Canyon from I-25 and Loveland, and continues through Rocky Mountain National Park to Granby. An alternative scenic route to Estes Park is Colo. 7, the "Peak-to-Peak Scenic Byway" that goes, under different designations, through Central City (Colo. 119), Nederland (Colo. 72), and Allenspark (Colo. 7).

By Plane   Visitors can fly into Denver International Airport and then rent a car or contact **Estes Park Shuttle** (© 970/586-5151; www.estesparkshuttle.com), which connects Estes Park with Boulder and Denver. Rates to Denver International Airport are $45 one-way and $85 round-trip.

ENTRY POINTS   Entry into the park is from the east (through Estes Park) or the west (through Grand Lake). **Trail Ridge Road** connects the two sides. Most visitors enter the park from the Estes Park side. The **Beaver Meadows entrance,** west of Estes Park on U.S. 36, is the national park's main entrance. U.S. 34 west from Estes Park takes you to the **Fall River entrance** (north of the Beaver Meadows entrance). Those entering the park from the west side should take U.S. 40 to Granby and then follow U.S. 34 north to the **Grand Lake entrance.**

GETTING AROUND   In summer, a free national park **shuttle bus** runs from Moraine Park Campground, Moraine Park Museum, and the Glacier Basin parking area to Bear Lake, with departures every 10 to 20 minutes. Shuttle buses also began operating in 2006 throughout the business district of Estes Park and from Estes Park into Rocky Mountain National Park. The buses run daily July through Labor Day; schedules are available at the Estes Park Visitor Center (see "Visitor Centers & Information," below).

Local taxi service is provided by **Stanley Brothers Taxi Company** (© 970/577-7433).

VISITOR CENTERS & INFORMATION   For information on where to stay and eat and what to do in the gateway community of Estes Park, contact the **Estes Park Convention and Visitors Bureau** (© 800/443-7837; www.estesparkcvb.com). There is a visitor center on U.S. 34, just east of its junction with U.S. 36, with access from both highways.

Unless otherwise noted, call the main park number (© 970/586-1206) for information on the following visitor centers.

Entering the park from Estes Park, the **Beaver Meadows Visitor Center,** U.S. 36, west of Colo. 66, has knowledgeable people to answer questions and give advice, a wide choice of books and maps for sale, and interpretive exhibits, including a relief model of the park. It's open daily from 8am to 9pm in summer and from 8am to 5pm the rest of the year.

Outside the park, just east of the Fall River entrance, is the **Fall River Visitor Center.** Located in a beautiful mountain lodge–style building, it was built with private funds but is staffed by park rangers and volunteers from the Rocky Mountain Nature Association. It contains exhibits on park wildlife, including some spectacular full-size bronzes of elk and other animals, plus a children's Discovery Room, an information desk, and a bookstore. Next door is a large (but somewhat pricey) souvenir-and-clothing shop plus a

(Fun Facts) **One Gutsy Lady!**

Isabella Lucy Bird, an intrepid Englishwoman returning home from the Hawaiian Islands in the fall of 1873, spent about 3 months exploring what we now call the Front Range of the Rockies, on horseback and mostly by herself. Crossing into the interior of the continent by rail from California, she left the train at Cheyenne, Wyoming, and headed south into Colorado. Her goal, she wrote, was "a most romantic place called Estes Park, at a height of 7,500 feet."

She arrived in late September and observed, "Longs Peak, 14,700 feet high, dwarfs all the surrounding mountains." (Actually, Longs Peak is 14,259 ft. in elevation). Five years after the first successful ascent of Longs Peak, Bird became the first woman to reach the top. "It was something at last to stand upon the storm-rent crown of this lonely sentinel of the Rocky Range. Uplifted above love and hate and storms of passion, calm amidst the eternal silences, fanned by zephyrs and bathed in living blue, peace rested for that one bright day on the Peak," she wrote to her sister.

Bird spent several weeks that autumn in a small cabin on Lake Estes. Nights were dark except for the brilliance of the stars, morning frosts were sharp, and water was carried from the lake. In late October she embarked on a tour of Colorado's Front Range, riding a bay pony, "a little beauty, with legs of iron, fast, enduring, gentle, and wise," disregarding warnings of hostile American Indians and the threat of snow and cold. Undeterred, Bird headed south across the plains, staying in lodgings when they were available, but camping out under the stars at other times. She followed rivers and trails through Denver to Old Colorado City, located in present-day Colorado Springs. Turning once more toward the mountains, she passed through the rich red rocks known as the Garden of the Gods, and listened to tales of the healing powers of the springs of Manitou. Winding her way back north, she endured snow blindness and bitter cold, before again reaching Estes Park, and writing, "Nothing I have seen in Colorado compares with Estes Park."

In early December, Isabella Bird left Estes Park for the final time, returning to the train at Cheyenne and eventually home to afternoon tea, fine linens, and a warm, soft bed in England. Although she later traveled to Japan, India, Turkey, and China, she never again visited the land she had fondly called the Wild West.

cafeteria-style restaurant with snacks and sandwiches. It's open daily from 9am to 6pm in summer and 9am to 5pm in spring and fall.

Near the park's west side entrance is the **Kawuneeche Visitor Center** (© **970/586-1513**), open daily from 8am to 6pm in summer, from 8am to 5pm in late spring, and from 8am to 4:30pm in fall and winter. Located high in the mountains (11,796 ft. above sea level) is the **Alpine Visitor Center,** at Fall River Pass, open from late spring through early fall, daily from 10:30am to 4:30pm; exhibits here explain life on the alpine tundra. Visitor facilities are also available at the **Moraine Park Museum** on Bear Lake Road, open daily from 9am to 4:30pm.

For more specifics on planning a trip, contact Rocky Mountain National Park, 1000 U.S. 36, Estes Park, CO 80517-8397 (📞 **970/586-1206** or 970/586-1333 for recorded information; www.nps.gov/romo). You can also get detailed information from the **Rocky Mountain Nature Association,** P.O. Box 3100, Estes Park, CO 80517 (📞 **970/586-0108;** www.rmna.org), which sells a variety of maps, guides, books, and videos.

FEES & REGULATIONS   Park admission for up to 7 days is $20 per vehicle, $10 per person for bicyclists, motorcyclists, and pedestrians.

As in many national parks, wilderness permits are required for all overnight backpacking trips, and camping is allowed only in specified campsites. Pets must be leashed at all times and are not permitted on trails or in the backcountry; in addition, the park insists that pets not be left in unattended vehicles. Both motor vehicles and bicycles must remain on the roads or in parking areas. Do not feed or touch any park animals, and do not pick any wildflowers.

SEASONS   Even though the park is technically open daily year-round, Trail Ridge Road, the main east–west thoroughfare through the park, is closed in winter. The road is usually open by late May (after the snow has been cleared) and closes between mid- and late October. However, it is not uncommon for snowstorms to close the road for several hours or even a full day at any time, especially in early June and October. The high country is open during the summer and as snow conditions permit in winter.

AVOIDING THE CROWDS   Because large portions of the park are closed half the year, practically everyone visits during the spring and summer. The busiest period is from mid-June to mid-August—essentially during school vacations. In order to avoid the largest crowds, try to visit just before or just after that period. For those who don't mind chilly evenings, late September and early October are less crowded and can be beautiful, although there's always the chance of an early winter storm. Regardless of when you visit, the absolute best way to avoid crowds is by putting on a backpack or climbing onto a horse. Rocky Mountain has about 350 miles of trails leading into all corners of the park (see "Sports & Outdoor Activities in & around the Park," below in this section).

RANGER PROGRAMS   Each visitor center offers campfire talks and other programs between June and September. Consult the park's free newspaper for scheduled activities, which vary from photo walks to fly-fishing and orienteering.

Seeing the Highlights

Although Rocky Mountain National Park is generally considered the domain of hikers and climbers, it's surprisingly easy to thoroughly enjoy this park without working up a sweat. For that we can thank **Trail Ridge Road.**

Built in 1932 and undoubtedly one of America's most scenic highways, it provides expansive and sometimes dizzying views in all directions. The drive from Estes Park to Grand Lake covers some 48 miles through the park, rising above 12,000 feet in elevation and crossing the Continental Divide. It offers spectacular vistas of snowcapped peaks, deep forests, and meadows of wildflowers, where bighorn sheep, elk, and deer browse. Allow at least 3 hours for the drive, and possibly more if you'd like to take a hike from one of the many vista points.

TRAIL RIDGE ROAD ★

Along Trail Ridge Road are numbered signs, from 1 to 12, starting on the east side of the park and heading west. These stops are described below, and the route is also discussed

Stop No. 1: Deer Ridge Junction. This spot offers views of the Mummy Mountain Range to the north. It is the official beginning of Trail Ridge Road, the highest continuous paved road in the United States, reaching an elevation of 12,183 feet. Here you're at a mere 8,940 feet.

Stop No. 2: Hidden Valley. Formerly the site of a downhill ski area, this scenic subalpine valley boasts forests of Engelmann spruce and fir. The elevation is 9,240 feet.

Stop No. 3: Many Parks Curve. This delightfully scenic stop, with one of the best roadside views in the park, is also a good location for birders, who are likely to spot the noisy Steller's jay and Clark's nutcracker. The term "park" is used in the sense of a level valley between mountain ranges (often an open, grassy area), which in this case was carved by glaciers some 10,000 years ago. The elevation is 9,620 feet.

Stop No. 4: Rainbow Curve. Just past a sign announcing your position 2 miles above sea level is Rainbow Curve, an area known for colorful rainbows that are often seen after thunderstorms. It's also famous for ferocious winds and brutal winters. Take a look at the trees that have branches only on their downwind side, where their trunks protect them from the elements. The excellent view from the overlook here extends past Longs Peak and into Hidden Valley and Horseshoe Park, where you can see rock, gravel, and other rubble left by a flood that struck in 1982 after a dam broke. The elevation is 10,829 feet.

Stop No. 5: Forest Canyon Overlook. From this stop's parking area, a short, paved walkway leads to an observation platform offering a beautiful but dizzying view into vast Forest Canyon, where the erosion work of glaciers is clearly evident. The peaks of the Continental Divide appear beyond. Near the overlook, watch for pikas (relatives of rabbits), marmots, and other small mammals. The elevation is 11,716 feet.

Stop No. 6: Rock Cut. Practically the highest point along Trail Ridge Road, this is alpine tundra at its harshest. Winds can reach 150 mph, winter blizzards are frequent, and temperatures in midsummer frequently drop below freezing. You'll have splendid views of the glacially carved peaks along the Continental Divide, and on the .5-mile **Tundra World Nature Trail,** you'll find signs identifying and discussing the hardy plants and animals that inhabit this cold and barren region. The elevation is 12,110 feet.

Stop No. 7: Lava Cliffs. Here you'll see a dark cliff, created by the carving action of glacial ice through a thick layer of tuff (volcanic ash and debris) that was deposited here about 28 million years ago during volcanic eruptions in the Never Summer Range, located about 8 miles west. If you look just below the cliff, you'll see a pretty meadow that is a popular grazing spot for elk. The elevation is 12,080 feet.

Stop No. 8: Fall River Pass. At this spot you'll get a good view of a huge amphitheater, and you can take a break at the Alpine Visitor Center. A viewing platform at the rear of the visitor center offers vistas of a wide, glacially carved valley of grasses, wildflowers, shrubs, and small trees where you're practically guaranteed to see elk grazing. This is also the junction of Trail Ridge Road and Old Fall River Road. The elevation is 11,796 feet.

Stop No. 9: Medicine Bow Curve. Views of a vast subalpine forest of spruce and fir and the distant Cache la Poudre River give way to the Medicine Bow Mountains, which extend into Wyoming. The elevation is 11,640 feet.

BOULDER

7

A SIDE TRIP TO ROCKY MOUNTAIN NATIONAL PARK

(Tips) **Old Fall River Road: A Step Back in Time**

For those who find Trail Ridge Road too civilized or too easy, there is an alternative: The park's original road still exists, and it's still mostly dirt, still steep, and just as narrow and winding as ever. Covering 11 miles (2 paved and 9 gravel), from Horseshoe Park to Fall River Pass, this one-way (west) road climbs 3,200 feet. It provides today's visitors with a glimpse into the experiences of those who explored this rugged land in Model T Fords and Stanley Steamers during the national park's early years.

Even before the establishment of Rocky Mountain National Park in 1915, there was interest in building a road through the mountains. In July 1913, work began with the arrival of 38 convicts from the Colorado State Penitentiary. The road was finally dedicated on September 14, 1920, and until Trail Ridge Road was built in 1932, Old Fall River Road was the only route from the east into the heart of the national park. Although the grading was new, the route of Old Fall River Road was not—it followed what Arapaho called the Dog's Trail, a path where they used dogs to pull crude V-shaped sleds through the mountains.

Today this road remains much as it was in the 1920s, with numerous drop-offs and switchbacks—not for anyone with a serious fear of heights! As you drive it, you'll see boulder fields, riparian areas, and cascading waterfalls, as well as some of the most rugged high-elevation sections of the park. Watch for the stone walls along the roadsides that were built during the 1920s in an often-unsuccessful effort to keep the road from being washed away. Snowmelt, freezing and thawing, and thunderstorms often caused damage to the road. A mudslide in July 1953 did so much harm that the park service was ready to give up on the road; public pressure led to a change of heart, and the historic Old Fall River Road reopened in 1968.

Stop No. 10: Milner Pass. This is the Continental Divide, the backbone of North America. From this point, water flows west to the Pacific or east toward the Atlantic. The divide also affects the park's weather—the west side is usually colder, is less windy, and receives much more precipitation than the east side. The elevation is 10,758 feet.

Stop No. 11: Farview Curve. This aptly named overlook provides a look at the beginnings of the Colorado River as it carves its way through the Kawuneeche Valley, 1,000 feet below the overlook, before flowing some 1,400 miles to the Gulf of California. There are also panoramic views of the Never Summer Mountains. Looking west from this point, you can see the Grand Ditch, which carries water across the Continental Divide to Colorado's thirsty eastern plains. Engelmann spruce and lodgepole pine grow here, and you'll see ground squirrels and chipmunks scurrying among the rocks. The elevation is 10,120 feet.

Stop No. 12: Holzwarth Trout Lodge Historic Site. Just past the Timber Creek Campground, this stop provides access to a short trail to **Holzwarth Trout Lodge Historic Site,** an early-20th-century homestead that started out as a working cattle ranch and

Passing through three ecosystems, the relatively short, slow drive provides a cross-section view of Rocky Mountain National Park, its plants and animals, its forests and valleys, and its famous alpine tundra, quite likely the bleakest but most fascinating terrain the majority of visitors will ever see. Open only in summer, Old Fall River Road begins at an elevation of 8,558 feet in the **montane** ecosystem. One of the milder sections of the park, it is home to ponderosa pine, Douglas fir, quaking aspen, numerous birds, and a wide variety of mammals, ranging from cottontail rabbits to elk and mountain lions. Continue your drive and you'll soon ease into the **subalpine** ecosystem, which is cooler and moister than the montane, with forests of Engelmann spruce, Colorado blue spruce, and subalpine fir. You'll find birds such as Clark's nutcracker, and mule deer, long-tailed weasels, and elk.

The upper limit of the subalpine ecosystem is at about 11,000 feet. Then there's a transition zone, where the same trees as in the subalpine ecosystem exist, but in a smaller size. Finally you're there—the end of the world. At almost 12,000 feet of elevation, the **alpine tundra** has no trees, and many of its other plants are almost too tiny to see. The wildlife includes golden eagles, hawks, mice and other rodents, and yellow-bellied marmots, plus bighorn sheep and elk.

Old Fall River Road ends at Fall River Pass at the Alpine Visitor Center—watch for elk as you approach the visitor center. There it joins Trail Ridge Road, which you can take back to the east side of the park, or go west to cross the Continental Divide at Milner Pass and continue into the park's western section. Old Fall River Road is open to motor vehicles and mountain bikes; trailers and motor homes over 25 feet long are wisely prohibited.

BOULDER

7

A SIDE TRIP TO ROCKY MOUNTAIN NATIONAL PARK

soon evolved into a dude ranch. Rangers give talks and guided walks here during the summer. The elevation is 8,884 feet.

Sports & Outdoor Activities in & Around the Park

In addition to Rocky Mountain National Park, many activities take place just outside the park in the 1,240-square-mile Roosevelt National Forest. In Estes Park, a **Forest Service Information Center** is located at 161 Second St. (© **970/586-3440**); it's usually open daily from 9am to 5pm in summer. For year-round information, contact the **Forest Service Information Center,** 2150 Centre Ave., Building E, Fort Collins, CO 80526 (© **970/295-6700;** www.fs.fed.us/r2).

BICYCLING   Bicyclists will have to share the roadways with motor vehicles along narrow roads with 5% to 7% grades. As in most national parks, bikes are not permitted off established roads. However, bicyclists still enjoy the challenge and scenery. One popular 16-mile ride is the **Horseshoe Park/Estes Park Loop,** which goes from Estes Park west on U.S. 34 past Aspenglen Campground and the park's Fall River entrance, and then heads east at the Deer Ridge Junction, following U.S. 36 through the Beaver Meadows park entrance. There are plenty of beautiful mountain views; allow 1 to 3 hours. A free park brochure provides information on safety, regulations, and other suggested routes. Tours, rentals, and repairs are available at **Colorado Bicycling Adventures,** 184 E. Elkhorn Ave., Estes Park (C **970/586-4241;** www.coloradobicycling.com). Bike rentals cost from $17 to $50 for a half-day and $25 to $91 for a full day, depending on the type of bike, which ranges from very basic to absolutely fantastic. The company offers guided downhill tours in the park for about $75 per person, and also leads a variety of free group bike rides in the Estes Park area from May to September (call or check the website for the current schedule).

CLIMBING & MOUNTAINEERING   **Colorado Mountain School,** 341 Moraine Ave., Estes Park, CO 80517 (C **800/836-4008;** www.totalclimbing.com), is an AMGA accredited year-round guide service, and the sole concessionaire for technical climbing and instruction in Rocky Mountain National Park. The school offers a wide range of programs. Among those I especially recommend are the 2-day mountaineering class for $425 and the guided group hike up Longs Peak for about $200 per person. The school also offers lodging in a hostel-type setting, at about $35 per night per person in summer with lower rates the rest of the year. (See also "Hiking & Backpacking," below.) Be sure to stop at the ranger station at the Longs Peak trail head for current trail and weather information before attempting to ascend Longs Peak.

EDUCATIONAL PROGRAMS   The **Rocky Mountain Nature Association** (see contact information under "Visitor Centers & Information," earlier in this chapter) offers a wide variety of seminars and workshops, ranging from 1 full day to several days. Subjects vary but might include songbirds, flower identification, edible and medicinal herbs, painting, wildlife photography, tracking park animals, and edible mushrooms. Rates are $85 to $100 for full-day programs and $170 and up for multiday programs.

FISHING   Four species of trout are fished in national park and national forest streams and lakes: brown, rainbow, brook, and cutthroat. (Only the cutthroat are natives.) A state fishing license is required (nonresidents: $9 for one day or $21 for 5 days, plus a $5 habitat stamp), and only artificial lures or flies are permitted in the park. A number of lakes and streams in the national park are closed to fishing, including Bear Lake. A free park brochure that's available at visitor centers lists open and closed bodies of water, plus regulations and other information.

HIKING & BACKPACKING   Park visitor centers sell U.S. Geological Survey topographic maps and guidebooks, and rangers can direct you to lesser-used trails. Keep in mind that all trails here start at over—sometimes well over—7,000 feet elevation, and even the easiest and flattest walks will likely be tiring for those accustomed to lower elevations.

One particularly enjoyable (and easy) hike is the **Alberta Falls Trail** from the Glacier Gorge Parking Area (.6 miles one-way), which rises in elevation only 160 feet as it follows Glacier Creek to pretty Alberta Falls.

A slightly more difficult option is the **Bierstadt Lake Trail,** accessible from the north side of Bear Lake Road about 6 1/3 miles from Beaver Meadows. This 1.6-mile (one-way) trail climbs 566 feet through an aspen forest to Bierstadt Lake, where you'll find excellent views of Longs Peak.

Starting at Bear Lake, the trail up to **Emerald Lake** offers spectacular scenery en route, past Nymph and Dream lakes. The .5-mile hike to Nymph Lake is easy, climbing 225 feet; from there the trail is rated moderate to Dream Lake (another .6 miles) and then on to Emerald Lake (another .7 miles), which is 605 feet higher than the starting point at Bear Lake. Another moderate hike is the relatively uncrowded **Ouzel Falls Trail,** which leaves from Wild Basin Ranger Station and climbs about 950 feet to a picture-perfect waterfall. The distance one-way is 2.8 miles.

Among my favorite moderate hikes here is the **Mills Lake Trail** ★, a 2.8-mile (one-way) hike, with a rise in elevation of about 700 feet. Starting from Glacier Gorge Junction, the trail goes up to a picturesque mountain lake, nestled in a valley among towering mountain peaks. This lake is an excellent spot for photographing dramatic Longs Peak, especially in late afternoon or early evening, and it's the perfect place for a picnic.

If you prefer a more strenuous adventure, you'll work hard but be amply rewarded with views of timberline lakes and alpine tundra on the **Timber Lake Trail,** in the western part of the park. It's 4.8 miles one-way, with an elevation gain of 2,060 feet. Another strenuous trail, only for experienced mountain hikers and climbers in top physical condition, is the 8-mile (one-way) **Longs Peak Trail,** which climbs some 4,855 feet along steep ledges and through narrows to the top of Longs Peak.

Backcountry permits (required for all overnight hikes) can be obtained at Park Headquarters and ranger stations (in summer) for $20 from May to October, free from November to April. For information, call ℂ **970/586-1242.** There is a 7-night backcountry camping limit from June to September, with no more than 3 nights at any one spot.

HORSEBACK RIDING   Many of the national park's trails are open to horseback riders. Several outfitters provide guided rides inside and outside the park, including a 1-hour ride (about $35) and the very popular 2-hour rides (about $50). There are also all-day rides ($120–$130; bring your own lunch) plus breakfast and dinner rides and multiday pack trips. Recommended companies include **SK Horses** (www.cowpokecornercorral. com), which operates **National Park Gateway Stables,** at the Fall River entrance of the national park on U.S. 34 (ℂ **970/586-5269**); and the **Cowpoke Corner Corral,** at Glacier Lodge, 3 miles west of town, 2166 Colo. 66 (ℂ **970/586-5890**). **Sombrero Ranches** (ℂ **970/586-4577;** www.sombrero.com) operates two stables inside park boundaries, **Moraine Park Stables** (ℂ **970/586-2327**) and **Glacier Creek Stables** (ℂ **970/586-3244**), as well as stables in Estes Park, Grand Lake, and Allenspark.

SKIING & SNOWSHOEING   Much of the park is closed to vehicular travel during the winter, when deep snow covers roads and trails. Snow is usually best January through March. A popular spot for cross-country skiing and snowshoeing in the park is Bear Lake, south of the Beaver Meadows entrance. A lesser-known area of the park is Wild Basin, south of the park's east entrances off Colo. 7, about a mile north of the community of Allenspark. A 2-mile road, closed to motor vehicles for the last mile in winter, winds through a subalpine forest to the Wild Basin Trailhead, which follows a creek to a waterfall, a rustic bridge, and eventually another waterfall. Total distance to the second falls is 2.8 miles. Along the trail, your chances are good for spotting birds such as Clark's nutcrackers, Steller's jays, and the American dipper. On winter weekends, the Colorado Mountain Club often opens a warming hut at the Wild Basin Ranger Station.

Before you set forth, stop by a visitor center for maps, information on where the snow is best, and a permit if you plan to stay out overnight. Rangers often lead guided snowshoe walks on winter weekends. Among shops that rent snowshoes and skis is **Estes Park Mountain Shop,** 2050 Big Thompson Ave. (ℂ **866/303-6548** or 970/586-6548; www.estesparkmountainshop.com). Daily rental costs $5 per pair of snowshoes or $8 for skis.

Rocky Mountain National Park is a premier wildlife-viewing area; fall, winter, and spring are the best times, although I saw plenty of elk and squirrels, plus a few deer, a marmot, and a coyote, during a mid-July visit. Large herds of elk and bighorn sheep can often be seen in the meadows and on mountainsides. In addition, you may spot mule deer, beavers, coyotes, and river otters. Watch for moose among the willows on the west side of the park. In the forests are lots of songbirds and small mammals; particularly plentiful are gray and Steller's jays, Clark's nutcrackers, chipmunks, and golden-mantled ground squirrels. There's a good chance of seeing bighorn sheep, marmots, pikas, and ptarmigan along Trail Ridge Road. For detailed and current wildlife-viewing information, stop by one of the park's visitor centers, and check on the many interpretive programs, including bird walks. Rangers stress that it is both illegal and foolish to feed any wildlife.

Camping

The park has five campgrounds with a total of almost 600 sites. There are 245 sites at **Moraine Park;** another 150 are at **Glacier Basin.** Moraine Park, **Timber Creek** (98 sites), and **Longs Peak** (26 tent sites) are open year-round; Glacier Basin and **Aspenglen** (54 sites) are seasonal. Camping in summer is limited to 3 days at Longs Peak and 7 days at other campgrounds; the limit is 14 days at all the park's campgrounds in winter. Arrive early in summer if you hope to snare one of these first-come, first-served campsites. Reservations for Moraine Park and Glacier Basin are accepted from Memorial Day to early September and are usually completely booked well in advance. However, any sites not reserved—as well as sites at Timber Creek, Longs Peak, and Aspenglen—are available on a first-come, first-served basis. Make reservations with the **National Park Reservation Service** (© 877/444-6777 or 518/885-3639 for international callers; www.recreation.gov). Campsites cost $20 per night during the summer, $14 in the off season when water is turned off. No showers or RV hookups are available.

There are also a number of commercial campgrounds in Estes Park, just outside the national park. All offer RV hookups and clean bathhouses, and are open from late spring to early fall only. They include **Estes Park KOA,** 2051 Big Thompson Ave., Estes Park, CO 80517 (© **800/562-1887** for reservations, or 970/586-2888; www.estesparkkoa. com), with RV rates for two of $32 to $42; **Mary's Lake Campground,** 2120 Mary's Lake Rd. (P.O. Box 2514), Estes Park, CO 80517 (© **800/445-6279** for reservations, or 970/586-4411; www.maryslakecampground.com), with RV rates for two of $38 to $41; and **Spruce Lake R.V. Park,** 1050 Mary's Lake Rd., Estes Park, CO 80517 (© **800/536-1050** or 970/586-2889; www.sprucelakerv.com), charging $40 to $48 for an RV site for two people. Estes Park KOA and Mary's Lake Campground also have tent sites at lower rates; Spruce Lake does not permit tents, but like the KOA offers rental cabins. (Mary's Lake rents pop-up campers as its premium alternative.)

ESTES PARK

Located just outside the east entrances to Rocky Mountain National Park, literally within a stone's throw, the community of Estes Park provides most of the lodging, dining, and other services for park visitors (there are no lodging facilities within the park boundaries). Unlike other Colorado mountain towns, most of which began as mining communities, Estes Park (elevation 7,522 ft.) has always been a resort town. Long known by the Utes and Arapaho, this area was explored in 1859 by rancher Joel Estes. But the growth of Estes Park is inextricably linked with two individuals: Freelan Stanley and Enos Mills.

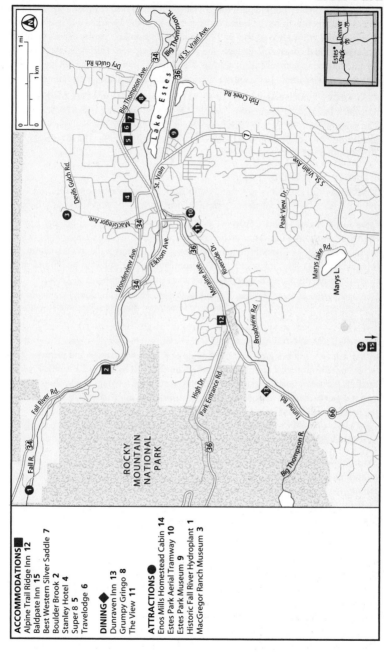

ACCOMMODATIONS ■
Alpine Trail Ridge Inn **12**
Baldpate Inn **15**
Best Western Silver Saddle **7**
Boulder Brook **2**
Stanley Hotel **4**
Super 8 **5**
Travelodge **6**

DINING ◆
Dunraven Inn **13**
Grumpy Gringo **8**
The View **11**

ATTRACTIONS ●
Enos Mills Homestead Cabin **14**
Estes Park Aerial Tramway **10**
Estes Park Museum **9**
Historic Fall River Hydroplant **1**
MacGregor Ranch Museum **3**

Stanley, a Bostonian who, with his brother Francis, invented the kerosene-powered Stanley Steamer automobile in 1899, settled in Estes Park in 1907, launched a Stanley Steamer shuttle service from Denver, and in 1909 built the landmark Stanley Hotel. Mills, an innkeeper-turned-conservationist, was one of the prime advocates for the establishment of Rocky Mountain National Park. President Woodrow Wilson signed the bill creating the 400-square-mile park in 1915; today it attracts some three million visitors annually.

FAST FACTS In an **emergency,** dial *C* **911.** The hospital, **Estes Park Medical Center,** which has a 24-hour emergency room, is at 555 Prospect Ave. ((*C* **970/586-2317**). The **post office** is at 215 W. Riverside Dr. (*C* **800/275-8777**). For statewide **road conditions,** call *C* **303/639-1111** or check www.cotrip.org. For **local weather,** call *C* **970/586-5555.**

What to See & Do

In addition to all the things to see and do in Rocky Mountain National Park, the community of Estes Park has plenty to offer in its own right.

Enos Mills Homestead Cabin This 1885 cabin and homestead belonged to the late-19th- and early-20th-century conservationist Enos A. Mills, a major force behind the establishment of Rocky Mountain National Park. A short walk down a nature trail brings you to the cabin, still owned by his descendants, with displays of his life and work. Also on the premises are a bookshop and a gallery. Allow 30 minutes to 1 hour.

6760 Colo. 7 (opposite Longs Peak Inn). *C* **970/586-4706.** $5 adults, $2.50 children 6–12, free for children under 6. Memorial Day to Labor Day usually Mon–Tues 11am–4pm, but call to confirm. By appointment Wed–Sun and off season.

Estes Park Aerial Tramway ★ This tram, which climbs 1,100 vertical feet in less than 5 minutes, offers a great ride up the side of Prospect Mountain and provides spectacular panoramic views of Longs Peak, the Continental Divide, and Estes Park village itself. Its lower terminal is a block south of the post office. You'll find a gift shop, a snack bar, and an observation deck at the upper terminal, and numerous trails converge atop the mountain. Allow at least 1 hour.

420 E. Riverside Dr. *C* **970/586-3675.** www.estestram.com. Admission $9 adults, $8 seniors 60 and older, $4 children 6–11, free for children under 6. Late May to mid-Sept daily 9am–6:30pm.

Estes Park Museum ★★ The lives of early homesteaders in Estes Park are depicted in this excellent museum, which includes a completely furnished turn-of-the-20th-century log cabin, an original Stanley Steamer car, and a changing exhibit gallery. The museum also features a permanent "Tracks in Time" exhibit that helps visitors see the impact that ordinary people, from the region's American Indians and women pioneers to today's area residents and travelers, have had on Estes Park. You can also see Rocky Mountain National Park's original headquarters building, which has been moved here. In addition, the museum sponsors a variety of programs and distributes a historical walking-tour brochure on downtown Estes Park. Allow 1¹/₂ hours.

Under the museum's administration, the **Historic Fall River Hydroplant,** at 1754 Fish Hatchery Rd., chronicles the 1909 construction and 1982 destruction of the town's one-time power supply, washed away when a dam inside Rocky Mountain National Park built by F. O. Stanley gave way. It's open Memorial Day through Labor Day, Tuesday through Sunday from 1 to 4pm.

200 Fourth St. at U.S. 36. *C* **970/586-6256.** www.estesnet.com/museum. Free admission; donations accepted. May–Oct Mon–Sat 10am–5pm, Sun 1–5pm; Nov–Apr Fri–Sat 10am–5pm, Sun 1–5pm.

MacGregor Ranch Museum   Listed on the National Register of Historic Places, the museum is on the one-time domain of the MacGregor family, a big name in local ranching lore. Originally founded in 1873, the ranch today is a lens into life on a cattle ranch in that era. Volunteer-led tours of the restored main house focus on the MacGregor family, but the grounds are full of other historic structures, not to mention a working cattle ranch—beef is for sale at the ranch office. Allow 1 hour.

180 MacGregor Lane. 𝄢 **970/586-3749.** www.macgregorranch.org. Admission $3 adults, free for those under 18. Jun–Aug Tues–Fri 10am–4pm. Closed rest of year.

Where to Stay

For help in finding accommodations, call the **Estes Park Convention and Visitors Bureau** (𝄢 **800/443-7837;** www.estesparkcvb.com). National chains here include **Best Western Silver Saddle,** 1260 Big Thompson Ave. (U.S. 34), Estes Park, CO 80517 (𝄢 **800/WESTERN** or 970/586-4476), with rates of $79 to $259 for a double from June to mid-September, $79 to $199 for a double during the rest of the year; **Super 8,** 1040 Big Thompson Ave., Estes Park, CO 80517 (𝄢 **800/800-8000** or 970/586-5338), charging $99 to $119 for a double in summer, $59 to $89 for a double during the rest of the year; and **Travelodge,** 1220 Big Thompson Ave., Estes Park, CO 80517 (𝄢 **800/ 578-7878** or 970/586-4421), charging $109 to $220 for a double in summer, $75 to $129 for a double during the rest of the year.

Although many lodging facilities in the Estes Park area do not have air-conditioning, it is seldom needed at this elevation. Unless otherwise noted, pets are not permitted at the following properties.

Alpine Trail Ridge Inn ★ Ⓥalue   This top-notch independent motel, right next to the entrance to Rocky Mountain National Park, offers nicely maintained rooms, many with private balconies, with basic Western decor and plenty of functionality. There are rooms with kings and queens, or two doubles, as well as a few two-room family units. Proprietors Jay and Fran Grooters are also great sources for hiking advice—Fran's **Trail Tracks** (www.trailtracks.com) publishes excellent 3-D hiking maps of Rocky Mountain National Park and other hiking meccas.

927 Moraine Ave., Estes Park, CO 80517. 𝄢 **800/233-5023** or 970/586-4585. Fax 970/586-6249. www. alpinetrailridgeinn.com. 48 units. Summer $80–$139 double, $140–$202 family unit. Closed mid-Oct to Apr. AE, DISC, DC, MC, V. **Amenities:** Restaurant (American); outdoor heated pool; business center. *In room:* A/C, cable TV, free Wi-Fi, fridge, coffeemaker, hair dryer, iron.

Baldpate Inn ★ Ⓕinds   Located 7 miles south of Estes Park, the Baldpate was built in 1917 and named for the novel *Seven Keys to Baldpate,* a murder mystery in which seven visitors believe each possesses the only key to the hotel. Guests today can watch several movie versions of the story, read the book, and contribute to the hotel's collection of more than 30,000 keys. Guests can also enjoy complimentary refreshments by the handsome stone fireplace in the lobby, relax on the large sun deck, or view free videos on the library VCR. But it might be difficult to stay inside once you experience the spectacular views from the inn's spacious porch and see the nature trails beckoning. Each of the early-20th-century–style rooms is unique, with handmade quilts on the beds. Several of the rooms are a bit small, and although most of the lodge rooms share bathrooms (five bathrooms for nine units), each room does have its own sink. Among my favorites are the Mae West Room (yes, she was a guest here), with a red claw-foot tub and wonderful views of the valley; and the Pinetop Cabin, which has a whirlpool tub, canopy bed, and gas fireplace. In summer, an excellent soup-and-salad buffet is served for lunch and dinner daily.

4900 S. Colo. 7 (P.O. Box 700), Estes Park, CO 80517. © 866/577-5397 or 970/586-6151. www.baldpate inn.com. 12 units (5 with private bathroom), 4 cabins. $110 double with shared bathroom, $135 double with private bathroom; $200 cabin per double ($15 per additional person). Rates include full breakfast. DISC, MC, V. Closed Nov–Apr. **Amenities:** Restaurant (seasonal). *In room:* No phone; free Wi-Fi.

Boulder Brook ★★ It would be hard to find a more beautiful setting for lodging than this. Surrounded by tall pines and cradled in a ruggedly majestic valley 2 miles from the park entrance, all suites face the Fall River, and all have private riverfront decks and full or partial kitchens. The spa suites are equipped with two-person spas, fireplaces, sitting areas with cathedral ceilings, and king-size beds. One-bedroom suites hold king-size beds, window seats, two TVs, and bathrooms with whirlpool tub/shower combinations. The grounds, a serene jumble of forest, rock, and running water, include an outdoor hot tub and barbecue area. Smoking is not allowed.

1900 Fall River Rd., Estes Park, CO 80517. © 800/238-0910 or 970/586-0910. Fax 970/586-8067. www.boulderbrook.com. 19 units. $109–$225 double. DISC, MC, V. **Amenities:** Year-round outdoor hot tub; large free video and DVD library. *In room:* Cable TV w/DVD/VCR, free Wi-Fi, kitchen, fridge, coffeemaker, hair dryer, iron.

Stanley Hotel ★★ F. O. Stanley, inventor of the Stanley Steamer, built this elegant hotel in 1909, and a flurry of recent projects have added a spa and a series of lavish condos. The equal of European resorts the day it opened, the Stanley was constructed in solid rock at an elevation of 7,800 feet on the eastern slope of the Colorado Rockies. Today the hotel and its grounds are listed on the National Register of Historic Places as the Stanley Historic District. Each room differs in size and shape, offering a variety of views of Longs Peak, Lake Estes, and surrounding hillsides. I prefer the deluxe rooms in the front of the building, which provide views of Rocky Mountain National Park.

333 Wonderview Ave. (P.O. Box 1767), Estes Park, CO 80517. © 800/976-1377 or 970/586-3371. Fax 970/586-4964. www.stanleyhotel.com. 140 units. $153–$240 double; $300–$400 suite; $400–$600 condominium; from $1,200 presidential cottage. AE, DISC, MC, V. **Amenities:** Restaurant (American); pool (heated outdoor); tennis court (outdoor, unlit); exercise room; spa. *In room:* Cable TV w/pay movies.

Where to Dine

Dunraven Inn ★★ ITALIAN This is a great spot to celebrate a special occasion in an intimate setting, but not so fancy that you wouldn't want to take the (well-behaved) kids. The decor is eclectic, to say the least: Images of the *Mona Lisa* are scattered about, ranging from a mustachioed lady to opera posters, and autographed dollar bills are posted in the lounge area. House specialties include shrimp scampi, lasagna, and my favorite, the Dunraven Italiano (a 10-oz. charbroiled sirloin steak in a sauce of peppers, onions, and tomatoes). There's a wide choice of pastas, fresh seafood, vegetarian plates, and desserts, plus a children's menu. The full bar is well stocked, and the wine list reasonably priced.

2470 Colo. 66. © 970/586-6409. www.dunraveninn.com. Reservations recommended. Main courses $10–$38. AE, DISC, MC, V. Daily 5–10pm; closes slightly earlier in winter.

Grumpy Gringo ★ (Kids) MEXICAN Dine in style at this classy Mexican restaurant without breaking the bank. The private booths, whitewashed plaster walls, green plants, bright poppies, and a few choice sculptures provide a posh atmosphere. And although the food is excellent and portions are large, the prices are surprisingly low. My choice here is a burrito. I also recommend the huge enchilada olé. It's actually three enchiladas: one each of cheese, beef, and chicken. The fajitas—either chicken or beef—are delicious.

There are six sauces from which to choose, each homemade, and rated mild, semihot, or hot. Burgers and sandwiches are also offered. The house specialty drink is the Gringo Margarita, made with Sauza Gold tequila from an original (and secret) recipe, and the signature dessert is deep-fried ice cream.

1560 Big Thompson Ave. (U.S. 34). ℂ **970/586-7705.** www.grumpygringo.com. Main courses $8–$14. AE, DISC, MC, V. Daily 11am–9pm summer, 11am–8pm fall through spring. On U.S. 34, 1 mile east of the junction of U.S. Hwy. 34 and Hwy. 36.

The View ★★ (Finds) STEAKS/SEAFOOD   Although the restaurant is named for the picture-perfect panorama of the town and surrounding mountainscape, the food is also terrific. Chef Russell Stephens shows an inventive eye for detail with such dishes as the walnut-crusted rainbow trout, served with garlic mashers and a grapefruit beurre blanc sauce, and a pan-seared rib-eye with garlic–blue cheese crust and merlot sauce. The atmosphere is woodsy but refined, with hardwood floors and red-and-white checkered tablecloths, and there is often jazz or a Celtic guitarist.

At Historic Crags Lodge, 300 Riverside Dr. ℂ **970/586-6066.** Reservations recommended. Main courses $15–$26 dinner. AE, MC, V. Daily 5–9pm. Closed mid-Oct to mid-May.

GRAND LAKE

The western entrance to Rocky Mountain National Park is at the picturesque little town of Grand Lake, in the shade of Shadow Mountain at the park's southwestern corner.

Here, in the crisp mountain air at 8,370 feet above sea level, you can stroll down an old-fashioned boardwalk as one of the locals rides by on horseback. In fact, take away the automobiles and electric lights, and this town looks and feels like the late 1800s. Located within the Arapaho National Recreation Area, Grand Lake is surrounded by three lakes—Grand Lake, Shadow Mountain Reservoir, and Lake Granby—each with a marina that offers boating (with rentals), fishing, and other watersports. Throughout the recreation area you'll also find miles of trails for hiking, horseback riding, four-wheeling, and mountain biking that become cross-country skiing and snowmobiling trails in winter.

Usually open daily from 11am to 5pm in summer, the **Kauffman House,** 407 Pitkin Ave., at Lake Avenue (ℂ **970/627-9644;** www.kauffmanhouse.org), is a log structure that was built as a hotel in 1892. It has been restored and now serves as the museum of the Grand Lake Historical Society, with many of its original furnishings and exhibits on what life was like here back when everyone arrived on horseback or by stagecoach. Admission is free, although donations are welcome.

Golfers may want to test their skills at the 18-hole championship **Grand Lake Golf Course** (ℂ **970/627-8008;** www.grandlakegolf.com), altitude 8,420 feet. Greens fees peak at $83 for 18 holes, although much lower twilight, off-season, and walking rates are available.

For further information on what to do in this area, stop at the **Visitor Information Center** on U.S. 34 at the turnoff into town (open daily 9am–5pm in summer, with shorter hours the rest of the year), or contact the **Grand Lake Area Chamber of Commerce,** P.O. Box 429, Grand Lake, CO 80447 (ℂ **800/531-1019,** or 970/627-3402; www.grandlakechamber.com). Information is also available from the Forest Service's **Sulphur Ranger District office** (P.O. Box 10, Granby, CO 80446), 9 Ten Mile Dr., off U.S. 40 about a half-mile south of Granby (ℂ **970/887-4100;** www.fs.fed.us/r2), open in summer Monday through Friday from 8am to 6pm, Saturday and Sunday 9am to 5pm, with shorter hours in winter.

There are plenty of lodging possibilities in Grand Lake. A good source for information is the **Grand Lake Area Chamber of Commerce** (see address above). In addition to the properties below, I like the **Grand Lake Terrace Inn,** 813 Grand Ave. (P.O. Box 1791), Grand Lake, CO 80447 (✆ **888/627-3001** or 970/627-3000; www.grandlaketerrace inn.com), a quaint mountain inn with three attractively decorated rooms plus a spacious suite, with rates of $60 to $150 for a double and $125 to $275 for the suite. The inn also has a restaurant serving three meals a day.

Black Bear Lodge   Located 3 miles south of town across from Shadow Mountain Lake, this comfortable and well-maintained establishment is a great bet if you're looking for an affordable motel with Rocky Mountain ambience. Some units have two rooms and some have kitchenettes. Of the 17 units, bathrooms in 8 have showers only; the rest have bathrooms with shower/tub combos. All units are nonsmoking.

12255 U.S. 34 (P.O. Box 609), Grand Lake, CO 80447. ✆ **800/766-1123** or 970/627-3654. www.blackbear grandlake.com. 17 units. $76–$135 double. MC, V. **Amenities:** Outdoor pool; 2 whirlpools (1 indoor, 1 outdoor); sauna. *In room:* Cable TV.

Daven Haven Lodge ★★   Set among pine trees across the street from the lake, this group of cabins is a good choice for those seeking peace and quiet in a secluded mountain resort–type setting. There's a welcoming stone fireplace in the lobby plus old Coke machines and several antique jukeboxes—they actually play 78 rpm records! The cabins vary in size, sleeping from two to eight people; each has its own picnic table and six have stone fireplaces. The decor and furnishings are contemporary Western. You'll also find a lovely patio, a volleyball court, horseshoes, and a bonfire pit. The Backstreet Steakhouse (see "Where to Dine," below) serves dinner nightly in summer and 4 nights a week in winter. All cabins are nonsmoking.

604 Marina Dr. (P.O. Box 1528), Grand Lake, CO 80447. ✆ **970/627-8144.** Fax 970/627-5098. www.daven havenlodge.com. 16 cabins. $94–$154 for units for 2–4 people; $164–$236 for units for 5–8 people. DISC, MC, V. 3-night minimum required on reservations during holidays. **Amenities:** Restaurant (steakhouse). *In room:* TV, free Wi-Fi, kitchen (no microwaves).

The Inn at Grand Lake ★   For modern lodging with an Old West feel, stay at this handsome restored historic building, originally constructed in 1881 as Grand Lake's courthouse and jail. Rooms have a variety of bed combinations, and several sleep up to six. They're equipped with Western-style furniture, ceiling fans, white stucco walls, and Indian-motif draperies and bedspreads. Many of the units have refrigerators and microwaves. About half of the units have tub/shower combinations, and the rest have showers only. The best views are on the street side of the building. The inn is located in the center of town, about a half-block from the lake. The Sagebrush BBQ & Grill (see "Where to Dine," below) serves three meals daily. All units are nonsmoking.

1103 Grand Ave. (P.O. Box 2087), Grand Lake, CO 80447. ✆ **800/722-2585** or 970/627-9234. www.innat grandlake.com. 18 units. $100–$150 double; $120–$180 suite. AE, DISC, MC, V. *In room:* TV, coffeemaker, hair dryer.

Where to Dine

Backstreet Steakhouse ★ STEAK   This cozy, country inn–style restaurant in the Daven Haven lodge (see above) offers fine dining in a down-home atmosphere. Steaks— from the 8-ounce filet mignon to the 12-ounce New York strip—are all USDA choice beef, cooked to perfection. The house specialty, Jack Daniel's pork chops (breaded, baked, and served with a creamy Jack Daniel's mushroom sauce), has been featured in

Bon Appétit magazine. Also on the menu are pasta, chicken, and fish dishes, plus slow-roasted prime rib, and children's items. Sandwiches and light entrees, such as the smoked salmon and wild game sausage platter, are served in the lounge.

In the Daven Haven Lodge, 604 Marina Dr. ℂ **970/627-8144.** www.davenhavenlodge.com. Reservations recommended in summer and on winter weekends. Main courses dining room $16–$36, lounge $7–$16. DISC, MC, V. Summer and Christmas holidays daily 5pm–close; winter Thurs–Sun 5pm–close.

Sagebrush BBQ & Grill AMERICAN   Come here to enjoy excellent barbecue plus steaks, sandwiches, and seafood in a historic building that also houses The Inn at Grand Lake. The atmosphere here is definitely Wild West, complete with Grand Lake's original jail doors, and so casual that you're encouraged to munch on peanuts and throw the shells on the floor. The specialty here is barbecue—try the super-tender fall-off-the-bone pork ribs—but I also suggest the New York strip steak, the pan-fried rainbow trout, and the elk medallions served with roasted raspberry chipotle sauce. Another good choice is the burrito—pork, chicken, or vegetarian—served with refried beans, green chile, cheese, tomato, and lettuce.

1101 Grand Ave. ℂ **970/627-1404.** www.sagebrushbbq.com. Main courses lunch and dinner $6–$24. MC, V. Sun–Thurs 7am–9pm; Fri–Sat 7am–10pm.

8

Colorado Springs

Magnificent scenic beauty, a favorable climate, and dreams of gold have lured visitors to Colorado Springs and neighboring Pikes Peak Country for well over 100 years.

In 1806, army Lt. Zebulon Pike led a company of soldiers on a trek around the base of an enormous mountain. He called it "Grand Peak," declared it unconquerable, and moved on. Today, the 14,110-foot mountain we know as Pikes Peak has been conquered so often that an auto highway and a cog railway take visitors to the top.

Unlike many Colorado towns, neither mineral wealth nor ranching was the cornerstone of Colorado Springs' economy during the 19th century—tourism was. In fact, Colorado Springs, founded in 1871, was the first genuine resort community west of Chicago. Gen. William J. Palmer, builder of the Denver & Rio Grande Railroad, established the resort on his rail line, at an elevation of 6,035 feet. The state's growing reputation as a health center, with its high mountains and mineral springs, convinced him to build at the foot of Pikes Peak. In an attempt to lure affluent easterners, he named the resort Colorado Springs, because most fashionable eastern resorts were called "springs." The mineral waters at Manitou Springs were only 5 miles away, and soon Palmer exploited them by installing a resident physician, Dr. Samuel Solly, who exuberantly trumpeted the benefits of Manitou's springs both in print and in person.

The 1890s gold strikes at Cripple Creek, on the southwestern slope of Pikes Peak, added a new dimension to life in Colorado Springs. Among those who cashed in on the boom was Spencer Penrose, a middle-aged Philadelphian and Harvard graduate who arrived in 1892, made some astute investments, and became quite rich. Penrose, who believed that the automobile would revolutionize life in the United States, promoted the creation of new highways. To show the effectiveness of motorcars in the mountains, he built the Pikes Peak Highway (1913–15), using more than $250,000 of his own money. Then, during World War I, at a cost of more than $2 million, he built the luxurious Broadmoor hotel at the foot of Cheyenne Mountain. World War II brought the military and defense industry to this area, and in 1958 the $200-million U.S. Air Force Academy opened.

Modern Colorado Springs is a growing city of about 400,000, with more than 600,000 in the metropolitan area. The majority of its residents are conservative, and the city is also home to some of the country's largest nondenominational churches and conservative groups.

To many visitors, the city retains the feel and mood of a small Western town. Most tourists come to see the Air Force Academy, marvel at the scenery at Garden of the Gods and Pikes Peak, and explore the history of America's West. I'm pleased to report that Colorado Springs also has some of the best lodging and dining in the state.

1 ORIENTATION

ARRIVING

By Plane

Major airlines offer nearly 100 flights a day to **Colorado Springs Airport,** located north of Drennan Road and east of Powers Boulevard in the southeastern part of the city (✆ **719/550-1972;** www.flycos.com).

Airlines serving Colorado Springs include **Allegiant** (✆ 702/505-8888; www.allegiant air.com), **American** (✆ 800/433-7300; www.aa.com), **Continental** (✆ 800/525-0280; www.flycontinental.com), **Delta** (✆ 800/221-1212; www.delta.com), **ExpressJet** (✆ 888/958-9538; www.expressjet.com), **Frontier** (✆ 800/432-1359; www.frontierairlines.com), **Northwest** (✆ 800/225-2525; www.nwa.com), **United** (✆ 800/864-8331; www.united.com), and **US Airways** (✆ 800/428-4322; www.usairways.com).

GETTING TO & FROM THE AIRPORT   Several companies provide airport shuttle services; call ✆ **719/550-1930** for information.

By Car

The principal artery to and from the north and south, I-25, bisects Colorado Springs. Denver is 70 miles north; Pueblo, 42 miles south. U.S. 24 is the principal east–west route through the city.

Visitors arriving on I-70 from the east can take exit 359 at Limon and follow U.S. 24 into the Springs. Arriving on I-70 from the west, the most direct route is exit 201 at Frisco, then Colo. 9 through Breckenridge 53 miles to U.S. 24 (at Hartsel), and finally east 66 miles to the Springs. This route is mountainous, so check road conditions before setting out in winter.

VISITOR INFORMATION

The **Experience Colorado Springs at Pikes Peak Convention and Visitors Bureau** is at 515 S. Cascade Ave., Colorado Springs, CO 80903 (✆ **800/888-4748** or 719/635-7506; fax 719/635-4968; www.experiencecoloradosprings.com). Ask for the free *Official Visitor Guide to Colorado Springs and the Pikes Peak Region,* a colorful booklet with a comprehensive listing of accommodations, restaurants, and other area visitor services, as well as a basic but efficient map. Inquire at the Visitor Information Center or local bookstores for more detailed maps. An excellent one is the Pierson Graphics Corporation's *Colorado Springs and Monument Valley Street Map.* The **Visitor Information Center,** at the southeast corner of Cascade Avenue and Cimarron Street, is open from 8:30am to 5pm daily in summer, Monday through Friday in winter. From I-25, take the Cimarron Street exit (exit 141), and head east about 4 blocks.

Visitors to Manitou Springs—and every Colorado Springs visitor should also get to Manitou Springs—can get information from the **Manitou Springs Chamber of Commerce & Visitors Bureau,** 354 Manitou Ave., Manitou Springs, CO 80829 (✆ **800/642-2567** or 719/685-5089; www.manitousprings.org). You can also contact the **Pikes Peak Country Attractions Association** at the same address (✆ **800/525-2250;** www.pikes-peak.com).

It's easy to get around central Colorado Springs, which is laid out on a classic grid pattern.

If you focus on the intersection of I-25 and U.S. 24, downtown Colorado Springs lies in the northeast quadrant, bounded on the west by I-25 and on the south by U.S. 24 (Cimarron St.). Boulder Street to the north and Wahsatch Avenue to the east complete the downtown frame. Nevada Avenue (Bus. 25 and Colo. 115) parallels the freeway for 15 miles through the city, intersecting it twice; Tejon Street and Cascade Avenue also run north–south through downtown between Nevada Avenue and the freeway. **Colorado Avenue** and **Platte Avenue** are the busiest east–west downtown cross streets.

> **Heads Up**
>
> At an elevation of 6,035 feet, Colorado Springs has two-thirds the oxygen found at sea level; Pikes Peak, at 14,110 feet, has only one-half the oxygen.

West of downtown, Colorado Avenue extends through the historic Old Colorado City district and the quaint foothill community of **Manitou Springs,** rejoining U.S. 24—a busy but less interesting artery—as it enters Pike National Forest.

South of downtown, **Nevada Avenue** intersects **Lake Avenue,** the principal boulevard into The Broadmoor hotel (see below), and proceeds south as Colo. 115 past Fort Carson to Cañon City.

North and east of downtown, **Academy Boulevard** (Colo. 83) is a good street name to remember. From the south gate of the Air Force Academy north of the Springs, it winds through residential hills, crosses Austin Bluff Parkway, and then runs without a curve 8 miles due south, finally bending west to intersect I-25 and Colo. 115 at Fort Carson. U.S. 24, which exits downtown east as Platte Avenue, and Fountain Boulevard, which leads to the airport, are among its cross streets. Austin Bluffs Parkway extends west of I-25 as **Garden of the Gods Road,** leading to that natural wonder.

City street addresses are divided by Pikes Peak Avenue into north and south; by Nevada Avenue into east and west.

2 GETTING AROUND

Although Colorado Springs has public transportation, most visitors prefer to drive. Parking and roads are good, and some of the best attractions, such as the Garden of the Gods (p. 191), are accessible only by car (or foot or bike for the truly ambitious).

BY CAR

For regulations and advice on driving in Colorado, see "Getting There & Getting Around," in chapter 3. The **American Automobile Association (AAA)** maintains an office in Colorado Springs at 3525 N. Carefree Circle (© **800/283-5222** or 719/591-2222; www.aaa.com), open Monday through Friday from 8:30am to 5:30pm and Saturday from 9am to 1pm.

CAR RENTALS   Car-rental agencies in Colorado Springs, some of which have offices in or near downtown as well as at the airport, include **Avis** (© 800/331-1212 or

719/596-2751), **Budget** (© 800/527-7000 or 719/473-6535), **Enterprise** (© 800/736- **175**
8222 or 719/636-3900), **Hertz** (© 800/654-3131 or 719/596-1863), and **National/
Alamo** (© 800/227-7368 or 719/574-8579). You can rent campers, travel trailers,
motor homes, and motorcycles from **Cruise America** (© 800/671-8042; www.cruise
america.com).

PARKING   Most downtown streets have parking meters; the rate is 25¢ for a half-hour.
Look for city-run parking lots, which charge 25¢ per half-hour and also offer day rates.
Outside downtown, free parking is generally available on side streets.

BY BUS

Mountain Metropolitan Transit (© **719/385-7433;** www.springsgov.com) provides
city bus service. Buses operate Monday through Friday from 5:10am to 10:45pm, Saturday from 5:30am to 10:45pm, and Sunday from 7:30am to 5:35pm, except major holidays. Fares on in-city routes are $1.50 for adults; 75¢ students, children 6 to 11, seniors,
and passengers with disabilities; and free for children under 6. There is also a free downtown shuttle and free seasonal trolley service in Manitou Springs. Bus schedules can be
obtained at terminals, city libraries, and the Colorado Springs Convention and Visitors
Bureau.

BY TAXI

Call **Yellow Cab** (© **719/634-5000**) for taxi service.

ON FOOT

Each of the main sections of town can easily be explored without a vehicle. It's fun, for
instance, to wander the winding streets of Manitou Springs or explore the Old Colorado
City "strip." Between neighborhoods, however, distances are considerable. Unless you're
particularly fit, it's wise to drive or take a bus or taxi.

(Fast Facts) Colorado Springs

American Express To report a lost card, call © **800/528-4800;** to report lost
traveler's checks, call © **800/221-7282.**

Area Code The telephone area code is **719.**

Babysitters Front desks at major hotels often can make arrangements.

Business Hours Most banks are open Monday through Friday from 9am to 5pm,
and some have Saturday hours. Major stores are open Monday through Saturday
from 9 or 10am until 5 or 6pm (sometimes until 9pm Fri), and often Sunday from
noon until 5pm. Stores that cater to tourists are usually open longer in the summer, with shorter hours in winter.

Car Rentals See "Getting Around," above.

Dentists For referrals for dentists who accept emergency patients, contact the
Colorado Springs Dental Society (© **719/598-5161**).

Doctors For referrals and other health information, call **HealthLink** (© **719/444-
2273**).

Drugstores **Walgreens,** 920 N. Circle Dr. (*©* **719/473-9090**), has a 24-hour prescription service.

Emergencies For police, fire, or medical emergencies, dial *©* **911.** To reach **Poison Control,** call *©* **800/332-3073.**

Eyeglasses You can get 1-hour replacement of lost or broken glasses at **Pearle Vision** in the Citadel Mall (*©* **719/597-0757**) and at **LensCrafters** in Erindale Centre on North Academy Boulevard (*©* **719/548-8650**).

Hospitals **Memorial Hospital,** 1400 E. Boulder St. (*©* **719/365-5000**), offers full medical services, including 24-hour emergency treatment, as does **Penrose–St. Francis Hospital,** 2215 N. Cascade Ave. (*©* **719/776-5000**).

Newspapers & Magazines The *Gazette* (www.gazette.com), published daily in Colorado Springs, is the city's most widely read newspaper. The *Denver Post* is also available at newsstands throughout the city. The glossy *Colorado Springs Style* magazine and the politically oriented *Independent* are other local periodicals. *USA Today* and the *Wall Street Journal* can be purchased on the street and at major hotels.

Photographic Needs There are dozens of photofinishing outlets throughout the city, including **Walgreens** and **Shewmaker's Camera Shop,** in the Woodmen Valley Shopping Center, 6902 N. Academy Blvd. (*©* **719/598-6412;** www.shewmakers. com). For camera and video supplies and repairs as well as photofinishing, go to the downtown location of **Shewmaker's,** 30 N. Tejon St. (*©* **719/636-1696**).

Post Office The main post office is downtown at 201 E. Pikes Peak Ave. Contact the U.S. Postal Service (*©* **800/275-8777;** www.usps.com) for hours and locations of other post offices.

Safety Although Colorado Springs is generally a safe city, it is not crime-free. Try to be aware of your surroundings at all times, and ask at your hotel or the visitor center about the safety of neighborhoods you plan to explore, especially after dark.

Taxes Total taxes on retail sales in Colorado Springs amount to about 7.4%; room taxes total about 9.4%. Rates in Manitou Springs are a bit higher.

Useful Telephone Numbers For **weather and road conditions,** including road construction, throughout the state, call *©* **303/639-1111** or visit www.cotrip.org.

3 WHERE TO STAY

You'll find a wide range of lodging possibilities here, from Colorado's ritziest resort—The Broadmoor—to basic budget motels. There are also several particularly nice bed-and-breakfasts; the **Colorado Bed and Breakfasts of the Pikes Peak Area** is a good resource (*©* 888/835-8900 or 719/685-1120; www.pikespeakareabnbs.com). The rates listed here are the officially quoted prices ("rack rates") and don't take into account individual or group discounts. Generally, rates are highest from Memorial Day to Labor Day, and lowest in the spring. During graduation and other special events at the Air Force Academy, rates can increase markedly, and you may have trouble finding a room at any price.

Rates listed below do not include the lodging tax (about 9% in Colorado Springs, 10% in Manitou Springs). Parking is free unless otherwise specified.

In addition to the accommodations described below, a number of moderately priced chain and franchise motels offer reliable lodging. These include the economical **Econo Lodge Downtown,** 714 N. Nevada Ave., Colorado Springs, CO 80903 (© **800/553-2666** or 719/636-3385), with doubles from $39 to $89; the attractive and well-maintained **Rodeway Inn & Suites Garden of the Gods,** 555 W. Garden of the Gods Rd., Colorado Springs, CO 80907 (© **800/828-4347** or 719/593-9119), with rates for two of $69 to $119; and **Super 8,** near Garden of the Gods at 4604 Rusina Rd., Colorado Springs, CO 80907 (© **800/800-8000** or 719/594-0964), which charges $42 to $57 for a double. Those looking for a more upscale chain won't go wrong with the **Doubletree Hotel World Arena,** 1775 E. Cheyenne Mountain Blvd. (I-25, exit 138), Colorado Springs, CO 80906 (© **800/222-TREE** or 719/576-8900), with double rates from $115 to $145 and suites from $300; or the **Crowne Plaza Colorado Springs Hotel,** 2886 S. Circle Dr. (I-25, exit 138), Colorado Springs, CO 80906 (© **800/981-4012** or 719/576-5900), with doubles from $89 to $199.

VERY EXPENSIVE

The Broadmoor ★★★ (Kids This storied resort keeps itself on the forefront of luxury, where it's been since Spencer Penrose originally opened it in 1918. (The first names entered on the guest register were those of John D. Rockefeller, Jr., and his party.) Today The Broadmoor is an enormous resort complex of historic pink Mediterranean-style buildings with modern additions, set at the foot of Cheyenne Mountain on magnificently landscaped 3,000-acre grounds about $3^{1}/_{2}$ miles southwest of downtown Colorado Springs. The original Italian Renaissance–style main building features marble staircase, chandeliers, Italian tile, hand-painted beams and ceilings, and a carved-marble fountain, not to mention a priceless art collection with original work by Toulouse-Lautrec and Ming dynasty ceramicists.

Behind the main building is lovely Cheyenne Lake; a swimming pool almost seamlessly attached to the west end looks like a part of the lake. This swimming complex will make you think you're at an oceanside beach resort, with water slides, two outdoor hot tubs, 13 cabanas, and an outdoor cafe. The guest rooms occupy a series of separate buildings centered on the lake and pool area. The spacious, luxurious rooms are beautifully decorated in European style, with chandeliers, Italian fabrics, rich wood, and limited-edition works of art. Most units hold two double beds or one king-size bed, desks and tables, plush seating, and two-line portable phones. Many rooms contain large soaking tubs and separate marble showers; some in the South Tower have high-tech touch screens that control the lights, the drapes, and even the "Privacy" and "Do Not Disturb" lights in the hall. The service is impeccable: The hotel averages two employees for every guest.

Lake Circle, at Lake Ave. (P.O. Box 1439), Colorado Springs, CO 80901. © **800/634-7711** or 719/634-7711. Fax 719/577-5700. www.broadmoor.com. 700 units. May–Oct $420–$565 double, $625–$1,000 standard suite; Nov–Apr $300–$420 double, $425–$850 standard suite; year-round up to $3,400 large suite. AE, DC, DISC, MC, V. Self-parking $14; valet $16. **Amenities:** 12 restaurants (all Continental, American, or Contemporary); 4 lounges; outdoor pool cafe; 3 swimming pools (indoor, outdoor with water slide, outdoor lap pool); 2 outdoor hot tubs; 3 18-hole golf courses; 9 all-weather tennis courts (1 clay court); state-of-the-art fitness center and full-service spa with aerobics classes, saunas, and whirlpool tubs; paddle boats; bicycle rentals; children's programs (summer); riding concierge; car-rental agency; shopping arcade; 24-hr. room service; in-room massage; valet laundry; stables; fly-fishing school; movie theater; shuttle bus between buildings; service station. *In room:* A/C, cable TV, free Wi-Fi, minibar, coffeemaker, hair dryer, iron, safe.

Colorado Springs Accommodations & Dining

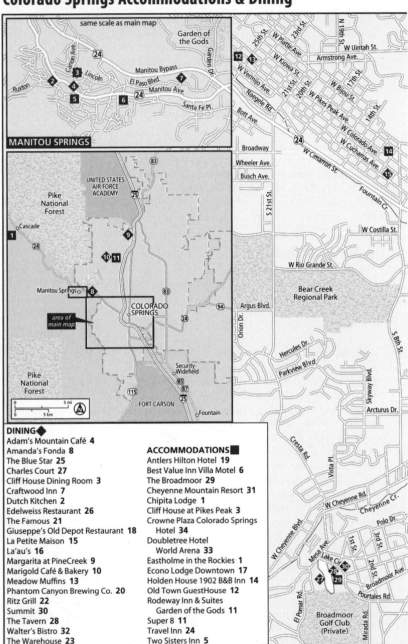

MANITOU SPRINGS

same scale as main map

Garden of the Gods

area of main map

Pike National Forest

UNITED STATES AIR FORCE ACADEMY

COLORADO SPRINGS

Bear Creek Regional Park

Pike National Forest

Security-Widefield

FORT CARSON

Fountain

DINING◆
Adam's Mountain Café **4**
Amanda's Fonda **8**
The Blue Star **25**
Charles Court **27**
Cliff House Dining Room **3**
Craftwood Inn **7**
Dutch Kitchen **2**
Edelweiss Restaurant **26**
The Famous **21**
Giuseppe's Old Depot Restaurant **18**
La Petite Maison **15**
La'au's **16**
Margarita at PineCreek **9**
Marigold Café & Bakery **10**
Meadow Muffins **13**
Phantom Canyon Brewing Co. **20**
Ritz Grill **22**
Summit **30**
The Tavern **28**
Walter's Bistro **32**
The Warehouse **23**

ACCOMMODATIONS■
Antlers Hilton Hotel **19**
Best Value Inn Villa Motel **6**
The Broadmoor **29**
Cheyenne Mountain Resort **31**
Chipita Lodge **1**
Cliff House at Pikes Peak **3**
Crowne Plaza Colorado Springs
    Hotel **34**
Doubletree Hotel
    World Arena **33**
Eastholme in the Rockies **1**
Econo Lodge Downtown **17**
Holden House 1902 B&B Inn **14**
Old Town GuestHouse **12**
Rodeway Inn & Suites
    Garden of the Gods **11**
Super 8 **11**
Travel Inn **24**
Two Sisters Inn **5**

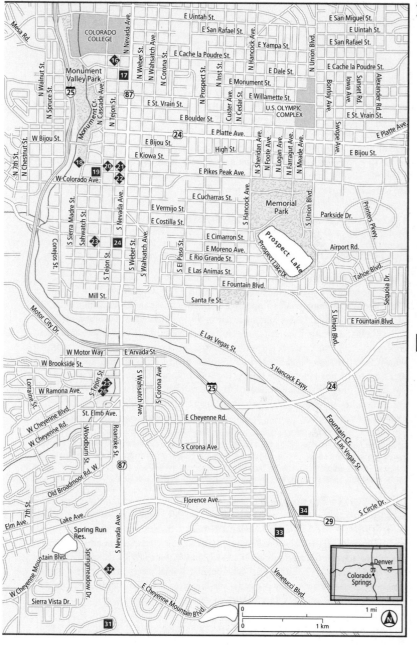

Antlers Hilton Hotel ★   The Antlers has been a Colorado Springs landmark for more than a century. Although it is in many ways geared to business travelers, for vacationers it offers the best accommodations within a short walking distance of many of downtown Colorado Springs' major attractions and restaurants. There have been three different Antlers on this site. The first, a turreted Victorian showcase built in 1883, was named for Gen. William Palmer's collection of deer and elk trophies. After it was destroyed by fire in 1898, Palmer built an extravagant Italian Renaissance–style building that survived until 1964, when it was leveled to make room for the more contemporary hotel, which Hilton renovated to the tune of $15 million in recent years. Antique black-walnut nightstands from the previous incarnation provide a touch of historic continuity to the spacious guest rooms, which are handsomely decorated in earth tones with rich wood furnishings. The corner rooms are larger, and I prefer the west-side rooms: They are more expensive, but worth every penny because of their unparalleled Pikes Peak views.

4 S. Cascade Ave., Colorado Springs, CO 80903. ℂ **877/754-9940** or 719/473-5600. Fax 719/389-0259. www.antlers.com. 292 units. Summer $139–$189 double; $250–$695 suite. AE, DC, DISC, MC, V. Self-parking $8; valet $12. **Amenities:** 2 restaurants (American); indoor pool; fitness center; whirlpool; salon; room service (6:30am–11pm); laundry. *In room:* A/C, cable TV, free Wi-Fi, coffeemaker, hair dryer, iron.

Cheyenne Mountain Resort ★★   Set at the foot of Cheyenne Mountain, this resort was built at a preexisting country club with a Pete Dye–designed golf course in 1985, and is something of a less-expensive alternative to the swank Broadmoor (above), just a few miles uphill. With a stunning view of the mountain from the lobby, the Cheyenne Mountain Resort features top-notch recreational facilities and attracts numerous conferences and meetings, but is an outstanding choice for tourists as well. The rooms—which are in a series of buildings set off from the main lodge—are rich and masculine, and have either one king or two queens (or both in some suites). The bathrooms are a cut above, with granite counters and tub/shower combos, as well as jetted soakers in the executive suites. All rooms have a private balcony, and most have great views.

3225 Broadmoor Valley Rd., Colorado Springs, CO 80906. ℂ **800/428-8886** or 719/538-4000. Fax 719/540-5779. www.cheyennemountain.com. 316 units, including 5 suites. Summer $169–$209 double; $485–$650 suite. Lower rates fall through spring. AE, DC, DISC, MC, V. **Amenities:** 2 restaurants (American); 2 lounges; indoor pool; 18-hole golf course; 18 indoor tennis courts; health club; Jacuzzi; sauna; bike rental; children's programs; concierge; business center; room service (7am–11pm); massage; dry cleaning. *In room:* A/C, cable TV w/pay movies, free Wi-Fi, coffeemaker, hair dryer, iron.

Cliff House at Pikes Peak ★★ (Finds)   Striving to compete with the best that Colorado has to offer (and doing a pretty good job), the Cliff House is an old yet new facility. Built in 1874, it was designated a National Historic Landmark in 1980, and has hosted such eminent guests as Theodore Roosevelt, Clark Gable, and Thomas Edison. A major fire forced the Cliff House to close in 1982, and it remained closed until a massive reconstruction in 1997. The project incorporated several pieces of the hotel's original decor, including ornate woodwork and a tile fireplace, and what the fire destroyed was replicated with an emphasis on attention to detail. Once again a grand and luxurious hotel, the Cliff House reopened in 1999.

Today the lovely, uniquely decorated accommodations vary in size and personality, although the overall decor is Queen Anne–Victorian. Units range from average-size, relatively simple studios to large, luxurious celebrity suites named for former guests. Some units have gas fireplaces, two-person spas, steam showers, and terrific views of the mountains. All have live flowering plants, robes, heated toilet seats, and working desks. I wouldn't turn down any room at the Cliff House, but my favorite is definitely the Clark Gable Suite ($475 double in summer), which is decorated in subdued Hollywood style— if you can call leopard-print wallpaper subdued—and contains a shower for two, a jetted tub, a wet bar and refrigerator, two TVs, a gas fireplace, and photos of Clark, who stayed at the hotel in the early 1940s.

There's a fine-dining restaurant (see "Where to Dine," below), and the entire property is nonsmoking.

306 Cañon Ave., Manitou Springs, CO 80829. ℂ **888/212-7000** or 719/685-3000. Fax 719/685-3913. www.thecliffhouse.com. 55 units. $145–$200 double; $189–$475 suite. Children under 13 stay free in parent's room. Rates include breakfast buffet. AE, DC, MC, V. **Amenities:** 2 restaurants (American/bar and grill); bar; fitness center; concierge; activities desk; airport pickup; room service 7am–11pm; on-call massage; valet laundry service. *In room:* A/C, cable TV w/ DVD players, CD player, free Wi-Fi, coffeemaker, hair dryer, iron, safe.

Old Town GuestHouse ★★   Just a half-block south of the main street of Colorado Springs' historic Old Colorado City stands this three-story redbrick inn. It may appear to be from the 1890s, but it actually dates from the 1990s. As a result, it features all the modern amenities, not to mention great service from innkeepers Don and Shirley Wick, who've owned the inn since 2005.

All eight of the individually decorated rooms are named for flowers: for example, Colorado Columbine, with mountain mural above the king bed; Moroccan Jasmine, with a Sahara Desert theme; Oriental Poppy, decorated with collectibles from the Orient; and romantic Victorian Rose. Each room has individual climate control, robes, and a queen or king bed. Several have gas-log fireplaces, seven have a private porch or balcony, and some have steam showers for two or private outdoor hot tubs. There's an elevator, and one room is ADA compliant.

The attractive library has a fireplace, music, and overstuffed chairs. Downstairs is a game room with pool table and exercise equipment, plus wireless Internet access throughout the inn.

115 S. 26th St., Colorado Springs, CO 80904. ℂ **888/375-4210** or 719/632-9194. Fax 719/632-9026. www.oldtown-guesthouse.com. 8 units. $99–$210 double. AE, DISC, MC, V. Free off-street parking. Children under 12 not accepted. *In room:* A/C, cable TV w/VCR/DVD player, free Wi-Fi, fridge, coffeemaker, hair dryer, iron.

MODERATE

Chipita Lodge ★★ (Finds)   In dinky Chipita Park, below the looming majesty of Pikes Peak—and above a peaceful lake—is the Chipita Lodge. The historic 1927 structure began as a hotel but served as both the local post office and a real-estate office before becoming an inn again in 1997. The common area has shelves of games, a TV, and a huge fireplace; there is also an outdoor hot tub. The rooms feature interesting furnishings—a vanity made from old P.O boxes, for one, and a rocker made from muleshoes; antiques and private baths help give the accommodations a woodsy elegance. The Chipita also rents nearby **cabins** for $135 to $165 a night with a 3-night minimum.

9090 Chipita Park Rd., Chipita Park, CO 80809. ℂ **877/CHIPITA [244-7482]** or 719/684-8454. www.chipita lodge.com. 8 units (6 with bathroom), including 2 cottages. $100–$135 double. Rates include full breakfast. AE, MC, V. 10 miles west of I-25, then 1.5 miles east on Chipita Park Rd. **Amenities:** Outdoor hot tub. *In room:* Free Wi-fi.

Eastholme in the Rockies ★   Nestled in the quaint Pikes Peak mountain village of Cascade, 10 miles west of downtown Colorado Springs, this Victorian B&B gives guests an opportunity to see the city and get away from it all in the same day. Originally built in 1885 as a resort hotel, this property has a storied history that includes a stint as a boarding house before becoming a guest inn in 1988. Today it's a favorite of vacationers who want to be within striking distance of city attractions, but whose main interests lie in the Rockies. The parlor holds a bay window, a fireplace, and antiques. Most of the inn's large rooms feature 10-foot ceilings, and all provide plush quilts and remarkable views. The Marriott and Eisenhower suites feature original furnishings and a plethora of antiques, and the cottages offer DVD players, fireplaces, and spacious bathrooms with whirlpool tubs.

4445 Hagerman Ave. (P.O. Box 98), Cascade, CO 80809. © **800/672-9901** or 719/684-9901. www. eastholme.com. 8 units (6 with bathroom), including 2 cottages. $95–$135 double; $135 suite; $150 cottage. Rates include full breakfast. DISC, MC, V. 10 miles west of I-25, about 1 mile off U.S. 24. **Amenities:** Outdoor hot tub. *In room:* Cable TV w/VCR, free Wi-fi, fridge, coffeemaker, hair dryer.

Holden House 1902 Bed & Breakfast Inn ★★ Innkeepers Sallie and Welling Clark restored this storybook 1902 Colonial Revival–style Victorian house, the adjacent carriage house, and the 1898 house next door, filling the rooms with antiques and family heirlooms. Located near Old Colorado City, the inn has a living room with a tile fireplace, a front parlor with a bay window, verandas, and a lovely garden out back. Guests enjoy 24-hour coffee-and-tea service with a bottomless cookie jar, an afternoon wine social, and a gourmet breakfast in the formal dining room. Two suites are in the main house, two are in the adjacent carriage house, and one is in the second home. Each guest room bears the name of a Colorado mining area and contains memorabilia of that district. All have sitting areas, queen-size beds, fireplaces, CD/DVD players, and tubs for two. The Cripple Creek suite features Victorian fretwork in the sitting area, a mahogany fireplace, and a magnificent Roman marble tub. The Independence Suite, in the adjacent building, is accessible to guests with disabilities. Smoking is not allowed and pets are not permitted—except the two resident cats, Mingtoy and Mei-Lin.

1102 W. Pikes Peak Ave., Colorado Springs, CO 80904. © **888/565-3980** or 719/471-3980. Fax 719/471-4740. www.holdenhouse.com. 5 suites. $140–$160 double. Rates include full breakfast. AE, DC, DISC, MC, V. Children not accepted. *In room:* A/C, TV w/DVD player, free Wi-Fi, fridge, hair dryer, iron.

Two Sisters Inn ★★ Built by two sisters in 1919 as a boarding house, this splendid bed-and-breakfast has been owned and operated by two women—sisters in spirit if not in blood—since 1990. Wendy Goldstein and Sharon Smith have furnished the four bedrooms and separate honeymoon cottage with family heirlooms and photographs, in a style best described as informal elegance. The rooms in the main house feature Victorian frills and furnishings, such as quilts and claw-foot bathtubs. The two rooms that

 Family-Friendly Hotels

Best Value Inn Villa Motel (p. 183) A swimming pool and easy access to parks and the attractions in Manitou Springs keep most kids occupied.

The Broadmoor (p. 177) A lake and pool area with a terrific water slide, plus tennis, golf, riding stables, and a great summer kids' program that includes a visit to the Cheyenne Mountain Zoo all add up to a wonderful family experience.

share a bathroom are only rented together ($79 for the second bedroom, plus $15 for an additional person), which is a great choice for two couples. Across a splendid garden area, the small cottage, with a separate bedroom and living room, has a feather bed, gas-log fireplace, refrigerator, and shower with skylight. Fresh flowers adorn each room, and homemade chocolates and baked goods are served upon arrival.

The rooms are great, but I especially like the breakfasts, which the proprietors describe as "healthy decadence." They often cook with herbs and vegetables from their garden, and they do some marvelous things with fruit. In the summer, Wendy and Sharon's lemonade, made fresh with naturally sparkling Manitou Springs water, is the perfect refreshment. Smoking is not permitted.

10 Otoe Place, Manitou Springs, CO 80829. *C* **800/2SISINN [274-7466]** or 719/685-9684. www.two sisinn.com. 5 units. $94–$188 double; $155 cottage. Rates include full breakfast. DISC, MC, V. Children under 10 not accepted. Located 1 block south of the town clock on Manitou Ave.

INEXPENSIVE

Best Value Inn Villa Motel (Kids)   A solid option right off the main drag in Manitou Springs, the Villa offers well-kept rooms and reasonable rates within walking distance of all of Manitou's restaurants and shops, as well as some older cottages that are the least expensive rooms on-site. The cottages have two double beds, the newer motel rooms have two queens or a king, and deluxe rooms have a jetted tub and a kitchenette to boot. For the kids, there's a small pool and easy access to the family-friendly attractions downtown.

481 Manitou Ave., Manitou Springs, CO 80829. *C* **888/315-2378** or 719/685-5492. www.villamotel.com. 47 units. Summer $82–$120 double; fall through spring $59–$109. AE, DC, DISC, MC, V. **Amenities:** Large outdoor pool. *In room:* A/C, cable TV, free Wi-Fi, fridge, coffeemaker, microwave, hair dryer, iron.

Travel Inn (Value)   Popular with both business travelers and vacationers on a budget, the Travel Inn offers a comfortable place to sleep at very reasonable rates. The two-story motel with bright turquoise trim is conveniently located near downtown Colorado Springs, with easy access to all the area attractions on I-25 and U.S. 24. The remodeled rooms are simple and comfortable, with white stucco walls and dark-wood furnishings. There is one apartment with a kitchenette that is designed for longer stays.

512 S. Nevada Ave., Colorado Springs, CO 80903. *C* **719/636-3986.** Fax 719/636-3980. 36 units (most with shower only). Summer $49–$89 double; fall through spring $40–$60 double. Rates include continental breakfast. AE, DC, DISC, MC, V. **Amenities:** Outdoor heated pool (seasonal); coin-op washers and dryers. *In room:* A/C, cable TV, free Wi-Fi, kitchenette.

CAMPING

Also see the section on **Mueller State Park,** under "Parks & Zoos," later in this chapter.

Garden of the Gods Campground   Located near Garden of the Gods (see "Attractions," p. 191), this large, tree-shaded campground offers 250 full RV hookups (30- and 50-amp service, some with modems and phones) and additional tent sites. Facilities include tables, barbecue grills, bathhouses, grocery store, wireless Internet access, laundry, heated swimming pool, whirlpool tub, playground, and clubhouse with pool tables and game room. The 12 camping cabins, which share the campground's bathhouse, rent for $45 to $50 for a double. There are also motel-style rooms for $60 to $110 for a double. The bunkhouse and the cabins are available in summer only.

3704 W. Colorado Ave., Colorado Springs, CO 80904. *C* **800/248-9451** or 719/475-9450. www.colorado campground.com. Summer $36–$49; fall through spring $22–$32. Extra person $3. DISC, MC, V. Take I-25, exit 141, head west on U.S. 24, then north (right) on 31st St., then left on Colorado Ave. for 6 blocks (keep right), and turn right to gate.

4 WHERE TO DINE

Colorado Springs has an excellent variety of above-average restaurants, with a good sampling of continental cuisine, Mexican restaurants, and steak joints. See also the section on dinner theaters in "Colorado Springs After Dark," later in this chapter. A good online resource for information on area restaurants and nightlife is **www.sceneinthesprings.com**.

VERY EXPENSIVE

Charles Court ★★ PROGRESSIVE AMERICAN   The English country-manor atmosphere of this outstanding restaurant at The Broadmoor resort (p. 177), with picture windows looking across Cheyenne Lake to the renowned hotel, lends itself to a fine-dining experience. The creative American menu, which changes seasonally, has a decidedly Rocky Mountain emphasis. You'll usually find such delicacies as a Colorado lamb rib eye, beef tenderloin, wild King salmon, Rocky Mountain trout, and a wild-game selection such as buffalo or venison. The wine list includes more than 600 selections, service is superlative, and the desserts are extraordinary. A seasonal outdoor patio provides splendid views of the mountains across the lake. A comparable experience can be had on the top of the tower on the other side of the lake at the **Penrose Room,** an equally refined eatery with a Continental bent and even more formality (jackets required).

Broadmoor W., in The Broadmoor, Lake Circle. ☏ 719/577-5733. www.broadmoor.com. Reservations recommended. Breakfast $8–$18; dinner main courses $23–$42. AE, DC, DISC, MC, V. Daily 7–11am and 6–10pm.

Cliff House Dining Room ★★ AMERICAN   The Cliff House Dining Room is an excellent choice for a romantic occasion. The Villeroy & Boch china, damask linen, crystal glassware, and 19th-century tiled fireplace evoke the charm of the Victorian era. The main event is dinner: old favorites expertly prepared in new ways. While the menu changes regularly, I recommend the filet mignon, charbroiled with roasted garlic pepper, and the seafood (trout to scallops and prawns) when they're available, but everything is quite good. As would be expected, service is impeccable. The breakfast menu offers traditional American selections, plus a nifty wild-mushroom Florentine with smoked bacon, and lunches are upscale sandwiches and entrees like quiche du jour and blackened ruby-red trout. The excellent wine list includes some 600 selections.

Cliff House Inn, 306 Cañon Ave., Manitou Springs. ☏ 719/785-2415. Reservations recommended. Breakfast and lunch main courses $7–$24; dinner main courses $19–$32. AE, DC, DISC, MC, V. Daily 6:30–10:30am, 11:30am–2:30pm, and 5:30–9:30pm.

Craftwood Inn ★★★ (Finds) COLORADO CUISINE   Ensconced in an English Tudor building with beamed ceilings, stained-glass windows, and a copper-hooded fireplace, the casually elegant Craftwood Inn, built in 1912, was originally a coppersmith's shop. Today this excellent restaurant specializes in regional game and also offers steak, seafood, and vegetarian dishes. The extensive selection of game—elk, venison, pheasant, quail, caribou, antelope, wild boar, ostrich, and buffalo—attracts the most acclaim. I especially recommend grilled Rocky Mountain elk steak (when available), marinated in herb and smoke-infused oil, and served with a cabernet sauvignon hunter's sauce. The adventurous might opt for the wild grill: elk, antelope, and venison, each accompanied by a distinctive sauce. Be sure to save room for one of the superb—and somewhat unusual—desserts, such as jalapeño white-chocolate mousse with raspberry sauce, or prickly pear sorbet. The outdoor patio provides wonderful views of Pikes Peak.

404 El Paso Blvd., Manitou Springs. © **719/685-9000.** www.craftwood.com. Reservations recommended. Main courses $24–$38. AE, DC, DISC, MC, V. Daily 5:30–8:30pm. Turn north off Manitou Ave. onto Mayfair Ave., go uphill 1 block, and turn left onto El Paso Blvd.; the Craftwood is on your right.

The Famous ★★ STEAK A swank urban steakhouse, The Famous is a magnet for beefeaters, serving up choice cuts of U.S. Prime. It's hard to go wrong here, but bring an appetite: Except for two filets, no steak is less than a pound. I like the Kansas City Bone-In Strip, but everything is top-shelf here, even the nonbeef fare, like fresh seafood (flown in daily), Colorado lamb, and chicken Oscar. The lunch menu is similarly carnivorous, with a few salads for good measure. There are shiny booths and jet-black tables, as well as a full bar and live piano every night.

31 N. Tejon St. © **719/227-7333.** Reservations recommended. Lunch main courses $10–$15; dinner main courses $28–$50. AE, DISC, MC, V. Mon–Fri 11am–3pm; Sun–Thurs 5–10pm; Fri–Sat 5–11pm.

Summit ★★★ CONTEMPORARY AMERICAN Flashy, modern, and new in 2006, Summit is a departure from The Broadmoor's typical eatery formula—Continental has long ruled the roost here—but it quickly rose to the top of the local culinary stratosphere. Designed by acclaimed architect Adam Tihany, the strikingly contemporary room is at once slick and romantic, with cloth chandeliers, contemporary metalwork on the windows and walls, and a glassed-in, rotating turret holding 432 bottles of wine behind the bar. The visual spectacle is aesthetically matched by the innovative and adventurous fare—the seasonal menu might have a terrific roasted beet salad or monkfish *osso buco*, but it depends on what's currently domestically available. The service is impeccable, and the sommelier is skilled at wine pairings, with a focus on biodynamic and organic wines, and wines from small wineries.

In The Broadmoor, 19 Lake Circle. © **719/577-5896.** www.summitatbroadmoor.com. Reservations recommended. Main courses $18–$32. AE, DC, DISC, MC, V. Daily 5:30–9pm.

Walter's Bistro ★★ CONTINENTAL Slick but not stuffy, Walter's manages to be classy, casual, and classic, all at once. Proprietor Walter Iser, a native of Salzburg, Austria, has long worked the front of the house in various upscale properties in the Springs and environs, but he's truly hit his stride with Walter's, which opened in 1999 and relocated to a handsome new location in 2004. Watching over four dining areas—including a richly decorated "red room" and a chef's table beneath windows into the kitchen—Iser has a gracious style and steady direction that inform an expertly prepared menu of Continental staples, which manage to simultaneously taste traditional but original. The menu changes regularly, but my visit included a terrific rack of lamb, herb-roasted and served with a creamy English pea risotto, pan-roasted Chilean sea bass, and a truly phenomenal bone-in filet mignon with an equally superlative bread pudding with wild mushrooms and andouille sausage. Desserts are decadent, including a chocolate "bag" filled with tiramisu, and the wine list is long and varied.

136 E. Cheyenne Mountain Blvd. © **719/630-0201.** Reservations recommended. Lunch main courses $7–$24; dinner main courses $24–$32. AE, DC, DISC, MC, V. Mon–Fri 11am–2pm; Mon–Sat 5:30–9pm.

EXPENSIVE

The Blue Star ★★ INTERNATIONAL FUSION In a quiet area just south of downtown, The Blue Star is one of the most popular eateries in Colorado Springs, and deservedly so. The menu changes monthly, but it always includes filet mignon, fresh fish (flown in daily), pork, and chicken, prepared with a nose for invention. The culinary inspiration comes from Mediterranean and Pacific Rim cultures, but it is ultimately unclassifiable, and in a local class of its own. The restaurant might serve Thai chile beef tips with avocado sorbet one week and beef bourguignon the next. Social and colorful, the bar features sleek wood and metal decor, and walls are adorned with well-lit artwork, whereas the dining room's atmosphere is milder with an open kitchen. Each room serves its own menu: The bar menu is "eating" (lunch and dinner in a social atmosphere), while the main room is serious "dining," dinner only in a more refined space. Blue Star has won *Wine Spectator*'s "Best of" Award of Excellence with its 8,500-bottle cellar since 2003.

1645 S. Tejon St. ℰ **719/632-1086.** www.thebluestar.net. Reservations recommended. Main courses $6–$14 lunch, $9–$25 dinner. AE, MC, V. Dining room Sun–Thurs 5:30–9pm; Fri–Sat 5:30–10pm. Bar open during restaurant hours; bar food service Mon–Wed 11:30am–10:30pm, Thurs–Fri 11:30am–midnight, Sat 3pm–midnight, Sun 3–10:30pm.

La Petite Maison ★★ CONTEMPORARY FRENCH   This delightful 1894 Victorian cottage houses a gem of a restaurant, chef-owned by Henri Chaperont. Since 1978, it has served a blend of classic French and eclectic modern cuisine in a friendly, intimate setting with jazz playing in the background. The food is innovative, interesting, and well presented; service is impeccable. The menus change monthly; if they're available, I suggest Colorado rack of lamb Provencale or the baked monkfish with three-grain mustard. Chaperont's skills are on full display with his three-course tasting menus, available for $30 Tuesday through Friday and Sunday; a typical meal could include traditional French onion soup, roasted pork tenderloin, and chocolate pate with lavender crème anglaise for dessert.

1015 W. Colorado Ave. ℰ **719/632-4887.** Reservations recommended. Main courses $19–$30. AE, DC, DISC, MC, V. Tues–Sun 5–10pm.

Margarita at PineCreek ★★ ECLECTIC   A delightful spot to sit and watch the sun set over Pikes Peak, the Margarita is tucked away above two creeks on the north side of the city. The decor is attractively simple, with tile floors and stucco walls; a tree-shaded outdoor patio is open in summer, and even features outdoor movies on occasion. Saturday evenings bring live harpsichord music to the dining room, and Friday nights often feature live acoustic music—from bluegrass to Celtic. Although the style of cooking may vary, depending on the chef's whim, the emphasis is on fresh ingredients, and everything is prepared from scratch, including breads and stocks. Lunches feature a choice of two homemade soups, salad, and fresh bread; there are also Southwestern and weekly specials. Six-course dinners offer three entree choices, usually fresh fish, veal, steak, pasta, lamb, or duckling.

7350 Pine Creek Rd. ℰ **719/598-8667.** Reservations recommended. Fixed-price lunch $10–$11; fixed-price dinner $30–$38; brunch $10–$15. AE, DISC, MC, V. Tues–Fri 11:30am–2pm; Tues–Sat 5:30–9pm; Sun 10:30am–2pm.

The Tavern ★★ STEAK/SEAFOOD   Authentic Toulouse-Lautrec lithographs on the walls and knotty pine furniture and paneling mark the Tavern, open since 1939, as a restaurant with unusual ambience. In the front dining room, nightly piano music is followed by a four-piece ensemble—guests are welcome to take a turn around the dance floor between courses. The quieter garden room, with luxuriant tropical foliage, gives the feeling of outdoor dining without being outdoors. Service in both rooms is impeccable.

Many selections are prepared in the restaurant's stone grill, and the emphasis is on fresh ingredients and classic cuisine. The lunch menu changes seasonally, but typically includes steaks, gourmet burgers, crab cakes, and a variety of sandwiches and salads. Dinners are more elaborate: Choose from slow-roasted prime rib, filet mignon, Rocky

Mountain trout, or roast chicken. All entrees come with a selection of homemade
breads.

Broadmoor Main, at The Broadmoor, Lake Circle. © **719/577-5733**. www.broadmoor.com. Reservations recommended. Main courses $10–$29 lunch, $16–$58 dinner. AE, DC, DISC, MC, V. Daily 11am–11pm.

The Warehouse ★★ CONTEMPORARY/FUSION This stalwart locals' joint, which opened in 1997, emanates the style that helped launch a revitalization of the south side of downtown Colorado Springs. The Warehouse is located in, yes, a converted century-old warehouse, a mixed-use building that's one of the most stylish addresses in the city. One side of the restaurant is the main dining area, with an array of tables centered on a copper-topped bar; across the hall is a gallery with couches where many people enjoy libations or wait for a table. The attractive industrial chic atmosphere is a nice match for the diverse menu, which is known for a filet "Oskar," seared beef tenderloin with lemon-pepper asparagus, blue crab, and Béarnaise sauce, and venison with a tart cherry sauce and mountain mushroom risotto. Lunch is lighter, mainly unique sandwiches and salads, and the wine and beer lists—focused on Colorado producers—are excellent.

25 W. Cimarron St. © **719475-8880**. www.thewarehouserestaurant.com. Reservations recommended. Main courses $8–$15 lunch, $15–29 dinner. AE, DISC, MC, V. Mon–Fri 11:30am–9pm; Sat 5–10pm.

MODERATE

Edelweiss Restaurant ★ (Kids) GERMAN The Edelweiss occupies an impressive stone building with a trio of fireplaces and an outdoor biergarten. It underscores its Bavarian atmosphere with strolling folk musicians on weekends, which gives it a party feel that makes this a fun place for kids. It offers a hearty menu of Jägerschnitzel, Wiener schnitzel, sauerbraten, bratwurst, and other old-country specials, as well as New York strip steak, fresh fish, and chicken. The fruit strudels are excellent, and there are some great beers, many of them German imports.

34 E. Ramona Ave. (southwest of I-25, 1 block west of Nevada Ave.). © **719/633-2220**. www.edelweiss rest.com. Reservations recommended. Main courses $7–$9 lunch, $12–$25 dinner. AE, DC, DISC, MC, V. Daily 11:30am–9pm.

Giuseppe's Old Depot Restaurant ★ (Kids) ITALIAN/AMERICAN Located in a restored Denver & Rio Grande train station with glass ticket windows lining the walls, Giuseppe's is a fun place with a lot of historic ambience. You can see freight trains going by just outside the windows. The same extensive menu is served all day. Spaghetti, lasagna (vegetarian spinach or spicy sausage and ground beef), and stone-baked pizza are house specialties. American dishes include my favorite—baby back pork ribs, smothered in Giuseppe's secret sauce—plus prime rib, grilled salmon filet, and fried chicken.

10 S. Sierra Madre St. © **719/635-3111**. www.giuseppes-depot.com. Menu items $8–$31; pizzas $11–$21. AE, DC, DISC, MC, V. Sun–Thurs 11am–9pm; Fri–Sat 11am–10pm.

Marigold Café and Bakery ★ (Finds) INTERNATIONAL This bustling restaurant and bakery is known for its fresh ingredients and homemade breads and pastries. A low wall separates the bakery counter from the cafelike dining area. Breakfast and lunch are casual, featuring traditional menus and gourmet-savvy items such as Greek pizzas and innovative sandwiches served on fresh breads. The restaurant takes on a more refined atmosphere at dinner, when the menu reflects a wide range of international influences. Favorites include flat iron steak, served with a balsamic and red-wine reduction, salmon with sautéed spinach and goat cheese and dried tomato pesto, jambalaya, and fresh pasta

188

Kids Family-Friendly Restaurants

Edelweiss Restaurant (p. 187) Kids will enjoy the strolling musicians who play German folk music on weekends, and they'll love the apple and cherry strudels.

Giuseppe's Old Depot Restaurant (p. 187) An original locomotive stands outside this old Denver & Rio Grande Railroad station. Most kids will adore the spaghetti and pizza.

Meadow Muffins (p. 190) The junk-store appearance and kid-friendly food (like a burger with peanut butter) make this place a hit with the younger set.

dishes. The bakery counter bustles through the early afternoon, offering splendid breads, pastries, and sandwiches. Box lunches, coffee, lattes, and cappuccinos are also available.

4605 Centennial Blvd. (at Garden of the Gods Rd.). ✆ **719/599-4776.** Main courses $5–$8.50 breakfast, $7–$10 lunch, $11–$32 dinner. AE, DC, DISC, MC, V. Restaurant Mon–Sat 7–10:30am, 11am–2:30pm, and 5–9pm. Coffee bar and bakery Mon–Fri 6am–9pm; Sat 7am–9pm. Closed Sun.

Phantom Canyon Brewing Co. ★ CONTEMPORARY AMERICAN This popular, busy brewpub is in the Cheyenne Building, home to the Chicago Rock Island & Pacific Railroad in the early 1900s. On any given day, 8 to 10 of Phantom Canyon's specialty beers are on tap, including homemade root beer. The signature beer is the Phantom, a traditional India pale ale; others include the Cascade Amber and a light ale called Queen's Blonde.

The dining room is large and wide open, with ceiling fans, hardwood floors, and the large brewing vats visible in the corner. Lunch is typical but well-prepared brewpub fare: hearty salads, half-pound burgers, fish and chips, and the like. The dinner menu is varied and more innovative, with choices such as roasted chicken and hot bacon salad, Queen's Blonde Ale soup, steak, and trout. The menus change periodically. On the second floor is a billiard hall with TVs and foosball. See also "Colorado Springs After Dark," later in this chapter.

2 E. Pikes Peak Ave. ✆ **719/635-2800.** Main courses $8–$13 lunch, $9–$25 dinner. AE, DC, DISC, MC, V. Mon–Thurs 11am–10pm; Fri–Sat 11am–midnight; Sun 10am–10pm. Bar open later.

Ritz Grill ★ NEW AMERICAN This lively restaurant-lounge with a large central bar is where it's at for many of the city's young professionals. The decor is Art Deco, the service fast and friendly. The varied, trendy menu offers such specialties as Garden Ritz veggie pizza, with fresh spinach, sun-dried tomatoes, bell peppers, onions, mushrooms, fresh pesto, and three cheeses; and Siamese tuna salad—served rare with wild greens, mango salsa, radish sprouts, pickled ginger chestnuts, and wasabi peas. I recommend Cajun chicken and shrimp, sautéed with bell peppers in a spicy alfredo sauce, or the peppered Ahi, spiced with pastrami and served with gingered white rice and sautéed spinach. See also "Colorado Springs After Dark," later in this chapter.

15 S. Tejon St. ✆ **719/635-8484.** www.ritzgrill.com. Main courses $7–$15 brunch and lunch, $12–$26 dinner. AE, MC, V. Mon–Thurs 11am–10pm; Fri–Sat 11am–10:30pm; Sun 9:30am–10pm. Bar open later with a limited menu.

Adam's Mountain Cafe ★★ (Finds) AMERICAN/VEGETARIAN Not strictly vegetarian, Adam's Mountain Cafe is one of the best restaurants in the area for those seeking vegetarian or healthy, largely organic—but not entirely meatless—fare. While Adam's relocated from its longtime Cañon Avenue address to the ground floor of the restored Spa Building in 2007, the country-meets-French–Victorian vibe is still there. The menu includes grilled items, fresh fish, and many Mediterranean-style entrees. Breakfast specialties include orange-almond French toast, my top choice, and the P. W. Busboy Special, consisting of two whole-grain pancakes, two scrambled eggs, and slices of fresh fruit. Lunch offerings include sandwiches, soups, salads, fresh pasta, and South-western plates. Come dinner, I recommend the harvest crepes, packed with roasted but-ternut squash and finished with a vegetarian red chile, and the Caribbean jerked chicken.

934 Manitou Ave. (in the Spa Building)., Manitou Springs. (C) **719/685-1430.** www.adamsmountain.com. Main courses $4.50–$9 breakfast and lunch, $8–$19 dinner. AE, DISC, MC, V. Daily 8am–3pm; Tues–Sat 5–9pm. Closed Mon Oct–Apr.

Amanda's Fonda ★ (Finds) AMERICAN My pick for Mexican food in Colorado Springs, Amanda's Fonda is the handiwork of a family that has owned Mexican restau-rants for six generations. Clearly they've honed the art of making remarkable chile in that time: Both the chile Colorado and the green chile are excellent; the former is red with big hunks of steak, the latter spicier with pork. The burritos, spinach-and-mushroom enchiladas, and seafood are also quite tasty, and on weekends the menu includes both *menudo* (tripe soup) and *pozole* (pork and hominy stew). The interior of the place is a funky maze, one part log cabin, one part family restaurant, and one part Mexican bar and grill. The shady creekside patio is a great place for a summertime meal.

3625 W. Colorado Ave. (C) **719/227-1975.** Main courses $6–$14. AE, DISC, MC, V. Mon–Sat 11:30am–9pm; Sun noon–9pm.

Dutch Kitchen ★ (Value) AMERICAN Good homemade food served in a casual, friendly atmosphere is the draw at this relatively small restaurant, which the Flynn family has owned and operated since 1959. I especially like the corned beef, pastrami, and ham sandwiches, and if you're there in summer, be sure to try the fresh rhubarb pie. Other house specialties include the pies (the buttermilk, pecan chocolate, and candied apple are award-winners) and homemade soups.

1025 Manitou Ave., Manitou Springs. (C) **719/685-9962.** Main courses $4–$8 lunch, $7–$13 dinner. No credit cards. Sat–Thurs 11:30am–3:30pm and 4:30–8pm. Closed Thurs in spring and fall. Closed Dec–Feb.

La'au's (Finds) HAWAIIAN TACOS An unexpected hybrid that works quite well, La'au's is a Colorado College student favorite that takes Mexican tradition and filters it through a Pacific Rim lens—it's one of the few taco joints on the mainland offering its customers chopsticks and sriracha sauce. With counter service and indoor and outdoor seating, Lau'au's tacos are topped with papaya or cabbage and often filled with Hawaiian staples like huli chicken or mahimahi. Besides tacos, borrachas (make-your-own taco plates), salads, and bowls (tacos minus the tortillas) are available, as are bottles of beer and pre-made margaritas.

830 N. Tejon St., ste. 110. (C) **719/578-5228.** Plates $5.50–$9. No credit cards. Mon–Sat 11am–10pm; Sun noon–8pm.

Meadow Muffins ★ (Value) (Kids) AMERICAN   A fun spot for a good, inexpensive meal in a lively atmosphere, Meadow Muffins is a boisterous bar packed with movie memorabilia and assorted oddities. The decorations range from two buckboard wagons (hung from the ceiling near the front door), which were supposedly used in *Gone with the Wind,* to a 5-ton cannon used in a number of war movies. The menu includes chicken wings, onion rings, sandwiches, salads, and the like. The burgers are especially good— just ask anyone in the Springs—but I have to admit that I couldn't bring myself to try the Jiffy Burger: a large ground-beef burger topped with bacon, provolone cheese, and— believe it or not—peanut butter. On most days, there are great food and drink specials. See also "Colorado Springs After Dark," later in this chapter.

2432 W. Colorado Ave., in Old Colorado City. ✆ **719/633-0583.** www.meadowmuffins.com. Most menu items $4.50–$9. AE, DISC, MC, V. Daily 11am–10pm. Bar open later with a limited menu.

5 ATTRACTIONS

Most of the attractions of the Pikes Peak region fit in two general categories: natural, such as Pikes Peak, Garden of the Gods, and Cave of the Winds; and historic/educational, including the Air Force Academy, Olympic Complex training center, museums, historic homes, and art galleries. There are also gambling houses in Cripple Creek.

If you visit Colorado from a sea-level area, you might want to schedule mountain excursions, such as the cog railway to the top of Pikes Peak, at the end of your stay. This will give your body time to adapt to the lower oxygen level at these higher elevations. See also "Health," in chapter 3.

THE TOP ATTRACTIONS

Colorado Springs Pioneers Museum ★★ (Value)   Housed in the former El Paso County Courthouse (1903), which is on the National Register of Historic Places, this museum is an excellent place to begin your visit to Colorado Springs. Exhibits depict the community's rich history, including its beginning as a fashionable resort, the railroad and mining eras, and its growth and development in the 20th century. Also here is the Victorian home of writer Helen Hunt Jackson.

You can ride an Otis birdcage elevator, which dates to the early 1900s, to the restored original courtroom, where several *Perry Mason* episodes were filmed. A recent renovation uncovered intriguing gold and silver images of goddesses, painted on the courtroom walls in part to represent the two key resources of the state's economy at the time. However, it's believed that they were also painted as a subtle protest when the country was changing from a gold and silver standard to a gold-only monetary standard. Another series of murals depicts over 400 years of Pikes Peak region history.

Changing exhibit areas house traveling shows such as quilts, historic photographs, aviation, American-Indian culture, and art pottery. The museum has hosted a wide range of events, including lectures on the American cowboy, antique-auto shows, jazz concerts, and Hispanic celebrations. The historic reference library and archives are available by appointment. Allow 1 to 3 hours.

215 S. Tejon St. ✆ **719/385-5990.** www.cspm.org. Free admission, donations accepted. Year-round Tues–Sat 10am–5pm. Take I-25, exit 141, east to Tejon St., turn right and go 4 blocks.

Garden of the Gods ★★★ (Value)   One of the West's unique geological sites, the 1,300-acre Garden of the Gods is a giant rock garden composed of spectacular red sandstone formations sculpted by rain and wind over millions of years. Located where several life zones and ecosystems converge, the beautiful city-run park harbors a variety of plant and animal communities. The oldest survivors are the ancient, twisted junipers, some 1,000 years old. The strangest animals are the honey ants, which gorge themselves on honey in the summer and fall, becoming living honey pots to feed their colonies during winter hibernation.

The park has a number of hiking trails—mostly easy to moderate—that offer great scenery and an opportunity to get away from the crowds. Leashed dogs are permitted on trails (owners should clean up after their pets). Many trails are also open to horseback riding and mountain biking. You can get trail maps for the park at the **visitor center,** which also offers exhibits on the history, geology, plants, and wildlife of the area; a cafeteria; and other conveniences.

A 12-minute multimedia theater presentation, *How Did Those Red Rocks Get There?* ($5 adults, $2 children 5–12, free for children under 5), newly remade by local filmmaker John Bourbonais in 2008 in high-definition with a unique BluRay projection system, is an excellent introduction to the geologic history of the area. In summer, park naturalists lead free 45-minute walks through the park and conduct free afternoon interpretive programs. You can also take a 20-minute bus tour of the park ($5 adults, $2.50 children 5–12, free for children under 5). You may spot technical rock climbers on some of the park spires; they are required to register at the visitor center.

Also in the park is the **Rock Ledge Ranch Historic Site** (see "More Attractions," below).

1805 N. 30th St. ✆ **719/634-6666.** www.gardenofgods.com. Free admission. Park May–Oct daily 5am–11pm; Nov–Apr daily 5am–9pm. Visitor Center Memorial Day to Labor Day daily 8am–8pm; Labor Day to Memorial Day daily 9am–5pm. Take Garden of the Gods Rd. west from I-25, exit 146, and turn south on 30th St.

Pikes Peak Cog Railway ★★   For those who enjoy rail travel, spectacular scenery, and the thrill of mountain climbing without all the work, this is the trip to take. The first

---

(Fun Facts)   **Fit for the Gods**

In 1859 large numbers of pioneers were arriving in Colorado hoping to find gold (their motto: "Pikes Peak or Bust"). Many of them established communities along what is now called the Front Range, including Colorado City, which was later incorporated within Colorado Springs.

Legend has it that certain pioneers who explored the remarkable sandstone formations in the area wanted to establish a beer garden there. However, one Rufus Cable objected: "Beer Garden! Why this is a fit place for a Garden of the Gods!"

Fortunately for posterity, Charles Elliott Perkins (head of the Burlington Railroad) bought the area some 20 years later and kept it in its natural state. Upon Perkins's death in 1907, his heirs gave the remarkable area to Colorado Springs on the condition that it be preserved as a park and open to the public. The park was dedicated in 1909 and is now a Registered National Landmark.

Colorado Springs Attractions

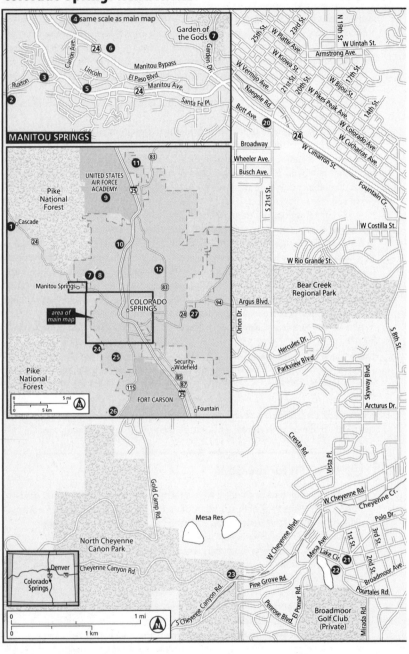

MANITOU SPRINGS

Garden of the Gods

Canon Ave.

Lincoln

Ruxton

Manitou Bypass

El Paso Blvd.

Manitou Ave.

Santa Fe Pl.

Garden Dr.

Pike National Forest

UNITED STATES AIR FORCE ACADEMY

Cascade

Manitou Springs

area of main map

COLORADO SPRINGS

Pike National Forest

Security-Widefield

FORT CARSON

Fountain

Gold Camp Rd.

North Cheyenne Cañon Park

Cheyenne Canyon Rd.

Mesa Res.

W Cheyenne Blvd.

S Cheyenne Canyon Rd.

Pine Grove Rd.

Penrose Blvd.

El Pomar Rd.

Mirada Rd.

Broadmoor Golf Club (Private)

Pourtales Rd.

Broadmoor Blvd.

Mesa Ave.

Lake Cir.

Polo Dr.

1st St.

2nd St.

3rd St.

Vista Pl.

W Cheyenne Rd.

Cheyenne Cr.

Cresta Rd.

Skyway Blvd.

Arcturus Dr.

Bear Creek Regional Park

W Rio Grande St.

W Costilla St.

Hercules Dr.

Parkview Blvd.

Orion Dr.

Argus Blvd.

COLORADO SPRINGS

Bott Ave.

Broadway

Wheeler Ave.

Busch Ave.

Naegele Rd.

W Vermijo Ave.

W Pikes Peak Ave.

W Colorado Ave.

W Cucharras Ave.

W Cimarron St.

Fountain Cr.

W Uintah St.

Armstrong Ave.

W Platte Ave.

W Kiowa St.

W Bijou St.

25th St.

23rd St.

21st St.

20th St.

17th St.

14th St.

19th St.

S 21st St.

S 8th St.

Denver

Colorado Springs

0   5 mi
0   5 km

0   1 mi
0   1 km

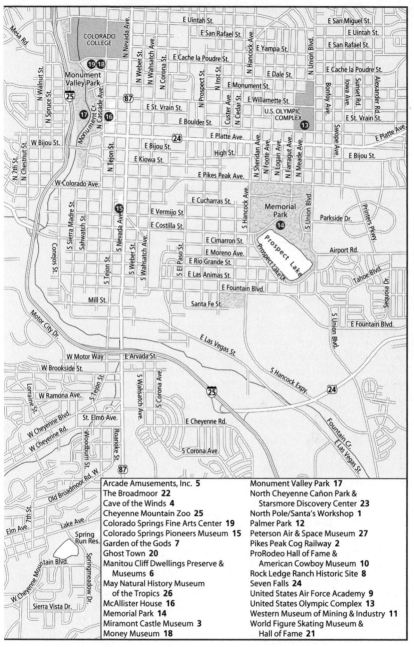

Arcade Amusements, Inc. **5**
The Broadmoor **22**
Cave of the Winds **4**
Cheyenne Mountain Zoo **25**
Colorado Springs Fine Arts Center **19**
Colorado Springs Pioneers Museum **15**
Garden of the Gods **7**
Ghost Town **20**
Manitou Cliff Dwellings Preserve &
 Museums **6**
May Natural History Museum
 of the Tropics **26**
McAllister House **16**
Memorial Park **14**
Miramont Castle Museum **3**
Money Museum **18**

Monument Valley Park **17**
North Cheyenne Cañon Park &
 Starsmore Discovery Center **23**
North Pole/Santa's Workshop **1**
Palmer Park **12**
Peterson Air & Space Museum **27**
Pikes Peak Cog Railway **2**
ProRodeo Hall of Fame &
 American Cowboy Museum **10**
Rock Ledge Ranch Historic Site **8**
Seven Falls **24**
United States Air Force Academy **9**
United States Olympic Complex **13**
Western Museum of Mining & Industry **11**
World Figure Skating Museum &
 Hall of Fame **21**

(Fun Facts) **Top of the Charts**

Teacher Katharine Lee Bates (1859–1929) wrote the patriotic song "America the Beautiful" after an 1895 wagon trip to the top of Pikes Peak.

passenger train climbed Pikes Peak on June 30, 1891, and diesel slowly replaced steam power between 1939 and 1955. Four custom-built Swiss twin-unit rail cars, each seating 216 passengers, went into service in 1989. The 9-mile route, with grades up to 25%, takes 75 minutes to reach the top of 14,110-foot Pikes Peak; the round-trip requires 3 hours and 10 minutes (including a 40-min. stopover at the top). Runs depart between 8am and 5pm in midsummer, with shorter hours at other times.

The journey is exciting from the start, but passengers really begin to ooh and aah when the track leaves the forest, creeping above timberline at about 11,500 feet. The view from the summit takes in Denver, 75 miles north; New Mexico's Sangre de Cristo range, 100 miles south; the Cripple Creek mining district, on the mountain's western flank; wave after wave of Rocky Mountain subranges to the west; and the seemingly endless sea of Great Plains to the east. This is also where you'll want to watch for Rocky Mountain bighorn sheep and yellow-bellied marmots. The Summit House at the top of Pikes Peak has a restaurant (sandwiches, snacks, beverages, and box lunches), a gift shop, and even a flavored oxygen bar.

Take a jacket or sweater—it can be cold and windy on top, even on warm summer days. This trip is not recommended if you have cardiac or respiratory problems. Even those in good health may feel faint or light-headed.

515 Ruxton Ave., Manitou Springs. ℂ **800/745-3773** or 719/685-5401. www.cograilway.com. $31–$33 adults, $17–$18 children under 12, free for children under 3 held on an adult's lap. Mid-Apr to mid-Nov, with 2–8 departures daily; call or check schedules online. Closed mid-Nov to mid-Apr, except for special events. Reservations required (available online). Take I-25, exit 141, west on U.S. 24 for 4 miles, turn onto Manitou Ave. west and go 1¹/₂ miles to Ruxton Ave., turn left and go about ¹/₂ mile.

Pikes Peak Highway ★   Perhaps no view in Colorado equals the 360-degree panorama from the 14,110-foot summit of Pikes Peak. Whether you go by cog railway (see above) or private vehicle, the ascent is a spectacular, exciting experience—although not for those with heart or breathing problems or a fear of heights. The 19-mile toll highway (paved for 10 miles, all-weather gravel thereafter) starts at 7,400 feet, some 4 miles west of Manitou Springs. There are numerous photo-op stops as you head up the mountain, and deer, mountain sheep, marmots, and other animals often appear on the slopes, especially above the timberline (around 11,500 ft.). This 156-curve road is the site of the annual Pikes Peak International Hill Climb (see "Spectator Sports," later in this chapter). Allow 3 hours minimum.

Off U.S. 24 at Cascade Ave. ℂ **800/318-9505** or 719/385-7325. www.pikespeakcolorado.com. Admission $10 adults, $5 children 6–15, free for children under 6, $35 maximum per car. Fri before Memorial Day to Labor Day daily 7am–7pm; Labor Day to late Sept daily 7am–5pm; Oct to Memorial Day daily 9am–3pm, weather permitting. Take I-25, exit 141, west on U.S. 24 about 10 miles.

United States Air Force Academy ★★   Colorado Springs' pride and joy got its start in 1954 when Congress authorized the establishment of a U.S. Air Force Academy and chose this 18,000-acre site from among 400 prospective locations. The first class of cadets enrolled in 1959, and each year since, about 4,000 cadets have enrolled for the 4 years of rigorous training required to become Air Force officers.

The Academy is 12 miles north of downtown; enter at the North Gate, off I-25, exit 156B. Soon after entering the grounds, at the intersection of North Gate Boulevard and Stadium Boulevard, you'll see an impressive outdoor B-52 bomber display. Where North Gate Boulevard becomes Academy Drive (in another mile or so), look to your left to see the Cadet Field House, where the basketball and ice-hockey teams play (see "Spectator Sports," later in this chapter), and the Parade Ground, where you can sometimes spot cadets marching.

Academy Drive soon curves to the left. Six miles from the North Gate, signs mark the turnoff to the Barry Goldwater Air Force Academy Visitor Center. Open daily, it offers a variety of exhibits and films on the academy's history and cadet life, extensive literature and self-guided tour maps, and the latest information and schedules on academy activities. There's also a large gift shop and coffee shop.

A short trail from the visitor center leads to the unmistakable Cadet Chapel. Its 17 gleaming aluminum spires soar 150 feet, and within the building are separate chapels for the major Western faiths as well as an "all faiths" room. The public can visit Monday through Saturday from 9am to 5pm; Sunday services at 10am are open to the public. The chapel is closed for 5 days around graduation and during special events.

Also within easy walking distance of the visitor center is Arnold Hall, the social center that houses historical exhibits, a cafeteria, and a theater featuring a variety of public shows and lectures.

Off I-25, exit 156B. *℃* **719/333-2025.** www.usafa.af.mil. Free admission. Visitor center daily 9am–5pm; grounds 8am–6pm; additional hours for special events.

United States Olympic Complex   So you think your local fitness center is state-of-the-art? Check out the 37-acre United States Olympic Complex, a sophisticated center where thousands of athletes train each year in a variety of Olympic sports. Free guided tours, available daily, take about an hour, and include a film depicting the U.S. Olympic effort. Visitors may also see athletes in training. The visitor center includes the U.S. Olympic Hall of Fame, interactive kiosks on Olympics subjects, various other displays, and a gift shop that sells Olympic-logo merchandise.

The complex includes the **Olympic Sports Center I,** with five gymnasiums and a weight-training room; **Sports Center II,** which accommodates 14 sports; the **Indoor Shooting Center,** the largest facility of its kind in the Western Hemisphere, with areas for rifle and pistol shooting, rapid-fire and women's sport pistol bays, running-target rifle ranges, and air-rifle and pistol-fire points; and the **Aquatics Center,** which contains a 50-by-25-meter pool with two movable bulkheads, 10 50m and 20 25m lanes, and more than 800,000 gallons of water. The U.S. Olympic Committee also operates the **7-Eleven Velodrome,** with a banked track for bicycle and roller speed skating, about 1 mile south of the Olympic Complex, in Memorial Park (see "Parks & Zoos," later in this chapter) off Union Boulevard. Olympic figure skaters train at the **World Arena,** southwest of downtown. Allow 1 to 2 hours.

1 Olympic Plaza, corner of Boulder St. (entrance) and Union Blvd. *℃* **888/659-8687** or 719/866-4618. www.usolympicteam.com. Free admission. Complex daily 9am–6pm. Guided tours begin every half-hour 9am–4pm (hourly Aug–May); reservations required for groups of 10 or more (*℃* 719/866-4656). From I-25, take exit 143.

Architectural Highlights

The Broadmoor This famous Italian Renaissance–style resort hotel has been a Colorado Springs landmark since Spencer Penrose built it in 1918. (See "Where to Stay," earlier in this chapter.) Stroll around the lake, have a drink at one of the watering holes, and look at the "Walk of Fame" near Charles Court, a hallway of photographs of celebrities at the resort, everyone from Jackie Gleason to the Shah of Iran to Aerosmith.

Lake Circle, at Lake Ave. ℂ **719/634-7711.** www.broadmoor.com. Free admission. Daily year-round.

Miramont Castle Museum Architecture buffs will love this place. Built into a hillside by a wealthy French priest as a private home in 1895 and converted by the Sisters of Mercy into a sanatorium in 1907, this unique Victorian mansion has always aroused curiosity. The structure incorporates at least nine identifiable architectural styles in its four stories, 46 rooms, 14,000 square feet of floor space, and 2-foot-thick stone walls. If you like tiny stuff, don't miss the room housing the miniatures museum. In summer, lunches, desserts, and tea are served Tuesday through Saturday from 11am to 4pm in the Queen's Parlour. The museum lies on the route from Manitou Avenue to the Pikes Peak Cog Railway. Allow at least 1 hour.

9 Capitol Hill Ave., Manitou Springs. ℂ **888/685-1011** or 719/685-1011. www.miramontcastle.org. Admission $6 adults, $5.50 seniors 60 and over, $2 children 6–15, free for children under 6. Memorial Day to Labor Day daily 9am–5pm; rest of year Tues–Sun 10am–4pm. Located 1 block west of the intersection of Manitou and Ruxton aves.

Historic Buildings

McAllister House This Gothic cottage, listed on the National Register of Historic Places, is a good place for a quick look at the Colorado of the late 19th century. It was built in 1873, and the builder, an army major named Henry McAllister, decided to construct the house with brick when he learned that the local wind was so strong it had blown a train off the tracks nearby. The house has many original furnishings, including three marble fireplaces. It is now owned by the Colonial Dames of America, whose knowledgeable volunteers lead guided tours. Allow about 1 hour.

423 N. Cascade Ave. (at St. Vrain St.). ℂ **719/635-7925.** Admission $5 adults, $4 seniors 62 and older, $3 children 6–12, free for children under 6. Summer Wed–Sat 10am–4pm, Sun noon–4pm; winter Thurs–Sat 10am–4pm. Take I-25, exit 141, east to Cascade Ave.; go left and continue for about 6 blocks.

Rock Ledge Ranch Historic Site Visitors can explore the history of three pioneer eras at this living-history farm, at the east entrance to Garden of the Gods Park. Listed on the National Register of Historic Places, the ranch presents the rigors of the homestead era at the 1860s Galloway Homestead, the agricultural difficulties of the working-ranch era at the 1880s Chambers Farm and Blacksmith Shop, and the more sophisticated estate period at the 1907 Orchard House. Special events, which take place frequently, include an old-fashioned Fourth of July celebration, an 1860s vintage baseball game in late summer, a Victorian Halloween party, and holiday celebrations Thanksgiving through Christmas. The General Store stocks a wide selection of historic reproductions, books, and gift items, and the proceeds help with preservation and restoration of the ranch. Allow 1 to 2 hours.

N. 30th St. and Gateway Rd., Garden of the Gods. ℂ **719/578-6777.** www.rockledgeranch.com. Admission $6 adults, $4 seniors 55 and older and students 13–18, $2 children 6–12, free for children under 6. June to Labor Day Wed–Sun 10am–5pm. Closed Labor Day–May. Take I-25, exit 146, and then follow signs west to Garden of the Gods.

Manitou Springs, which centers on Manitou Avenue off U.S. 24 West, is a separate town with its own government. It is one of the country's largest National Historic Districts. Legend has it that Utes named the springs Manitou, their word for "Great Spirit," because they believed that the Great Spirit had breathed into the waters to create the natural effervescence of the springs. Pikes Peak soars above the town nestled at its base.

Today, the community offers visitors a chance to step back to a slower and quieter time. It boasts numerous elegant Victorian buildings, many of which house delightful shops, galleries, restaurants, and lodgings. Manitou Springs is also home to many fine artists and artisans, whom you might spot painting or sketching about town. A small group of sculptors began the Manitou Art Project in 1992; it installed more than 20 sculptures in various locations downtown and in the parks, creating a large sculpture garden for all to enjoy. The works, which stay on display for a year, are for sale, with 25% of the proceeds used to purchase permanent sculpture for the city.

Visitors are encouraged to take the self-guided tour of the nine restored mineral springs of Manitou. Pick up the *Manitou Springs Visitor's Guide,* which contains a map and descriptions to help you find each spring. It's available at the **Manitou Springs Chamber of Commerce & Visitors Bureau,** 354 Manitou Ave. (① **800/642-2567** or 719/685-5089; www.manitousprings.org), which is open daily.

Old Colorado City, Colorado Avenue between 21st and 31st streets, was founded in 1859, 12 years before Colorado Springs. The town boomed in the 1880s after General Palmer's railroad came through. Tunnels led from the respectable side of town to this saloon and red-light district so that the city fathers could carouse without being seen coming or going—or so the legend goes. Today this historic district has an interesting assortment of shops, galleries, and restaurants.

Museums & Galleries

Colorado Springs Fine Arts Center ★   The center's permanent American collection includes works by legends like Georgia O'Keeffe, John James Audubon, John Singer Sargent, Charles Russell, Dale Chihuly, and other famed painters and sculptors, as well as a world-class collection of Native American and Latin American works. Opened in 1936 and fabulously expanded in 2007, the center also houses a 450-seat performing-arts theater, a 32,000-volume art-research library, the Bemis School of Art, a tactile gallery for those who are visually impaired, and a delightful sculpture garden. The expansion doubled the gallery space and won raves from architectural critics. Changing exhibits showcase local collections as well as touring international exhibits. Designed by renowned Santa Fe architect John Gaw Meem (whose work is nicely complemented by Denver-based David Tryba's colorful expansion), the Art Deco–style building reflects Southwestern mission and Pueblo influences. There is **Cafe 36** for lunch and the **Deco Lounge** for coffee and cocktails on weekend nights. Allow 1 to 3 hours.

30 W. Dale St. (west of N. Cascade Ave.). ① **719/634-5581.** www.csfineartscenter.org. Admission to galleries and museum $7.50 adults, $6.75 seniors and students 5–17, free for children under 5. Separate admission for performing-arts events. Galleries and museum Tues–Fri and Sun 10am–5pm; Sat 10–8pm. Open 1st Thurs of every month until 9pm for wine tasting. Closed federal holidays. Take I-25, exit 143, east to Cascade St., turn right to Dale St., and then turn right again.

Ghost Town (Kids)   A fun place to take the family, Ghost Town is part historic attraction, part theme park. Made up of authentic 19th-century buildings relocated from other parts of Colorado, this "town" is sheltered from the elements in Old Colorado City.

There's a sheriff's office, jail, saloon, general store, livery stable, blacksmith shop, rooming house, and assay office. Animated frontier characters tell stories of the Old West, while a shooting gallery, antique arcade machines, and nickelodeons provide additional entertainment. During the summer you can even pan for real gold. Allow about 2 hours.

400 S. 21st St. (on U.S. 24). ✆ **719/634-0696.** www.ghosttownmuseum.com. Admission $6.50 adults, $3.50 children 6–16, free for children under 6. June–Aug Mon–Sat 9am–6pm, Sun 11am–6pm; Sept–May Mon–Sat 10am–5pm, Sun 11am–5pm. Take I-25, exit 141; town is just west of exit.

Manitou Cliff Dwellings Preserve & Museums ★ (Kids)
The cliff-dwelling ruins here are real, although originally they were located elsewhere. This put me off at first—they would be more authentic if they were in their original location—but the move here may have saved them. In the early 1900s, archaeologists, who saw such dwellings being plundered by treasure hunters, dismantled some of the ancient buildings, gathered artifacts found there, and hauled them away. Some of these ruins, constructed from A.D. 1200 to 1300, can be seen here in a village reconstructed by archaeologists. There are also two museums with exhibits on prehistoric American Indian life, and several gift shops that sell American-Indian–made jewelry, pottery, and other crafts, plus Colorado souvenirs. American-Indian dancers perform during the summer. Allow 2 hours.

U.S. 24, Manitou Springs. ✆ **800/354-9971** or 719/685-5242. www.cliffdwellingsmuseum.com. Admission $9.50 adults, $8.50 seniors 60 and over, $7.50 children 7–11, free for children under 7. May–Sept daily 9am–6pm; Oct–Nov and Mar–Apr daily 9am–5pm; Dec–Feb daily 10am–4pm. Closed Thanksgiving and Dec 25. Take I-25, exit 141, and go west on U.S. 24 about 5 miles.

May Natural History Museum of the Tropics (Kids)
Here you'll find one of the world's best public collections of giant insects and other tropical invertebrates, not to mention a statue out front touted to be the world's largest Hercules beetle. James F. W. May (1884–1956) spent more than half a century exploring the world's jungles while compiling his illustrious collection, which has grown to more than 100,000 invertebrates, about 8,000 of which are on display at any given time. The specimens are irreplaceable, because many came from areas that are now so politically unstable that no one is willing or able to explore the backcountry to collect them again. Exhibits change periodically.

Also on the grounds is the **Museum of Space Exploration,** where you can take a pictorial trip through the history of space exploration, beginning with man's first attempts to fly and continuing through the most recent photos from NASA. Also on display are numerous models of early aircraft, World War II planes, and spacecraft. Take time to view one or more of the NASA space films, which include the first moon landing. Allow 2 to 3 hours for both museums. There's also a 500-site campground ($24–$26 for campsites) with hiking trails, fishing, and a playground area.

710 Rock Creek Canyon Rd. ✆ **719/576-0450.** www.maymuseum-camp-rvpark.com. Admission (includes Museum of Space Exploration) $6 adults, $5 seniors 60 and older, $3 children 6–12, free for children under 6. May–Sept daily 9am–6pm. Closed Oct–Apr except for groups of 10 or more. Take Colo. 115 and drive southwest out of Colorado Springs for 9 miles; watch for signs and the Hercules Beetle of the West Indies that mark the turnoff to the museum.

Money Museum ★ (Finds)
Operated by the American Numismatic Association, this museum is the largest collection of its kind west of the Smithsonian Institution, consisting of four galleries of coins, tokens, medals, and paper money from around the world. Of special note is the earliest reale (Spanish coin) struck in the New World (Mexico),

dating from 1536. There's also an 1804 dollar, a 1913 "V" nickel, and a nice collectors' **199** library. Allow 1 hour.

818 N. Cascade Ave., on the campus of Colorado College. © **719/632-2646.** www.money.org. Free admission, donations welcome. Tues–Fri 9am–5pm; Sat 10am–5pm; Sun noon–5pm. Take I-25, exit 143, east to Cascade Ave., then turn right, and go about 6 blocks.

Peterson Air & Space Museum Through its exhibits, this museum traces the history of Peterson Air Force Base, NORAD, the Air Defense Command, and Air Force Space Command. Of special interest are 16 historic aircraft, including P-47 Thunderbolt and P-40 Warhawk fighters from World War II, plus a number of missiles and jets from the Korean War to the present. To mark the 50th anniversary of the U.S. Air Force, a memorial grove of 58 conifer trees honoring the USAF Medal of Honor recipients was planted. There's also a small gift shop. Allow 1 to 2 hours. *Note:* Visitors must have a military ID or give administration at least 24 hours' advance notice to get on the base (72 hours for Saturday visits).

Peterson Air Force Base main gate, off U.S. 24 7 miles east of downtown. © **719/556-4915.** www. petemuseum.org. Free admission. Tues–Sat 9am–4:30pm. Closed holidays and occasionally during military exercises; call ahead. Take I-25, exit 141, and then follow U.S. 24 east about 7¹/₂ miles.

ProRodeo Hall of Fame & American Cowboy Museum ★★ (Kids) No rhinestone cowboys here. This is the real thing, with exhibits on the development of rodeo, from its origins in early ranch work to major professional sport. You'll learn about historic and modern cowboys, including those brave (or crazy) enough to climb onto bucking broncos and wild bulls, in Heritage Hall. The Hall of Champions displays photos, gear, personal memorabilia, and trophies honoring rodeo greats. There are two multimedia presentations, and the museum features changing exhibits of Western art. Outside you'll find a replica rodeo arena, live rodeo animals, and a sculpture garden. Allow 2 hours.

101 ProRodeo Dr. (off Rockrimmon Blvd.). © **719/528-4764.** www.prorodeohalloffame.com. Admission $6 adults, $5 seniors 55 and older, $3 children 6–12, free for children under 6. Memorial Day to Aug daily 9am–5pm; Sept to day before Memorial Day Wed–Sun 9am–5pm. Closed Jan 1, Easter, Thanksgiving, and Dec 25. Take I-25 to exit 147.

Western Museum of Mining & Industry ★★ Machines are fun, and the bigger the better. Historic hard-rock mining machinery and other equipment from Cripple Creek and other late-19th-century Colorado gold camps form the basis of this museum's 4,000-plus-item collection. Visitors can see an operating Corliss steam engine with an enormous 17-ton flywheel, a life-size underground mine reconstruction, and an exhibit on mining-town life showing how early Western miners and their families lived. You can also pan for gold—there's a wheelchair-accessible trough—and view a 23-minute video presentation on life in the early mining camps. Various hands-on family activities focus on themes such as life in a mining town, minerals in everyday products, and recycled art. Free guided tours are available; call for information and times. Allow at least 2 hours.

1025 North Gate Rd., at I-25, exit 156A (off Gleneagle Dr. just east of the north gate of the U.S. Air Force Academy). © **800/752-6558** or 719/488-0880. www.wmmi.org. Admission $8 adults, $6 seniors 60 and older and students 13–17, $4 children 3–12, free for children under 3. Mon–Sat 9am–4pm. Guided tours begin at 10am and 1pm. Located just east of I-25 via Gleneagle Dr.

World Figure Skating Museum & Hall of Fame This is the only museum of its kind in the world, exhibiting 1,200 years of ice skates—from early versions of carved bone to highly decorated cast-iron examples and finally the steel blades of today. There

Impressions

The air is so refined that you can live without much lungs.
—Shane Leslie, *American Wonderland*, 1936

are also skating costumes, medals, and other memorabilia; changing exhibits; films; a library; and a gift shop. A gallery displays skating-related paintings, including works by the 17th-century Dutch artist Pieter Brueghel and Americans Winslow Homer and Andy Warhol. The museum is recognized by the International Skating Union, the sport's international governing body, as the repository for the history and official records of figure skating and the sport's official hall of fame. Here also are the U.S. national, regional, sectional, and international trophies. Allow 1 to 2 hours.

20 1st St. ℂ **719/635-5200.** www.worldskatingmuseum.org. Admission $3 adults, $2 seniors 60 and over and children 6–12, free for children under 6. Summer Mon–Sat 10am–4pm; closed Sat rest of year. Closed major holidays. Take I-25, exit 138, west on Lake Ave.; just before The Broadmoor, turn right onto 1st St.

Natural Attractions

Cave of the Winds ★ (**Kids**)   Discovered by two boys on a church outing in the 1880s, this impressive underground cavern has offered public tours for well over a century. It provides a good opportunity to see the beauty of the underworld. The 45-minute Discovery Tour takes visitors along a well-lit ³/₄-mile passageway through 20 subterranean chambers, complete with classic stalagmites, stalactites, crystal flowers, and limestone canopies. In the Adventure Room, modern lighting techniques return visitors to an era when spelunking was done by candle and lantern. The 1¹/₂-hour Lantern Tour follows unpaved and unlighted passageways and corridors. This tour is rather strenuous, with some stooping required in areas with low ceilings; it might muddy your shoes, but not your clothes.

Kids especially like the outdoor laser shows (with stereophonic sound) presented nightly during the summer at 9pm ($10 adults, $5 children 6–15, free for children under 6).

U.S. 24, Manitou Springs. ℂ **719/685-5444.** www.caveofthewinds.com. Discovery Tour $18 adults, $9 children 6–15, free for children under 6. Tours depart every 15–30 min. Memorial Day to Labor Day daily 9am–8pm; early Sept–late May daily 10am–4:30pm. Lantern Tours (3 times daily in summer and on weekends; other times by reservation) $22 adults, $12 children 6–15, children under 6 are not permitted. Visitors with heart conditions, visual impairment, or other physical limitations are advised not to take Lantern Tour. Take I-25, exit 141, and go 6 miles west on U.S. 24.

Seven Falls   This is a good choice for those who have not yet gotten their fill of Colorado's spectacular mountain scenery. A picturesque 1-mile drive through a box canyon takes you between the Pillars of Hercules, where the canyon narrows to just 42 feet, ending at these cascading falls. Seven separate waterfalls dance down a granite cliff, cascading some 181 feet. A free elevator takes visitors to the Eagle Nest viewing platform. A mile-long trail atop the plateau passes the grave of 19th-century novelist Helen Hunt Jackson, the author of *Ramona,* and ends at a panoramic view of Colorado Springs. Watch for birds and other wildlife along the way. Allow 2 hours.

At the end of S. Cheyenne Canyon Rd. ℂ **719/632-0765.** www.sevenfalls.com. Day admission $9 adults, $8 seniors, $5.50 children 6–15, free for children under 6; night admission $11 adults, $9.50 seniors, $6.50 children 6–15, free for children under 6; lower rates in winter. Mid-May to Memorial Day daily

Parks & Zoos

Cheyenne Mountain Zoo ★ (Kids)   On the lower slopes of Cheyenne Mountain, at 6,800 feet above sea level, this medium-size zoological park is my top choice for a family outing. The zoo's 800-plus animals, many in "natural" environments, include wolves, lions, leopards, red pandas, elephants, hippos, monkeys, giraffes, reptiles, snakes, and lots of birds. Rocky cliffs have been created for the mountain goats; there's a pebbled beach for penguins and a new animal-contact area for children. The zoo is home to more than 30 endangered species, including the Siberian tiger, Amur leopard, and black-footed ferret. The zoo's giraffe herd is the largest and most prolific captive herd in the world; there have been about 200 live births since the 1950s. Visitors can actually feed the long-necked beasts ($1 for three crackers).

There's also a colorful antique carousel, built in 1926, the year the zoo was founded. New in 2008, the $8.2-million **Rocky Mountain Wild** lets visitors get up close and personal with mountain lions, grizzly bears, moose, and other local denizens. A stroller- and wheelchair-accessible tram makes a full loop of the zoo in about 15 minutes; it operates from Memorial Day to Labor Day. Admission to the zoo includes road access to the nearby **Will Rogers Shrine of the Sun,** a granite tower built in 1937, with photos and information on the American humorist. The tower also affords great views of the city and surrounding countryside. Strollers, double strollers, wheelchairs, and wagons are available for rent at Thundergod Gift and Snack Shop. Allow 2 to 4 hours for the zoo and an extra 45 minutes for the shrine.

4250 Cheyenne Mountain Zoo Rd. ✆ **719/633-9925.** www.cmzoo.org. Admission $14 adults, $12 seniors 65 and over, $7.25 children 3–11, free for children under 3. Summer daily 9am–6pm; off season daily 9am–5pm. Take I-25, exit 138; drive west to The Broadmoor hotel and follow signs.

Memorial Park   One of the largest parks in the city, Memorial is home to the Mark "Pa" Sertich Ice Center and the Aquatics and Fitness Center, as well as to the famed 7-Eleven Velodrome, which is used for world-class bicycling events. Other facilities include baseball and softball fields, volleyball courts, tennis courts, a bicycle criterium, and jogging trails. The park also stages a terrific fireworks display on Independence Day. See the sections on ice-skating, swimming, and tennis under "Outdoor Activities," below.

1605 E. Pikes Peak Ave. (between Hancock Ave. and Union Blvd.). ✆ **719/385-5940.** www.springsgov. com (follow links). Free admission. Daily year-round. Located 1 mile east of downtown.

Monument Valley Park   This long, slender park follows Monument Creek through downtown Colorado Springs. At its south end are formal zinnia, begonia, and rose gardens, and in the middle are demonstration gardens of the Horticultural Art Society. Facilities include softball and baseball fields, a swimming pool (open daily in summer; $5.50 adults, $4 children), volleyball and tennis courts, children's playgrounds, and picnic shelters. Also in the park are the 4.3-mile Monument Creek Trail for walkers, runners, and cyclists, and the 1-mile Monument Valley Fitness Trail at the north end, beside Bodington Field.

170 W. Cache La Poudre Blvd. ✆ **719/385-5940.** www.springsgov.com (follow links). Free admission. Daily year-round.

Mueller State Park ★★★ (Finds) Somewhat like a junior version of Rocky Mountain National Park, Mueller contains over 5,000 acres of prime scenic beauty along the west slope of Pikes Peak. The 55 miles of trails, designated for hikers, horseback riders, and mountain bikers, provide opportunities to observe elk, bighorn sheep, black bear, and the park's other wildlife. The best times to spot wildlife are spring and fall, just after sunrise and just before sunset. In the summer, rangers lead hikes and offer campfire programs in a 100-seat amphitheater. The park has 132 campsites (© **800/678-2267** for reservations), with fees ranging from $14 for walk-in sites to $18 for drive-in sites with electricity; coin-operated pay showers are available from mid-May to mid-October. Also available are two- to four-bedroom cabins for $120 to $240 a night,

P.O. Box 39, Divide, CO 80814. © **719/687-2366**. www.parks.state.co.us. Admission $6 per vehicle. Take U.S. 24 west from Colorado Springs to Divide (25 miles), and then go 3¹/₂ miles south on Colo. 67.

North Cheyenne Cañon Park and Starsmore Discovery Center ★★ A
delightful escape on a hot summer day, this 1,600-acre park includes North Cheyenne Creek, which drops 1,800 feet over the course of 5 miles in a series of cascades and waterfalls. The heavily wooded park contains picnic areas and about 15 miles of hiking/biking/horseback riding trails. The small visitor center at the foot of scenic Helen Hunt Falls has exhibits on history, geology, flora, and fauna. The **Starsmore Discovery Center** (© **719/385-6086**) at the entrance to the park holds maps, information, and interactive exhibits for both kids and adults, including audiovisual programs and a climbing wall where you can learn about rock climbing. Call for current climbing-wall hours. During the summer, the center schedules a series of free programs on subjects such as rock climbing, butterflies, and hummingbirds, and guided walks and hikes (call for the current schedule). The park also has excellent rock-climbing areas for experienced climbers; pick up information at the Starsmore Discovery Center or Helen Hunt Falls Visitor Center.

2120 S. Cheyenne Cañon Rd. (west of 21st St.). © **719/578-6146**. www.springsgov.com (follow links). Free admission. Park daily year-round. Starsmore Discovery Center summer daily 9am–5pm; call for hours at other times. Helen Hunt Falls Visitor Center Memorial Day to Labor Day daily 9am–5pm; closed rest of year. Located just west of the Broadmoor Golf Club via Cheyenne Blvd.

Palmer Park Deeded to the city in 1899 by Colorado Springs founder Gen. William Jackson Palmer, this 737-acre preserve offers hiking, biking, and horseback riding across a mesa overlooking the city. It contains a variety of minerals (including quartz, topaz, jasper, and tourmaline), rich vegetation (including a yucca preservation area), and considerable wildlife. The Edna Mae Bennet Nature Trail is a self-guided excursion, and there are numerous other trails. Other facilities include 12 separate picnic areas, softball and baseball fields, and volleyball courts.

3650 Maizeland Rd. off Academy Blvd. © **719/385-5940**. www.springsgov.com (follow links). Free admission. Daily year-round. Located 3 miles east of I-25 via Austin Bluffs Pkwy. (exit 146).

ESPECIALLY FOR KIDS
In addition to the listings below, children will probably enjoy the **Cheyenne Mountain Zoo** (p. 201), **May Natural History Museum**, (p. 198), and **Ghost Town** (p. 197).

Arcade Amusements, Inc. ★ (Kids) Among the West's oldest and largest amusement arcades, this game complex just might be considered a hands-on arcade museum as well as a fun place for kids of all ages. Some 250 machines range from original working penny pinball machines to modern video games, skee-ball, and 12-player horse racing.

900 Block Manitou Ave., Manitou Springs. © **719/685-9815**. Free admission; arcade games from 1¢. Early May to Labor Day daily 10am–10pm. Call for winter hours. Located in downtown Manitou Springs.

Workshop is busy from mid-May until December 24. Not only can kids visit shops where elves have some early Christmas gifts for sale, but they can also see Santa and whisper their requests in his ear. This 26-acre village features numerous rides, including a miniature train, a 60-foot Ferris wheel, and a space-shuttle replica that swings to and fro, as well as magic shows and musical entertainment, snack shops, and an ice-cream parlor.

At the foot of Pikes Peak Hwy. off U.S. 24, 5 miles west of Manitou Springs. (© **719/684-9432.** www.santas-colo.com. Admission (includes all rides, shows, and attractions) $17 ages 2–59, free for seniors 60 and over and children under 2. Mid-May to late June daily 10am–5pm; late June to mid-Aug daily 10am–5:30pm; mid-Aug to Dec 23 (weather permitting) Fri–Tues 10am–5pm; Dec 24 10am–4pm. Closed Dec 25 to mid-May. Take I-25, exit 141, and go west on U.S. 24 about 10 miles.

ORGANIZED TOURS

Half- and full-day bus tours of Colorado Springs, Pikes Peak, the Air Force Academy, and other nearby attractions are offered by **Gray Line of Colorado Springs,** 3704 W. Colorado Ave. (© **800/345-8197** or 719/633-1181; www.coloradograyline.com). Prices range from $35 to $50 per person.

A free downtown **walking tour** brochure, with a map and descriptions of more than 30 historic buildings, is available at the Colorado Springs Convention and Visitors Bureau, as well as at local businesses.

Another free brochure, *Old Colorado City,* shows the location of more than a dozen historic buildings and lists shops, galleries, and other businesses.

The **Manitou Springs Chamber of Commerce & Visitors Bureau** (see "Visitor Information," earlier in this chapter) distributes the free *Manitou Springs Visitor's Guide,* which includes a self-guided walking-tour map of Mineral Springs, as well as information on where to find a variety of outdoor sculptures. See "Historic Neighborhoods," earlier in this chapter.

6 OUTDOOR ACTIVITIES

For information on the city's parks and programs, contact the **Colorado Springs Parks and Recreation Department** (© 719/385-5940; www.springsgov.com). Most of the state and federal agencies concerned with outdoor recreation are headquartered in Denver. There are branch offices in Colorado Springs for **Colorado State Parks,** 2128 N. Weber St. (© **719/471-0900;** www.parks.state.co.us); the **Colorado Division of Wildlife,** 4255 Sinton Rd. (© **719/227-5200;** www.wildlife.state.co.us); and the **U.S. Forest Service,** Pikes Peak Ranger District of the Pike National Forest, 601 S. Weber St. (© **719/636-1602;** www.fs.fed.us/r2/psicc/pp).

You can get hunting and fishing licenses at many sporting-goods stores, as well as at the Colorado Division of Wildlife office listed above.

AERIAL SPORTS The **Black Forest Soaring Society,** 24566 David C. Johnson Loop, Elbert, CO 80106 (© **303/648-3623;** www.soarbfss.org), some 50 miles northeast of Colorado Springs, offers glider rides, rentals, and instruction. Rides start at about $100 for a 15-minute ride; rentals (to those with gliding licenses) and instruction are also available. Advance reservations are required.

The area's commercial ballooning companies include **High but Dry Balloons,** 4164 Austin Bluffs Pkwy., #146, Colorado Springs, CO 80918 (© **719/260-0011;** www.

highbutdryballoons.com), for tours, champagne flights, and weddings. Sunrise flights are scheduled daily year-round, weather permitting. Cost depends on the number of passengers, locations, and type of flight, but start at about $195 per person. Generally, flights last 2 or 3 hours, with a minimum of 1 hour. On Labor Day weekends since 1977, the **Colorado Springs Balloon Classic ★★** (© **719/471-4833;** www.balloonclassic. com) sees over 100 hot-air balloons launched from the city's Memorial Park. Admission is free.

BICYCLING Aside from the 4.3-mile loop trail around Monument Valley Park (see "Parks & Zoos," under "Attractions," above), there are numerous other urban trails for bikers. You can get information at the city's Visitor Information Center (see "Visitor Information," earlier in this chapter). For rentals ($30 per day), contact **Colorado Springs West Bikes,** 2403 W. Colorado Ave. (© **719/633-5565**).

FISHING Most serious Colorado Springs anglers drive south 40 miles to the Arkansas River or west to the Rocky Mountain streams and lakes, such as those found in Eleven Mile State Park and Spinney Mountain State Park on the South Platte River west of Florissant. Bass, catfish, walleye pike, and panfish are found in the streams of eastern Colorado; trout is the preferred sport fish of the mountain regions.

   Angler's Covey, 295 S. 21st St. (© **800/75-FISHN [753-4746]** or 719/471-2984; www.anglerscovey.com), is a specialty fly-fishing shop and a good source of general fishing information for southern Colorado. It offers guided half- and full-day trips ($245–$395 for one to three persons), as well as state fishing licenses, rentals, flies, tackle, and clinics.

GOLF Public courses include the **Patty Jewett Golf Course,** 900 E. Española St. (© **719/385-6950**); and **Valley Hi Golf Course,** 610 S. Chelton Rd. (© **719/385-6917**). Nonresident greens fees range from $26 to $28 for 18 holes (not including a cart). **Pine Creek Golf Club,** 9850 Divot Trail (© **719/594-9999**), is another public course, with greens fees of $42 to $52.

   The finest golf courses in the Colorado Springs area are private. Guests of The Broadmoor hotel (p. 177) can play the 54-hole **Broadmoor Golf Club** (© **719/577-5790**).

HIKING Opportunities abound in municipal parks (see "Parks & Zoos," under "Attractions," above) and Pike National Forest, which borders Colorado Springs to the west. The U.S. Forest Service district office can provide maps and general information (see address and phone number in the introduction to this section).

   Especially popular are the 7.5-mile **Waldo Canyon Trail,** with its trailhead just east of Cascade Avenue off U.S. 24; the 6-mile **Mount Manitou Trail,** starting in Ruxton Canyon above the hydroelectric plant; and the 12-mile **Barr Trail** to the summit of Pikes Peak. **Mueller State Park** (© **719/687-2366**), 3¹/₂ miles south of Divide en route to Cripple Creek, has 50 miles of trails. See "Parks & Zoos" under "Attractions," above.

Impressions

Could one live in constant view of these grand mountains without being elevated by them into a lofty plane of thought and purpose?

—Gen. William J. Palmer, founder of Colorado Springs, 1871

HORSEBACK RIDING   You'll find good opportunities at city parks, including Garden of the Gods, North Cheyenne Cañon Park, and Palmer Park, plus Mueller State Park (see "Attractions," earlier in this chapter). The **Academy Riding Stables,** 4 El Paso Blvd., near the Garden of the Gods (☎ **888/700-0410** or 719/633-5667; www.academyriding stables.com), offers guided trail rides for children and adults by reservation ($38 for 1 hr., $55 for 2).

ICE-SKATING   The **Mark "Pa" Sertich Ice Center** at Memorial Park (☎ **719/385-5983**) is open daily and offers prearranged instruction and rentals. (Admission is $1.50 to $5; skate rentals are $2.) The U.S. Olympic Complex operates the **Colorado Springs World Arena Ice Hall,** 3185 Venetucci Blvd. (☎ **719/477-2150;** www.worldarena.com), with public sessions daily. Admission is $1 to $4; skate rentals are $2. If you have hockey equipment, you can join a pickup game ($7); call for times. To get there, take I-25, exit 138, go west on Circle Drive to Venetucci Boulevard, and go south to the arena.

MOUNTAIN BIKING   There are abundant mountain-biking opportunities in the Colorado Springs area; contact the U.S. Forest Service for details (see address and phone number in the introduction to the section). From May to early October, **Challenge Unlimited,** 204 S. 24th St. (☎ **800/798-5954** or 719/633-6399; www.bikithikit.com), hosts fully equipped, guided rides for every level of experience. Your guide on the 19-mile ride down the Pikes Peak Highway, from the summit at 14,110 feet to the tollgate at 7,000 feet, presents an interpretation of the nature, history, and beauty of the mountain. Participants must be at least 10 years old; advance reservations are recommended. Rates are $45 to $110 per person. For rentals ($30 per day), contact **Colorado Springs West Bikes,** 2403 W. Colorado Ave. (☎ **719/633-5565**).

RIVER RAFTING   Colorado Springs is 40 miles from the Arkansas River near Cañon City. Several licensed white-water outfitters tackle the Royal Gorge. **Echo Canyon River Expeditions,** 45000 U.S. 50 West, Cañon City, CO 81212 (☎ **800/755-3246** or 719/275-3154; www.raftecho.com), offers half-day to 3-day trips on "mild to wild" stretches of river. The company uses state-of-the-art equipment, including self-bailing rafts. Costs range from $49 (half-day, adult) to $645 for a 4-day expedition. **Arkansas River Tours,** P.O. Box 337, Cotopaxi, CO 81223 (☎ **800/321-4352** or 719/942-4362; www.arkansasrivertours.com), offers white-water trips of lengths from a quarter of a day to a full day for $32 to $110, and 2-day trips for $259 to $289.

SWIMMING & TENNIS   Many city parks have pool or lake swimming, for which they charge a small fee, and free tennis courts. Contact the Colorado Springs Parks and Recreation Department (☎ **719/385-5940**) for locations and hours.

7 SPECTATOR SPORTS

The **Air Force Academy Falcons** football team dominates the sports scene, and there are also competitive baseball, basketball, ice hockey, and soccer teams. Call for schedules and ticket information (☎ **800/666-USAF [8723]** or 719/472-1895; www.goairforce falcons.com).

AUTO RACING   The **Pikes Peak International Hill Climb** (☎ **866/464-2626** for tickets or 719/685-4400; www.ppihc.com), known as the "Race to the Clouds," takes place annually in late June or early July. An international field of drivers negotiates the hairpin turns of the final 12$^{1}/_{3}$ miles of the Pikes Peak Highway to the top of the

14,110-foot mountain. On the way up, there are 156 turns, 2,000-foot cliffs, and no guardrails.

BASEBALL   The **Colorado Springs Sky Sox,** of the Pacific Coast League, the AAA farm team for the Colorado Rockies of Denver, play a full 144-game season, with 72 home games at Security Service Field, 4385 Tutt Blvd., off Barnes Road east of Powers Boulevard (© **719/591-7699** for tickets or 719/597-1449; www.skysox.com). The season runs from April to Labor Day. Tickets cost $6 to $11.

HOCKEY   In addition to Air Force Academy hockey (see above), the **World Arena,** 3185 Venetucci Blvd. (© **719/477-2100;** www.worldarena.com), is home to the perennial power Colorado College Tigers (© **719/389-6324;** www.cctigers.com). Tickets are $13 to $18.

RODEO   Held annually since 1941, the **Pikes Peak or Bust Rodeo** (© **719/576-2626** for tickets or 719/635-3547; www.coloradospringsrodeo.com), which takes place in mid-July, is a major stop on the Professional Rodeo Cowboys Association circuit. Its purse of more than $150,000 makes it the second-largest rodeo in Colorado, after Denver's National Western Stock Show. It takes place at the **Norris-Penrose Events Center,** 945 W. Rio Grande St., and tickets run $5 to $30. Various events around the city, including a parade and a street breakfast, mark the rodeo.

8 SHOPPING

Five principal areas attract shoppers in Colorado Springs. The Manitou Springs and Old Colorado City neighborhoods are fun places to browse for art, jewelry, arts and crafts, books, antiques, and other specialty items. The Chapel Hills and Citadel malls combine major department stores with a variety of national chain outlets. Downtown Colorado Springs also has numerous shops.

SHOPPING A TO Z
Antiques
Antique Emporium at Manitou Springs   The shop's 4,000-square-foot floor space provides ample room for displaying its collection of antique furniture, china, glassware, books, collectibles, and primitives. 719 Manitou Ave., Manitou Springs. © **719/685-9195.**

Colorado Country Antique Mall   This well-established multidealer mall, covering some 10,000 square feet, is filled with a wide variety of antiques and collectibles, including a good selection of lower-priced items. 2109 Broadway St. © **719/520-5680.**

Art Galleries
Business of Art Center   Primarily an educational facility to help artists learn the business end of their profession, the center also has workshops, classes, and lectures, plus numerous artists' studios (open for viewing), six exhibition galleries, and a gift shop. Featured are renowned Colorado artists and juried exhibits of regional art. The shop offers a varied selection of regional artwork, including prints, photographs, jewelry, sculpture, ceramics, wearable art, hand-blown glass, and carved-wood objects. Theater, music, and dance performances are occasionally staged. 513 Manitou Ave., Manitou Springs. © **719/685-1861.** www.thebac.org.

Commonwheel Artists Co-op   Original art and fine crafts by area artists fill this excellent gallery, where you'll find a good selection of paintings, photography, sculpture, jewelry, textiles, and other items. 102 Cañon Ave., Manitou Springs. ℭ **719/685-1008.** www. commonwheel.com.

Flute Player Gallery   This gallery offers contemporary and traditional American Indian silver and turquoise jewelry, Pueblo pottery, Navajo weavings, and Hopi kachina dolls. 2511 W. Colorado Ave., Old Colorado City. ℭ **719/632-7702.** www.fluteplayergallery.com.

Michael Garman's Gallery Ⓚⓘ⓭ﬆ   A showcase for Garman's sculptures and casts depicting urban and Western life, this gallery also holds "Magic Town," a large model of an old-time inner city, with sculptures and holographic actors. Admission to Magic Town is $5 for adults, $3.50 for seniors, $1.50 for children 7 to 12, and free for children under 7. 2418 W. Colorado Ave., Old Colorado City. ℭ **800/731-3908** or 719/471-9391. www.michael garman.com.

Books

There are numerous chain bookstores around the city, including **Barnes & Noble,** 795 Citadel Dr. E., just east of the Citadel Mall (ℭ **719/637-8282**).

Book Sleuth Ⓕⓘ⓷⓭ﬆ   For all your mystery needs, visit this bookstore. In addition to a wide selection of mystery novels (including a good stock of out-of-print books), the shop offers numerous puzzles and games. 2501 W. Colorado Ave., #105, Old Colorado City. ℭ **719/632-2727.**

Crafts

Van Briggle Art Pottery   Founded in 1899 by Artus Van Briggle, who applied Chinese matte glaze to Rocky Mountain clays molded into imaginative Art Nouveau shapes, this is one of the oldest active art potteries in the United States. Artisans demonstrate their craft, from throwing on the wheel to glazing and firing. Free tours are available, and finished works are sold in the showroom. 600 S. 21st St., Old Colorado City. ℭ **800/847-6341** or 719/633-7729. www.vanbriggle.com.

Jewelry

Manitou Jack's Jewelry & Gifts   Black Hills gold, 10- and 14-karat, is the specialty here. There's also an extensive collection of American-Indian jewelry, pottery, sand paintings, and other art. The shop will create custom jewelry and make repairs. 814 Manitou Ave., Manitou Springs. ℭ **719/685-5004.**

Velez Galeria   This well-established downtown Colorado Springs store sells the work of indigenous jewelers from the Southwest and Mexico, as well as artworks in many media. 220 N. Tejon St. ℭ **719/630-3710.**

Malls & Shopping Centers

Chapel Hills Mall   Macy's, JCPenney, and Dillard's are among the 150 stores at this mall, which also houses a glow-in-the-dark mini-golf course, a children's play area, a 15-screen movie theater, and about two dozen food outlets. 1710 Briargate Blvd. (N. Academy Blvd., at I-25, exit 150A). ℭ **719/594-0110.** www.chapelhillsmall.com.

The Citadel   This is southern Colorado's largest regional shopping mall, with Dillard's, Macy's, JCPenney, and more than 170 specialty shops and restaurants. 750 Citadel Dr. E. (N. Academy Blvd. at E. Platte Ave.). ℭ **719/591-5516.** www.shopthecitadel.com.

The Promenade Shops at Briargate   Among the shops and restaurants at this chic outdoor shopping center on the city's northern suburban fringe are Pottery Barn, Ann Taylor, P.F. Chang's China Bistro, and Ted's Montana Grill. 1885 Briargate Pkwy., ℂ 719/265-6264; www.thepromenadeshopsatbriargate.com.

Sporting Goods

In business since 1968, the independent **Mountain Chalet,** 226 N. Tejon St. (ℂ 719/633-0732; www.mtnchalet.com), sells camping gear, outdoor clothing, hiking and climbing gear, and winter sports equipment. Another good source for all sorts of outdoor clothing and equipment is **Sports Authority,** with stores at 7730 N. Academy Blvd. (ℂ **719/532-1020**) and 1409 N. Academy Blvd. (ℂ **719/574-1400**).

Western Wear

Lorig's Western Wear ★   This Colorado Springs institution is where real cowboys get their hats, boots, jeans, and those fancy belts with the big buckles. 15 N. Union Blvd. ℂ 719/633-4695.

Wine & Liquor

Cheers Liquor Mart   This 35,000-square-foot liquor supermarket has a huge selection of beer and wine, including Colorado wines, at good prices. 1105 N. Circle Dr. ℂ 719/574-2244.

The Wines of Colorado   This tasting room and sales outlet offers the greatest number of Colorado wines available for tasting under one roof. There are also gift items, and the restaurant offers a grill menu. 8045 W. U.S. 24, Cascade (about 10 miles west of Colorado Springs). ℂ 719/684-0900.

9 COLORADO SPRINGS AFTER DARK

The Colorado Springs entertainment scene spreads throughout the metropolitan area. Pikes Peak Center, the Colorado Springs Fine Arts Center, City Auditorium, Colorado College, and various facilities at the U.S. Air Force Academy are all outstanding venues for the performing arts. The city also supports dozens of cinemas, nightclubs, bars, and other after-dark attractions. Downtown is the major nightlife hub, but Old Colorado City and Manitou Springs also have their fair share of interesting establishments.

Weekly entertainment schedules appear in the Friday *Gazette.* Also look at the listings in the *Independent,* free entertainment tabloids. A good online resource for information on events and nightlife, as well as for restaurants, is **www.sceneinthesprings.com**.

Tickets for many major entertainment and sporting events can be obtained from **Ticketmaster** (ℂ **719/520-9090;** www.ticketmaster.com).

THE CLUB & MUSIC SCENE

Black Sheep   A good bet for punk and indie rock, the Black Sheep features graffiti art on the walls and an edgy vibe throughout. 2106 E. Platte Ave. ℂ 719/227-7625.

Cowboys   Two-steppers and country-and-western music lovers flock to this east-side club, which boasts the largest dance floor in the area. It's open Wednesday to Sunday, and dance lessons are available. 25 N. Tejon St. ℂ 719/596-1212.

Poor Richard's Restaurant An eclectic variety of performers appear at this bohemian landmark 1 or 2 nights a week, presenting everything from acoustic folk to Celtic melodies to jazz to bluegrass. The menu includes pizza, sandwiches, and the Springs' best nachos (blue corn chips and mozzarella), as well as beer and wine. Adjacent are Poor Richard's Bookstore and Little Richard's Toy Store, all owned by local politico Richard Skorman. 324½ N. Tejon St. ℂ 719/632-7721.

Rum Bay Located in the renovated Woolworth Building downtown, the lively Rum Bay is a massive nightclub sporting a wall full of rum bottles and a tropical theme. Disc jockeys spin records for two dance floors; there's also a piano bar featuring dueling players. The entire block contains a number of additional bars under the same management, ranging from Cowboys (see above), to "the world's smallest bar," to Rum Bay–like clubs focusing on tequila and bourbon. 20 N. Tejon St. ℂ 719/634-3522.

The Underground This popular hangout attracts a diverse crowd, from college students and other young people to baby boomers and retirees. Patrons come to dance or just listen to the equally eclectic music (live or recorded), which ranges from rock to jazz to reggae, with some occasional folk. 110 N. Nevada Ave. ℂ 719/578-7771.

THE BAR SCENE

Bijou Bar and Grill Southern Colorado's longest-standing gay and lesbian bar, the Bijou Bar has a Mexican menu, regular drink specials, Wednesday karaoke nights, and DJs spinning dance music on Fridays and Saturdays. 2510 E. Bijou Ave. ℂ 719/473-5718.

15C An unmarked speak-easy–style joint with an alley entrance, 15C is a slick martini-and-cigar bar with an upscale ambience accented by dim lighting and leather couches. Located just off Bijou St. in the alley between Cascade Ave. and Tejon St. ℂ 719/635-8303.

Golden Bee ⓂMoments An opulent 19th-century English pub was disassembled, shipped from Great Britain, and reassembled piece by piece to create this delightful drinking establishment. You can have imported English ale by the yard or half-yard while enjoying steak-and-potato pie, Devonshire cheddar-cheese soup, sandwiches, or other British specialties. Evenings bring a ragtime pianist to enliven the atmosphere; interested guests are given songbooks for singalongs. Lower-level entrance of the Broadmoor International Center, Lake Circle. ℂ 719/634-7711.

Meadow Muffins A boisterous barroom packed to the gills with movie memorabilia and assorted knickknacks, Meadow Muffins certainly doesn't lack personality. It features DJs or live music several nights a week. The food is standard bar fare, but the burgers are great. On most days, there are several specials, with happy hour from 4 to 7pm daily (until closing on Fri). There are pool tables, a pair of big-screen TVs, and arcade games. See also the restaurant listing on p. 190. 2432 W. Colorado Ave., in Old Colorado City. ℂ 719/633-0583.

Oscar's Featuring aquariums above the bar, this downtown hangout shucks more oysters than anyplace in the Springs, including The Broadmoor's eateries. The menu here is Cajun, the crowd eclectic, the music tending toward jazz and blues. 333 S. Tejon St. ℂ 719/471-8070.

Phantom Canyon Brewing Co. This popular brewpub generally offers 8 to 10 of its specialty beers, including homemade root beer. The beers are unfiltered and unpasteurized, served at the traditional temperature for the style. I recommend Railyard Ale, a light amber ale with a smooth, malty taste; Hefeweizen, a traditional German wheat beer;

and a very hoppy India pale ale. A billiard hall is on the second floor. See also the restaurant listing on p. 188. 2 E. Pikes Peak Ave. ℂ 719/635-2800.

Ritz Grill   Especially popular with young professionals after work and the chic clique later in the evening, this noisy restaurant-lounge, known for its martinis and large central bar, brings an Art Deco feel to downtown Colorado Springs. There's live music (usually rock) starting at 9pm Thursday through Saturday. See also the restaurant listing on p. 188. 15 S. Tejon St. ℂ 719/635-8484.

Tony's   Laden with plenty of brick and Green Bay Packers memorabilia, this neighborhood bar just north of Acacia Park has a laid-back vibe, Wisconsin roots, and the best fried cheese curds in the state. 311 N. Tejon St. ℂ 719/228-6566.

THE PERFORMING ARTS

Among the major venues for performing arts is the 8,000-seat **Colorado Springs World Arena,** 3185 Venetucci Blvd., at I-25, exit 138 (ℂ 719/477-2100; www.worldarena. com). The area's newest entertainment center, it presents big-name country and rock concerts and a wide variety of sporting events. Other major facilities include the handsome **Pikes Peak Center,** 190 S. Cascade Ave. (ℂ 719/520-7469 for the ticket office or 719/477-2100; www.pikespeakcenter.org), a 2,000-seat concert hall in the heart of downtown that has been acclaimed for its outstanding acoustics. The city's symphony orchestra and dance theater call the Pikes Peak Center home, and top-flight touring entertainers, Broadway musicals, and symphony orchestras appear here as well. The **Colorado Springs Fine Arts Center,** 30 W. Dale St. (ℂ 719/634-5581 for general information, or 719/634-5583 for the box office; www.csfineartscenter.org), is a historic facility (see "Museums & Galleries" under "Attractions," earlier in this chapter) that includes a children's theater program, a repertory theater company, dance programs and concerts, and classic films. Recent productions have included *Annie* and *Oklahoma.* At the historic **City Auditorium,** 221 E. Kiowa St. (ℂ 719/385-5969; www.springsgov. com, follow links), you can often attend a trade show or big-name concert—Willie Nelson has performed here—or drop in at the Lon Chaney Theatre for a dramatic production.

Theater & Dance

BlueBards   The Air Force Academy's cadet theater group performs Broadway and other productions; it recently staged *Kiss Me Kate.* Arnold Hall Theater, U.S. Air Force Academy. ℂ 719/333-4497.

Colorado Springs Dance Theatre   This nonprofit organization presents international dance companies from September to May at Pikes Peak Center, Colorado College's Armstrong Hall, and other venues. Notable productions have included Mikhail Baryshnikov, Alvin Ailey Repertory Ensemble, Ballet Folklorico of Mexico, and other traditional, modern, ethnic, and jazz dance programs. Each year, three to five performances are scheduled, and master classes, lectures, and other programs often coincide with the performances. Tickets typically run $20 to $40. 7 E. Bijou St., Suite 209. ℂ 719/630-7434. www.csdance.org.

Star Bar Players   Each year, this resident theater company presents several full-length plays, ranging from Greek comedies to modern murder mysteries. Recent productions have included *The Heidi Chronicles* and *The Rabbit Hole.* Tickets are typically $10 to $15. Osborne Studio Theatre, Theatreworks, 3955 Cragwood Dr. ℂ 719/573-7411. www.starbar players.org.

Flying W Ranch ★   This working cattle and horse ranch, just north of the Garden of the Gods, encompasses a Western village of more than a dozen restored buildings and a mine train. There are also demonstrations of Navajo weaving and horse-shoeing. A Western stage show features bunkhouse comedy, cowboy balladry, and foot-stompin' fiddle, mandolin, and guitar music. From mid-May to September the town opens each afternoon at 5pm (Thurs–Sun in Sept); a chuck-wagon dinner (barbecued beef or chicken, potatoes, beans, biscuits, and cake) is served ranch-style at 7pm, and the show begins at 8pm. The winter steakhouse is open October to December and March to May on Friday and Saturday, with seatings at 5 and 8pm and a Western stage show at each seating.

3330 Chuckwagon Rd. (✆) 800/232-FLYW or 719/598-4000. www.flyingw.com. Reservations recommended. Chuck wagon dinners $20 adults, $10 children 6–12; winter steakhouse $24–$26 adults, $12–$15 children under 9.

Iron Springs Chateau Melodrama ★   Located near the foot of the Pikes Peak Cog Railway, this popular comedy and drama dinner theater urges patrons to boo the villain and cheer the hero. Past productions have included *Farther North to Laughter or Buck of the Yukon, Part Two,* and *When the Halibut Start Running or Don't Slam the Door on Davy Jones' Locker.* A family-style dinner, with free seconds, includes oven-baked chicken and barbecued beef brisket, mashed potatoes, green beans almandine, pineapple coleslaw, and buttermilk biscuits. A singalong and a vaudeville-style olio show follow the performance. Iron Springs Chateau is open from April to mid-October and in December. Dinner is served on Tuesday, Wednesday, Friday, and Saturday between 6 and 6:45pm; the show follows at 8pm.

444 Ruxton Ave., Manitou Springs. (✆) **719/685-5104** or 719/685-5572. Reservations required. Dinner and show $29 adults, $27 seniors, $16 children; show only $16 adults, $15 seniors, $9.50 children.

---

10 SIDE TRIPS FROM COLORADO SPRINGS

FLORISSANT FOSSIL BEDS NATIONAL MONUMENT ★★

Approximately 35 miles west of Colorado Springs on U.S. 24 is the small village of Florissant, which means "flowering" in French. It couldn't be more aptly named—every spring its hillsides virtually blaze with wildflowers. Just 2 miles south is one of the most spectacular, yet relatively unknown, fossil deposits in the world, Florissant Fossil Beds National Monument. From Florissant, follow the signs along Teller County Road 1.

The fossils in this 6,000-acre National Park Service property are preserved in the rocks of ancient Lake Florissant, which existed 34 million years ago. Volcanic eruptions spanning half a million years trapped plants and animals under layers of ash and dust; the creatures were fossilized as the sediment settled and became shale.

The detailed impressions, first discovered in 1873, offer the most extensive record of its kind in the world. Scientists have removed thousands of specimens, including 1,100 separate species of insects. Dragonflies, beetles, and ants; more fossil butterflies than anywhere else in the world; plus spiders, fish, some mammals, and birds are all perfectly preserved from 34 to 35 million years ago. Leaves from willows, maples, and hickories; extinct relatives of birches, elms, and beeches; and needles of pines and sequoias are also plentiful. These fossil plants, markedly different from those living in the area today, show how the climate has changed over the centuries.

Mudflows also buried forests during this long period, petrifying the trees where they stood. Nature trails pass petrified tree stumps; one sequoia stump is 10 feet in diameter and 11 feet high. There's a display of carbonized fossils at the visitor center, which also offers interpretive programs. An added attraction within the monument is the homestead of Adeline Hornbek, who pioneered the area with her children in 1878. The national monument also has over 14 miles of hiking trails.

Nearby, about ¹/₂ mile north of the monument, there's superb fishing for German browns and cutthroats at Spinney Mountain Reservoir.

Admission to the monument is $3 per adult and free for children under 15, making a visit here an incredibly affordable outing. It's open from 8am to 6pm daily in summer and 9am to 5pm daily the rest of the year (closed Jan 1, Thanksgiving, and Dec 25). Contact Florissant Fossil Beds National Monument, P.O. Box 185, Florissant, CO 80816-0185 (© 719/748-3253; www.nps.gov/flfo).

CRIPPLE CREEK

This old mining town on the southwestern flank of Pikes Peak was known as the world's greatest gold camp after the precious metal was first discovered here in 1890. During its heyday at the beginning of the 20th century, Cripple Creek (elevation 9,494 ft.) had a stock exchange, two opera houses, five daily newspapers, 16 churches, 19 schools, and 73 saloons, plus an elaborate streetcar system and a railroad depot that saw 18 arrivals and departures a day. By the time mining ceased in 1961, more than $800 million worth of ore had been taken from the surrounding hills.

Today Cripple Creek has several dozen limited-stakes gambling casinos, most lining Bennett Avenue. They cash in not only on the lure of gambling but also on the nostalgia for the gambling houses that were once prominent throughout the Old West. Although gamblers must be at least 21 years old, some casinos offer special children's areas, along with other family activities. Among the more interesting of the many casinos in town is the **Imperial Casino Hotel,** 123 N. 3rd St. at Bennett Avenue (P.O. Box 869), Cripple Creek, CO 80813 (© 800/235-2922 or 719/689-7777; www.imperialcasinohotel. com). Built in 1896 following a disastrous fire that razed most of the city, the fully renovated Imperial offers Victorian accommodations in a handsome historic building, a casino, and several restaurants and bars.

One of the town's unique attractions is a herd of wild donkeys, descendants of the miners' runaways, that roam freely through the hills and into the streets. The year's biggest celebration, **Donkey Derby Days** in late June, culminates with a donkey race.

Although gambling takes place year-round, many of the historic attractions are open in summer only or have limited winter hours. Among those you'll want to check out is the 1891 **Mollie Kathleen Gold Mine,** 1 mile north of Cripple Creek on Colo. 67 (© 719/689-2466; www.goldminetours.com). It offers visitors a rare chance to join hard-rock miners on a 1,050-foot underground descent into a genuine gold mine and take home a gold-ore specimen as a souvenir. Tours last about 40 minutes; temperatures in the mine are 45°F to 50°F (7°C–10°C), and jackets are provided. Admission is $15 for adults, $10 for children 3 through 12, and free for children under 3. The mine is open from early April to mid-September daily from 9am to 5pm with shorter hours the rest of the year (call ahead).

The **Cripple Creek District Museum,** at the east end of Bennett Avenue (© 719/ 689-2634; www.cripple-creek.org), includes three historic buildings packed with late-19th-century relics, including mining and railroad memorabilia. There's a gold-ore exhibit,

Victorian fashions and furniture, exhibits on local wildlife, historic photos, a fully restored Victorian-era flat, and an assay office where fire-testing of local ores took place. The museum is open daily from 10am to 5pm Memorial Day through September, and Friday to Sunday from 10am to 4pm the rest of the year. Admission is $5 adults, $3 seniors and children. There is another museum, the Old Homestead Museum, covering the world's oldest profession in a family-friendly tour for $4 adults and $3 kids and seniors.

The **Cripple Creek & Victor Narrow Gauge Railroad Co.** ★★, at the Midland Terminal Depot, east end of Bennett Avenue at 5th Street (© **719/689-2640;** www.cripplecreekrailroad.com), takes visitors on a 4-mile narrated tour. The route runs past abandoned mines and over a reconstructed trestle to the ghost town of Anaconda, powered by a 15-ton "iron horse" steam locomotive. The train operates daily from mid-May to mid-October. The first train leaves the station at 10am and subsequent trains leave about every 40 minutes, until 5pm. Tickets are $13 for adults, $11 for seniors, $7.75 for children 3 to 12, and free for kids under 3.

Cripple Creek is 45 miles west of Colorado Springs; take U.S. 24 west and Colo. 67 south. For additional information, contact the **Cripple Creek Chamber of Commerce,** P.O. Box 430, Cripple Creek, CO 80813 (© **877/858-4653** or 719/689-3461; www.cripple-creek.co.us).

Nearby Scenic Drives

When you leave Cripple Creek, two drives of particular beauty offer alternatives to Colo. 67. Neither is paved and both are narrow and winding, but both are usually acceptable for everyday vehicles under dry conditions. Each is roughly 30 miles long but requires about 90 minutes to negotiate. First, take Colo. 67 south out of Cripple Creek for 6 miles to the historic mining town of **Victor,** a delightful, picturesque destination.

The **Gold Camp Road** leads east from Victor to Colorado Springs via the North Cheyenne Cañon. Teddy Roosevelt said that this trip up the old Short Line Railroad bed had "scenery that bankrupts the English language." The **Phantom Canyon Road** leads south from Victor to Florence, following another old narrow-gauge railroad bed known as the Gold Belt Line. A number of ghost towns and fossil areas mark this route.

11 A SIDE TRIP TO ROYAL GORGE

From Colorado Springs, the breathtaking **Royal Gorge** and **Royal Gorge Bridge and Park** and the historic town of Cañon City make an easy day trip. The Royal Gorge, one of the most impressive natural attractions in the state, lies 8 miles west of Cañon City off U.S. 50, at the head of the Arkansas River valley. From the Springs, head southwest on Colo. 115 for about 33 miles, turn west for about 12 miles on U.S. 50 to Cañon City (about 45 miles altogether), and then go south to the Royal Gorge.

This narrow canyon, 1,053 feet deep, was cut through solid granite by 3 million years of water and wind erosion. When Zebulon Pike saw the gorge in 1806, he predicted that man would never conquer it. But by 1877 the Denver & Rio Grande Railroad had laid a route through the canyon, and it soon became a major tourist attraction.

The gorge is spanned by what is said to be the world's highest suspension bridge and an aerial tramway, built for no other reason than to thrill tourists. The ¼-mile-long bridge was constructed in 1929, suspended from two 300-ton cables, and reinforced in 1983. An incline railway, believed to be the world's steepest, was completed in 1931; it plunges from the rim of the gorge 1,550 feet to the floor at a 45° angle, giving passengers the view from the bottom as well as from the top. The 35-passenger tram, added in 1968, provides views of the gorge and the bridge from a height of 1,178 feet above the Arkansas River.

Owned by Cañon City, the park also holds a 260-seat multimedia theater (where visitors can see a video presentation on the area's history and construction of the bridge), miniature railway, trolley, old-fashioned carousel, various thrill rides and children's attractions, restaurants, gift shops, a petting zoo with free burro rides, and herds of tame mule deer. Live entertainment and a variety of special events take place throughout the year.

The bridge is open year-round, daily from 7 or 8am to dusk; the rest of the park is open daily late April through October from 10am until 5 to 7pm. Admission—$22 for adults, $19 for seniors, $17 for children 4 to 11, free for children under 4—includes crossing the bridge and all other park rides and attractions. For information, contact **Royal Gorge Bridge & Park,** P.O. Box 549, Cañon City, CO 81215 (© **888/333-5597** or 719/275-7507; www.royalgorgebridge.com).

An interesting way to view the canyon is from the **Royal Gorge Route Railroad,** 401 Water St. (south of U.S. 50 on 3rd St.), Cañon City, CO 81212 (© **888/724-5748** or 303/569-1000; www.royalgorgeroute.com). The train takes passengers on a 2-hour, 24-mile trip through the canyon. From early May to early October, the train departs daily at 9:30am and 12:30pm; there are also 3:30pm departures in summer and 7pm dinner rides on select evenings. Coach tickets cost $33 for adults, $22 for children 3 to 12, and are free for children under 3 who sit on a guardian's lap. Reservations are recommended. Observation-dome tickets are $25 more and dinner rides are $85 a person ($110 in the observation dome).

To see this beautiful gorge from the river while also enjoying some thrills, consider a raft trip. Rates for adults run $100 to $120 for a full-day trip, including lunch; a half-day trip is about $50 to $65. Most Royal Gorge raft trips include rough white-water stretches of the river; those preferring calmer sections should inquire with local rafting companies. Major outfitters include **Arkansas River Tours** (© **800/321-4352** or 719/942-4362; www.arkansasrivertours.com), **Echo Canyon River Expeditions** (© **800/748-2953;** www.raftecho.com), and **Wilderness Aware Rafting** (© **800/462-7238** or 719/395-2112; www.inaraft.com). See also "River Rafting," under "Outdoor Activities," earlier in this chapter.

OTHER AREA ATTRACTIONS

Cañon City was a popular film setting during the industry's early days, and it was a special favorite of silent screen actor Tom Mix, who reputedly worked as a cowboy in the area before becoming a film star. The drowning death of a prominent actress temporarily discouraged film companies from coming here, but the area's beautiful scenery and Old West heritage lured the industry back in the late 1950s, helped along by the creation of Buckskin Joe, a Western theme park and movie set where dozens of films have been shot, including *How the West Was Won, True Grit,* and *Cat Ballou.*

Although movies are rarely shot here nowadays, **Buckskin Joe Frontier Town & Railway** (© **719/275-5149;** www.buckskinjoe.com), about 8 miles west of Cañon City on U.S. 50, remains a popular tourist attraction. The authentic-looking Old West town was created from genuine 19th-century buildings relocated from across the state. Visitors can watch gunfights, pan for gold, see a magic show, ride horseback (or in a horse-drawn trolley), and wander through a Western maze. The **Scenic Railway** (© **719/275-5485**) offers a 30-minute trip through rugged Royal Gorge country, where you're likely to see deer and other wildlife, to the rim of the Royal Gorge for a panoramic view of the canyon and bridge.

Frontier Town is open May through September and mid-October to Halloween as a dark attraction. Hours are 10am to 5pm daily in May, 9:30am to 6pm daily from June to August, and 10am to 5pm Thursday to Monday in September. The railway runs from March to December. Hours from Memorial Day to Labor Day are 9am to 7pm; call for hours at other times. Combination admission tickets, which include the Scenic Railway, a horse-drawn trolley, and all the Frontier Town attractions and entertainment, are $18 for adults, $14 for children 4 to 11, and free for children under 4. Tickets for the railway are only $11 for adults and $10 for children; tickets for Frontier Town only are $14 for adults and $12 for children. Expect to spend 2 to 4 hours here.

Other Cañon City attractions include the **Museum of Colorado Prisons ★**, 201 N. 1st St. (*② 719/269-3015*; www.prisonmuseum.org), especially interesting for those with an appreciation of the macabre. Housed in the state's former women's prison, just outside the walls of the original territorial prison that opened in 1871, it contains an actual gas chamber, historic photos of life behind bars, weapons confiscated from inmates, the last hangman's noose used legally in the state, a simulation of a lethal-injection system and of the "Old Gray Mare" (a cruel apparatus used to punish misbehaving prisoners), and other artifacts and exhibits. There's also a gift shop selling arts and crafts made by inmates at a medium-security prison next door. The museum is open May through September daily from 8:30am to 6pm; October through April, Friday through Sunday from 10am to 5pm. Admission is $7 for adults, $6 for seniors 65 and older, $5 for children 6 to 12, and free for children under 6. Allow about an hour.

Those interested in Colorado history might also enjoy stopping at the **Royal Gorge Regional Museum and History Center,** 612 Royal Gorge Blvd. (*② 719/276-5279*), which holds displays of American-Indian artifacts, guns, gems, minerals, wild-game trophies, historic photos, old dolls, pioneer household items, and other memorabilia. These are pretty much the kinds of things you'll find in most small-town museums in the American West, but what sets this museum apart somewhat are several renovated and authentically furnished buildings out back. Here is the 1860 log cabin built by Anson Rudd, local blacksmith and first warden of the Colorado Territorial Prison. The museum is typically open from 10am to 4pm Wednesday through Saturday. It's closed December 24 plus all state and federal holidays. Admission is free. Allow a half-hour.

Another local attraction, especially fascinating for young would-be dinosaur hunters, is **Dinosaur Depot ★**, 330 Royal Gorge Blvd. (*② 800/987-6379* or 719/269-7150; www.dinosaurdepot.com). The depot's main claim to fame is the dinosaur lab, where paleontologists are working to remove various dinosaur fossils from the rock that has encased them for the past 150 million years. There are also several interpretive exhibits, including fossilized bones that visitors can hold, a fossilized tree, a children's Discovery Room with plenty of hands-on exhibits, and a gift shop. Dinosaur Depot also sells brochures for self-guided tours of the internationally renowned **Garden Park Fossil Area** just north of town, which is the source of many of the museum's exhibits, and to see some 90-million-year-old dinosaur tracks nearby. The museum is open daily from 9am to 5pm late May to mid-August; shorter hours the rest of the year. Admission is $4 for adults, $2 for children 4 to 12, and free for children under 4. Allow 45 minutes at Dinosaur Depot, and another 1 to 2 hours at Garden Park Fossil Area.

Cañon City has several midprice lodging options, including the **Best Western Royal Gorge Motel,** 1925 Fremont Dr., Cañon City, CO 81212 (*② 800/231-7317* or

719/275-3377), with double rates ranging from $69 to $109 in summer. A more off-the-beaten-path option is **The Orchard Bed & Breakfast,** 1824 Pinion Ave., Brookside, CO 81212 (℃ **877/212-0497** or 719/275-0072; www.theorchardbandb.com), tucked away in an agricultural area on the edge of an apple orchard south of town. Double rooms are $90, with full breakfast included. **Merlino's Belvedere,** 1330 Elm Ave. (℃ **719/275-5558;** www.belvedererestaurant.com), is my pick for a meal, specializing in gourmet Italian cuisine, steaks, and seafood at lunch and dinner daily. Most dinner main courses run $15 to $35.

For more information on where to stay and eat and a walking tour of historic downtown Cañon City, as well as details on scenic drives and other attractions, contact the **Cañon City Chamber of Commerce,** 403 Royal Gorge Blvd., Cañon City, CO 81212 (℃ **800/876-7922** or 719/275-2331; www.canoncitychamber.com).

---

12 A SIDE TRIP TO PUEBLO

Among Colorado's most underrated cities, Pueblo is just 42 miles south of Colorado Springs via I-25. As you drive through, along the interstate, it might appear that this bland, industrial city—with its railroad tracks, warehouses, and factories—doesn't warrant a stop. But don't let your first impression fool you. Once you get off the highway you'll discover the real Pueblo, with historic homes, fine Western art, a well-run zoo, a delightful riverfront park, and a number of outdoor recreational opportunities.

Although Zebulon Pike and his U.S. Army exploratory expedition camped at the future site of Pueblo in 1806, there were no white settlements here until 1842, when El Pueblo Fort was constructed as a fur-trading outpost. It was abandoned following a Ute massacre in late 1854, but when the Colorado gold rush began 5 years later, the town of Pueblo was born on the site of the former fort.

In the early 20th century, the city grew as a major center for coal mining and steel production. Job opportunities attracted large numbers of immigrants, especially from Mexico and Eastern Europe. Pueblo today is home to high-tech industries as well as the University of Southern Colorado. As the largest city (pop. a bit over 100,000) in southeastern Colorado, it is the market center for a 15-county region extending to the borders of New Mexico, Oklahoma, and Kansas. Elevation is 4,695 feet.

ESSENTIALS

GETTING THERE **By Car** I-25 links Pueblo directly with Colorado Springs, Denver, and points north; and Santa Fe, Albuquerque, and other New Mexico cities to the south. U.S. 50 runs east to La Junta and west to Cañon City, Gunnison, and Montrose.

By Plane **Pueblo Memorial Airport,** 31201 Bryan Circle, Keeler Parkway off U.S. 50 East (℃ **719/553-2760;** www.pueblo.us), is served by **Great Lakes Airlines** (℃ **800/554-5111;** www.greatlakesav.com) with daily flights to Denver only as a United partner. Agencies providing rental cars at the airport include **Avis** (℃ **800/331-1212** or 719/948-9665) and **Hertz** (℃ **800/654-3131** or 719/948-3345).

VISITOR INFORMATION Contact the **Greater Pueblo Chamber of Commerce,** 302 N. Santa Fe Ave. (P.O. Box 697), Pueblo, CO 81003 (℃ **800/233-3446** or 719/542-1704; www.pueblochamber.org and www.destinationpueblo.com), for most travel-related needs. The **Visitor Information Center** is located at the chamber office, which

ACCOMMODATIONS ■
Abriendo Inn **5**
Best Western Eagle Ridge
  Inn & Suites **3**
Comfort Inn **3**
Hampton Inn **3**

DINING ◆
La Renaissance **6**
Patti's Restaurant **12**
Star Bar & Lunch **15**

ATTRACTIONS ●
El Pueblo History Museum **11**
Hose Company #3 **7**
Infozone News Museum **8**
The Nature & Raptor Center **1**
Pueblo Weisbrod Aircraft Museum **14**
Pueblo Zoo **2**
Rosemount Museum **4**
Sangre de Cristo Arts & Conference Center **13**
Southeastern Colorado Heritage Center **9**
Steelworks Museum of Industry & Culture **16**
Vail Hotel **10**

COLORADO SPRINGS

8

A SIDE TRIP TO PUEBLO

is open year-round Monday through Friday from 8am to 5pm, and some Saturdays from 10am to 2pm.

GETTING AROUND   Pueblo lies on the eastward-flowing Arkansas River, at its confluence with Fountain Creek. The downtown core is located north of the Arkansas and west of the Fountain, immediately west of I-25. Santa Fe Avenue and Main Street, 1 block west, are the principal north–south thoroughfares; the cross streets are numbered (counting northward), with Fourth and Eighth streets the most important. Pueblo Boulevard circles the city on the south and west, with spurs leading to the nature center and Lake Pueblo State Park.

FAST FACTS   Medical services, including for emergencies, are provided by **Parkview Medical Center,** 400 W. 16th St. (© **719/584-4000;** www.parkviewmc.com); and **St. Mary-Corwin Medical Center,** 1008 Minnequa Ave. (© **719/557-4000;** www.stmary corwin.org). The main **post office** is located at 1022 Fontino Blvd.; call the U.S. Postal Service (© **800/275-8777;** www.usps.com) for hours and locations of other post offices.

Historic Pueblo runs along Union Avenue north from the Arkansas River to First Street, a distance of about 5 blocks. More than 40 buildings in the **Union Avenue Historic District** (www.seepueblo.com) are listed on the National Register of Historic Places, including the **Vail Hotel** (217 S. Grand Ave.), headquarters of the **Pueblo County Historical Society** museum and library (𝄞 **719/543-6772;** www.pueblohistory.org), with railroad memorabilia, locally made saddles, and some 8,000 books, historical maps, and photographs depicting Pueblo's history. **Union Depot,** with its mosaic-tile floors and beautiful stained-glass windows, houses retail stores and offices, yet still serves rail freight lines. **Walking-tour maps** can be obtained at the Visitor Information Center (see "Visitor Information," above), as well as from Union Avenue businesses.

Located in a historic fire station built in 1881 is **Hose Company #3—Pueblo's Fire Museum,** 116 Broadway Ave. (𝄞 **719/553-2830;** www.pueblofire.org). Open for guided tours by appointment only (free admission; donations encouraged), the museum contains antique fire engines, firefighting equipment, photographs, and other firefighting-related displays.

El Pueblo History Museum ★★ This beautiful museum is a splendid introduction to the region. Located at the intersection of West First Street, Union Avenue, and Grand Avenue, the museum also serves as the Scenic Byways Visitor Center and as a gateway to the Arkansas Riverwalk (see "Outdoor Activities," below) and the historic district.

Evocative of a mid-1800s trading post, the museum's design replicates a square adobe building with a central plaza, reminiscent of Bent's Old Fort. The museum showcases the traditions of the numerous cultural and ethnic groups in the area, utilizing maps and photos plus displays specific to each era. It begins with such items as beaded garments, pouches, American-Indian baskets, and stonework; then it moves into the Spanish, French, and American exploration of the area, highlighting the fur traders and Bent's Fort. The founding of the city through farming, ranching, and the early steel and mining industries is next, followed by early-20th-century labor issues.

The museum also explores the area's continued industrial expansion, which brought a tremendous influx of immigrants, resulting in a rich cultural mix. Other exhibits explain how outdoor activities drew visitors to the area in the 20th century, and will likely tempt visitors outside to explore the Riverwalk. Allow at least an hour and a half.

301 N. Union Ave. 𝄞 719/583-0453. www.coloradohistory.org. Admission $4 adults; $3 seniors 65 and older, students with IDs, and children 6–12; free for children under 6; free for children 12 and under on Saturday. Tues–Sat 10am–4pm.

Infozone News Museum Ⓚⁱᵈˢ Say whatever you want about this museum—one of its primary goals is to increase our knowledge and understanding of Americans' rights to freedom of speech and freedom of the press. Located on the fourth floor of the public library, this state-of-the-art facility also provides a look at the history of Pueblo and its newspapers, and has hands-on activities that youths will especially enjoy. There's a working Linotype typesetting machine to examine, as well as a 100-seat movie theater where a variety of films are shown. Interactive touch-screen computer kiosks turn visitors into reporters as they go on assignment, interview those close to the action, and then see the story in print. Allow 45 minutes.

Robert Hoag Rawlings Public Library, 100 E. Abriendo Ave. 𝄞 719/562-5604. www.infozonenews museum.com. Free admission. Mon–Thurs 9am–9pm; Fri–Sat 9am–6pm; Sun 1–5pm. Closed major holidays.

The Nature and Raptor Center ★   A major recreation and education center, this area provides access to more than 36 miles of paved biking and hiking trails along the Arkansas River and around Lake Pueblo. There are also a 150-foot fishing dock, volley-ball courts, horseshoe pits, an amphitheater, nature trails, picnic areas, and a large chil-dren's playground. Boats and canoes can be put into the Arkansas River here. An interpretive center displays exhibits on the flora and fauna of the area, there are demon-stration gardens along the river, and the Cafe del Rio serves American and Southwestern dishes. At the Raptor Center, injured eagles, owls, and other birds of prey are nursed back to health and released into the wild. The center also houses several resident birds of prey. Allow at least an hour.

5200 Nature Center Rd., via W. 11th St. ✆ **719/549-2414** main office, 719/549-2327 Raptor Center. www. gncp.org. Free admission (donations welcome). On-site parking $3. Grounds open daily sunrise–sunset; Raptor Center Tues–Sun 11am–4pm; Interpretive Center and gift shop Tues–Sat 9am–5pm.

Pueblo Weisbrod Aircraft Museum   The place to come to see some fascinating old airplanes, this museum has more than two dozen historic aircraft—World War II and postwar—on display, as well as numerous exhibits and photographs depicting the B-24 bomber and its role in World War II. It's hard to miss the restored Boeing B-29 Super-fortress, with its 141-foot wingspan, which dominates a large hangar. Also on display are a Douglas A-26 Invader, a Grumman F-9 Cougar, a Douglas C-47 Skytrain (or, as the GI's dubbed it, a Gooney Bird), RA5C Vigilante, and a McDonnell Douglas F-101A Voodoo. There's a well-stocked souvenir shop, offering hard-to-find military and general aviation-related items. Allow 1 to 2 hours.

31001 Magnuson Ave. ✆ **719/948-9219.** www.pwam.org. Admission $7; free for children under 10. Mon–Sat 10am–4pm; Sun 1–4pm. At Pueblo Memorial Airport, 6 miles east of downtown via U.S. 50.

Pueblo Zoo (Kids)   More than 400 animals representing some 130 species live in this 25-acre zoo, listed on the National Register of Historic Places for several buildings and other structures (including a moat) that were constructed of native sandstone during the Depression by WPA workers. Attractions include a Northern River Otter exhibit, a tropical rainforest, and a black-footed penguin underwater exhibit. You'll find all sorts of reptiles and insects in the herpetarium; kangaroos and emus in the Australia Station; an excellent African lion exhibit; and endangered species such as cotton-top tamarins, pre-hensile tail skinks, and maned wolves. You'll also see zebras, Malayan sun bears, and Lar gibbons. Kids in a participatory mood should flock to Pioneer Farm, where they can feed a variety of rare domesticated animals, and to the Discovery Room, which features hands-on exhibits for all ages. Stop by the Watering Hole snack bar or the Wild Things gift shop, which boasts a better-than-average selection of animal-related items. Allow 2 to 4 hours.

City Park, 3455 Nuckolls Ave. ✆ **719/561-1452.** www.pueblozoo.org. Admission $7.50 adults, $6.50 seniors 65 and older, $5 children 3–12, free for children 2 and under. Memorial Day weekend through Labor Day daily 9am–5pm; rest of year Mon–Sat 9am–4pm and Sun noon–4pm. Closed from noon on the day before Thanksgiving, Christmas, and New Year's and all day on those three holidays.

Rosemount Museum ★   Were you a rich and sophisticated westerner in a previous life? Then you probably lived in an elegant home like this. Completed in 1893 for the pioneer Thatcher family, this 37-room mansion is one of the finest surviving examples of late-19th-century architecture and decoration in North America. The three-story, 24,000-square-foot home was built entirely of pink rhyolite stone. Inside you'll find

A SIDE TRIP TO PUEBLO

handsome oak, maple, and mahogany woodwork; remarkable works of stained glass; hand-decorated ceilings; exquisite Tiffany lighting fixtures; period furniture; and 10 fireplaces. Allow 1 hour for the guided tour.

419 W. 14th St. (at Grand Ave.). ☎ **719/545-5290.** www.rosemount.org. Admission $6 adults, $5 seniors 60 and over, $4 childen 6–18, free for children under 6. Tues–Sat 10am–4pm (last tour begins at 3:30pm). Closed major holidays and Jan. Take the I-25 exit for 13th St.

Sangre de Cristo Arts & Conference Center ★ (Kids Pueblo's cultural hub is a three-building complex that houses a 500-seat theater, two dance studios, four art galleries (including one with a fine collection of Western art), a gift shop, a restaurant, and the state-of-the-art Buell Children's Museum, which covers 12,000 square feet with a wide variety of hands-on arts and science exhibits. The center also hosts concerts and other performing-arts events, including a children's theater program (call for details). Allow 2 to 3 hours.

210 N. Santa Fe Ave. ☎ **719/295-7200.** www.sdc-arts.org. $4 adults, $3 children 15 and under. Galleries and children's museum Tues–Sat 11am–4pm, restaurant Tues–Sat 11am–2pm.

Southeastern Colorado Heritage Center Located across the street from the historic Union Depot train station, this facility includes exhibits on southeastern Colorado's pioneer days, including a mid-1800s store and early communications equipment. There are also railroad exhibits, presented in cooperation with the Pueblo Railway Museum, which also maintains the outdoor exhibits of locomotives, passenger cars, and freight cars just west of the depot at 132 W. B Street (www.pueblorailway.org). Allow at least 1 hour for the museum and railyard.

201 W. B St. ☎ **719/295-1517.** www.theheritagecenter.us. Free admission. Tues–Sat 10am–4pm.

Steelworks Museum of Industry & Culture New in 2007, this facility focuses on the history and impact of the Colorado Fuel and Iron Corporation, which began in the 1870s to provide steel rails for the region's railroads and grew to include mining and steel and iron production, and then merged with a fuel company. At one time it operated mines and quarries throughout the West, and the company was the single largest private landowner in Colorado.

Housed in a historic medical-dispensary building, the museum's exhibits examine the history of mining and steel production, including the company's sometimes-violent labor relations, plus railroading and general history of the area. Among the displays are a one-of-a-kind mine rescue railcar and exhibits on industrial medicine. There is also a gift shop. Allow 1 hour.

1612 E. Abriendo Ave. ☎ **719/564-9086.** www.cfisteel.org. Admission $5 adults, $3 children 3–11, free for children under 3. Mon–Sat 10am–4pm; in summer also Sun noon–4pm.

OUTDOOR ACTIVITIES

Pueblo's mild climate makes it a popular destination for boating, fishing, and other outdoor recreation, with several major stops for the region's outdoor enthusiasts.

Watersport aficionados are drawn to **Lake Pueblo State Park ★** (also called Pueblo Reservoir), which has some 4,500 surface acres of water and 60 miles of shoreline. The lake is popular among **anglers** trying for rainbow trout, brown trout, crappie, black bass, and channel catfish, and there's a free fish-cleaning station.

It's also a huge attraction for **boaters,** who come from all over southern Colorado, and the park offers swimming, hiking, and biking. The park's **North Shore Marina** (☎ 719/547-3880; www.noshoremarina.com) provides a gas dock, boating and fishing supplies, groceries, and a restaurant. The **South Marina** (✆ 719/564-1043; www.thesouthshore marina.com) provides the same services and also rents pontoon boats ($135–$175 for 4 hr. and $240–$320 for 9 hr., plus fuel), April through October.

The **Rock Canyon Swim Beach** (✆ 719/564-0065), at the east end of the park, is open from Memorial Day to Labor Day Thursday to Monday 11am to 7pm and has lifeguards on duty. There's a five-story, three-flume **water slide** ($1.75 per ride or $10 all day), plus rentals of paddle boats ($6 per half-hour), and a snack bar. Entrance to the beach costs only $1. These fees are in addition to the $6 general park admission fee.

The park has about 400 **campsites,** some with electric and water hookups. A dump station and showers are available, and camping rates are $14 to $18 May 1 through Labor Day, $12 to $20 the rest of the year. Camping reservations are available for an extra charge of $8 by calling ✆ **800/678-2267** or through the state parks website (see following paragraph). Day use costs $6 per vehicle, and campers must pay this in addition to camping fees.

From Pueblo, take U.S. 50 west for 4 miles, turn south onto Pueblo Boulevard and go another 4 miles to Thatcher Avenue, then turn west, and go 6 miles to the park. For information, contact the park office at ✆ **719/561-9320,** or go to **www.parks.state.co.us**.

The **Historic Arkansas Riverwalk of Pueblo ★★** is a beautifully landscaped waterfront park that covers some 26 acres and offers pedestrian and bike paths, benches, sculptures, gardens, and natural areas that provide good wildlife-viewing opportunities. Pedal-boat rentals are available from early April to late September on a small lake along the Riverwalk, weekends only in April and daily the rest of the season. Rates are $6 per half-hour for a one-person boat and $10 per half-hour for a two-to-four-seat boat. Excursion boat rides along the Arkansas take place on weekends in April, and operate daily from May to late September. Rates for the narrated 25-minute tours are $5 for adults, $4 for seniors and members of the military, and $3 for children 3 to 12. Hours for both pedal-boat rentals and the excursion-boat rides vary throughout the season; call the boathouse (✆ 719/595-1589) for the schedule. The Riverwalk is located near the south end of the Union Avenue Historic District (see "What to See & Do," above), and is easily accessed via Main Street. For information, contact Historic Arkansas Riverwalk of Pueblo Authority, 200 W. First St., Suite 303, Pueblo, CO 81003 (✆ **719/595-0242;** www.puebloharp.com).

Also while you're in town, stop at **City Park,** northeast of the intersection of Pueblo Boulevard (Colo. 45) and Thatcher Avenue. Home to the Pueblo Zoo (see above), the park covers some 200 acres and offers two fishing lakes, tennis courts, a swimming pool (open in summer), and playgrounds. There's also a beautiful hand-carved antique carousel, built in 1911, with music provided by a 1920 Wurlitzer Military Band Organ. The carousel is open evenings and Sunday afternoons in summer; the park is open daily year-round. For information, call the Pueblo Parks and Recreation Department (✆ **719/553-2790;** www.pueblo.us).

There are plenty of opportunities for hiking, backpacking, mountain biking, fishing, and camping nearby in lands under the jurisdiction of the U.S. Forest Service. For information, contact the headquarters of the **Pike and San Isabel National Forests and Comanche and Cimarron National Grasslands,** 2840 Kachina Dr., Pueblo, CO 81008 (✆ **719/553-1400;** www.fs.fed.us/r2).

Local **golf courses** open to the public include **Walking Stick,** 1301 Walking Stick Blvd. (✆ **719/553-1180**), at the northwest corner of the University of Southern Colorado. Rated among Colorado's best courses and best values, this 18-hole course has a driving range and charges $28 to $30 for 18 holes and $11 for a cart. Other local courses include **Elmwood** at City Park, 3900 Thatcher Ave. (✆ **719/561-4946**), with an 18-hole regulation course plus executive 9-hole course. Greens fees for 18 holes are $22. **Desert Hawk Golf Course at Pueblo West,** 251 S. McCulloch Blvd. (✆ **719/547-2280**), is an 18-hole regulation course with greens fees for 18 holes from $26 to $28.

SPECTATOR SPORTS

MOTOR SPORTS   Stock-car races are held every Saturday evening from April to September at **I-25 Speedway,** off I-25 at exit 108 (✆ **303/798-4387;** www.i25speedway. com). Nationally sanctioned drag racing, Sports Car Club of America road racing, and other motor sports take place at the **Pueblo Motorsports Park,** U.S. 50 and Pueblo Boulevard in Pueblo West (✆ **719/583-0907;** www.pueblomotorsportspark.com), April through September.

RODEO   Those visiting Pueblo from mid-August to early September can take in the **Colorado State Fair** (✆ **800/876-4567** or 719/561-8484; www.coloradostatefair.com), which includes a professional rodeo, carnival rides, food booths, industrial displays, horse shows, animal exhibits, and household-name entertainers.

WHERE TO STAY

There are numerous lodging possibilities in Pueblo, with many of the national chains represented. Rates are highest in summer, especially during the State Fair (mid-Aug to early Sept). Among the reliable major chains are the **Best Western Eagle Ridge Inn & Suites,** 4727 N. Elizabeth St. (✆ **800/WESTERN** [937-8376] or 719/543-4644), with double rates of $85 to $150; **Comfort Inn,** 4645 N. Freeway (✆ **800/424-6423** or 719/542-6868), with doubles ranging from $69 to $119; and **Hampton Inn,** 4703 N. Freeway, just west of I-25, exit 102 (✆ **800/972-0165** or 719/544-4700), where double rates range from $119 to $159. Room tax adds just under 12%.

Abriendo Inn ★★   This delightful B&B, built in 1906 as a mansion for brewing magnate Martin Walter, his wife, and their eight children, is the best place to stay for those who want to soak up some of the region's history without sacrificing modern comforts and conveniences. A traditional foursquare-style house listed on the National Register of Historic Places, the Abriendo Inn has won a deserved number of awards. It's also very conveniently located in Pueblo's historic district, close to shops, the Riverwalk, and other attractions.

The comfortable guest rooms are decorated with antique furniture and period reproductions, plus king- or queen-size brass or four-poster beds. Four units have showers only; the rest have tub/shower combos or whirlpool tubs for two. Delicious homemade breakfasts, which might include egg-sausage soufflé or baked apricot French toast, are served in the oak-wainscoted dining room or on the outdoor patio. Smoking is permitted on the veranda only.

300 W. Abriendo Ave., Pueblo, CO 81004. ✆ **719/544-2703.** Fax 719/542-6544. www.abriendoinn.com. 10 units. $98–$155 double. Rates include full breakfast and 24-hr. refreshments. AE, MC, V. *In room:* A/C, cable TV, free Wi-Fi, fridge (some), hair dryer.

Camping

There are two KOA campgrounds in the Pueblo area, both open year-round and with all the usual commercial-campground amenities, including seasonal swimming pools. The

Pueblo KOA is 5 miles north of the city at I-25, exit 108 (© **800/562-7453** for reservations, or 719/542-2273; www.koa.com), and charges $25 to $29 for tent sites and $33 to $39 for RV hookup sites. The **Pueblo South KOA,** about 20 miles south of Pueblo at I-25, exit 74 (© **800/562-8646** for reservations, or 719/676-3376; www.koa.com), charges $24 for tent sites and $35 to $42 for RV hookup sites. Both also have camping cabins (you share the bathhouse with campers) with rates in the $45 to $50 range. There are also some 400 campsites at **Lake Pueblo State Park** (see "Outdoor Activities," above).

WHERE TO DINE

For a comfortable, down-home dining experience, I like the American and Italian food served for breakfast, lunch, and dinner at **Patti's Restaurant,** 241 S. Santa Fe Ave. (© **719/543-2371**). Located on the Riverwalk, in the same location since 1936, Patti's offers American favorites, including sandwiches, burgers, steak, and seafood, plus Italian specialties, in a relaxed family-friendly atmosphere. Available at both breakfast and lunch, I recommend the Half Breed—a spicy Italian sausage wrapped in a tortilla and smothered with spaghetti and green-chile sauce. Hours are 6:30am to 8pm Wednesday and Thursday, 6:30am to 9pm Friday and Saturday, and 7:30am to 8pm Sunday (closed Mon and Tues). Lunch and dinner prices run $6 to $15 and MasterCard, Visa, and Discover cards are accepted. You'll find more in the way of local color and local delicacies at the venerable **Star Bar & Lunch,** 300 Spring St. (© **719/542-9718**). The house special is the green-chile slopper, an aptly named dish composed of a hamburger submerged in a bowl of green chile.

La Renaissance ★★ STEAK/SEAFOOD   Housed in a historic 1880s Presbyterian church, La Renaissance, a favorite of locals since it opened in 1974, offers casually elegant dining in a unique atmosphere. The decor includes stained-glass windows, high vaulted ceilings, and oak pews, which provide some of the seating. Dinners begin with an appetizer and a tureen of soup and finish with dessert, which might be the delightful cream puffs. Although the menu changes periodically, entrees might include the tender slow-roasted prime rib, steamed Alaskan king crab legs, rack of lamb in a rosemary glaze, baby back pork ribs, or breast of chicken with sautéed mushrooms. There's a wide variety of domestic and imported wine and beer, and service is attentive and friendly.

217 E. Routt Ave. © **719/543-6367.** Reservations recommended. 5-course dinner $15–$30. AE, DC, DISC, MC, V. Mon–Sat 5–9pm. From I-25, exit 97B, take Abriendo Ave. northwest for 4 blocks, turn left onto Michigan St., and go 2 blocks to the restaurant.

Appendix: Fast Facts, Toll-Free Numbers & Websites

1 FAST FACTS: DENVER, BOULDER & COLORADO SPRINGS

AMERICAN EXPRESS The American Express travel agency, 555 17th St., Denver (📞 **303/383-5050**), is open Monday through Friday from 8am to 5pm. It offers full member services and currency exchange.

AREA CODES In Denver and Boulder, the telephone area codes are **303** and **720.** In Colorado Springs, the area code is **719.**

ATM NETWORKS/CASHPOINTS See "Money & Costs," in chapter 3.

AUTOMOBILE ORGANIZATIONS Motor clubs will supply maps, suggested routes, guidebooks, accident and bail-bond insurance, and emergency road service. The **American Automobile Association (AAA)** is the major auto club in the United States. If you belong to a motor club in your home country, inquire about AAA reciprocity before you leave. You may be able to join AAA even if you're not a member of a reciprocal club; to inquire, call AAA (📞 **800/222-4357;** www.aaa.com). AAA is actually an organization of regional motor clubs, so look under "AAA Automobile Club" in the White Pages of the telephone directory. AAA has a nationwide emergency road service telephone number (📞 **800/AAA-HELP**).

BUSINESS HOURS Generally, business offices are open weekdays from 9am to 5pm and government offices are open from 8am until 4:30 or 5pm. Stores are open 6 days a week, with many also open on Sunday; department stores usually stay open until 9pm at least 1 day a week. Discount stores and supermarkets are often open later than other stores, and some supermarkets are open 24 hours a day.

Banks are usually open weekdays from 9am to 5pm, occasionally a bit later on Friday, and sometimes on Saturday. There's 24-hour access to automated teller machines (ATMs) at most banks, plus in many shopping centers and other outlets.

CAR RENTALS See "Toll-Free Numbers & Websites," p. 231.

DRINKING LAWS The legal age for purchase and consumption of alcoholic beverages is 21; proof of age is required and often requested at bars, nightclubs, and restaurants, so it's always a good idea to bring ID when you go out.

Do not carry open containers of alcohol in your car or any public area that isn't zoned for alcohol consumption. The police can fine you on the spot. And nothing will ruin your trip faster than getting a citation for DUI ("driving under the influence"), so don't even think about driving while intoxicated.

In 2008, Colorado retracted its "blue laws," which had banned the sale on Sundays of liquor and beer containing more than 3.2% alcohol.

DRIVING RULES See "Getting There and Getting Around," in chapter 3.

ELECTRICITY Like Canada, the United States uses 110–120 volts AC (60 cycles), compared to 220–240 volts AC (50 cycles) in most of Europe, Australia, and New Zealand. Downward converters that change 220–240 volts to 110–120 volts are difficult to find in the United States, so bring one with you.

EMBASSIES & CONSULATES All embassies are located in the nation's capital, Washington, D.C. Some consulates are located in major U.S. cities, and most nations have a mission to the United Nations in New York City. If your country isn't listed below, call for directory information in Washington, D.C. (© 202/555-1212) or check www.embassy.org/embassies.

The embassy of **Australia** is at 1601 Massachusetts Ave. NW, Washington, DC 20036 (© 202/797-3000; www.austemb.org). There are consulates in New York, Honolulu, Houston, Los Angeles, and San Francisco.

The embassy of **Canada** is at 501 Pennsylvania Ave. NW, Washington, DC 20001 (© 202/682-1740; www.canadianembassy.org). Other Canadian consulates are in Buffalo (New York), Detroit, Los Angeles, New York, and Seattle.

The embassy of **Ireland** is at 2234 Massachusetts Ave. NW, Washington, DC 20008 (© 202/462-3939; www.irelandemb.org). Irish consulates are in Boston, Chicago, New York, San Francisco, and other cities. See website for complete listing.

The embassy of **New Zealand** is at 37 Observatory Circle NW, Washington, DC 20008 (© 202/328-4800; www.nzemb.org). New Zealand consulates are in Los Angeles, Salt Lake City, San Francisco, and Seattle.

The embassy of the **United Kingdom** is at 3100 Massachusetts Ave. NW, Washington, DC 20008 (© 202/588-7800; www.britainusa.com). Other British consulates are in Atlanta, Boston, Chicago, Cleveland, Houston, Los Angeles, New York, San Francisco, and Seattle.

EMERGENCIES Call © 911. For the Colorado Poison Center, call © 303/739-1123. For the Rape Crisis and Domestic Violence Hotline, call © 303/318-9989.

GASOLINE (PETROL) At press time, the cost of gasoline (also known as gas, but never petrol), was about $2 a gallon in Denver and vicinity. Taxes are already included in the printed price. One U.S. gallon equals 3.8 liters or .85 imperial gallons. Fill-up locations are known as gas or service stations.

HOLIDAYS Banks, government offices, post offices, and many stores, restaurants, and museums are closed on the following legal national holidays: January 1 (New Year's Day), the third Monday in January (Martin Luther King, Jr., Day), the third Monday in February (Presidents' Day), the last Monday in May (Memorial Day), July 4 (Independence Day), the first Monday in September (Labor Day), the second Monday in October (Columbus Day), November 11 (Veterans' Day/Armistice Day), the fourth Thursday in November (Thanksgiving Day), and December 25 (Christmas). The Tuesday after the first Monday in November is Election Day, a federal government holiday in presidential-election years (held every 4 years, and next in 2012).

For more information on holidays see the "Calendar of Events," in chapter 3.

HOSPITALS See the "Fast Facts" in chapters 5, 7, and 8.

INSURANCE Medical Insurance Although it's not required of travelers, health insurance is highly recommended. Most health insurance policies cover you if you get sick away from home—but check your coverage before you leave.

International visitors to the U.S. should note that unlike many European countries, the United States does not usually offer free or low-cost medical care to its citizens or visitors. Doctors and hospitals are expensive, and in most cases will require advance payment or proof of coverage before they render their services. Good policies will cover the costs of an accident, repatriation, or death. Packages such as **Europ Assistance's "Worldwide Healthcare Plan"** are sold by European automobile clubs and travel agencies at attractive rates. **Worldwide Assistance Services, Inc.** (© 800/777-8710; www.worldwideassistance.com) is the agent for Europ Assistance in the United States.

Though lack of health insurance may prevent you from being admitted to a hospital in nonemergencies, don't worry about being left on a street corner to die: The American way is to fix you now and bill the daylights out of you later.

If you're ever hospitalized more than 150 miles from home, **MedjetAssist** (© 800/527-7478; www.medjetassistance.com) will pick you up and fly you to the hospital of your choice in a medically-equipped and -staffed aircraft 24 hours a day, 7 days a week. Annual memberships are $225 individual, $350 family; you can also purchase short-term memberships.

Canadians should check with their provincial health plan offices or call **Health Canada** (© 866/225-0709; www.hc-sc.gc.ca) to find out the extent of their coverage and what documentation and receipts they must take home in case they are treated in the United States.

Travelers from the U.K. should carry their European Health Insurance Card (EHIC), which replaced the E111 form as proof of entitlement to free/reduced cost medical treatment abroad (© 0845/606-2030; www.ehic.org.uk). Note, however, that the EHIC only covers "necessary medical treatment," and for repatriation costs, lost money, lost baggage, or cancellation, travel insurance from a reputable company should always be sought (www.travelinsuranceweb.com).

Travel Insurance The cost of travel insurance varies widely, depending on the destination, the price and length of your trip, your age and health, and the type of trip you're taking, but expect to pay between 5% and 8% of the vacation itself. You can get estimates from various providers through **InsureMyTrip.com.** Enter your trip cost and dates, your age, and other information, for prices from more than a dozen companies.

U.K. citizens and their families who make more than one trip abroad per year may find an annual travel insurance policy works out cheaper. Check **www.moneysupermarket.com**, which compares prices across a wide range of providers for single- and multi-trip policies.

Most big travel agents offer their own insurance and will probably try to sell you their package when you book a holiday. Think before you sign. **Britain's Consumers' Association** recommends that you insist on seeing the policy and reading the fine print before buying travel insurance. **The Association of British Insurers** (© 020/7600-3333; www.abi.org.uk) gives advice by phone and publishes *Holiday Insurance,* a free guide to policy provisions and prices. You might also shop around for better deals: Try **Columbus Direct** (© 0870/033-9988; www.columbusdirect.net).

Trip Cancellation Insurance Trip-cancellation insurance will help retrieve your money if you have to back out of a trip or depart early, or if your travel supplier goes bankrupt. Trip cancellation traditionally covers such events as sickness, natural disasters, and State Department advisories. The latest news in trip-cancellation insurance is the availability of expanded hurricane coverage and the "any-reason" cancellation coverage—which costs more but covers cancellations made for any reason. You won't get back 100% of your prepaid trip cost, but you'll be refunded a substantial portion. **TravelSafe** (② **888/885-7233**; www.travelsafe.com) offers both types of coverage. Expedia also offers any-reason cancellation coverage for its air-hotel packages. For details, contact one of the following recommended insurers: **Access America** (② 866/807-3982; www.accessamerica.com); **Travel Guard International** (② 800/826-4919; www.travelguard.com); **Travel Insured International** (② 800/243-3174; www.travelinsured.com); and **Travelex Insurance Services** (② 888/457-4602; www.travelexinsurance.com).

INTERNET ACCESS Coffee shops, libraries, FedEx Kinko's locations, and most hotels offer Internet access on Colorado's Front Range. Also see "Staying Connected," in chapter 3.

LAUNDROMATS There are numerous Laundromats in Denver, Boulder, and Colorado Springs; consult local phone books.

LEGAL AID If you are "pulled over" for a minor infraction (such as speeding), never attempt to pay the fine directly to a police officer; this could be construed as attempted bribery, a much more serious crime. Pay fines by mail, or directly into the hands of the clerk of the court. If accused of a more serious offense, say and do nothing before consulting a lawyer. Here the burden is on the state to prove a person's guilt beyond a reasonable doubt, and everyone has the right to remain silent, whether he or she is suspected of a crime or actually arrested. Once arrested, a person can make one telephone call to a party of his or her choice. International visitors should call your embassy or consulate.

LOST & FOUND Be sure to tell all of your credit card companies the minute you discover your wallet has been lost or stolen and file a report at the nearest police precinct. Your credit card company or insurer may require a police report number or record of the loss. Most credit card companies have an emergency toll-free number to call if your card is lost or stolen; they may be able to wire you a cash advance immediately or deliver an emergency credit card in a day or two. Visa's U.S. emergency number is ② **800/847-2911** or 410/581-9994. American Express cardholders and traveler's check holders should call ② **800/221-7282.** Master-Card holders should call ② **800/307-7309** or 636/722-7111. For other credit cards, call the toll-free number directory at ② **800/555-1212.**

If you need emergency cash over the weekend when all banks and American Express offices are closed, you can have money wired to you via **Western Union** (② **800/325-6000;** www.westernunion.com).

MAIL At press time, domestic postage rates were 26¢ for a postcard and 42¢ for a letter. For international mail, a first-class letter of up to 1 ounce costs 90¢ (69¢ to Canada and Mexico); a first-class postcard costs the same as a letter. For more information go to **www.usps.com** and click on "Calculate Postage."

If you aren't sure what your address will be in the United States, mail can be sent to you, in your name, c/o General Delivery at the main post office of the city or region where you expect to be. (Call ② **800/275-8777** for information on the nearest post office.) The addressee must pick up mail in person and must produce proof of identity (driver's license, passport, etc.). Most post offices will hold your mail for up to 1 month, and are open Monday to Friday from 8am to 6pm, and Saturday from 9am to 3pm.

Always include zip codes when mailing items in the U.S. If you don't know your zip code, visit www.usps.com/zip4.

MAPS The region's best map store, **Mapsco Map and Travel Center,** 800 Lincoln St., Denver, CO 80203 (© **800/456-8703** or 303/830-2373; www.mapsco.com), offers USGS and recreation maps, state maps and travel guides, raised relief maps, and globes.

MEDICAL CONDITIONS If you have a medical condition that requires **syringe-administered medications,** carry a valid signed prescription from your physician; syringes in carry-on baggage will be inspected. Insulin in any form should have the proper pharmaceutical documentation. If you have a disease that requires treatment with **narcotics,** you should also carry documented proof with you—smuggling narcotics aboard a plane carries severe penalties in the U.S.

For **HIV-positive visitors,** requirements for entering the United States are somewhat vague and change frequently. For up-to-the-minute information, contact **AIDSinfo** (© **800/448-0440** or 301/519-6616 outside the U.S.; www.aidsinfo.nih.gov) or the **Gay Men's Health Crisis** (© **212/367-1000;** www.gmhc.org).

NEWSPAPERS & MAGAZINES The *Denver Post* (www.denverpost.com) is Colorado's largest daily newspaper, with coverage of the Denver metropolitan area plus news of the state. The *Rocky Mountain News* (www.rockymountainnews.com) also covers the metropolitan area. Each publishes a weekday edition; only the *News* prints on Saturday, and only the *Post* appears on Sunday. A widely read free weekly, *Westword* (www.westword.com), is known as much for its controversial jabs at local politicians and celebrities as for its entertainment listings. In Boulder and Colorado Springs, the daily newspapers are the *Daily Camera* and *The Gazette,* respectively.

PASSPORTS The websites listed provide downloadable passport applications as well as the current fees for processing applications. For an up-to-date, country-by-country listing of passport requirements around the world, go to the "International Travel" tab of the U.S. State Department at **http://travel.state.gov.** International visitors to the U.S. can obtain a visa application at the same website. *Note:* Children are required to present a passport when entering the United States at airports. More information on obtaining a passport for a minor can be found at http://travel.state.gov. Allow plenty of time before your trip to apply for a passport; processing normally takes 4–6 weeks (3 weeks for expedited service) but can take longer during busy periods (especially spring). And keep in mind that if you need a passport in a hurry, you'll pay a higher processing fee.

For Residents of Australia You can pick up an application from your local post office or any branch of Passports Australia, but you must schedule an interview at the passport office to present your application materials. Call the **Australian Passport Information Service** at © **131-232,** or visit the government website at www.passports.gov.au.

For Residents of Canada Passport applications are available at travel agencies throughout Canada or from the central **Passport Office,** Department of Foreign Affairs and International Trade, Ottawa, ON K1A 0G3 (© **800/567-6868;** www.ppt.gc.ca). *Note:* Canadian children who travel must have their own passport. However, if you hold a valid Canadian passport issued before December 11, 2001, that bears the name of your child, the passport remains valid for you and your child until it expires.

For Residents of Ireland You can apply for a 10-year passport at the **Passport Office,** Setanta Centre, Molesworth Street,

Dublin 2 (© **01/671-1633;** www.irlgov.
ie/iveagh). Those under age 18 and over
65 must apply for a 3-year passport. You
can also apply at 1A South Mall, Cork
(© **21/494-4700**), or at most main post
offices.

For Residents of New Zealand You can
pick up a passport application at any New
Zealand Passports Office or download it
from their website. Contact the **Passports
Office** at © **0800/225-050** in New Zealand or 04/474-8100, or log on to www.
passports.govt.nz.

For Residents of the United Kingdom
To pick up an application for a standard
10-year passport (5-yr. passport for children under 16), visit your nearest passport
office, major post office, or travel agency,
or contact the **United Kingdom Passport
Service** at © **0870/521-0410** or search its
website at www.ukpa.gov.uk.

POLICE Call © **911** for emergencies.

SMOKING Since 2006, smoking has
been banned in all public places in Colorado, including restaurants and bars.

TAXES Colorado has a 2.9% state sales
tax; local jurisdictions often add another
4% or 5%. Lodging tax is typically 10% to
15%. The United States has no value-
added tax (VAT) or other indirect tax at
the national level. Every state, county, and
city may levy its own local tax on all purchases, including hotel and restaurant
checks and airline tickets. These taxes will
not appear on price tags.

TELEPHONES Many convenience groceries and packaging services sell **prepaid
calling cards** in denominations up to $50;
for international visitors these can be the
least expensive way to call home. Many
public pay phones at airports now accept
American Express, MasterCard, and Visa
credit cards. **Local calls** made from pay
phones in most locales cost either 25¢ or
35¢ (no pennies, please). Most long-distance and international calls can be dialed

directly from any phone. **For calls within
the United States and to Canada,** dial 1
followed by the area code and the seven-
digit number. **For other international
calls,** dial 011 followed by the country
code, city code, and the number you are
calling.

Calls to area codes **800, 888, 877,** and
866 are toll-free. However, calls to area
codes **700** and **900** (chat lines, bulletin
boards, "dating" services, and so on) can
be very expensive—usually a charge of 95¢
to $3 or more per minute, and they some-
times have minimum charges that can run
as high as $15 or more.

For **reversed-charge or collect calls,**
and for **person-to-person calls,** dial the
number 0 then the area code and number;
an operator will come on the line, and you
should specify whether you are calling collect, person-to-person, or both. If your
operator-assisted call is international, ask
for the overseas operator.

For **local directory assistance** ("information"), dial 411; for long-distance
information, dial 1, then the appropriate
area code and 555-1212.

TELEGRAPH, TELEX & FAX Tele-
graph and telex services are provided
primarily by **Western Union** (© **800/325-
6000;** www.westernunion.com). You can
telegraph (wire) money, or have it tele-
graphed to you, very quickly over the
Western Union system, but this service
can cost as much as 15 to 20 percent of the
amount sent.

Most hotels have **fax machines** available for guest use (be sure to ask about the
charge to use it). Many hotel rooms are
wired for guests' fax machines. A less
expensive way to send and receive faxes
may be at stores such as **The UPS Store.**

TIME All of Colorado is in the **Mountain Standard Time Zone.** The continental United States is divided into **four time
zones:** Eastern Standard Time (EST),
Central Standard Time (CST), Mountain

Standard Time (MST), and Pacific Standard Time (PST). Alaska and Hawaii have their own zones. For example, when it's 9am in Los Angeles (PST), it's 7am in Honolulu (HST), 10am in Denver (MST), 11am in Chicago (CST), noon in New York City (EST), 5pm in London (GMT), and 2am the next day in Sydney.

Daylight saving time is in effect from 1am on the second Sunday in March to 1am on the first Sunday in November, except in Arizona, Hawaii, the U.S. Virgin Islands, and Puerto Rico. Daylight saving time moves the clock 1 hour ahead of standard time.

TIPPING In Denver, Boulder, and Colorado Springs, tips are a very important part of certain workers' income, and gratuities are the standard way of showing appreciation for services provided. (Tipping is certainly not compulsory if the service is poor!) In hotels, tip **bellhops** at least $1 per bag ($2–$3 if you have a lot of luggage) and tip the **chamber staff** $1 to $2 per day (more if you've left a disaster area for him or her to clean up). Tip the **doorman** or **concierge** only if he or she has provided you with some specific service (for example, calling a cab for you or obtaining difficult-to-get theater tickets). Tip the **valet-parking attendant** $1 every time you get your car.

In restaurants, bars, and nightclubs, tip **service staff** 15% to 20% of the check, tip **bartenders** 10% to 15%, tip **checkroom attendants** $1 per garment, and tip **valet-parking attendants** $1 per vehicle.

As for other service personnel, tip **cab drivers** 15% of the fare; tip **skycaps** at airports at least $1 per bag ($2–$3 if you have a lot of luggage); and tip **hairdressers** and **barbers** 15% to 20%.

TOILETS You won't find public toilets or "restrooms" on the streets in most U.S. cities but they can be found in hotel lobbies, bars, restaurants, museums, department stores, railway and bus stations, and service stations. Large hotels and fast-food restaurants are often the best bet for clean facilities. Restaurants and bars in resorts or heavily visited areas may reserve their restrooms for patrons.

USEFUL PHONE NUMBERS City of Denver (nonemergency): ✆ **311;** Colorado Road Conditions: ✆ **303/639-1111;** U.S. Dept. of State Travel Advisory: ✆ **202/647-5225** (manned 24 hrs.); U.S. Passport Agency: ✆ **202/647-0518;** U.S. Centers for Disease Control International Traveler's Hotline: ✆ **404/332-4559.**

VISAS For information about U.S. Visas go to **http://travel.state.gov** and click on "Visas." Or go to one of the following websites:

Australian citizens can obtain up-to-date visa information from the **U.S. Embassy Canberra,** Moonah Place, Yarralumla, ACT 2600 (✆ **02/6214-5600**), or by checking the U.S. Diplomatic Mission's website at **http://usembassy-australia. state.gov/consular.**

British subjects can obtain up-to-date visa information by calling the **U.S. Embassy Visa Information Line** (✆ **0891/200-290**) or by visiting the "Visas to the U.S." section of the American Embassy London's website at **www.usembassy.org.uk.**

Irish citizens can obtain up-to-date visa information through the **Embassy of the USA Dublin,** 42 Elgin Rd., Dublin 4, Ireland (✆ **353/1-668-8777**), or by checking the "Consular Services" section of the website at **http://dublin.usembassy.gov.**

Citizens of **New Zealand** can obtain up-to-date visa information by contacting the **U.S. Embassy New Zealand,** 29 Fitzherbert Terrace, Thorndon, Wellington (✆ **644/472-2068**), or get the information directly from the website at **http:// wellington.usembassy.gov.**

MAJOR U.S. AIRLINES

(* flies internationally as well)

Alaska Airlines/Horizon Air
✆ 800/252/7522
www.alaskaair.com

American Airlines*
✆ 800/433-7300 (in U.S. or Canada)
✆ 020/7365-0777 (in U.K.)
www.aa.com

ATA Airlines
✆ 800/435-9282
www.ata.com

Continental Airlines*
✆ 800/523-3273 (in U.S. or Canada)
✆ 084/5607-6760 (in U.K.)
www.continental.com

Delta Air Lines*
✆ 800/221-1212 (in U.S. or Canada)
✆ 084/5600-0950 (in U.K.)
www.delta.com

Frontier Airlines
✆ 800/432-1359
www.frontierairlines.com

JetBlue Airways
✆ 800/538-2583 (in U.S.)
✆ 080/1365-2525 (in U.K. or Canada)
www.jetblue.com

Midwest Airlines
✆ 800/452-2022
www.midwestairlines.com

Northwest Airlines*
✆ 800/225-2525 (in U.S.)
✆ 870/0507-4074 (in U.K.)
www.flynaa.com

Southwest Airlines
✆ 800/435-9792
www.southwest.com

United Airlines*
✆ 800/864-8331 (in U.S. and Canada)
✆ 084/5844-4777 (in U.K.)
www.united.com

US Airways*
✆ 800/428-4322 (in U.S. and Canada)
✆ 084/5600-3300 (in U.K.)
www.usairways.com

MAJOR INTERNATIONAL AIRLINES

Aeroméxico
✆ 800/237-6639 (in U.S.)
✆ 020/7801-6234 (in U.K.,
information only)
www.aeromexico.com

Air France
✆ 800/237-2747 (in U.S.)
✆ 800/375-8723 (in U.S. and Canada)
✆ 087/0142-4343 (in U.K.)
www.airfrance.com

Air India
✆ 212/407-1371 (in U.S.)
✆ 91 22 2279 6666 (in India)
✆ 020/8745-1000 (in U.K.)
www.airindia.com

Air Jamaica
✆ 800/523-5585 (in U.S. or Canada)
✆ 208/570-7999 (in Jamaica)
www.airjamaica.com

Air New Zealand
✆ 800/262-1234 (in U.S.)
✆ 800/663-5494 (in Canada)
✆ 0800/028-4149 (in U.K.)
www.airnewzealand.com

Alitalia
✆ 800/223-5730 (in U.S.)
✆ 800/361-8336 (in Canada)
✆ 087/0608-6003 (in U.K.)
www.alitalia.com

American Airlines
© 800/433-7300 (in U.S. and Canada)
© 020/7365-0777 (in U.K.)
www.aa.com

British Airways
© 800/247-9297 (in U.S. and Canada)
© 087/0850-9850 (in U.K.)
www.british-airways.com

China Airlines
© 800/227-5118 (in U.S.)
© 022/715-1212 (in Taiwan)
www.china-airlines.com

Continental Airlines
© 800/523-3273 (in U.S. and Canada)
© 084/5607-6760 (in U.K.)
www.continental.com

Delta Air Lines
© 800/221-1212 (in U.S. and Canada)
© 084/5600-0950 (in U.K.)
www.delta.com

EgyptAir
© 212/581-5600 (in U.S.)
© 020/7734-2343 (in U.K.)
© 09/007-0000 (in Egypt)
www.egyptair.com

El Al Airlines
© 972/3977-1111 (outside Israel)
© *2250 (from any phone in Israel)
www.elal.co.il

Emirates Airlines
© 800/777-3999 (in U.S.)
© 087/0243-2222 (in U.K.)
www.emirates.com

Finnair
© 800/950-5000 (in U.S. and Canada)
© 087/0241-4411 (in U.K.)
www.finnair.com

Iberia Airlines
© 800/722-4642 (in U.S. and Canada)
© 087/0609-0500 (in U.K.)
www.iberia.com

Icelandair
© 800/223-5500 ext 2 prompt 1
(in U.S. and Canada)

© 084/5758-1111 (in U.K.)
www.icelandair.com
www.icelandair.co.uk (in U.K.)

Israir Airlines
© 877/477-2471 (in U.S. and Canada)
© 700/505-777 (in Israel)
www.israirairlines.com

Japan Airlines
© 012/025-5931 (international)
www.jal.co.jp

Korean Air
© 800/438-5000 (in U.S. and Canada)
© 0800/413-000 (in U.K.)
www.koreanair.com

Lan Airlines
© 866/435-9526 (in U.S.)
© 305/670-9999 (in other countries)
www.lanchile.com

Lufthansa
© 800/399-5838 (in U.S.)
© 800/563-5954 (in Canada)
© 087/0837-7747 (in U.K.)
www.lufthansa.com

North American Airlines
© 800/359-6222
www.flynaa.com

Olympic Airlines
© 800/223-1226 (in U.S.)
© 514/878-9691 (in Canada)
© 087/0606-0460 (in U.K.)
www.olympicairlines.com

Philippine Airlines
© 800/I-Fly-Pal (800/435-9725)
(in U.S. and Canada)
© 632/855-8888 (in Philippines)
www.philippineairlines.com

Quantas Airways
© 800/227-4500 (in U.S.)
© 084/5774-7767 (in U.K.)
© 13 13 13 (in Australia)
www.quantas.com

South African Airways
© 271/1978-5313 (international)
© 0861 FLYSAA (086/135-9122)
(in South Africa)
www.flysaa.com

Swiss Air
- ℂ 877/359-7947 (in U.S. and Canada)
- ℂ 084/5601-0956 (in U.K.)
- www.swiss.com

TACA
- ℂ 800/535-8780 (in U.S.)
- ℂ 800/722-TACA (8222) (in Canada)
- ℂ 087/0241-0340 (in U.K.)
- ℂ 503/2267-8222 (in El Salvador)
- www.taca.com

Thai Airways International
- ℂ 212/949-8424 (in U.S.)
- ℂ 020/7491-7953 (in U.K.)
- www.thaiair.com

CAR RENTAL AGENCIES

Advantage
- ℂ 800/777-5500 (in U.S.)
- ℂ 021/0344-4712 (outside of U.S.)
- www.advantagerentacar.com

Alamo
- ℂ 800/GO-ALAMO (800/462-5266)
- www.alamo.com

Avis
- ℂ 800/331-1212 (in U.S. and Canada)
- ℂ 084/4581-8181 (in U.K.)
- www.avis.com

Budget
- ℂ 800/527-0700 (in U.S.)
- ℂ 800/268-8900 (in Canada)
- ℂ 087/0156-5656 (in U.K.)
- www.budget.com

Dollar
- ℂ 800/800-4000 (in U.S.)
- ℂ 800/848-8268 (in Canada)
- ℂ 080/8234-7524 (in U.K.)
- www.dollar.com

Turkish Airlines
- ℂ 90 212 444 0 849
- www.thy.com

United Airlines*
- ℂ 800/864-8331 (in U.S. and Canada)
- ℂ 084/5844-4777 (in U.K.)
- www.united.com

US Airways*
- ℂ 800/428-4322 (in U.S. and Canada)
- ℂ 084/5600-3300 (in U.K.)
- www.usairways.com

Virgin Atlantic Airways
- ℂ 800/821-5438 (in U.S. and Canada)
- ℂ 087/0574-7747 (in U.K.)
- www.virgin-atlantic.com

Enterprise
- ℂ 800/261-7331 (in U.S.)
- ℂ 514/355-4028 (in Canada)
- ℂ 012/9360-9090 (in U.K.)
- www.enterprise.com

Hertz
- ℂ 800/645-3131
- ℂ 800/654-3001 (for international reservations)
- www.hertz.com

National
- ℂ 800/CAR-RENT (800/227-7368)
- www.nationalcar.com

Payless
- ℂ 800/PAYLESS (800/729-5377)
- www.paylesscarrental.com

Rent-A-Wreck
- ℂ 800/535-1391
- www.rentawreck.com

Thrifty
- ℂ 800/367-2277
- ℂ 918/669-2168 (international)
- www.thrifty.com

MAJOR HOTEL & MOTEL CHAINS

Best Western International
- ℂ 800/780-7234 (in U.S. and Canada)
- ℂ 0800/393-130 (in U.K.)
- www.bestwestern.com

Clarion Hotels
- ℂ 800/CLARION or 877/424-6423 (in U.S. and Canada)
- ℂ 0800/444-444 (in U.K.)
- www.choicehotels.com

Comfort Inns
© 800/228-5150
© 0800/444-444 (in U.K.)
www.ComfortInnChoiceHotels.com

Courtyard by Marriott
© 888/236-2427 (in U.S.)
© 0800/221-222 (in U.K.)
www.marriott.com/courtyard

Crowne Plaza Hotels
© 888/303-1746
www.ichotelsgroup.com/crowneplaza

Days Inn
© 800/329-7466 (in U.S.)
© 0800/280-400 (in U.K.)
www.daysinn.com

Doubletree Hotels
© 800/222-TREE (800/222-8733)
  (in U.S. and Canada)
© 087/0590-9090 (in U.K.)
www.doubletree.com

Econo Lodges
© 800/55-ECONO (800/552-3666)
www.choicehotels.com

Embassy Suites
© 800/EMBASSY (800/362-2779)
www.embassysuites.hilton.com

Fairfield Inn by Marriott
© 800/228-2800 (in U.S. and Canada)
© 0800/221-222 (in U.K.)
www.marriott.com/fairfieldinn

Four Seasons
© 800/819-5053 (in U.S. and Canada)
© 0800/6488-6488 (in U.K.)
www.fourseasons.com

Hampton Inn
© 800/HAMPTON (800/426-4766)
www.hamptoninn.hilton.com

Hilton Hotels
© 800/HILTONS (800/445-8667)
  (in U.S. and Canada)
© 087/0590-9090 (in U.K.)
www.hilton.com

Holiday Inn
© 800/315-2621 (in U.S. and Canada)
© 0800/405-060 (in U.K.)
www.holidayinn.com

Howard Johnson
© 800/446-4656 (in U.S. and Canada)
www.hojo.com

Hyatt
© 888/591-1234 (in U.S. and Canada)
© 084/5888-1234 (in U.K.)
www.hyatt.com

InterContinental Hotels & Resorts
© 800/424-6835 (in U.S. and Canada)
© 0800/1800-1800 (in U.K.)
www.ichotelsgroup.com

La Quinta Inns & Suites
© 800/642-4271 (in U.S. and Canada)
www.lq.com

Loews Hotels
© 800/23LOEWS (800/235-6397)
www.loewshotels.com

Marriott
© 877/236-2427 (in U.S. and Canada)
© 0800/221-222 (in U.K.)
www.marriott.com

Motel 6
© 800/4MOTEL6 (800/466-8356)
www.motel6.com

Omni Hotels
© 888/444-OMNI (888/444-6664)
www.omnihotels.com

Quality
© 877/424-6423 (in U.S. and Canada)
© 0800/444-444 (in U.K.)
www.QualityInn.ChoiceHotels.com

Radisson Hotels & Resorts
© 888/201-1718 (in U.S. and Canada)
© 0800/374-411 (in U.K.)
www.radisson.com

Ramada Worldwide
© 888/2-RAMADA (888/272-6232)
  (in U.S. and Canada)
© 080/8100-0783 (in U.K.)
www.ramada.com

Red Carpet Inns
© 800/251-1962
www.bookroomsnow.com

Red Lion Hotels
© 800/RED-LION (800/733-5466)
www.redlion.rdln.com

Red Roof Inns
© 866/686-4335 (in U.S. and Canada)
© 614/601-4075 (international)
www.redroof.com

Renaissance
© 888/236-2427
www.renaissance.com

Residence Inn by Marriott
© 800/331-3131
© 800/221-222 (in U.K.)
www.marriott.com/residenceinn

Rodeway Inns
© 877/424-6423
www.RodewayInn.ChoiceHotels.com

Sheraton Hotels & Resorts
© 800/325-3535 (in U.S.)
© 800/543-4300 (in Canada)
© 0800/3253-5353 (in U.K.)
www.starwoodhotels.com/sheraton

Super 8 Motels
© 800/800-8000
www.super8.com

Travelodge
© 800/578-7878
www.travelodge.com

Westin Hotels & Resorts
© 800-937-8461 (in U.S. and Canada)
© 0800/3259-5959 (in U.K.)
www.starwoodhotels.com/westin

Wyndham Hotels & Resorts
© 877/999-3223 (in U.S. and Canada)
© 050/6638-4899 (in U.K.)
www.wyndham.com

INDEX

See also Accommodations and Restaurant indexes, below.

FROMMER'S® COMPLETE TRAVEL GUIDES

Alaska
Amalfi Coast
American Southwest
Amsterdam
Argentina
Arizona
Atlanta
Australia
Austria
Bahamas
Barcelona
Beijing
Belgium, Holland & Luxembourg
Belize
Bermuda
Boston
Brazil
British Columbia & the Canadian
  Rockies
Brussels & Bruges
Budapest & the Best of Hungary
Buenos Aires
Calgary
California
Canada
Cancún, Cozumel & the Yucatán
Cape Cod, Nantucket & Martha's
  Vineyard
Caribbean
Caribbean Ports of Call
Carolinas & Georgia
Chicago
Chile & Easter Island
China
Colorado
Costa Rica
Croatia
Cuba
Denmark
Denver, Boulder & Colorado Springs
Eastern Europe
Ecuador & the Galapagos Islands
Edinburgh & Glasgow
England
Europe
Europe by Rail

Florence, Tuscany & Umbria
Florida
France
Germany
Greece
Greek Islands
Guatemala
Hawaii
Hong Kong
Honolulu, Waikiki & Oahu
India
Ireland
Israel
Italy
Jamaica
Japan
Kauai
Las Vegas
London
Los Angeles
Los Cabos & Baja
Madrid
Maine Coast
Maryland & Delaware
Maui
Mexico
Montana & Wyoming
Montréal & Québec City
Morocco
Moscow & St. Petersburg
Munich & the Bavarian Alps
Nashville & Memphis
New England
Newfoundland & Labrador
New Mexico
New Orleans
New York City
New York State
New Zealand
Northern Italy
Norway
Nova Scotia, New Brunswick &
  Prince Edward Island
Oregon
Paris
Peru

Philadelphia & the Amish Country
Portugal
Prague & the Best of the Czech
  Republic
Provence & the Riviera
Puerto Rico
Rome
San Antonio & Austin
San Diego
San Francisco
Santa Fe, Taos & Albuquerque
Scandinavia
Scotland
Seattle
Seville, Granada & the Best of
  Andalusia
Shanghai
Sicily
Singapore & Malaysia
South Africa
South America
South Florida
South Korea
South Pacific
Southeast Asia
Spain
Sweden
Switzerland
Tahiti & French Polynesia
Texas
Thailand
Tokyo
Toronto
Turkey
USA
Utah
Vancouver & Victoria
Vermont, New Hampshire & Maine
Vienna & the Danube Valley
Vietnam
Virgin Islands
Virginia
Walt Disney World® & Orlando
Washington, D.C.
Washington State

FROMMER'S® DAY BY DAY GUIDES

Amsterdam
Barcelona
Beijing
Boston
Cancun & the Yucatan
Chicago
Florence & Tuscany

Hong Kong
Honolulu & Oahu
London
Maui
Montréal
Napa & Sonoma
New York City

Paris
Provence & the Riviera
Rome
San Francisco
Venice
Washington D.C.

PAULINE FROMMER'S GUIDES: SEE MORE. SPEND LESS.

Alaska
Hawaii
Italy

Las Vegas
London
New York City

Paris
Walt Disney World®
Washington D.C.

FROMMER'S® PORTABLE GUIDES

Acapulco, Ixtapa & Zihuatanejo
Amsterdam
Aruba, Bonaire & Curacao
Australia's Great Barrier Reef
Bahamas
Big Island of Hawaii
Boston
California Wine Country
Cancún
Cayman Islands
Charleston
Chicago
Dominican Republic

Florence
Las Vegas
Las Vegas for Non-Gamblers
London
Maui
Nantucket & Martha's Vineyard
New Orleans
New York City
Paris
Portland
Puerto Rico
Puerto Vallarta, Manzanillo & Guadalajara

Rio de Janeiro
San Diego
San Francisco
Savannah
St. Martin, Sint Maarten, Anguila & St. Bart's
Turks & Caicos
Vancouver
Venice
Virgin Islands
Washington, D.C.
Whistler

FROMMER'S® CRUISE GUIDES

Alaska Cruises & Ports of Call

Cruises & Ports of Call

European Cruises & Ports of Call

FROMMER'S® NATIONAL PARK GUIDES

Algonquin Provincial Park
Banff & Jasper
Grand Canyon

National Parks of the American West
Rocky Mountain
Yellowstone & Grand Teton

Yosemite and Sequoia & Kings Canyon
Zion & Bryce Canyon

FROMMER'S® WITH KIDS GUIDES

Chicago
Hawaii
Las Vegas
London

National Parks
New York City
San Francisco

Toronto
Walt Disney World® & Orlando
Washington, D.C.

FROMMER'S® PHRASEFINDER DICTIONARY GUIDES

Chinese
French

German
Italian

Japanese
Spanish

SUZY GERSHMAN'S BORN TO SHOP GUIDES

France
Hong Kong, Shanghai & Beijing
Italy

London
New York
Paris

San Francisco
Where to Buy the Best of Everything.

FROMMER'S® BEST-LOVED DRIVING TOURS

Britain
California
France
Germany

Ireland
Italy
New England
Northern Italy

Scotland
Spain
Tuscany & Umbria

THE UNOFFICIAL GUIDES®

Adventure Travel in Alaska
Beyond Disney
California with Kids
Central Italy
Chicago
Cruises
Disneyland®
England
Hawaii

Ireland
Las Vegas
London
Maui
Mexico's Best Beach Resorts
Mini Mickey
New Orleans
New York City
Paris

San Francisco
South Florida including Miami & the Keys
Walt Disney World®
Walt Disney World® for Grown-ups
Walt Disney World® with Kids
Washington, D.C.

SPECIAL-INTEREST TITLES

Athens Past & Present
Best Places to Raise Your Family
Cities Ranked & Rated
500 Places to Take Your Kids Before They Grow Up
Frommer's Best Day Trips from London
Frommer's Best RV & Tent Campgrounds in the U.S.A.

Frommer's Exploring America by RV
Frommer's NYC Free & Dirt Cheap
Frommer's Road Atlas Europe
Frommer's Road Atlas Ireland
Retirement Places Rated